ICTS
155
Special Education Learning Behavior Specialist I
Teacher Certification Exam

By: Sharon Wynne, M.S
Southern Connecticut State University

"And, while there's no reason yet to panic, I think it's only prudent that we make preparations to panic."

XAMonline, INC.
Boston

Copyright © 2007 XAMonline, Inc.

All rights reserved. No part of the material protected by this copyright notice may be reproduced or utilized in any form or by any means, electronic or mechanical, including photocopying, recording or by any information storage and retrievable system, without written permission from the copyright holder.

To obtain permission(s) to use the material from this work for any purpose including workshops or seminars, please submit a written request to:

XAMonline, Inc.
21 Orient Ave.
Melrose, MA 02176
Toll Free 1-800-509-4128
Email: info@xamonline.com
Web www.xamonline.com
Fax: 1-781-662-9268

Library of Congress Cataloging-in-Publication Data

Wynne, Sharon A.
    ICTS Special Education Learning Behavior Specialist I 155: Teacher Certification
    / Sharon A. Wynne ISBN 978-1-58197-975-6
    1. Special Education Learning Behavior Specialist I   2. Study Guides.   3. ICTS
    4. Teachers' Certification & Licensure.   5. Careers

Disclaimer:

The opinions expressed in this publication are the sole works of XAMonline and were created independently from the National Education Association, Educational Testing Service, or any State Department of Education, National Evaluation Systems or other testing affiliates.

Between the time of publication and printing, state specific standards as well as testing formats and website information may change that is not included in part or in whole within this product. Sample test questions are developed by XAMonline and reflect similar content as on real tests; however, they are not former tests. XAMonline assembles content that aligns with state standards but makes no claims nor guarantees teacher candidates a passing score. Numerical scores are determined by testing companies such as NES or ETS and then are compared with individual state standards. A passing score varies from state to state.

Printed in the United States of America   œ-1

ICTS: Special Education Learning Behavior Specialist I
ISBN: 978-1-58197-975-6

Table of Contents

Great Study and Testing Tips!

What to study in order to prepare for the subject assessments is the focus of this study guide but equally important is *how* you study.

You can increase your chances of truly mastering the information by taking some simple, but effective steps.
Study Tips:

1. Some foods aid the learning process. Foods such as milk, nuts, seeds, rice, and oats help your study efforts by releasing natural memory enhancers called CCKs (*cholecystokinin*) composed of *tryptophan*, *choline*, and *phenylalanine*. All of these chemicals enhance the neurotransmitters associated with memory. Before studying, try a light, protein-rich meal of eggs, turkey, and fish. All of these foods release the memory enhancing chemicals. The better the connections, the more you comprehend.

Likewise, before you take a test, stick to a light snack of energy boosting and relaxing foods. A glass of milk, a piece of fruit, or some peanuts all release various memory-boosting chemicals and help you to relax and focus on the subject at hand.

2. Learn to take great notes. A by-product of our modern culture is that we have grown accustomed to getting our information in short doses (i.e. TV news sound bites or USA Today style newspaper articles.)

Consequently, we've subconsciously trained ourselves to assimilate information better in neat little packages. If your notes are scrawled all over the paper, it fragments the flow of the information. Strive for clarity. Newspapers use a standard format to achieve clarity. Your notes can be much clearer through use of proper formatting. A very effective format is called the *"Cornell Method."*

Take a sheet of loose-leaf lined notebook paper and draw a line all the way down the paper about 1-2" from the left-hand edge.

Draw another line across the width of the paper about 1-2" up from the bottom. Repeat this process on the reverse side of the page.

Look at the highly effective result. You have ample room for notes, a left hand margin for special emphasis items or inserting supplementary data from the textbook, a large area at the bottom for a brief summary, and a little rectangular space for just about anything you want.

3. <u>Get the concept then the details.</u> Too often we focus on the details and don't gather an understanding of the concept. However, if you simply memorize only dates, places, or names, you may well miss the whole point of the subject. A key way to understand things is to put them in your own words. If you are working from a textbook, automatically summarize each paragraph in your mind. If you are outlining text, don't simply copy the author's words.

Rephrase them in your own words. You remember your own thoughts and words much better than someone else's, and subconsciously tend to associate the important details to the core concepts.

4. <u>Ask Why?</u> Pull apart written material paragraph by paragraph and don't forget the captions under the illustrations.

Example: If the heading is "Stream Erosion", flip it around to read "Why do streams erode?" Then answer the questions.

If you train your mind to think in a series of questions and answers, not only will you learn more, but it also helps to lessen the test anxiety because you are used to answering questions.

5. <u>Read for reinforcement and future needs.</u> Even if you only have 10 minutes, put your notes or a book in your hand. Your mind is similar to a computer; you have to input data in order to have it processed. *By reading, you are creating the neural connections for future retrieval.* The more times you read something, the more you reinforce the learning of ideas.

Even if you don't fully understand something on the first pass, *your mind stores much of the material for later recall.*

6. <u>Relax to learn so go into exile.</u> Our bodies respond to an inner clock called biorhythms. Burning the midnight oil works well for some people, but not everyone.

If possible, set aside a particular place to study that is free of distractions. Shut off the television, cell phone, pager and exile your friends and family during your study period.

If you really are bothered by silence, try background music. Light classical music at a low volume has been shown to aid in concentration over other types.

Music that evokes pleasant emotions without lyrics are highly suggested. Try just about anything by Mozart. It relaxes you.

7. <u>Use arrows not highlighters.</u> At best, it's difficult to read a page full of yellow, pink, blue, and green streaks.

Try staring at a neon sign for a while and you'll soon see my point, the horde of colors obscure the message.

8. <u>Budget your study time.</u> Although you shouldn't ignore any of the material, *allocate your available study time in the same ratio that topics may appear on the test.*

Testing Tips:

1. <u>Get smart, play dumb.</u> Don't read anything into the question. Don't make an assumption that the test writer is looking for something else than what is asked. Stick to the question as written and don't read extra things into it.

2. <u>Read the question and all the choices *twice* before answering the question.</u> You may miss something by not carefully reading, and then re-reading both the question and the answers.

If you really don't have a clue as to the right answer, leave it blank on the first time through. Go on to the other questions, as they may provide a clue as to how to answer the skipped questions.

If later on, you still can't answer the skipped ones . . . ***Guess.***
The only penalty for guessing is that you *might* get it wrong. Only one thing is certain; if you don't put anything down, you will get it wrong!

3. <u>Turn the question into a statement.</u> Look at the way the questions are worded. The syntax of the question usually provides a clue. Does it seem more familiar as a statement rather than as a question? Does it sound strange?

By turning a question into a statement, you may be able to spot if an answer sounds right, and it may also trigger memories of material you have read.

4. <u>Look for hidden clues.</u> It's actually very difficult to compose multiple-foil (choice) questions without giving away part of the answer in the options presented.

In most multiple-choice questions you can often readily eliminate one or two of the potential answers. This leaves you with only two real possibilities and automatically your odds go to Fifty-Fifty for very little work.

5. <u>Trust your instincts.</u> For every fact that you have read, you subconsciously retain something of that knowledge. On questions that you aren't really certain about, go with your basic instincts. **Your first impression on how to answer a question is usually correct.**

6. <u>Mark your answers directly on the test booklet.</u> Don't bother trying to fill in the optical scan sheet on the first pass through the test.

7. <u>Watch the clock!</u> You have a set amount of time to answer the questions. Don't get bogged down trying to answer a single question at the expense of 10 questions you can more readily answer.

THIS PAGE BLANK

SUBAREA I. **FOUNDATIONS AND CHARACTERISTICS**

COMPETENCY 1.0 **UNDERSTAND PROCESSES OF HUMAN DEVELOPMENT AND FACTORS, INCLUDING DISABILITY THAT AFFECT DEVELOPMENT AND LEARNING.**

Skill 1.1 **Demonstrate knowledge of the similarities and differences among the cognitive, physical, sensory, cultural, social, and emotional development and needs of individuals with and without disabilities.**

PHYSICAL DEVELOPMENT, INCLUDING MOTOR AND SENSORY

It is important for the teacher to be aware of the physical stage of development and how the child's physical growth and development affect the child's learning. Factors determined by the physical stage of development include: ability to sit and attend, the need for activity, the relationship between physical skills and self-esteem, and the degree to which physical involvement in an activity (as opposed to being able to understand an abstract concept) affects learning.

Children with physical impairments possess a variety of disabling conditions. Although there are significant differences among these conditions, similarities also exist. Each condition usually affects one particular system of the body: the cardiopulmonary system (i.e. blood vessels, heart, and lungs), the musculoskeletal system (i.e. spinal cord, brain nerves). Some conditions develop during pregnancy, birth, or infancy because of the known or unknown factors, which may affect the fetus or newborn infant. Other conditions occur later due to injury (trauma), disease, or factors not fully understood.

In addition to motor disorders, individuals with physical disabilities may have multi-disabling conditions such as concomitant hearing impairments, visual impairments, perceptual disorders, speech defects, behavior disorders, or mental handicaps, performance, and emotional responsiveness.

Some characteristics of individuals with physical disabilities and other health impairments are:

1. Lack of physical stamina; fatigue
2. Chronic illness; poor endurance
3. Deficient motor skills; normal movement may be prevented
4. May cause physical limitations or impede motor development; a prosthesis or an orthosis may be required.
5. Mobility and exploration of one's environment may be limited.
6. Limited self-care abilities.
7. Progressive weakening and degeneration of muscles.
8. Frequent speech and language defects; communication may be prevented; echolatia orthosis may be present.
9. May experience pain and discomfort throughout the body.
10. May display emotional (psychological) problems, which require treatment.
11. Social adjustments may be needed; may display maladaptive social behavior.
12. May necessitate long-term medical treatment, which maybe become a financial burden on the family
13. May have embarrassing side effects from certain diseases or treatment.
14. May exhibit erratic or poor attendance patterns, which leads to the child missing many skills and the parent or caregiver to miss days of work.

In 1981, the condition of autism was moved from the exceptionality category to the seriously emotionally disturbed to that of other health impaired by virtue of a change in language in the original definitions under Public Law 94-142 ("Education of Handicapped Children." Federal Register, 1977). With IDEA, in 1990, autism was made into a separate exceptionality category.

Children whose behavior deviates from society's standards for normal behavior at certain ages and stages of development may be considered as displaying emotional difficulties.

Behavioral expectations vary from setting to setting – for example, it is acceptable to yell on the football field, but not as the teacher is explaining a lesson to the class. Different cultures have their standards of behavior, further complicating the question of what constitutes a behavioral problem. People also have their personal opinions and standards for what is tolerable and what is not. Some behavioral problems are openly expressed; others are inwardly directed and not very obvious. As a result of these factors, the terms behavioral disorders and emotional disturbance have become almost interchangeable.

While almost all children at times exhibit behaviors that are aggressive, withdrawn, or otherwise inappropriate, the IDEA definition of serious emotional disturbance focuses on behaviors that persist over time, are intense, and impairs a child's ability to function in society.

The behaviors must not be caused by temporary stressful situations or other causes (i.e. depression over the death of a grandparent, or anger over the parents' impending divorce). In order for a child to be considered seriously emotionally disturbed, he or she must exhibit one or more of the following characteristics over a **long period of time** and to a **marked degree** that **adversely affects** a child's educational performance.

- Inability to learn, that cannot be explained by intellectual, sensory, or health factors
- Inability to maintain satisfactory interpersonal relationships
- Inappropriate types of behaviors
- General pervasive mood of unhappiness or depression
- Physical symptoms or fears associated with personal or school problems
- Schizophrenic children are covered under this definition, and social maladjustment by itself does not satisfy this definition unless it is accompanied by one of the other conditions of SED

The diagnostic categories and definitions used to classify mental disorders come from the American Psychiatric Association's publication Diagnostic and Statistical Manual of Mental Disorders (DSM-V), the handbook that is used by psychiatrists and psychologists. The DSM-V is a multiaxial classification system consisting of dimensions (axes) coded along with the psychiatric diagnosis. The axes are:

- Axis I----Principal psychiatric diagnosis (e.g. overanxious disorder)

- Axis II---Developmental problems (e.g. developmental reading disorder)

- Axis III---Physical disorders (e.g. allergies)

- Axis IV--Psychosocial stressors (e.g. divorce)

- Axis V---Rating of the highest level of adaptive functioning (includes intellectual and social). Rating is called Global Assessment Functioning (GAF) score.

While the DSM-V is one way of diagnosing serious emotional disturbance, there are other ways of classifying the various forms that behavior disorders manifest themselves. The following tables summarize some of these classifications.

Externalizing Behaviors	Internalizing Behaviors
Aggressive behaviors expressed outwardly toward others.	Withdrawing behaviors that are directed inward to oneself.
Manifested as hyperactivity, persistent aggression, irritating behaviors that are impulsive and distractible	Social withdrawal
Examples: hitting, cursing, stealing, arson, cruelty to animals, hyperactivity,	Depression, fears, phobias, elective mutism, withdrawal, anorexia and bulimia

Well-known instruments used to assess children's behavior have their own categories (scales) to classify behaviors. The following table illustrates the scales used in some of the widely used instruments. Disturbance may also be categorized in degrees: mild, moderate or severe. The degree of disturbance will affect the type and degree of interventions and services required by emotionally handicapped students. Degree of disturbance also must be considered when determining the least restrictive environment and the services named fro free, appropriate education for these students. An example of a set of criteria for determining the degree of disturbance is the one developed by P.L. Newcomer:

CRITERIA	DEGREE OF DISTURBANCE		
	Mild	Moderate	Severe
Precipitating events	Highly stressful	Moderately stressful	Not stressful
Destructiveness	Not destructive	Occasionally destructive	Usually destructive
Maturational appropriateness	Behavior typical for age	Some behavior untypical for age	Behavior too young or too old
Personal functioning	Cares for own needs	Usually cares for own needs	Unable to care for own needs
Social functioning	Usually able to relate to others	Usually unable to relate to others	Unable to relate to others
Reality index	Usually sees events as they are	Occasionally sees events as they are	Little contact with reality
Insight index	Aware of behavior	Usually aware of behavior	Usually not aware of behavior
Conscious control	Usually can control behavior	Occasionally can control behavior	Little control over behavior
Social responsiveness	Usually acts appropriately	Occasionally acts appropriately	Rarely acts appropriately

Source: Understanding and Teaching Emotionally Disturbed Children and Adolescents, (2nd ed., p. 139), by P.L. Newcomer, 1993, Austin, TX: Pro-De. Copyright 1993. Reprinted with permission.

Cognitive Development

Children go through patterns of learning beginning with pre-operational thought processes and move to concrete operational thoughts. Eventually they begin to acquire the mental ability to think about and solve problems in their head because they can manipulate objects symbolically. Children of most ages can use symbols such as words and numbers to represent objects and relations, but they need concrete reference points. It is essential children be encouraged to use and develop the thinking skills that they possess in solving problems that interest them. The content of the curriculum must be relevant, engaging, and meaningful to the students.

The teacher of special needs students must have a general knowledge of cognitive development. Although children with special needs cognitive development rate maybe different than other children, a teacher needs to be aware of some of the activities of each stage as part of the basis to determine what should be taught and when it should be taught.

The following information about cognitive development was taken from the Cincinnati Children's Hospital Medical Center at www.cincinattichildrens.org

Some common features indicating a progression from more simple to more complex cognitive development include the following:

Children (ages 6-12)
- Begin to develop the ability to think in concrete ways. Concrete operations are operations performed in the presence of the object and events that are to be used.
- Examples: how to combine (addition), separate (subtract or divide), order (alphabetize and sort/categorize), and transform (change things such as 25 pennies=1 quarter) objects and actions

Adolescence (ages 12-18)
- Adolescence marks the beginning development of more complex thinking skills, including abstract thinking, the ability to reason from known principles (form own new ideas or questions), the ability to consider many points of view according to varying criteria (compare or debate ideas or opinions), and the ability to think about the process of thinking.

What cognitive developmental changes occur during adolescence?

During adolescence (between 12 and 18 years of age), the developing teenager acquires the ability to think systematically about all logical relationships within a problem. The transition from concrete thinking to formal logical operations occurs over time. Every adolescent progresses at varying rates in developing his / her ability to think in more complex ways. Each adolescent develops his / her own view of the world. Some adolescents may be able to apply logical operations to school work long before they are able to apply them to personal dilemmas. When emotional issues arise, they often interfere with an adolescent's ability to think in more complex ways. The ability to consider possibilities, as well as facts, may influence decision making, in either positive or negative ways.

Some common features indicating a progression from more simple to more complex cognitive development include the following:

Early Adolescence
During early adolescence, the use of more complex thinking is focused on personal decision making in school and home environments, including the following:

- Begins to demonstrate use of formal logical operations in school work.
- Begins to question authority and society standards.
- Begins to form and verbalize his / her own thoughts and views on a variety of topics, usually more related to his / her own life, such as:
    - Which sports are better to play.
    - Which groups are better to be included in.
    - What personal appearances are desirable or attractive.
    - What parental rules should be changed.

Middle Adolescence
With some experience in using more complex thinking processes, the focus of middle adolescence often expands to include more philosophical and futuristic concerns, including the following:

- Often questions more extensively.
- Often analyzes more extensively.
- Thinks about and begins to form his / her own code of ethics.
  Thinks about different possibilities and begins to develop own identity.
- Thinks about and begins to systematically consider possible future goals.
- Thinks about and begins to make his / her own plans.
- Begins to think long term.
- Use of systematic thinking begins to influence relationships with others.

Late adolescence

During late adolescence, complex thinking processes are used to focus on less self-centered concepts as well as personal decision making, including the following:

- Develops idealistic views on specific topics or concerns.
- Debate and develop intolerance of opposing views.
- Begins to focus thinking on making career decisions.
- Begins to focus thinking on emerging role in adult society.
- Increased thoughts about more global concepts such as justice, history, politics, and patriotism.

What encourages healthy cognitive development during adolescence?

The following suggestions will help to encourage positive and healthy cognitive development in the adolescent:

- Include adolescents in discussions about a variety of topics, issues, and current events.
- Encourage adolescents to share ideas and thoughts with adults.
- Encourage adolescents to think independently and develop their own ideas.
- Assist adolescents in setting their own goals.
- Stimulate adolescents to think about possibilities of the future.
- Compliment and praise adolescents for well thought out decisions.
- Assist adolescents in re-evaluating poorly made decisions for themselves.

Certain stages of child development have their own sets of problems, and it should be kept in mind that short-term undesirable behaviors can and will occur over these stages. Child development is also a continuum, and children may manifest these problem behaviors somewhat earlier or later than their peers.

About 15-20% of the school-aged population between 6 and 17 years old receive special education services.. The categories of learning disabilities and emotional disturbance are the most prevalent. Exceptional students are very much like their peers without disabilities. The main difference is that they have an intellectual, emotional, behavioral, or physical deficit that significantly interferes with their ability to benefit from education.

Skill 1.2 **Demonstrate knowledge of communication theory, language development, and the role of language, communication modes, and communication patterns in learning for individuals with and without disabilities.**

Language is the means whereby people communicate their thoughts, make requests and respond to others. Communication Competence is an interaction of cognitive competence, social knowledge, and language competence. Communication problems may result from in any or all of these areas, which directly impact the student's ability to interact with others. Language consists of several components, each of which follows a sequence of development. Brown and colleagues were the first to describe language as a function of developmental stages rather than age (Reid, 1988 p 44). He developed a formula to group the mean length of utterances (sentences) into stages. Counting the number of morphemes per 100 utterances, one can calculate a mean length of utterance, MLU. Total number of morphemes / 100 = MLU e.g. 180/100 = 1.8

Summary of Brown's findings about MLU and language development:

Stage	MLU	Developmental Features
L	1.5-2.0	14 basic morphemes (e.g. in, on, articles, possessives)
LI	2.0-2.5	Beginning of pronoun use, auxiliary verbs
LII	2.5-3.0	Language form approximate adult forms. Beginning of questions and negative statements
IV	3.0-3.5	Use of complex (embedded)sentences
V	3.5-4.0	Use of compound sentences.

COMPONENTS OF LANGUAGE
Language learning is composed of five components. Children progress through developmental stages through each component.

Phonology
Phonology is the system of rules about sounds and sound combinations for a language. A phoneme is the smallest unit of sound that combines with other sounds to make words. A phoneme, by itself, does not have a meaning; it must be combined with other phonemes. Problems in phonology may be manifested as developmental delays in acquiring consonants, or reception problems, such as misinterpreting words because a different consonant was substituted.

Morphology

Morphemes are the smallest units of language that convey meaning. Morphemes are root words, or free morphemes that can stand alone (e.g. walk), and affixes (e.g. ed, s, ing). Content words carry the meaning in a sentence, and functional words join phrases and sentences. Generally, students with problems in this area may not use inflectional endings in their words, may not be consistent in their use of certain morphemes or may be delayed in learning morphemes such as irregular past tenses.

Syntax

Syntax rules, commonly known as grammar, govern how morphemes and words are correctly combined. Wood, (1976) describes six stages of syntax acquisition (Mercer, p 347).

- **Stages 1 and** 2- Birth to about 2 years: Child is learning the semantic system.
- **Stage 3** – Ages 2 – 3 years: Simple sentences contain subject and predicate.
- **Stage 4**- Ages 2 ½ to 4 years: Elements such as question words are added to basic sentences (e.g. where), word order is changed to ask questions. The child begins to use "and" to combine simple sentences, and the child begins to embed words within the basic sentence.
- **Stage 5**- About 3 ½ to 7 years: The child uses complete sentences that include word classes of adult language. The child is becoming aware of appropriate semantic functions of words and differences within the same grammatical class.
- **Stage 6**- About 5 to 20 years: The child begins to learn complex sentences and sentences that imply commands, requests and promises.

Syntactic deficits are manifested by the child using sentences that lack length or complexity for a child that age. The child may have problems understanding or creating complex sentences and embedded sentences.

Semantics
Semantics is language content: objects, actions, and relations between objects. As with syntax, Wood (1976) outlines stages of semantic development:

- **Stage 1**- Birth to about 2 years: The child is learning meaning while learning his first words. Sentences are one-word, but the meaning varies according to the context. Therefore, "doggie" may mean, "This is my dog," or, "There is a dog," or "The dog is barking."
- **Stage 2**- About 2 to 8 years: The child progresses to two-word sentences about concrete actions. As more words are learned, the child forms longer sentences, until about age 7, things are defined in terms of visible actions. The child begins to respond to prompts (e.g. pretty/flower), and at about age 8, the child can respond to a prompt with an opposite (e.g. pretty/ugly).
- **Stage 3**- Begins at about age 8: The child's word meanings relate directly to experiences, operations and processes. Vocabulary is defined by the child's experiences, not the adult's. At about age 12, the child begins to give "dictionary" definitions, and the semantic level approaches that of adults.

Semantic problems take the form of:

- Limited vocabulary
- Inability to understand figurative language or idioms; interprets literally
- Failure to perceive multiple meanings of words, changes in word meaning from changes in context, resulting in incomplete understanding of what is read
- Difficulty understanding linguistic concepts (e.g. before/after), verbal analogies, and logical relationships such as possessives, spatial, and temporal
- Misuse of transitional words such as "although," "regardless"

Pragmatics
Commonly known as the speaker's intent, pragmatics are used to influence or control the actions or attitudes of others. **Communicative competence** depends on how well one understands the rules of language, as well as the social rules of communication such as taking turns and using the correct tone of voice.

Pragmatic deficits are manifested by failures to respond properly to indirect requests after age 8 (e.g. "Can't you turn down the TV"? elicits a response of "No" instead of "Yes" and the child turning down the volume). Children with these deficits have trouble reading cues that indicate the listener does not understand them. Whereas a person would usually notice this and adjust one's speech to the listener's needs the child with pragmatic problems does not do this.

Pragmatic deficits are also characterized by inappropriate social behaviors such as interruptions or monopolizing conversations. Children may use immature speech and have trouble sticking to a topic. These problems can persist into adulthood, affecting academic, vocational and social interactions.

Problems in language development often require long-term interventions, and can persist into adulthood. Certain problems are associated with different grade levels:

Preschool and Kindergarten: The child's speech may sound immature, the child may not be able to follow simple directions, and often cannot name things such as the days of the week and colors. They child may not be able to discriminate between sounds and the letters associated with the sounds. The child might substitute sounds and have trouble responding accurately to certain types of questions. The child may play less with his peers or participate in non-play or parallel play.

Elementary School: Problems with sound discrimination persist, and the child may have problems with temporal and spatial concepts (e.g. before/after). As the child progresses through school, he may have problems making the transition from narrative to expository writing. Word retrieval problems may not be very evident because the child begins to devise strategies such as talking around the word he cannot remember, or using fillers, and descriptors. The child might speak more slowly, have problems sounding out words, and get confused with multiple-meaning words. Pragmatic problems show up in social situations such as failure to correctly interpret social cues and adjust to appropriate language, inability to predict consequences, and inability to formulate requests to obtain new information.

Secondary School: At this level, difficulties become more subtle. The child lacks the ability to use and understand higher-level syntax, semantics, and pragmatics. If the child has problems with auditory language, he may also have problems with short-term memory. Receptive and/or expressive language delays impair the child's ability to learn effectively. The child often lacks the ability to organize categorize the information received in school. Problems associated with pragmatic deficiencies persist but because the child is aware of them, he becomes inattentive, withdrawn or frustrated.

Communication is the transference of information from one party to another and occurs in many different manners. Sometimes, it is oral while other times it may be conveyed through facial expressions or body language. There is also written language, which is used to convey many different messages as well. This process of transferring information and sharing it with another person is known as communication theory

Over the years, theories regarding language development have been very vocal and disagreed in many levels. The major disagreement can be tracked back to the 1950's where two predominant theories emerged.
Behaviorism developed and believed that language was the direct result of the situations surrounding the child. Behaviorists believed that the environment controlled all language and solely these outside forces influenced its development.

On the other hand, nativism theorists believed that all language was similar to genetic traits. They believed that language was determined before birth and developed in a similar manner to other innate characteristics. They ruled out that any outside factors could influence the development process.

Currently, these two opposing viewpoints have been combined to form the interactionist theories. This term indicates that children's language skills are a direct result of inherent predetermined skills and the surrounding environment.

It is this combination approach that is most accepted in today's society. In relation to reading, it is important to understand the fact that reading is language based. Children who struggle in language developmental will almost certainly have difficulty obtaining a solid foundation in reading skills.

As language developments, students begin to understand how sounds blend together to form words, how words go together to form sentences, and how sentences go together to form stories. It is through these stories and sentences that meaning is conveyed from one party to another.

If a student is unable to convey that meaning or draw conclusions from the message that someone else is sending, they miss a key component of language development. With this skill missing, the natural progression that text conveys meaning is also missed. Since the ultimate goal of reading is comprehension or understanding, one can see the significant deficit these children experience.

Speech pathologists that specialize in language development can therefore be an essential component to preventing and helping children with language disorders. In this way, these trained specialists can also help in preventing and remediating language issues, which will help reading skills.

In summary, language development is crucial to the progress students will experience in life. There are many different modes and patterns of communication as discussed in the opening paragraphs. Students will find a variety of methods to communicate in the school setting including: oral, augmentative, sign language, Braille, written, use of technological aids, and picture symbol systems. It is important to be familiar with each system on a general level and more specifically with those students you encounter use.

Oral language development occurs over time and at varying rates. Children start with developing their own rules and learn the correct pronunciation and grammar by listening to and being corrected by adults. Over time they learn the correct syntax, but they do need time to develop their oral language skills. There are three basic components to oral language development:

- Phonological - combination of sounds
- Semantics – sounds and words go together to form other words
- Syntactics – combining words to form sentences

Students come to kindergarten in varying degrees of oral language development. Teachers should not try to focus on problems or the inability to pronounce certain words or letter sounds. If, however, after providing enormous support, the child cannot make the proper speech sounds, then he/she should be referred to a speech pathologist. This situation exists for only a small number of children. Many children will outgrow the oral language problems with the proper coaching and modeling provided by the teacher.
Teachers should nurture oral language development by:

- Providing a wealth of oral language opportunities in the classroom
- Respecting the diversity of backgrounds and cultures that the students bring to the classroom.
- Engaging the students in conversation while instructing.
- Encouraging conversation between the students

Skill 1.3 Demonstrate knowledge of typical and atypical motor development.

All people develop in their own ways and at their own paces, however, there are generally accepted milestones for motor development on which we can gauge the progress of children. These milestones occur in a sequential fashion and when children deviate in significant manner from the norm may have difficulty achieving in different ways.

Motor is typically described in two ways: gross and fine. Gross motor refers to large muscle movements, while fine motor refers to small muscle movements. Both areas have their own milestones. Keeping in mind that in order to progress to the next skill, a child must first attain a lower skill, it is important to keep track of the development of the children.

Here is a very brief and general overview of the typical motor development, atypical development would include any patterns which do not follow the descriptions.

Birth – Six Weeks:
- Movement of arms and legs
- Begin to lift head
- Sudden jerking movements

Six Weeks – Three Months:
- Stabilize head on own
- Muscle control begins

Three Months – Six Months:
- Will begin to support own weight on arms
- Begin to roll over
- Can sit up on own or when propped with supportive pillows

Six Months – Nine Months:
- Sits alone
- Scooting
- Stand with support and help
- Rolling over
- Grasping objects
- Try to hold cup/bottle

Nine Months – 1 year:
- Crawling
- Walking
- Pushing up to standing position
- Picking up objects by using pincher grasp (thumb and first finger)

1 year – 2 years:
- Walking
- Kicking and rolling balls
- Learning to maneuver stairs
- Using utensils to eat
- Putting toys in buckets or bowls
- Marking with crayons (fist grasp)
- Stacking blocks (2-3)
- Tries to take things apart

2 years to 3 years:
- Running
- Jumping with two feet
- Using stairs alone
- Balancing on one foot for 1-2 seconds
- Scribbling
- Beginning to use scissors
- Stringing beads

3 years – 5 years:
- Throwing and catching balls
- Hopping
- Skipping
- Climbing
- Pedaling a bike with training wheels
- Pouring from one container to another
- Buttoning
- Zipping and unzipping
- Development of pincher grasp when writing

5 years – 7 years:
- Pumping on a swing
- Jumping rope
- Swimming
- Visual-motor coordination develops to complex levels
- Catching balls
- Balancing on one foot for 10-20 seconds
- Draw shapes, letters and words
- Drawing recognizable pictures
- Tying shoes

Skill 1.4 **Demonstrate knowledge of the effects on behavior and learning of family, community, and a child's and family's cultural and environmental milieu.**

As a child develops, whether typically or with some developmental delays, there are impacts on all those who surround him. In the best of circumstances, a supportive, nurturing relationship develops and stress is limited to very little. However, when a child is born with, or develops with delays there can be significant effects not only on that child but all others involved.

Beginning with the family, there can be additional stress which impacts greatly bonding and relationship development. This stress can require additional intervention and support from within the community. As the developmental delays occur, there can also be impacts specifically for the child which may impact behavior and learning.

Depending on the severity of the issues involved, there may be additional skills with the family has to now become proficient. For example, a child may require specific medical treatments which the parents and other family members may be required to perform on a regular basis. In this case, there may be a significant amount of learning in a very short period of time.
The available community resources, support from cultural systems, and other outside factors may also require those involved in care to immerse themselves in new and detailed education. This can be overwhelming for anyone.

This stress can lead to behavioral changes in many different ways as well. The family may argue because they do not have a communication system in place to share their fears, frustrations, concerns, questions, or other issues which may be affecting them. Additionally, other outside people from the community may be adding to the stress with their reactions to the difficulties the child is facing.

Often well meaning, sometimes people are uncertain how to respond when a child displays differences. The entire process is difficult at best and when together the factors can lead to a trying situation for all involved.

COMPETENCY 2.0   UNDERSTAND VARIOUS TYPES OF DISABILITIES
                   AND THE CHARACTERISTICS OF STUDENTS WITH
                   SPECIAL NEEDS

Skill 2.1   Demonstrate knowledge of major genetic and environmental
              etiologies of cognitive, sensory, emotional, and physical
              disabilities.

THE CAUSATION AND PREVENTION OF A DISABILITY

No one knows exactly what causes learning disabilities. There is a wide range of possibilities that make it almost impossible to pin point the exact cause. Listed below are some factors that can attribute to the development of a disability.

Problems in Fetal Brain Development - During pregnancy things can go wrong in the development of the brain, which alters how the neurons form or interconnect. Throughout pregnancy, brain development is vulnerable to disruptions. If the disruption occurs early, the fetus may die, or the infant may be born with widespread disabilities and possibly mental retardation. If the disruption occurs later, when the cells are becoming specialized and moving into place, it may leave errors in the cell makeup, location, or connections. Some scientists believe that these errors may later show up as learning disorders.

Genetic Factors - Learning disabilities can run in families, which show that there may be a genetic link. For example, children who do not have certain reading skills, such as hearing the separate sounds of words, are likely to have a parent with a similar problem. A parent's learning disability can take a slightly different form in the child. Due to this, it is unlikely that specific learning disorders are directly inherited.

Environment - Additional reasons for why learning disabilities appear to run in families stem from the family environment. Parents with expressive language disorders may talk less to their children or their language may be muffled. In this case the lack of a proper role model for acquiring good language skills causes the disability.

Tobacco, Alcohol, and Other Drug Use -- Many drugs taken by the mother pass directly to the fetus during pregnancy. Research shows that a mother's usage of cigarettes, alcohol, or other drugs during pregnancy may have damaging effects on the unborn child. Mothers who smoke during pregnancy are more likely to have smaller birth weight babies. Newborns, who weigh less than 5 pounds, are more at risk for learning disorders.

Heavy alcohol use during pregnancy has been linked to Fetal Alcohol Syndrome (FAS), a condition resulting in low birth weigh, intellectual impairment, hyperactivity, and certain physical defects.

Problems During Pregnancy or Delivery -- Complications during pregnancy can also cause learning disabilities. The mother's immune system can react to the fetus and attack it as if it were an infection. This type of problem appears to cause newly formed brain cells to settle in the wrong part of the brain. In addition, during delivery, the umbilical cord can become twisted and temporarily cut off oxygen to the fetus, resulting in impaired brain functions.

Toxins in the Environment -- New brain cells and neural networks are produced for a year after the child is born. These cells are vulnerable to certain disruptions.

There are certain environmental toxins that may lead to learning disabilities. Cadmium and lead are becoming a leading focus of neurological research. Cadmium is used in making some steel products. It can get into the soil and then into the foods we eat. Lead was once common in paint and gasoline, and is still present in some water pipes.

Children with cancer who have been treated with chemotherapy or radiation at an early age can also develop learning disabilities. This is very prevalent in children with brain tumors who received radiation to the skull.

In order to prevent disabilities from occurring, information on the causes of disabilities should be widely available so that parents can take the necessary steps to safeguard their children from conception up until the early years of life. While some of the causes of disability are unavoidable or incidental, there are many causes that can be prevented.

IDENTIFY THE CHARACTERISTICS OF EMOTIONALLY DISTURBED CHILDREN

Children with emotional disturbances or behavioral disorders are not always easy to identify. It is, of course, easy to identify the acting-out child who is constantly fighting, who cannot stay on task for more than a few minutes, or who shouts obscenities when angry. It is not always easy to identify the child who internalizes his or her problems, on the other hand, or may appear to be the "model" student, but suffers from depression, shyness, or fears. Unless the problem becomes severe enough to impact school performance, the internalizing child may go for long periods without being identified or served.

Studies of children with behavioral and emotional disorders, share some general characteristics:

Lower academic performance: While it is true that some emotionally disturbed children have above average IQ scores, the majority are behind their peers in measures of intelligence and school achievement. Most score in the "slow learner" or "mildly mentally retarded" range on IQ tests, averaging about 90. Many have learning problems that exacerbate their acting out or "giving-up" behavior. As the child enters secondary school, the gap between or her and non-disabled peers widens until the child may be as many as 2 to 4 years behind in reading and/or math skills by high school. Children with severe degrees of impairment may be difficult to evaluate.

Social skills deficits: Students with deficits may be uncooperative, selfish in dealing with others, unaware of what to do in social situations, or ignorant of the consequences of their actions. This may be a combination of lack of prior training, lack of opportunities to interact, and dysfunctional value systems and beliefs learned from their family.

Classroom behaviors: Often, emotionally disturbed children display classroom behavior that is highly disruptive to the classroom setting. Emotionally disturbed children are often out of their seat or running around the room, hitting, fighting, or disturbing their classmates, stealing or destroying property, defiant and noncompliant, and/or verbally disruptive. They do not follow directions and often do not complete assignments.

Aggressive behaviors: Aggressive children often fight or instigate their peers to strike back at them. Aggressiveness may also take the form of vandalism or destruction of property. Aggressive children also engage in verbal abuse.

Delinquency: As emotionally disturbed, acting-out children enter adolescence, they may become involved in socialized aggression (i.e. gang membership) and delinquency. Delinquency is a legal term, rather than a medical, and describes truancy, and actions that would be criminal if they were committed by adults. Not every delinquent is classified as emotionally disturbed, but children with behavioral and emotional disorders are especially at risk for becoming delinquent because of their problems at school (the primary place for socializing with peers), deficits in social skills that may make them unpopular at school, and/or dysfunctional homes.

Withdrawn behaviors: Children who manifest withdrawn behaviors may consistently act in an immature fashion or prefer to play with younger children. They may daydream or complain of being sick in order to "escape". They may also cry often, cling to the teacher, and ignore those who attempt to interact, or suffer from fears or depression.

Schizophrenia and psychotic behaviors: Children may have bizarre delusions, hallucinations, incoherent thoughts, and disconnected thinking. Schizophrenia typically manifests itself between the ages of 15 and 45, and the younger the onset, the more severe the disorder. These behaviors usually require intensive treatment beyond the scope of the regular classroom setting.

Gender: Many more boys than girls are identified as having emotional and behavioral problems, especially hyperactivity and attention Deficit disorder, autism, childhood psychosis and problems with under control (aggression, socialized aggression). Girls, on the other hand, have more problems with over control (i.e. withdrawal and phobias). Boys are much more prevalent than girls in problems with mental retardation and language and learning disabilities.

Age Characteristics: When they enter adolescence, girls tend to experience affective or emotional disorders such as anorexia, depression, bulimia, and anxiety at twice the rate of boys, which mirrors the adult prevalence pattern.

Family Characteristics: Having a child with an emotional or behavioral disorder does not automatically mean that the family is dysfunctional. However, there are family factors that create or contribute to the development of behavior disorders and emotional disturbance.

- Abuse and neglect
- Lack of appropriate supervision
- Lax, punitive, and/or lack of discipline
- High rates of negative types of interaction among family members
- Lack of parental concern and interest
- Negative adult role models
- Lack of proper health care and/or nutrition
- Disruption in the family

Some characteristics of students with **mild learning and behavioral disabilities** are as follows:

- Lack of interest in schoolwork
- Prefer concrete rather than abstract lessons
- Possess weak listening skills
- Low achievement; limited verbal and/or writing skills
- Respond better to active rather than passive learning tasks
- Have areas of talent or ability often overlooked by teachers
- Prefer to receive special help in regular classroom
- Higher dropout rate than regular education students
- Achieve in accordance with teacher expectations
- Require modification in classroom instruction and are easily distracted.

Identify characteristic of students who have a learning disability:

- Hyperactivity: a rate of motor activity higher than normal
- Perceptual difficulties: visual, auditory, and perceptual problems
- Perceptual-motor impairments: poor integration of visual and motor systems, often affecting fine motor coordination.
- Disorders of memory and thinking: memory deficits, trouble with problem-solving, concept formation and association, poor awareness of own metacognitive skills (learning strategies)
- Impulsiveness: acts before considering consequences, poor impulse control, often followed by remorselessness.
- Academic problems in reading, math, writing or spelling; significant discrepancies in ability levels.

Identify characteristics of individuals with mental retardation or intellectual Disabilities:

- IQ of 70 or below
- Limited cognitive ability; delayed academic achievement, particularly in language-related subjects
- Deficits in memory which often relate to poor initial perception, or inability to apply stored information to relevant situations
- Impaired formulation of learning strategies
- Difficulty in attending to relevant aspects of stimuli: slowness in reaction time or in employing alternate strategies.

Identify characteristics of individuals with Autism
This exceptionality appears very early in childhood. Six common features of autism are:

- **Apparent sensory deficit** –The child may appear not to see or hear or react to a stimulus, then react in an extreme fashion to a seemingly insignificant stimulus.
- **Severe affect isolation**—The child does not respond to the usual signs of affection such as smiles and hugs.
- **Self-stimulation** – Stereotyped behavior takes the form of repeated or ritualistic actions that make no sense to others, such as hand flapping, rocking, staring at objects, or humming the same sounds for hours at a time.
- **Tantrums and self-injurious behavior (SIB)** – Autistic children may bite themselves, pull their hair, bang their heads, or hit themselves. They can throw severe tantrums, and direct aggression and destructive behavior toward others.
- **Echolalia**—also known as "parrot talk." The autistic child may repeat what is played on television, for example, or respond to others by repeating what was said to him. Alternatively, he may simply not speak at all.

Severe deficits in behavior and self-care skills. Autistic children may behave like children much younger than themselves.

Skill 2.2   Demonstrate knowledge of differential characteristics including levels of severity and multiple disabilities, of individuals with disabilities across the age range.

Eligibility for special education services is based on a student having one of the above disabilities (or a combination thereof) and demonstration of educational need through professional evaluation.

Seldom does a student with a disability fall into only one of the characteristics listed in the law. For example, a student with a hearing impairment may also have a specific learning disability, or a student on the autism spectrum may also demonstrate a language impairment. In fact, language impairment is inherent in autism. Sometimes the eligibility is defined as a multiple disabilities (with one listed as a primary eligibility on the IEP and the others listed as secondary). Sometimes there are overlapping needs that are not necessarily listed as a secondary disability.

Teachers of special education students should be aware of the similarities between areas of disabilities as well as differences.

Students with disabilities (in all areas) may demonstrate difficulty in social skills. For a student with hearing impairment, social skills may be difficult because of not hearing social language. However, the emotionally disturbed student may have difficulty because of a special type of psychological disturbance. An autistic student, as a third example, would be unaware of the social cues given with voice, facial expression, and body language. Each of these students would need social skill instruction but in a different way.

Students with disabilities (in all areas) may demonstrate difficulty in academic skills.

A student with mental retardation will need special instruction across all areas of academics while a student with a learning disability may need assistance in only one or two subject areas.

Students with disabilities may demonstrate difficulty with independence or self-help skills. A student with a visual impairment may need specific mobility training while a student with a specific learning disability may need a checklist to help in managing materials and assignments.

Special Education Teachers should be aware that although students across disabilities may demonstrate difficulty in similar ways, the causes may be very different. For example, some disabilities are due to specific sensory impairments (hearing or vision), some due to cognitive ability (mental retardation), and some due to neurological impairment (autism or some learning disabilities). The reason for the difficulty should be a consideration when planning the program of special education intervention.

Additionally, Special Education Teachers should be aware that each area of disability has a range of involvement. Some students may have minimal disability and require no services. Others may need only a few accommodations and have 504 Plan. Some may need an IEP that outlines a specific special education program which might be implemented in an inclusion/resource program, self-contained program, or in a residential setting.

A student with ADD may be able to participate in the regular education program with a 504 Plan that outlines a checklist system to keep the student organized and additional communication between school and home. Other students with ADD may need instruction in a smaller group with fewer distractions and would be served in a resource room.

Special educators should be knowledgeable of the cause and severity of the disability and its manifestations in the specific student when planning an appropriate special education program. Because of the unique needs of the child, such programs are documented in the child's IEP – Individualized Education Program.

Student with a disability means a student with a disability who has not attained the age of 21 prior to September 1st and who is entitled to attend public schools and who, because of mental, physical or emotional reasons, has been identified as having a disability and who requires special services and programs approved by the department. The terms used in this definition are defined as follows:

(1) *Autism* means a developmental disability significantly affecting verbal and nonverbal communication and social interaction, generally evident before age 3 that adversely affects a student's educational performance. Other characteristics often associated with autism are engagement in repetitive activities and stereotyped movements, resistance to environmental change or change in daily routines, and unusual responses to sensory experiences. The term does not apply if a student's educational performance is adversely affected primarily because the student has an emotional disturbance. A student who manifests the characteristics of autism after age 3 could be diagnosed as having autism if the criteria in this paragraph are otherwise satisfied.

(2) *Deafness* means a hearing impairment that is so severe that the student is impaired in processing linguistic information through hearing, with or without amplification that adversely affects a student's educational performance.

(3) *Deaf-blindness* means concomitant hearing and visual impairments, the combination of which causes such severe communication and other developmental and educational needs that they cannot be accommodated in special education programs solely for students with deafness or students with blindness.

(4) *Emotional disturbance* means a condition exhibiting one or more of the following characteristics over a long period of time and to a marked degree that adversely affects a student's educational performance:

   (i) an inability to learn that cannot be explained by intellectual, sensory, or health factors.

   (ii) an inability to build or maintain satisfactory interpersonal relationships with peers and teachers;

   (iii) inappropriate types of behavior or feelings under normal circumstances;

   (iv) a generally pervasive mood of unhappiness or depression; or

   (v) a tendency to develop physical symptoms or fears associated with personal or school problems.

The term includes schizophrenia. The term does not apply to students who are socially maladjusted, unless it is determined that they have an emotional disturbance.

(5) *Hearing impairment* means an impairment in hearing, whether permanent or fluctuating, that adversely affects the child's educational performance but that is not included under the definition of *deafness* in this section.

(6) *Learning disability* means a disorder in one or more of the basic psychological processes involved in understanding or in using language, spoken or written, which manifests itself in an imperfect ability to listen, think, speak, read, write, spell, or to do mathematical calculations. The term includes such conditions as perceptual disabilities, brain injury, minimal brain dysfunction, dyslexia and developmental aphasia. The term does not include learning problems that are primarily the result of visual, hearing or motor disabilities, of mental retardation, of emotional disturbance, or of environmental, cultural or economic disadvantage.

(7) *Mental retardation* means significantly sub-average general intellectual functioning, existing concurrently with deficits in adaptive behavior and manifested during the developmental period that adversely affects a student's educational performance.

(8) *Multiple disabilities* means concomitant impairments (such as mental retardation-blindness, mental retardation-orthopedic impairment, etc.), the combination of which cause such severe educational needs that they cannot be accommodated in a special education program solely for one of the impairments. The term does not include deaf-blindness.

(9) *Orthopedic impairment* means a severe orthopedic impairment that adversely affects a student's educational performance. The term includes impairments caused by congenital anomaly (*e.g.*, clubfoot, absence of some member, etc.), impairments caused by disease (*e.g.*, poliomyelitis, bone tuberculosis, etc.), and impairments from other causes (*e.g.*, cerebral palsy, amputation, and fractures or burns which cause contractures).

(10) *Other health-impairment* means having limited strength, vitality or alertness, including a heightened alertness to environmental stimuli, that results in limited alertness with respect to the educational environment, that is due to chronic or acute health problems, including but not limited to a heart condition, tuberculosis, rheumatic fever, nephritis, asthma, sickle cell anemia, hemophilia, epilepsy, lead poisoning, leukemia, diabetes, attention deficit disorder or attention deficit hyperactivity disorder or Tourettes syndrome, which adversely affects a student's educational performance.

(11) *Speech or language impairment* means a communication disorder, such as stuttering, impaired articulation, a language impairment or a voice impairment that adversely affects a student's educational performance.

(12) *Traumatic brain injury* means an acquired injury to the brain caused by an external physical force or by certain medical conditions such as stroke, encephalitis, aneurysm, and anoxia or brain tumors with resulting impairments that adversely affect educational performance. The term includes open or closed head injuries or brain injuries from certain medical conditions resulting in mild, moderate or severe impairments in one or more areas, including cognition, language, memory, attention, reasoning, abstract thinking, judgment, problem solving, sensory, perceptual and motor abilities, psychosocial behavior, physical functions, information processing, and speech. The term does not include injuries that are congenital or caused by birth trauma.

(13) *Visual impairment including blindness* means an impairment in vision that, even with correction, adversely affects a student's educational performance. The term includes both partial sight and blindness.

Skill 2.3 **Demonstrate knowledge of basic functions of the body's systems in relation to common medical conditions and health impairments affecting individuals with disabilities.**

Having a general understanding of basic anatomy and physiology is essential when working with students with various medical conditions and health impairments. Generally, there will be specific information about the individual needs of students from parents, doctors, or other specially trained personnel. However, as the teacher knowing the basic functions of the body's systems can be quite helpful.

For example, having an understanding of how the muscles contract to cause movement can provide you with a general and more personal understanding of the contractures a student with cerebral palsy may be experiencing.

The human body is very complex and at any given time numerous activities are occurring at the same time. Keeping this in mind, along with the knowledge that each organ or part of the body has it's own purpose and function and is equally important to help the person function, will provide the teacher with a basic level of understanding to the fact that when one part is not working appropriately due to disability it will affect many other components.

Some of the basic functions of the human body are:

- Movement
- Reproduction
- Growth
- Responsiveness
- Metabolism
- Organization
- Differentiation
- Respiration
- Digestion
- Excretion

When any one of these functions is impaired due to disability or there are environmental factors impacting them, the person will have difficulty completing tasks presented. It is essential to find adaptations to allow for improved quality of life.

It is also important to keep in mind the fact that meeting these basic biological needs comes before any other higher level needs, such as academics. Students need to have appropriate modifications to attend to these basic system needs in the school setting before any sort of academic issues can be addressed.

Skill 2.4 **Demonstrate knowledge of the effects of sensory disabilities on language development and cognition, including the effects on cultural development and familial structures.**

As previously discussed, all systems within the human body are integral to each other. Therefore, when one is impacted by disability there will be others which are effected as well. In the case of sensory disabilities, they can affect language development and cognition.

When a student is unable to see, hear or has other sensory issues, instinctively other senses begin to compensate for the one which is not functioning appropriately. Stories are told over and over how the blind man could hear sounds the seeing man could not, or other anecdotes which demonstrate this phenomenon.

So while other senses try to compensate for the damaged one, other areas are affected and may not progress through proper developmental milestones. For example, the student who can not hear may have difficulties acquiring normal language. Due to the fact that language is an oral process, the fact that a child is unable to hear eliminates all of the natural processes in place for developing this skill. Therefore, extraordinary measures need to be taken to ensure language develops.

Other examples could be provided for each possible sensory disability. The blind child would have a hard time understanding the concepts of color, as they are unable to see color and it has no texture. There are other sensory issues, where students may have a sensitivity to certain textures of foods, clothes, etc.

In general, children who have only sensory disabilities are not impacted cognitively. They may, as discussed previously, have difficulties with some concepts due to their disability, but this is not a cognitive deficit. As with any disability, there may be more than one area impacted, in which case cognitive skills may be addressed.

Any disability may cause stress within the family or close community surrounding the child. In some cultures, disabilities of any sort are considered shameful. It is important to understand and respect their individual beliefs. It is not the place of the school system to make judgments. This can be a difficult situation and become tense and uncomfortable at times when values and beliefs clash. It is important to remain impartial and simply keep your professional distance. Providing the best information and educational recommendations is of continued importance, but also being respectful of the wishes of the family when they may disagree with proposals is equally important.

Skill 2.5   Demonstrate knowledge of resources that provide information on exceptional conditions.

There are numerous different exceptionalities and it is impossible for one person to be aware of all of them. For this reason, it is important for Special Education Teachers to have knowledge of available resources from which they can gain information.

First, there is a tremendous amount of information available via the Internet to provide any information a teacher may need in regards to various exceptionalities. For conditions which are medically based or require medical intervention, a wealth of information in clearly explained terms can be found at www.webmd.com. This site can provide the teacher with a clearer understanding of the medical issues children and families are dealing with on a daily basis. Another site which is a great source of information is the Council for Exceptional Children's (CEC) website at www.cec.sped.org. This site provides information for teachers in a variety of areas including:

- Legislation
- Accreditation and licensure
- Various Exceptionalities
- Research-based best educational practices
- Accommodation and modification instructional strategies
- Subject area specific information
- Professional role, responsibility and topics
- Support for teachers

The CEC website also has a store component which has a wealth of professional texts and resource books. These materials can give the teacher additional information about many different exceptionalities.

Within your district or school system there are generally large amounts of knowledge pools waiting to be tapped. The school psychologist can help to clarify issues about specific children or conditions. Resources for school psychologists can be found at www.schoolpsychology.net . There information can be gathered on a number of different exceptional conditions.

Continuing professional development is also critical to finding information about the exceptionalities. Sometimes, the necessary professional development activities will be presented by medical establishments and not necessarily through known educational sources. For example, when dealing with a student with a seizure disorder, the Epileptic Foundation offers tremendous training opportunities, which provide a wealth of information. Sometimes, it takes effort on the part of the educator to find the necessary resources to meet your needs, but information is plentiful with a diligent effort.

COMPETENCY 3.0 UNDERSTAND THE SIGNIFICANCE OF DISABILITIES FOR HUMAN DEVELOPMENT AND LEARNING.

Skill 3.1 **Demonstrate knowledge of the effect of language disorders, processing deficits, cognitive disorders, behavioral/emotional/ social disorders, and physical and sensory disabilities on learning.**

Learning is the ultimate goal of all schooling systems. When a student has an exceptionality in one or more areas quite often learning is impacted. In cases where learning is impacted, special education services are warranted. Various exceptionalities can impact learning in a variety of ways, all of which are unique to each student individually. However, there are some overriding generalizations which can be drawn.

Language Disorders: Students with language disorders have difficulty understanding language, expressing themselves, or communicating. When this occurs, learning is impacted significantly. As language of some form is the main method in which information to be learned is conveyed to the student, a breakdown is imminent. Students with language disorders may need specific clarification, visual cuing and support, and other modifications to overcome these difficulties.

Processing Deficits: Processing deficits affect the manner in which students take the information presented and transfer it into something meaningful to themselves. When a student has difficulties processing information, they often will arrive at misconceptions. These misconceptions require specific clarification for the correct learning to occur.

Cognitive Disorders: Cognitive disorders affect the ability the student has to acquire new information. There are many different levels of cognitive disorders all of which affect the types and amount of new information which can be learned by these students.

Behavior/Emotional/Social Disorders: Students who struggle in these domains often have difficulty learning. The difficulties arise from the inability of the more basic needs the student may have being met before more higher level (learning) can take place. For these students, management of the behavior and emotions needs to occur and be secure before students are able to take in the more academic concepts.

Physical/Sensory Disabilities: Students with physical disabilities alone may need accommodations to be able to access the information presented. Learning needs to be maneuvered in such a manner as to allow the student to have equal opportunity to engage in the same learning experiences as those with no physical issues. Once these opportunities are presented, learning will follow in a manner similar to those without physical disabilities.

Skill 3.2 **Demonstrate knowledge of the effect of language disorders, processing deficits, cognitive disorders, behavioral/emotional /social disorders, and physical and sensory disabilities on behavior.**

As with learning, student's behavior can be impacted by a great many factors. As disabilities overlap, it is sometimes difficult to weed out the specific cause of behavior problems, but it is an important process to work through. Though there are no clear cut rules when it comes to the effect of disorders on a student's behavior there are some broad generalizations which can be drawn.

Language Disorders: When students struggle with either understanding or expressing themselves, they can become quite frustrated. This constant battle to be heard or to understand can be hard to take. Students with language disorders may have no other method of handling this frustration other than acting out or misbehaving. Addressing the underlying causes of the behavior problems may in fact, solve the problem totally.

Processing Deficits: Students who have difficulty processing information may misread situations and therefore respond inappropriately. Because they are unable to look at the events, make sense of what is occurring, and then pull from various strategies to respond appropriately, the students may become impulsive or choose inappropriate ways to react.

Cognitive Disorders: When a child has a cognitive disorder, their ability to appropriately understand events and situations is impaired. This impairment can make it difficult for the students to have appropriate behavioral responses. Additionally, they may not have adequate understanding of what is right and wrong when it comes to behavior in various situations.

Behavior/Emotional/Social Disorders: Students who struggle and perhaps have an organic or mental health diagnosed disorder will have difficulties displaying socially acceptable behavior within society. These disorders affect many different aspects of behavior and require specialized intervention in order to address the underlying cause behind the disorder, usually through the medical profession.

Physical/Sensory Disabilities: Students with physical/sensory disabilities can express similar difficulties to those with language disorders when it comes to behaviors. These students deal with a great deal of frustration on a regular basis trying to participate in society. These frustrations continue to build and can cause intense anger or other unacceptable behavioral issues.

Skill 3.3   Recognize the uses and effects of classes of medications (e.g., stimulant, antidepressant, seizure) on individuals' educational, cognitive, physical, sensory, and emotional behaviors.

Students with disabilities who take medications often experience medication side effects that can impact their behavior and educational development. Teachers may perceive the child is unmotivated or drowsy, not fully understanding the cognitive effects that medications can have on a child.

Some medications may impair concentration, which can lead to poor processing ability, lower alertness, and cause drowsiness and hyperactivity. Students who take several medications may have an increased risk of behavioral and cognitive side effects.

The student's parents should let the school know when the student is beginning or changing their medication so they can look out for possible side effects.

Antidepressants:
There are three different classes of antidepressants that students can take. One type is called the selective serotonin-reuptake inhibitors (SSRIs). The SSRIs block certain receptors from absorbing serotonin. Over time, SSRIs may cause changes in brain chemistry. The side effects of SSRIs include dry mouth, insomnia or restless sleep, increased sweating, and nausea. It can also cause mood swings in people with bipolar disorders.

A second type of antidepressant that may be used is the tricyclic antidepressants. They are considered good for treating depression and obsessive-compulsive behavior. They cause similar side effects to the SSRIs such as sedation, tremor, seizures, dry mouth, light sensitivity, and mood swings in people with bipolar disorders.

A third type of antidepressant is the monoamine oxidase inhibitors (MAOIs). They are not as widely used as the other two types because many have unpleasant and life-threatening interactions with many other drugs, including common over-the-counter medications. People taking MAOIs must also follow a special diet, because these medications interact with many foods. The list of foods to avoid includes chocolate, aged cheeses, and more.

Stimulants are often prescribed to help with attention deficit disorder and attention deficit hyperactivity disorder. The drugs can have many side effects including agitation, restlessness, aggressive behavior, dizziness, insomnia, headache, or tremor.

In severe cases of anxiety an anti-anxiety medication (tranquilizer) may be prescribed. Most tranquilizers have a potential for addiction and abuse. They tend to be sedating, and can cause a variety of unpleasant side effects, including blurred vision, confusion, sleepiness, and tremors.

If educators are aware of the types of medication that their students are taking along with the myriad of side effects they will be able to respond more positively when some of the side effects of the medication change their students behavior, response rate, and attention span.

There are numerous available seizure medications currently used to treat seizure disorders. The majority of the drugs are what are known as blood level drugs, which indicates they need to be taken one or more times daily and take time to build up to treatment level within the person's bloodstream. If doses are missed it can significantly affect the control of the seizures. Some of the more commonly prescribed seizure medications include: Depakote, Lamictal, Carbamazepine, Tegretol, Topamax, Gabapentin, and Klonopin.

Regardless of the medication or its intended use, there can be side effects for students. These side effects can affect the ability of the child to learn, use both fine or gross motor, or their behavior within the school. It is important to be in regular contact with the parents and/or doctors of children taking medications to report issues occurring within the school setting. Some side effects may be able to be controlled through dosage or changing the medication. However, there are still other times when it is a give and take situation, where it is necessary to accept certain things in order to treat the underlying medical issue. Open dialogue and communication is the most important factor whenever dealing with students taking medications.

Skill 3.4   Demonstrate knowledge of the unique effect of two or more disabilities (e.g., deaf/blind, social/emotional disorder and language disorder) on learning and behavior.

Students sometimes demonstrate more than one disability. In this case, the impact on both learning and behavior increases significantly. As previously discussed, students struggling with one area of deficit often have a difficult time taking in the information presented in the school setting. When this is compounded by more than one disability it requires specialized planning and instructional techniques to ensure adequate learning occurs.

The same can be said for behavior. The frustrations a student experiences from dealing with one disability can provide a difficult situation to manage. When additional disabilities are added, the stress increases and so can misbehaviors. While neither learning difficulties or behavioral situations are guaranteed for students with more than one disability, it is something to keep in mind and consider.

Students who are both deaf and blind present a unique challenge within the school setting. These students need all information presented in a manner with which their remaining sense can be utilized to maximize the learning opportunities. Since two of five senses are eliminated and schools are set up and designed to provide instruction using both of these eliminated senses it can be difficult for students to feel a part of the school setting. In this way, both learning and behavior can become problems which will need to be specifically addressed through the child's Individual Education Plan (IEP).

Another example of compounding disabilities which can be of significant concern in the school setting are children who have language disorders and social/emotion difficulties as well. For these children, they lack the ability to understand and express themselves using language and by interpreting social situations. This can lead to a variety of misunderstandings. As the students lack the ability to respond appropriately in social situations, they have no means with which to respond to presented issues. In this case, the students may need to find alternate ways to express their frustrations, anger, or other feelings in order for learning to progress.

No matter what the combination of disabilities, students will need to have specific strategies and techniques put into place to help them find appropriate compensation strategies to increase their ability to display appropriate behavior within the school setting and to progress through the curriculum. Sometimes this will involve many professionals besides the teacher, but with the end goal of providing an appropriate education to the students in mind, it will occur. After all, education includes learning how to respond in social situations as well as the academic curriculum.

SUBAREA II.   ASSESSING STUDENTS AND
                               DEVELOPING INDIVIDUALIZED PROGRAMS

COMPETENCY 4.0   UNDERSTAND TYPES AND CHARACTERISTICS OF
                  ASSESSMENT INSTRUMENTS AND METHODS

Skill 4.1   Demonstrate knowledge of the role of assessment as an
             educational process.

One of the most important aspects of education today is the process of
completing assessments. Assessment is integral in all parts of the educational
process and should occur in a cyclical manner. It is only through assessment
that growth can be determined. Additionally, in today's world with the
implementation of the No Child Left Behind Act (NCLB), assessment is a critical
component to showing progress at the individual student level and at a broader
school level.

The process begins with the completion of an assessment. Data is gathered and
interpreted to determine the instructional program the student should be involved
in during the school. After this plan is developed, the next phase is to implement
the teaching program. Throughout teaching, the student's progress should be
monitored on a regular basis.

Progress monitoring allows the teacher to make instructional adjustments to
ensure the material covered is being internalized and learned by the students. If
the teacher notices that progress has stagnated or is not occurring, s/he can
make changes right away. This prevents losing too much time waiting for end of
year assessments.

Formalized assessments may occur at regular intervals to check overall progress
toward state or national standards. These assessments can provide buildings
with information as to the adequacy of their curriculum in relation to those
standards. Typically however, this information is returned to late for use
instructionally during the current school year.

Overall, this process of assessing, teaching, checking progress, and reassessing
is what drives all instruction. It is often said in education today, that without the
data, it is simply an opinion. The only way to gain the necessary data is through
assessment.

Additionally, in the case of special education, students are generally given
additional individualized assessments to determine their qualification status for
services. In some places, this is also being reevaluated and a Response to
Intervention (RTI) model is being used.

In a RTI model, the progress monitoring assessment data is used to make qualification determinations. An individual plan is developed, specific for the students and then implemented. The student's progress is charted and kept track of over a period of time (typically more than a year). If despite adequate intervention, the student continues to make inadequate progress, the child would become eligible for services. No matter the model, in all education today, assessment is what drives all instruction.

Skill 4.2 Demonstrate knowledge of terminology used in assessment.

The following terms are frequently used in behavioral as well as academic testing and assessment. They represent basic terminology and not more advanced statistical concepts.

Baseline—also known as establishing a baseline. This procedure means collecting data about a target behavior or performance of a skill before certain interventions or teaching procedures are implemented. Establishing a baseline will enable a person to determine if the interventions are effective.

Criterion-Referenced Test – A test in which the individual's performance is measured against mastery of curriculum criteria rather than comparison to the performance of other students. Criterion-referenced tests may be commercially or teacher made. Since these tests measure what a student can or cannot do, results are especially useful for identifying goals and objectives for IEPs and lesson plans.

Curriculum-Based Assessment—Assessment of an individual's performance of objectives of a curriculum, such as a reading or math program. The individual's performance is measured in terms of what objectives were mastered.

Duration Recording-- measuring the length of time a behavior lasts, i.e. tantrums, time out of class, or crying.

Error Analysis—The mistakes on an individual's test are noted and categorized by type. For example, an error analysis in a reading test could categorize mistakes by miscues, substituting words, omitted words or phrases, and miscues that are self corrected.

Event recording—The number of times a target behavior occurs during an observation period.

Formal Assessment—Standardized tests that have specific procedures for administration, norming, scoring and interpretation. These include intelligence and achievement tests.

Frequency—the number of times a behavior occurs in a time interval, such as out-of-seat behavior, hitting, and temper tantrums.

Frequency Distribution—Plotting the scores received on a test and tallying how many individuals received those scores. A frequency distribution is used to visually determine how the group of individuals performed on a test, illustrate extreme scores, and compare the distribution to the mean or other criterion.

Informal Assessment—Non-standardized tests such as criterion referenced tests and teacher-prepared tests. There are no rigid rules or procedures for administration or scoring.

Intensity—The degree of a behavior as measured by its frequency and duration.

Interval Recording—This technique involves breaking the observation into an equal number of time intervals, such as 10-second intervals during a 5-minute period. At the end of each interval, the observer notes the presence or absence of the target behavior. The observer can then calculate a percentage by dividing the number of intervals in which the target behavior occurred by the total number of intervals in the observation period. This type of recording works well for behaviors which occur with high frequency or for long periods of time, such as on or off-task behavior, pencil tapping, or stereotyped behaviors. The observer does not have to constantly monitor the student, yet can gather enough data to get an accurate idea of the extent of the behavior.

Latency—the length of time that elapses between the presentation of a stimulus (e.g. a question), and the response (e.g. the student's answer).

Mean—The arithmetic average of a set of scores, calculated by adding the set of scores and dividing the sum by the number of scores. For example, if the sum of a set of 35 scores is 2935, dividing that sum by 35, (the number of scores), yields a mean of 83.9.

Median—The middle score: 50% of the scores are above this number and 50% of the scores are below this number. In the example above, if the middle score were 72, 17 students would have scored less than 72, and 17 students would have scored more than 72.

Mode: The score most frequently tallied in a frequency distribution. In the example above, the most frequently tallied score might be 78. It is possible for a set of scores to have more than one mode.

Momentary Time Sampling—This is a technique used for measuring behaviors of a group of individuals or several behaviors from the same individual. Time samples are usually brief, and may be conducted at fixed or variable intervals. The advantage of using variable intervals is increased reliability, as the students will not be able to predict when the time sample will be taken.

Multiple Baseline Design—This may be used to test the effectiveness of an intervention in a skill performance or to determine if the intervention accounted for the observed changes in a target behavior. First, the initial baseline data is collected, followed by the data during the intervention period. To get the second baseline, the intervention is removed for a period of time and data is collected again. The intervention is then reapplied, and data collected on the target behavior. An example of a multiple baseline design might be ignoring a child who calls out in class without raising his hand. Initially, the baseline could involve counting the number of times the child calls out before applying interventions. During the time the teacher ignores the child's call-outs, data is collected. For the second baseline, the teacher would resume the response to the child's call-outs in the way she did before ignoring. The child's call-outs would probably increase again, if ignoring actually accounted for the decrease. If the teacher reapplies the ignoring strategy, the child's call-outs would probably decrease again.
Multiple baseline designs may also be used with single-subject experiments where:

- The same behavior is measured for several students at the same time. An example would be observing off-task or out-of-seat behavior among three students in a classroom.
- Several behaviors may be measured for one student. The teacher may be observing call-outs, off-task, and out-of-seat, behavior for a particular child during an observation period.
- Several settings are observed to see if the same behaviors are occurring across settings. A student's aggressive behavior toward his classmates may be observed at recess, in class, going to or from class, or in the cafeteria.

Norm-Referenced Test- An individual's performance is compared to the group that was used to calculate the performance standards in this standardized test. Some examples are the CTBS, WISC-R and Stanford-Binet.

Operational Definition-The description of a behavior and its measurable components. In behavioral observations, the description must be specific and measurable so that the observer will know exactly what constitutes instances and non-instances of the target behavior. Otherwise, reliability may be inaccurate.

Pinpoint- Specifying and describing the target behavior for change in measurable and precise terms. "On time for class" may be interpreted as arriving physically in the classroom when the tardy bell has finished ringing or it may mean being at the pencil sharpener or it may mean being in one's in seat and ready to begin work when the bell has finished ringing. Pinpointing the behavior makes it possible to accurately measure the behavior.

Profile-plotting an individual's behavioral data on a graph.

Rate-The frequency of a behavior over a specified time period, such as 5 talk-outs during a 30-minute period, or typing 85 words per minute.

Raw Score-The number of correct responses on a test before they have been converted to standard scores. Raw scores are not meaningful because they have no basis of comparison to the performance of other individuals.

Reliability—The consistency (stability) of a test over time to measure what it is supposed to measure. Reliability is commonly measured in four ways:

- Test-retest method—The test is administered to the same group or individual after a short period of time and the results are compared.
- Alternate form (equivalent form)—measures reliability by using alternative forms to measure the same skills. If both forms are administered to the same group within a relatively short period of time, there should be a high correlation between the two sets of scores if the test has a high degree of reliability.
- Interrater—This refers to the degree of agreement between two or more individuals observing the same behaviors or observing the same tests.
- Internal reliability—is determined by statistical procedures or by correlating one-half of the test with the other half of the test.

Standard Deviation—The standard deviation is a statistical measure of the variability of the scores. The more closely the scores are clustered around the mean, the smaller the Standard Deviation will be.

Standard Error of Measurement—This statistic measures the amount of possible error in a score. If the Standard error of Measurement for a test is + or - 3, and the individual's score is 35, then, the actual score may be 32 to 35.

Standard Score—A derived score with a set mean, (usually 100) and a standard deviation. Examples are T-scores (mean of 50 and a standard deviation of 10), Z-scores (mean of 0 and standard deviation of 1), and scaled scores. Scaled scores may be given for age groups or grade levels. IQ scores, for instance, use a mean of 100 and a standard deviation of 15.

Task Analysis --Breaking an academic or behavioral task down into its sequence of steps. Task analysis is necessary when preparing criterion-referenced tests and performing error analysis. A task analysis for a student learning to do laundry might include:

1. Sort the clothes by type(white, permanent press, delicate)
2. Choose a type and select the correct water temperature and setting
3. If doing a partial load, adjust the water level
4. Measure the detergent
5. Turn on the machine
6. Load the clothes
7. Add bleach, fabric softener at the correct time
8. Wait for the machine to stop spinning completely before opening it
9. Remove the clothes from the machine and place in a dryer (A task analysis could be done for drying and folding as well)

Validity—The degree to which a test measures what it claims to measure, such as reading readiness, self-concept, or math achievement. A test may be highly reliable but it will be useless if it is not valid. There are several types of validity to examine when selecting or constructing an assessment instrument.

- Content – This type of validity examines the question of whether the types of tasks in the test measure the skill or construct the test claims to measure. That is, a test, which claims to measure mastery in algebra, would probably not be valid if the majority of the items involved basic operations with fractions and decimals.
- Criterion – referenced validity involves comparing the test results with a valid criterion. For example, a doctoral student preparing a test to measure reading and spelling skills may check the test against an established test such as the WRAT-T or another valid criterion such as school grades.
- Predictive Validity - refers to how well a test will relate to a future criterion level, such as the ability of a reading test administered to a first-grader to predict that student's performance at third or fifth grade.
- Concurrent validity – refers to how well the test relates to a criterion measure given at the same time. For example, a new test, which probably measures reading achievement, may be given to a group, which also takes the WRAR-R which has established validity. The test results are compared using statistical measures. The recommended coefficient is 80 or better.
- Construct validity – refers to the ability of the test to measure a theoretical construct, such as intelligence, self-concept, and other non-observable behaviors. Factor analysis and correlation studies with other instruments that measure the same construct are ways to determine construct validity.

Skill 4.3 **Demonstrate knowledge of procedures for using assessment to identify students' learning characteristics and modes of communication, monitor student progress, and evaluate learning strategies and instructional approaches.**

As previously discussed assessment is integral to all aspects of education today. Beyond the scope of general instruction, assessment data can also be used to identify students' learning characteristics, modes of communication, monitor student progress and evaluate learning strategies/instructional approaches.

Identifying Students' Learning Characteristics: Students learn in a variety of different manners and formats. Howard Gardner's theory of multiple intelligences describes at least seven different learning strengths people demonstrate. In school, teachers need to use assessment data to clearly identify how students learn best, in order to meet their needs. In regards to assessment, there are a number of learning style inventories, indexes, and observation tools which allow the teacher and student to help better determine the learning style most suited for the students individually. An example of an learning style inventory can be found at: http://www.ncsu.edu/felder-public/ILSpage.html .

Modes of Communication: Assessing the modes of communication demonstrated by a student is best done through performance assessment in which a student is completing an activity. There are three modes of communication typically discussed. They are: interpretative communication, interpersonal communication and presentational communication; these three modes work together allowing communication to occur. Interpretative communication typically correlates with comprehension, and is described as what the student understands. Interpersonal communication is the ability of the student to respond and react to others opinions, comments or suggestions. Finally, the presentational communication includes the sharing of findings, ideas and information. These modes can be assessed through many other instructional activities.

Progress Monitoring: As touched on briefly in the above skills, progress monitoring is essential in every classroom. It is through this form of assessment, the teacher is able to make informed decisions about instructional changes, adaptations and modifications. Charting and keeping track of the progress individual students are making provides the teacher with detailed and specific information on which to base future lessons. It is through this that s/he can evaluate whether or not the instructional strategies and procedures being implemented are working for that student. Using normative growth rate data and trend lines of performance, teachers can make specific instructional changes and have the data to support the reasoning behind those changes.

Skill 4.4   Demonstrate knowledge of methods and strategies for assessing students' skills within curricular areas, including academic, social, and vocational.

Assessment needs to occur across all areas of the curriculum. This includes all academic areas, social skills and in the case of older students, vocational skills. Valid and reliable methods should be instituted to ensure data is meaningful and useful within the classroom.

Assessment can be informal or formal in nature. Informal assessment methods include observation, running records, checklists, and other nonstandardized procedures. Formal assessment includes norm-referenced, criterion referenced, and any other standardized measurement tools. Teacher made or text book specific tests are more formalized types of assessments, but without appropriate benchmarks are truly more informal measures. Both kinds of assessments provide a great deal of information to the teacher and parents in regards to instruction and future implications.

Academic area assessments are generally in place in most school settings. There are district level and state level assessments to measure the progress of students in reading, writing, math, science, etc. These assessments provide a great deal of information, but still more may need to be gathered. Teachers will need to look at the available results and determine if additional data is required. If it is, they will also need to look for appropriate tools from which to gather it. Having a basic understanding of formal and informal assessments is key.

Using reading as an example, the state level test results will not provide specific day to day instructional level information for students. Teachers may need to administer a reading inventory to determine instructional reading levels or a more skill specific assessment, such as a phonics assessment to gain the insight they need to drive the day to day instruction.

When considering social skills assessments, observational data and other checklists or inventories may be used to gather the information of the skills needed to be developed. The school psychologist and Guidance Counselor may be integral in helping with the completion of these types of assessments. Almost all social skills assessments used in schools are informal in nature.

Vocational assessments, like social skills assessments, are typically informal. In the case of vocational assessments, sometimes situations are created, similar to work settings, and the student is asked to complete the assessment as s/he would in a real work setting. Observations, aptitude tests, interest inventories and other such tools are used in the process of completing vocational assessments as well.

Skill 4.5 **Demonstrate knowledge of ways to assess reliable methods of response in individuals who lack typical communication and performance abilities.**

When students are unable to communicate with the evaluator in a typical fashion, the person completing the assessment needs to find a reliable method for interpreting the responses of the student. Without this assurance, the results of any assessment would not be useful in anyway.

Students who are unable to speak, may require another method with which to respond to oral items. One system which is reliable and effective is to use an augmentative communication device. This may be as simple as a set of pictures which represent typical words used in sentences on a chart. The student then would point to the picture which represents the appropriate answer. There are other types of augmentative communication devices which the student may use on a regular basis that could be used and still ensure reliability.

There are also specific developed tests for children who are unable to respond in a typical format. In the case of intelligence testing, there are tests of nonverbal intelligence developed to be used by students who have difficulties or are unable to complete a more usual intelligence test. Other tests have similar formats which can be utilized when communication difficulties are present.

Sometimes it may be necessary to engage the services of an interpreter. In this case, it can be a very reliable situation if the person doing the interpretation is clear in understanding items need to be completed verbatim. There can be no extra explanations or clarifications outside the realm of what the evaluator deems appropriate. With this type of agreement in place, using an interpreter can be valuable to gaining a more accurate set of assessment information.

Finally, utilizing the knowledge of the speech and language pathologist can be one of the most effective methods to finding an accurate and reliable method for assessing students with communication difficulties. As experts in the area of communication, these professionals often may have specific tests to help gather more information in an appropriate manner. If there are not additional assessments, there may be suggestions they can provide to ensure reliable data is the result.

Skill 4.6   Demonstrate knowledge of the strengths and limitations of various formal and informal assessment tools.

Formal assessments include standardized criterion, norm-referenced instruments, and commercially prepared inventories, which are developmentally appropriate for students across the spectrum of disabilities. Criterion-referenced tests compare a student's performance to a previously established criterion rather than to other students from a normative sample. Norm-referenced tests use normative data for scoring which include performance norms by age, gender, or ethnic group. Formal assessments allow teachers to make comparisons in regards to students. This is particularly helpful when determining if the student is making the necessary progress. However, sometimes due to a variety of factors, these types of assessments provide but a snippet of data which may not be representational of true performance.

Informal assessment strategies include non-standardized instruments such as checklists, developmental rating scales, observations, error analysis, interviews, teacher reports and performance-based assessments that are developmentally appropriate students across disabilities. Informal evaluation strategies rely upon the knowledge and judgment of the professional and are an integral part of the evaluation. An advantage of using informal assessments is the ease of design and administration, and the usefulness of information the teacher can gain about the student's strength and weaknesses. A weakness of informal assessments can be seen as to the fact that it is difficult to report progress in a meaningful manner when using only informal assessments. Often they are somewhat objective in nature and can be interpreted differently by different evaluators.

Some instruments can be both formal and informal tools. For example, observation may incorporate structured observation instruments as well as other informal observation procedures, including professional judgment. When evaluating a child's developmental level, a professional may use a formal adaptive rating scale while simultaneously using professional judgment to assess the child's motivation and behavior during the evaluation process.

IDEA requires that a variety of assessment tools and strategies are utilized when conducting assessments. Before utilizing a formal or informal tool, the practitioner should make sure that the tool is the most appropriate one that can be used for that particular population group. Many assessment tools can be used across disabilities. Dependent upon the disability in question, such as blindness, autism, or hearing impaired, some assessment tools will give more information than others.

Some of the informal and formal assessments that can be used across disabilities are curriculum-based assessments, multiple baseline design, norm-referenced test and momentary time sampling.

Adaptive behavior refers to the knowledge, behavior, and daily living skills that are required to function effectively and independently in a number of different settings.

An adaptive behavior measure is a specific comprehensive assessment of independent living skills. The measurement of adaptive behavior assesses the skills of an individual relative to the skills of his same-age peers. It is a significant tool in eligibility consideration for students with mental handicaps and in the development of effective educational interventions.

Adaptive behaviors commonly include communication and social skills, daily living skills, personal care skills, and other skills that are needed to function at home, at school, and in the community.

Adaptive behavior measurement is important for pinpointing specific skills that need to be taught. Most students acquire adaptive behavior skills through practical experiences. Students with disabilities may need direct instruction in order to acquire the necessary adaptive behavior skills.

Measurement of adaptive behavior should take into account the student's behavior and skills in a number of settings including the classroom, school, home, and neighborhood. In order to get an accurate assessment, the adaptive behavior should be measured by a variety of different people in different settings.

The primary method of measuring adaptive behavior is via structured interviews with teachers and parents. A person trained to administer an adaptive behavior rating scale, such as a school counselor, interviews the student's parents and teachers. The responses are recorded on a rating scale that assesses the student's skills and abilities in various settings. The information obtained from the interview is more valid when the people being interviewed are familiar with the student's knowledge and skills. It is important that parents and teachers provide the most accurate and objective assessment as possible.

Additional methods of measuring adaptive behavior include analyzing the student's records from schools, watching the student in specific circumstances, and testing the student's skills by giving him specific tasks to complete.

The rating scales are created to address the following areas:

- Communication—skills in communicating with others, talking, writing
- Self-care—skills in toileting, eating, dressing, hygiene, and grooming
- Home-living—clothing care, housekeeping, property maintenance, food preparation and cooking, planning and budgeting for shopping
- Social—getting along with others in social situations, interacting with others, forming relationships
- Community use—travel within community, shopping, obtaining services in community (doctor, dentist, setting up utilities), public transportation
- Self-direction—making choices in allocation of time and effort, following a schedule, seeking assistance, deciding what to do in new situations
- Health and safety—making choices about what to eat, illness identification and treatment, avoiding danger, relationships
- Functional academics—skills taught in school that are used every day including reading, writing, computation skills, telling time, using numbers
- Leisure—using available time when not working or in school, choosing age- appropriate activities
- Work—employment skills including work related attitudes and social behaviors, completion of tasks, persistent effort.

Some of the most common adaptive behavior instruments include the following:

Measure	Format	Useful Derived Information
American Association of Mental Retardation (AAMR) 1993	Rating scale or interview	Factor scores of Personal, Social and Community plus 2 Maladaptive Domains
Adaptive Behavior Assessment System – second edition 2003– school, parent, and adult forms	Multiple formats including rating scale, interview, and self report for adults; multiple formats encouraged	Composite, plus scores in 10 adaptive skills areas.
Comprehensive Test of Adaptive Behavior (Revised 2000)	Rating scale with behavioral composite plus "tests" that are used if the behavior has not been observed	7 domains, self-help, home, independence, social, sensory, motor, and language/academic
Scales of Independent Behavior – Revised (1996)	Highly structured interview conducted by professional or paraprofessional.	Composite plus motor, social interaction and communication, personal living, and community living; maladaptive behaviors included
Vineland Adaptive Behavior Scales (1984)	Semi-structured interview requiring well-trained professional; school form uses a rating scale format.	Composite plus Communication, Daily Living, Motor (0-6 yrs), and Socialization. No maladaptive behavior content

Types of Assessment
It is useful to consider the types of assessment procedures that are available to the classroom teacher. The types of assessment discussed below represent many of the more common types, but the list is not comprehensive.

Anecdotal Records
These are notes recorded by the teacher concerning an area of interest or concern with a particular student. These records should focus on observable behaviors and should be descriptive in nature. They should not include assumptions or speculations regarding effective areas such as motivation or interest. These records are usually compiled over a period of several days to several weeks. Limitations occur when the notes provide a bias of some manner toward the student based on behavioral notes logged by a previous teacher. However, sometimes these records can provide a great deal of insight into instructional strategies.

Rating Scales & Checklists

These assessments are generally self-appraisal instruments completed by the students or observations-based instruments completed by the teacher. The focus of these is frequently on behavior or effective areas such as interest and motivation. Rating scales can be helpful, but are subjective in nature and this should be kept in mind when interpreting the data.

Portfolio Assessment

The use of student portfolios for some aspect of assessment has become quite common. The purpose, nature, and policies of portfolio assessment vary greatly from one setting to another. In general, a student's portfolio contains samples of work collected over an extended period of time. The nature of the subject, age of the student, and scope of the portfolio, all contribute to the specific mechanics of analyzing, synthesizing, and otherwise evaluating the portfolio contents.

In most cases, the student and teacher make joint decisions as to which work samples go into the student's portfolios. A collection of work compiled over an extended time period allows teacher, student, and parents to view the student's progress from a unique perspective. Qualitative changes over time can be readily apparent from work samples. Such changes are difficult to establish with strictly quantitative records typical of the scores recorded in the teacher's grade book.

Questioning

One of the most frequently occurring forms of assessment in the classroom is oral questioning by the teacher. As the teacher questions the students, she collects a great deal of information about the degree of student learning and potential sources of confusing for the students. While questioning is often viewed as a component of instructional methodology, it is also a powerful assessment tool.

Formal/Informal testing

Please refer to skill 3.02 for definitions and descriptions.

Additional Types of tests

Tests and similar direct assessment methods represent the most easily identified types of assessment. Thorndike (1997) identifies three types of assessment instruments:

1. Standardized achievement tests
2. Assessment material packaged with curricular materials
3. Teacher-made assessment instruments
      Pencil and paper test
      Oral tests
      Product evaluations
      Performance tests
      Effective measures (p.199)

Kellough and Roberts (1991) take a slightly different perspective. They describe "three avenues for assessing student achievement:

a) What the learner says
b) What the learner does, and
c) What the learner writes..." (p.343)

Purposes for Assessment

There are a number of different classification systems used to identify the various purposes for assessment. A compilation of several lists identifies some common purposes such as the following:

1. Diagnostic assessments are used to determine individual weakness and strengths in specific areas.
2. Readiness assessments measure prerequisite knowledge and skills.
3. Interest and Attitude assessments attempt to identify topics of high interest or areas in which students may need extra motivational activities.
4. Evaluation assessments are generally programmed or teacher focused.
5. Placement assessments are used for purposes of grouping students or determining appropriate beginning levels in leveled materials.
6. Formative assessment provide on-going feedback student progress and the success of instructional methods and materials.
7. Summative assessment define student accomplishment with the intent to determine the degree of student mastery or learning that has taken place.

For most teachers, assessment purposes vary according to the situation. It may be helpful to consult several sources to help formulate an overall assessment plan. Kellough and Roberts (1991) identify six purposes for assessment. These are:

1. To evaluate and improve student learning
2. To identify student strengths and weaknesses
3. To assess the effectiveness of a particular instructional strategy
4. To evaluate and improve program effectiveness
5. To evaluate and improve teacher effectiveness
6. To communicate to parents their children's progress (p.341)

Limitations of Various Types of Assessment

The existence of various types of assessment stems from the unique needs of children with disabilities and the environments in which the disabilities are most troublesome. A student who demonstrates difficulty interacting with peers and acts impulsively may not be effectively evaluated with a portfolio. Anecdotal records, questioning and certain checklists may give a better picture of the extent to which such peer interactions are detrimental to the student's (and others') well being and success. Conversely, a student who displays academic difficulty is better assessed with samples of work (portfolio) and carefully chosen formal tests. In short, assessments are as valuable as the appropriate choice and use thereof.

Skill 4.7   Demonstrate knowledge of legal provisions, regulations, and guidelines regarding the assessment of individuals with disabilities.

If instructional modifications in the regular classroom have not proven successful, a student may be referred for multidisciplinary evaluation. The evaluation is comprehensive and includes norm and criterion-referenced tests (e.g. IQ and diagnostic tests), curriculum-based assessment, systematic teacher observation (e.g. behavior frequency checklist), samples of student work, and parent interviews. The results of the evaluation are twofold: to determine eligibility for special education services and to identify a student's strengths and weaknesses in order to plan an individual education program.

The wording in federal law is very explicit about the manner in which evaluations must be conducted, and about the existence of due process procedures that protect against bias and discrimination. Provisions in the law include the following as listed.

1. The testing of children in their native or primary language unless it is clearly not feasible to do so.
2. The use of evaluation procedures selected and administered to prevent cultural or ethnic discrimination.
3. The use of assessment tools validated for the purpose for which they are being used (e.g. achievement levels, IQ scores, adaptive skills).
4. Assessment by a multidisciplinary team utilizing several pieces of information to formulate a placement decision.

Furthermore, parental involvement must occur in the development of the child's educational program. According to the law, parents must:

1. Be notified before initial evaluation or any change in placement by a written notice in their primary language describing the proposed school action, the reasons for it, and the available educational opportunities.
2. Consent, in writing, before the child is initially evaluated.

Parents may:

1. Request an independent educational evaluation if they feel the school's evaluation is inappropriate.
2. Request an evaluation at public expense if a due process hearing decision is that the public agency's evaluation was inappropriate.
3. Participate on the committee that considers the evaluation, placement, and programming of the student.

All students referred for evaluation for special education should have the results of a relatively current vision and hearing screening on file. This will determine the adequacy of sensory acuity and ensure that learning problems are not due to a vision and/or hearing problem.

All portions of the Special Education process from assessment to placement is strictly confidential to parties outside of the people who will directly be servicing the student. Under no circumstances should information be shared outside of the realm of parent/guardian and those providing related services without the consent of the parent/guardian.

With the latest reauthorization of IDEA, new legislation brings into play the Response to Intervention (RTI) model for the identification of students with disabilities. Under this model, the progress of students is monitored over time. Using this progress or lack thereof, student qualification status is determined.

COMPETENCY 5.0 **UNDERSTAND PROCEDURES AND CRITERIA FOR IMPLEMENTING ASSESSMENT ACTIVITIES THAT ARE APPROPRIATE FOR THE INDIVIDUAL NEEDS OF STUDENTS WITH DISABILITIES.**

Skill 5.1 **Apply knowledge of procedures for gathering background information regarding students' academic history and methods for creating and maintaining accurate records for use in selecting, adapting, or developing appropriate assessments for students with disabilities.**

Relevant background information regarding the student's academic, medical, and family history should be used to identify students with disabilities and evaluate their progress.

An evaluation report should include the summary of a comprehensive diagnostic interview by a qualified evaluator. A combination of candidate self-report interviews, with families and others, and historical documentation, such as transcripts and standardized test scores, is recommended.

The evaluator should use professional judgment as to which areas are relevant to determining a student's eligibility for accommodations due to disabilities. In order to properly identify students with disabilities and evaluate their progress, the evaluator should include background information regarding academic, medical, cultural, and family history when making an evaluation. The evaluation should include a developmental history; relevant medical history, including the absence of a medical basis for the present symptoms; academic history including results of prior standardized testing; reports of classroom performance; relevant family history, including primary language of the home and the candidate's current level of fluency of English; relevant psychosocial history; a discussion of dual diagnosis, alternative or co-existing mood, behavioral, neurological, and/or personality disorders along with any history of relevant medication use that may affect the individual's learning; and exploration of possible alternatives that may mimic a learning disability.

By utilizing all possible background information in the assessment, the evaluator can rule out alternative explanations for academic problems such as poor education, poor motivation and study skills, emotional problems, and cultural and language differences. If the student's entire background and history is not taken into account, it is not always possible to institute the most appropriate educational program for the student with disabilities.

As evaluations are designed and ready to be completed with students it is critical adequate records be kept on all aspects of the process. Some students may require adaptations and modifications during the assessment process due to their disabilities. For example, a student who cannot hear may need information presented in sign language. These kinds of adaptations should be clearly and precisely noted.

Also, it is important to have clear reasons for deciding which assessments will be given to a student. This too should be explained in clear terms within the final report where results are shared with the appropriate persons. In this way, all those involved with the student will have a clear understanding of all background, testing, and adaptations made during the evaluation procedure.

Skill 5.2   Apply knowledge of the principles and procedures for identifying students' educational priorities by developing and conducting an individualized inventory of the student's home, community, social and vocational environments, and integrated curriculum needs.

The assessment process is an essential part of developing an individualized program for students. The needs of the whole child must be considered in order to address all of the needs of each child. Therefore information should be gathered by using various sources of information.

Besides the general education teacher, a vital person or persons in the assessment process should be the parent. The parent can provide needed background information on the child, such as a brief medical, physical, and developmental history. Paraprofessionals, doctors, and other professionals are also very helpful in providing necessary information about the child. Additionally, other community members, persons involved with the student in social settings or vocational settings should also be tapped for appropriate and pertinent information.

Ways of gathering information:

Interview: Interviews can be in person or on paper. The related parties can be invited to a meeting to conduct the interview, if the parent does not respond after several attempts, the paper interview may be sent or mailed home.

Questionnaires: Questionnaires are also a good way of gathering information. Some questionnaires maybe open ended questions and some maybe several questions that are to be answered using a rating scale. The answerer is to circle ratings ranging from 1 to 5 or 1 to 7 meaning Strongly Disagree to Strongly Agree.

Conference/ Meeting: With parents' permission, it may be useful to conduct a meeting, one on one, or in a group setting, to gather information about the child. Everyone involved with the child that may be able to offer any information about the child, the child's academic progress, physical development, social skills, behavior, or medical history and/or needs should be invited to attend.

Skill 5.3   Apply knowledge of the principles and procedures for modifying or adapting formal nationally standardized, state, and local assessments, including the Illinois Alternative Assessment.

Yearly, the Illinois Department of Education revises and reexamines the procedures for acceptable modifications for assessments. It is important to stay current in reading these procedures and only use allowable accommodations when administering the exams. All modifications should be included as part of the students IEP and reviewed at least annually.

Skill 5.4   Apply knowledge of considerations and procedures used in assessing the extent and quality of an individual's accessibility to and progress through the general education curriculum.

The ultimate goal of special education services is to return the student to regular education. In this way, it is important for the special educator to become very familiar with the regular education curriculum and appropriate modifications and adaptations which can be made to it to ensure student success. The more aspects of the general education curriculum students are able to complete and access, the more feasibility there is in eventually returning them to regular education.

When considering the general curriculum, the first step is to analyze it for areas where the student may be successful with no support from special education. There may be individual areas of strength the student demonstrates where there will need to be no accommodations in place. The next step is to work out a manageable plan of action to allow the student to have this access.

Once all areas have been identified with which the student will have no difficulty accessing the regular curriculum, it is now time to look at what areas may require simple accommodations and modifications. An example might include a student who has a great deal of difficulty reading, but understands the underlying concepts being introduced in a science class. In this case, the student may just need simple accommodations to compensate for the reading difficulties. Some possible accommodations might include: text on tape, partnering for reading assignments with a stronger student, or providing outlines of the chapters to be read written in language the student is able to read.

Many students are able to access the regular education curriculum with some simple accommodations and modifications. Sometimes this takes a concerted effort on the part of the special educator and regular educator. Shared planning times can be helpful or at the minimum regular opportunities to dialogue and share instructional objectives. Additionally, team teaching can be a tremendously beneficial strategy to all students within a classroom.

Some students with disabilities will have more difficulty with the academic areas of the regular curriculum, but will be able to participate in less academic areas. Perhaps they have a special musical or artistic ability. Inclusion in these subject areas should also be considered whenever possible for students.

To determine the extent with which as student can participate in the general education curriculum, the teacher must look in detail at the strengths and weaknesses of the student, how s/he can support the student to ensure success, and the objectives of the regular education curriculum. A thorough and complete examination of these areas will provide the teacher with a well-developed plan for providing the most appropriate inclusion of students' with disabilities in the regular education curriculum.

Skill 5.5   Apply knowledge of methods for adapting formal assessment devices to accommodate a student's typical mode of communication and response and of considerations for matching appropriate assessment procedures to purposes of assessment.

See Skill 4.5

Skill 5.6   Demonstrate knowledge of the influences of disabilities, culture, and language on the assessment process.

The process of completing assessments is often affected and influenced by a number of factors. For this reason, it is important the person administering the assessment be sure to include statements explaining anything which may have impacted the results of the assessment or should be taken into consideration when interpreting the results.

Both in the original authorization and the reauthorization of the Individual with Disabilities Education Act (IDEA), statements were to be considered and included when making determination as to whether or not a student has a disability. Some of these areas to be considered are: skill level is not the result of a lack of appropriate instruction, one disability is not influencing appropriate results from being obtained in other areas, cultural differences and impacts, and that assessments are conducting in the students native language to ensure there is not a second language acquisition problem which appears similar to a disability.

Lack of appropriate instruction can occur for many different reasons. A student with many medical issues may miss a large portion of school and therefore not receive the necessary instruction to progress to the next level. Moving through many different schools in short periods of time can also significantly impact the instruction students receive.

Compounding disabilities need to be considered when assessing students. Is there a learning disability or is the student struggling with learning due to the fact she is unable to hear. If it is due to the hearing issue, that student should not be given the additional label of having a learning disability, and more appropriate changes and modifications should be put in place to increase accessibility to the regular education curriculum.

Cultural differences may be impacting students in their education. Students might miss certain units of instruction due to cultural celebrations. In other examples, students may not have the necessary vocabulary to understand concepts presented. It is important, that when conducting an evaluation, the person consider and rule out that the results have not been impacted in a negative manner due to cultural differences.

When students are acquiring a second language, it is important to complete assessments in both languages to ensure valid and reliable information is gathered. Is it true that the student does not know the word red, or do they understand what red is when presented with it in their native language? The process of acculturation is a long and slow process taking from two through seven years. Students should not be given labels and placed in special education for what are normal second language acquisition issues.

COMPETENCY 6.0   UNDERSTAND PROCEDURES AND STRATEGIES FOR ASSESSING THE EDUCATIONAL STRENGTHS AND NEEDS OF STUDENTS WITH DISABILITIES FOR THE PURPOSE OF DESIGNING AND EVALUATING INSTRUCTION.

Skill 6.1   Apply knowledge of principles for interpreting information from formal and informal assessment instruments, developing individualized assessment strategies, and evaluating the results of instruction.

Having the knowledge of interpreting and applying formal and informal assessment data is very important to the development of IEPs. An individualized educational instructional program is designed around the child's strengths and weaknesses. An educator must have knowledge of interpreting formal and informal assessment data to assist him in determining some of those strengths and weaknesses.

<u>**Formal Assessments:**</u>
Results of formal assessments are given in derived scores, which compare the student's raw score to the performance of a specified group of subjects. Criteria for the selection of the group may be based on characteristics such as age, sex, or geographic area. The test results of formal assessments must always be interpreted in light of what type of tasks the individual was required to perform. The most commonly used derived scores follow.

A. Age and Grade Equivalents. These scores are considered developmental scores because they attempt to convert the student's raw score into an average performance of a particular age or grade group.

Age Equivalents are expressed in years and months, i.e. 7-3. In the standardization procedure, a mean is calculated for all individuals of the particular age who took the test. If the mean or median number of correct responses for children 7 years and 3 months was 80, then an individual whose raw score was 80 would be assigned an age-equivalent of 7 years and 3 months.

Grade Equivalents are written as years and tenths of years, e.g., 6.2 would read sixth grade, second month. Grade equivalents are calculated on the average performance of the group, and have been criticized for their use to measure gains in academic achievement and to identify exceptional students.

Quartiles, Deciles, and Percentiles indicate the percentage of scores that fall below the individual's raw score. Quartiles divide the score into four equal parts; the first quartile is the point at which 25% of the scores fall below, the full score. Deciles divide the distribution into ten equal parts; the seventh decile would mark the point below which 70% of the scores fall. Percentiles are the most frequently used, however. A percentile rank of 45 would indicate that the person's raw score was at the point below which 45% of the other scores fell.

B. Standard Scores are raw scores with the same mean (average) and standard deviation (variability of asset of scores). In the standardization of a test, about 68% of the scores will fall above or below 1 standard deviation of the mean of 100. About 96% of the scores will fall within the range of 2 standard deviations above or below the mean. A standard deviation of 20, for example, will mean that 68% of the scores will fall between 80 and 120, with 100 as the mean. The most common are T scores, z scores, stanines, and scaled scores. Standard scores are useful because they allow for direct comparison of raw scores from different individuals. In interpreting scores, it is important to note what type of standard score is being used.

C. Criterion Referenced Tests and Curriculum-based Assessments are interpreted on the basis of the individual's performance on the objectives being measured. Such assessments may be commercially prepared or teacher-made, and can be designed for a particular curriculum or a scope and sequence. These assessments are made by selecting objectives, task analyzing those objectives, and selecting measures to test the skills necessary to meet those tasks. Results are calculated for each objective, such as Cindy was able to divide 2-digit numbers by 1-digit numbers 85% of the time and was able to divide 2-digit numbers by 2-digit numbers 45% of the time. These tests are useful for gaining insight into the types of error patterns the student makes. Because the student's performance is not compared to others in a group, results are useful for writing IEPs as well as deciding what to teach.

Norm-referenced Assessments
Norm-referenced tests (NRT) are used to classify students for homogenous groupings based on ability levels or basic skills into a ranking category. In many school communities, NRTs are used to classify students into AP (Advanced Placement), honors, regular or remedial classes that can significantly impact student future educational opportunities or success. NRTs are also used by national testing companies such as Iowa Test of Basic Skills (Riverside), Florida Achievement Test (McGraw-Hill) and other major test publishers to test a national sample of students to norm against standard test-takers. Stiggins (1994) states "Norm-referenced tests (NRT) are designed to highlight achievement differences between and among students to produce a dependable rank order of students across a continuum of achievement from high achievers to low achievers."

Educators may select NRTs to focus on students with lower basic skills which could limit the development of curriculum content that needs to provide students with academic learning's that accelerate student skills from basic to higher skill application to address the state assessments and core subject expectations.

NRT ranking ranges from 1-99 with 25% of students scoring in the lower ranking of 1-25 and 25% of students scoring in the higher ranking of 76-99. Florida uses a variety of NRTs for student assessments that range from Iowa Basic Skills Testing to California Battery Achievement testing to measure student learning in reading and math.

Criterion-referenced Assessments

Criterion-referenced assessments look at specific student learning goals and performance compared to a norm group of student learners. According to Bond (1996) "Educators or policy makers may choose to use a Criterion-referenced test (CRT) when they wish to see how well students have learned the knowledge and skills which they are expected to have mastered." Many school districts and state legislation use CRTs to ascertain whether schools are meeting national and state learning standards. The latest national educational mandate of "No Child Left Behind" (NCLB) and Adequate Yearly Progress (AYP) use CRTs to measure student learning, school performance, and school improvement goals as structured accountability expectations in school communities. CRTs are generally used in learning environments to reflect the effectiveness of curriculum implementation and learning outcomes.

Performance-based Assessments

Performance-based assessments are currently being used in a number of state testing programs to measure the learning outcomes of individual students in subject content areas. Washington State uses performance-based assessments for the WASL (Washington Assessment of Student Learning) in Reading, Writing, Math and Science to measure student-learning performance. Attaching a graduation requirement to passing the required state assessment for the class of 2008 has created a high-stakes testing and educational accountability for both students and teachers in meeting the expected skill based requirements for 10th grade students taking the test.

In today's classrooms, performance-based assessments in core subject areas must have established and specific performance criteria that start with pre-testing in a subject area and maintain daily or weekly testing to gauge student learning goals and objectives. To understand a student's learning is to understand how a student processes information. Effective performance assessments will show the gaps or holes in student learning which allows for an intense concentration on providing fillers to bridge non-sequential learning gaps. Typical performance assessments include oral and written student work in the form of research papers, oral presentations, class projects, journals, student portfolio collections of work, and community service projects.

Summary

With today's emphasis on student learning accountability, the public and legislature demands for school community accountability for effective teaching and assessment of student learning outcomes will remain a constant mandate of educational accountability. In 1994, thirty-one states use NRTs for student assessments, while thirty-three states use CRTs in assessing student learning outcomes (Bond, 1996). Performance-based assessments are being used exclusively for state testing of high school students in ascertaining student learning outcomes based on individual processing and presentation of academic learning. Before a state, district, or school community can determine which type of testing is the most effective, there must be a determination of testing outcome expectation; content learning outcome; and deciding effectiveness of the assessments in meeting the learning goals and objectives of the students.

Informal Assessments:

Some of the most common informal assessments include: checklists, observations, and performance assessments/tasks. There are a variety of checklists available. Some, like the Conners Checklist, have standardized procedures for scoring and provide specific details as to the adequate interpretation of the information gained. Other less specific checklists can be interpreted in a broader manner to provide general guidance in writing goals and objectives for the IEP. For example, if on checklists completed by several parties who have regular interaction with the student, the student is rated as having poor organization skills, when writing the IEP a goal might be developed to increase organization.

Observational data and performance assessments can be used in a similar manner as checklists. It is important to keep in mind that one should complete more than one before listing the area in the IEP as either a strength or need. General accepted practice looks to at least three measures before considering an area to have validity and reliability.

Sometimes it is necessary to develop assessment strategies specific to the student to build in accommodations for any issues which may be related to the disability. It is important to be very specific when detailing this information to the parents or in reports/IEPs. The reasons behind the need for these individualized strategies, the nature of them and the scope should all be clearly explained.

As instruction occurs, it is important for the special educator to have a means to evaluate the appropriateness of said instruction. Regular progress monitoring with assessment measures specifically designed for progress monitoring is the most appropriate way to evaluate the success of instruction. Along with the tool, it is important to set realistic goals and aim lines based on normative data for the rates of growth in specific skills. An example of this can be found in improving reading fluency. If the goal is to improve reading fluency, it is helpful to understand that on average children make about one word more correct per minute each week of instruction. With this information available, one can set an appropriate academic objective within the IEP. Then, progress monitoring using reading fluency measures can occur weekly to ensure the student is making expected growth. If the child is not, then further examination of the reasons need to occur.

Skill 6.2 **Demonstrate knowledge of strategies for assessing learning environments, for designing and implementing functional assessments of individuals' behavior within those environments, and for matching necessary supports to individual learners' needs.**

The special educator needs to be involved in constant assessment to ensure the students are making the progress as related to their Individual Education Plan (IEP) goals and objectives. In this way, a method must be developed for assessing different environments the student may experience throughout the school day. This assessment data can then be used to design a functional behavioral assessment in order to better support the students' needs in these learning situations.

First, the special educator must find appropriate methods for assessing learning environments. Typically, the use of direct observation is used to accomplish this task. There are numerous protocols available for completing a direct observation from more standardized procedures. In direct observation, trained personnel observe and records possible cause of the behavior (antecedents) and the end result of the behavior (consequence). The observer charts the various causes, behaviors and consequent events over a period of time. Data analysis is then used to develop a hypothesis statement and strategies to decrease the amount of misbehavior and increase positive behaviors.

Sometimes more indirect methods of observation are used as well to gather additional information about the student's behaviors. In this case, interviews and checklists are used as methods to gather the data. This combination of direct and indirect observation, data analysis and the development of the hypothesis statement is known as a Functional Behavioral Assessment (FBA). FBAs are a regular occurrence when students are struggling within the school environment to help develop a plan of action the faculty and staff involved with the student can use to help the child improve his behavioral skills.

Once the data has been collected and the hypothesis statement is written, a team of professionals gather together to write a Behavioral Intervention Plan (BIP). The BIP is a specific plan of action with strategies, accommodations, modifications, supplementary aids, support systems, program, and positive behavioral strategies. This plan becomes a part of the child's IEP and is implemented across all learning environments.

The BIP is written by a team of professionals involved with the education of the student exhibiting difficulties. It is essential the general education teacher and Special Education Teacher delivering services to the student be present and active participants in the development of the BIP. Since they spend the most time with the student, they have the ability to share current classroom expectations and structures in place to support the student and can relay appropriate behavioral expectations for the various learning environments.

Skill 6.3 **Demonstrate knowledge of models of reading diagnosis that include student proficiency with print conventions, phonemic awareness, word recognition, vocabulary, fluency, comprehension, and self-monitoring which assist in determining individual students' reading strengths and needs and independent, instructional, and frustrational reading levels.**

"If we want children to become strategic readers, then we create classrooms that reinforce the strategies we've demonstrated and allow children to practice on books that match their needs."
Sharon Taberski

Models of Reading Diagnosis:
The use of Data and Ongoing Reading Assessment to adjust Instruction to meet students' reading needs.

Assessment is the practice of collecting information about something from children's responses and evaluating is the process of judging the children's responses to determine how well they are achieving particular goals or demonstrating reading skills.

When a teacher asks a child to retell a story, this is a form of assessment. After the child retells the story, the teacher judges how accurate it was and gives it a grade or score and sometimes also makes anecdotal comments about the child in the course of listening to the child's retelling of the story.

Assessment and evaluation have to be intricately connected in the literacy classroom Assessment is necessary because teachers need ways to determine what students are learning and how they are progressing. In addition, assessment can be a tool which can also help students take ownership of their own learning and become partners in their ongoing development as readers and writers. In this day of public accountability, clear, definite and reliable assessment engenders confidence in public education.

There are two broad categories of assessment:

Informal Assessment utilizes observations, and other non-standardized procedures to compile anecdotal and observation data/evidence of children's progress.

Formal Assessment is comprised of standardized tests and procedures carried out under circumscribed conditions.

Informal Assessments include but are not limited to: checklists, observations, and performance assessments/tasks.

Formal Assessments include: state tests, standardized achievement tests, NAEP tests, etc.

Effective assessments should have the following characteristics:

I. An ongoing process with the teacher making some kind of an informal or formal assessment almost every time the child speaks, listens, reads, writes, or views something in the classroom. The assessment should be a natural part of the instruction and not intrusive.

2. Be integrated into ongoing instruction. Throughout the teaching and learning day, the child's written, spoken and reading contributions to the class or lack thereof, need to and can be continually accessed.

3. Reflect the actual reading and writing experiences which classroom learning has prepared the child for. The child should be able to show that he or she can read and explain or react to a similar literary or expository work.

4. Be a collaborative and reflective process. Teachers can learn from what the children reveal about their own individual assessments. Children, even as early as grade two, should be supported by their teacher to continually and routinely ask themselves questions assessing their reading (and other skill progress). They might ask: "How have I done in understanding what the author wanted to say?," " What can I do to improve my reading?" and "How can I use what I have read to learn more about this topic?"

   Teachers need to be informed by their own professional observation AND by children's comments as they assess and customize instruction for children.

5. Multidimensional and may include but not be limited to: samples of writings, student retellings, running records, anecdotal teacher observations, self-evaluations, records of independent reading, etc. From this multidimensional data, the teacher can derive a consistent level of performance and design additional instruction that will enhance the level of student performance.

6. Take into account children's age and ethnic/cultural patterns of learning.

7. Assess to teach children from their strengths, not their weaknesses. Find out what reading behaviors, children demonstrate well and then design instruction to support those behaviors.

8. Be a part of the children's learning process and not done ON them, but rather done WITH them.

It should also be noted that that for these purposes the term PERCENTILE is defined as a score on a scale of 100 showing the percentage of a distribution that is equal to it or below it.

For the teacher's information the following are examples of key criterion-referenced tests which measure a child's performance against a standard:

DEGREES OF READING POWER (DRP) –This test is targeted to assess how well children understand the meaning of written text in real life situations. This test is supposed to measure the process of children's reading, not the products of reading such as identifying the main idea and author's purpose.

CTPIII- This is a criterion-referenced test which measures verbal and quantitative ability in grades 3-12. It is targeted to help differentiate among the most capable students those who rank above the 80th percentile on other standardized tests. This is a test that emphasizes higher order thinking skills and process-related reading comprehension questions.

TERRA NOVA/COMPREHENSIVE TEST OF BASIC SKILLS (CTBS)

The following are examples of Norm-Referenced Tests which fall into this category because test scores are reported as percentile ratings.

IOWA Test of Basic Skills (ITBS)

CONCEPTS OF VALIDITY, RELIABILITY, and BIAS in Testing

Validity is how well a test measures what it is supposed to measure. Teacher made tests are therefore not generally extremely valid, although they may be an appropriate measure for the validity of the concept the teacher wants to assess for his/her own children's achievement.

Reliability is the consistency of the test. This is measured by whether the test will indicate the same score for the child who takes it twice.

Bias in testing occurs when the information within the test or the information required to respond to a multiple choice question or constructed response (essay question on the test) is information that is not available to some test takers who come from a different cultural, ethnic, linguistic or socio-economic background than do the majority of the test takers. Since they have not had the same prior linguistic, social or cultural experiences that the majority of test takers have had, these test takers are at a disadvantage in taking the test and no matter what their actual mastery of the material taught by the teacher, can not address the "biased" questions. Generally other "non-biased" questions are given to them and eventually the biased questions are removed from the examination.

To solidify what might be abstract to the reader, on a recent reading test in my school system, the grade four reading comprehension multiple choice had some questions about the well known fairy tale of the gingerbread boy. These questions were simple and accessible for most of the children in the class. But two children who were recent new arrivals from the Dominican Republic had learned English there. They were reading on grade four level, but in their Dominican grade school, the story of the Gingerbread Boy was not a major one. Therefore a question about this story on the standardized reading test did demonstrate examiner bias and was not fair to these test takers.

Holistic scoring involves assessing a child's ability to construct meaning through writing. It uses a scale called a RUBRIC which ranges from 0 to 4 –

O- This rubric would be for a piece which can not be scored. It does not respond to the topic asked or is illegible.

1- Would be a writing which does respond to the topic, but does not cover it accurately.

2- Would be for a response which is on the questions, but lacks sufficient details to convey the purpose and to accomplish the writing task requested.

3- Would be a paper which in general fulfills the purpose of the writing assignment and demonstrates that the reader correctly constructed meaning. The reader showed that he or she understands the writer's purpose and message.

4- This response has the most details, best organization, and presents a well expressed reaction to the original writer's piece.

MISCUE ANALYSIS

This is a procedure that allows the teacher a look at the reading process. By definition, the miscue is an oral response different from the text being read. Sometimes miscues are also called unexpected responses or errors. By studying a student's miscues from an oral reading sample, the teacher can determine which cues and strategies, the student is correctly using or not using in constructing meaning. Of course, the teacher can customize instruction to meet the needs of this particular student.

INFORMAL READING INVENTORIES (IRI)
These are a series of samples of texts prearranged in stages of increasing difficulty. Listening to children read through these inventories, the teacher can pinpoint their skill level and the additional concepts they need to work on.

GROUP VERSUS INDIVIDUAL READING ASSESSMENTS
Part of the successful teaching of reading is the organizational strategy of using flexible groups in contrast to whole class and individual activities. Flexible groups may consist of two, three or more students working together to accomplish a specific purpose.

In evaluating school reform improvements for school communities, educators may implement and assess student academic performance using norm-referenced, criterion-referenced, and performance-based assessments. Effective classroom assessment can provide educators with a wealth of information on student performance and teacher instructional practices. Using student assessment can provide teachers with data in analyzing student academic performance and making inferences on student learning plans that can foster increased academic achievement and success for students.

PHONOLOGICAL AWARENESS:

Phonological awareness means the ability of the reader to recognize the sound of spoken language. This recognition includes how these sounds can be blended together, segmented (divided up), and manipulated (switched around). This awareness then leads to phonics, a method for teaching children to read. It helps them "sound out words."

Development of phonological skills may begin during pre-K years. Indeed by the age of 5, a child who has been exposed to rhyme can recognize a rhyme. Such a child can demonstrate phonological awareness by filling in the missing rhyming word in a familiar rhyme or rhymed picture book. I surprised my mother by filling in missing rhymes in a familiar nursery rhyme book at the age of four. She was trying to rush ahead to complete the book, but I wouldn't be cheated of even one rhyme!! Little did I know that I was phonologically aware at four!!

You teach children phonological awareness when you teach them the sounds made by the letters, the sounds made by various combinations of letters and to recognize individual sounds in words.

Phonological Awareness Skills include:

I. Rhyming and syllabification
2. Blending sounds into words—such as pic-tur-bo-k
3. Identifying the beginning or starting sounds of words and the ending or closing
   sounds of words
4. Breaking words down into sounds-also called "segmenting" words
5. Recognizing other smaller words in the big word, by removing starting sounds, "hear" to ear

The role of Phonological Awareness in reading development
Instructional methods to teach phonological awareness may include any or all of the following:

1. Auditory games and drills during which children recognize and manipulate the sounds of words, separate or segment the sounds of words, take out sounds, blend sounds, add in new sounds, or take apart sounds to recombine them in new formations are good ways to foster phonological awareness.

2. Snap game- the teacher says two words. The children snap their fingers if the two words share a sound, which might be at the beginning, middle or end of the word. Silence occurs if the words share no sounds. Children love this simple game and it also helps with classroom management. Language games model for children identification of rhyming words. These games help inspire children to create their own rhymes.

3. Word strip activities and experiences help children concretely experience how words are made up of syllables and that words can be broken down into separate sounds. Word strips help kinesthetic and spatial learners work to enhance this auditory skill.

4. Read books that rhyme such as *Sheep in Jeep* by Nancy Shaw or *The Fox on a Box* by Barbara Gregorich.

5. Share books with children that use alliteration (words that all begin with the same sound) such as *Avalanche, A to Z*.

Assessment of Phonological Awareness
These skills can be assessed by having the child listen to the teacher say two words. Then ask the child to decide if these two words are the same word repeated twice or two different words.

When you make this assessment, if you do use two different words, make certain that they only differ by one phoneme, such as /d/ and /g/.

Children can be assessed on words which are not real words that are familiar to them. Words used can be make-believe words.

Word Recognition:

Word Identification- Selective Cue Stage. Sometimes children have not yet experienced an awareness of the conventions of print and labeling in their own home environments. The teacher or an aide may have to go on a label adventure and support children in recognizing or affixing labels to parts of the classroom, halls and school building. A neighborhood walk with a digital or hand held camera may be required to help children identify uses and functions of print in society. A classroom photo essay or bulletin board could be the outgrowth of such an activity.

Sight Vocabulary- Beginning readers may enjoy outdoing Dolch (1936), who compiled the best known sight vocabulary word list. They can create their own class version of this list with illustrations and even some comments about why they have nominated certain words for the list.

Vocabulary:

Using Phonics to Decode Words in Connected Text

Identifying New Words
Some strategies to share with children during conferences or as part of shared reading include the following prompts:

Look at the beginning letter/s... What sound do you hear?

Stop to think about the text or story. What word with this beginning letter would make sense here?

Look at the book's illustrations. Do they provide you with help in figuring out the new word?

Think of what word would make sense, sound right, and match the letters that you see. Start the sentence over, making your mouth ready to say that word.

Skip the word, read to the end of the sentence, and then come back to the word. How does what you've read help you with the word?

Listen to whether what you are reading makes sense and matches the letters (this is asking the child to self-monitor). If it doesn't make sense, see if you can correct it on your own. Look for spelling patterns you know from the spelling pattern wall.

Look for smaller words you might know within the larger word.

Think of any place you may have seen this word before or story read to you or by you, where you met up with this word.

Read on a little, and then return to the part that confused you.

Use of Semantic and Syntactic Cues

Semantic Cues
Prompts that the teacher can use which will alert the children to semantic cues include:

You said (the child's statement and incorrect attempt). Does that make sense to you?

If someone said (repeat the child's attempt), would you know what he or she meant?

You said (child's incorrect attempt). Would you write that?

Children need to use meaning to predict what the text says so that the relevant information can prompt the correct words to surface as they identify the words. If children come to a word they can't immediately recognize, they need to try to figure it out using their past reading (or being read to) experiences background knowledge, and what they can deduce so far from the text itself.

Syntactic Cues
You said (child's incorrect attempt). Does that sound right?
You said (child's incorrect attempt). Can we say it like that?

Phonics terminology-
Morpheme, Base word, root, inflection and/or any other affix.

Development of Phonics Skills in Individual Students

English Language Learners
In *ON SOLID GROUND* (2000), researcher and educator Sharon Taberski said that it is much harder for children from ELL backgrounds and children from homes where other English dialects are spoken to use syntactic cues to attempt to self-correct.

These children, through no fault of their own, do not have sufficient experience hearing Standard English spoken to use this cueing system as they read. These children need a teacher who is sensitive to their linguistic or cultural background to guide them through these issues.

Highly Proficient Readers

Highly proficient readers can be paired as buddy tutors for ELL or special needs classroom members or to assist the resource room teacher during their reading time. They can use the CVC Game developed by Jacki Montrieth to support their peers and can even modify the game to meet the needs of classroom peers. My elementary years were filled with buddy partnering and peer tutoring which stood me in good stead when I actually began to take my elementary education courses. Of course, this also offers the highly proficient reader the opportunity to do a service learning project, while still in elementary school. It also introduces the learner to another dimension of reading, the role of the reader as trainer and recruiter of other peers into the circle of readers and writers!

If the highly proficient readers are so motivated or if their teachers so desire, the peer tutors can also maintain an ongoing reading progress journal for their tutees. This will be a wonderful way to realize the goals of the reading and writing workshop.

Content area vocabulary is the specific vocabulary related to the particular concepts of various academic disciplines (social science, science, math, art, etc.). While teachers tend to think of content area vocabulary as something that should just be focused on at the secondary level (middle and high school), even elementary school-aged students studying various subjects will understand concepts better when the vocabulary used to describe them is explicitly explained. But it is true that in the secondary level, where students go to teachers for the various subjects, content area vocabulary becomes more important. Often, educators believe that vocabulary should just be taught in the Language Arts class, not realizing that (a) there is not enough time for students to learn the enormous vocabulary in order to be successful with a standards-based education, and (b) that the teaching of vocabulary, related to a particular subject, is a very good way to help students understand the subject better.

Now, how do content area teachers teach vocabulary? First and foremost, teachers should help students learn strategies to figure out the meanings for difficulty vocabulary when they encounter it on their own.

Teachers can do this by teaching students how to identify the meanings of words in context (usually through activities where the word is taken out, and the students have to figure out a way to make sense of the sentence). In addition, dictionary skills must be taught in all subject areas. Teachers should also consider that teaching vocabulary is not just the teaching of words: rather, it is the teaching of complex concepts, each with histories and connotations.

When teachers explicitly teach vocabulary, it is best when they connect new words to words, ideas, and experiences that students are already familiar with. This will help to reduce the strangeness of the new words. Furthermore, the more concrete the examples are, the more likely students will know how to use the word in context.

Finally, students need plenty of exposure to the new words. They need to be able to hear and use the new words in many naturally-produced sentences. The more one hears and uses a sentence in context, the more the word is solidified in the person's long-term vocabulary.

Fluency:

Use of Oral Reading Fluency in Facilitating Comprehension
At some point it is crucial, that just as the nervous, novice bike rider, finally relaxes and speeds happily off; so too must the early reader integrate graphophonic cues with semantic and structural ones. Before this is done, the oral quality of early reader's has a stilted beat to it, which of course, does not promote reading engagement and enjoyment.

The teacher needs to be at his/her most theatrical to model for children the beauties of voice and nuance that are contained in the texts whose print they are tracking so anxiously. Children love nothing more than to mimic their teacher and can do so legitimately and without hesitation, if the teacher takes time each day to theatrically recite a poem with them. The poem might be posted on chart paper and be up on the board for a week.

First the teacher can model the fluent and expressive reading of this poem. Then with a pointer, the class can recite it with the teacher. As the week progresses, the class can recite it on their own.

Comprehension:

Knowledge of levels of reading comprehension and strategies for promoting comprehension of imaginative literary texts at all levels
Sharon Taberski (2000) recommends that initially strategies for promoting comprehension of imaginative literary texts at all levels, be done with the whole class.

Here are Taberski's four main strategies for promoting comprehension of imaginative literary texts. She feels that if repeated sufficiently during the k-3 years and even if introduced as late as grade 4, these strategies will even serve the adult lifelong reader in good stead.

Strategy One: "Stopping to Think" –reflecting on the text as a whole. .
As part of this strategy, the reader is challenged to come up with the answer to these three questions:

1. What do I think is going to happen? (Inferential)
2. Why do I think this is going to happen? (Evaluative and inferential)
3. How can I prove that I am right by going back to the story? (inferential)

Taberski recommends that teachers introduce these key strategies with books that can be read in one sitting and recommends the use of picture books for these instructive strategies.

Taberski also suggests that books which are read aloud and used for this strategy also contain: a strong storyline, some degree of predictability, a text that invites discussion and a narrative with obvious stopping points.

Strategy Two for promoting comprehension of imaginative/literary texts that Taberski recommends, which is familiar to most elementary teachers, is story mapping.

For stories which suit this strategy, Taberski selects those which have distinct episodes, few characters and obvious problems. In particular, she tries to use a story where a single, central problem or issue is introduced at the beginning of the story and then resolved or at least followed through by the close of the story. To make a story map of a particular story, Taberski divides the class into groups and asks one group of children to illustrate the "Characters" in the book. Another group of children are asked to draw the "Setting," while a third and fourth group of children tackle "Problem " and "Resolution."

The story may also help children to hold together their ideas for writing in the writing workshop as they take their reading of an author's story to a new level. Best suited to the story mapping techniques are those books which have a story with a conflict resolution format such as a main problem introduced at the beginning of the story which is at least somewhat resolved at the end of the story.

Strategy Three: The Character Mapping strategy also used by Taberski focuses the children as readers on the ways in which the main character's personal traits can determine what will happen in the story. Character mapping works best when the character: is not your daily run of the mill individual, has been featured perhaps in other books by the same author, has a personality that is somewhat predictable, and is capable of changing behavior as a consequence of what happens.

Using writing to share, deepen, and expand understanding of literary texts is a cornerstone of the balanced literacy approach.

Strategy Four: In line with the modeled writing component of balanced literacy, where the teacher first reads something that inspires the teacher's writing and then shares that individual "modeled" (teacher written) writing with the children, Taberski advocates reading sections of stories aloud and then having the teacher pause to reflect on what's happened in the story and then write down a response to it.

Within the confines of the elementary classroom, the teacher can use a chart to record his/her response to the vents or personalities of a particular story being read and the children can also contribute their comments for the chart. Later on, the children can start reflective reader's notebooks or journals where they will record their reactions to their readings independently. These independent reactions may or may not be shared with the teacher or with their families.

The best types of texts for this type of response are: those that relate to age appropriate issues for young children (i.e. homework, testing, bullies, and friendship), a plot that can be interpreted in different ways, a text that is filled with questions, and a text full of suspense or wonder.

Self-Monitoring:

Self-Monitoring- When students self-monitor, they are able to keep track of all the factors themselves involved in the process. In this way, they are able to process the information in the manner that is best for them.

Reading Levels:

When considering both formal and informal assessment data gathered on students, it is important to quantify the information into terms easily recognized by other teachers, administrators and parents. In reading, general practice is to categorize the information into levels of reading. These levels go across both kinds of assessments. They are compromised of a combination of a word accuracy percentage and a comprehension percentage.

Independent. This level is the level at which the child can read text totally on their own. When reading books at the independent level, students will be able to decode between 95 and 100% of the words and comprehend the text with 90% or better. Many bodies of research indicate that about 98% accuracy makes for a good independent reader; however, there is other research that goes as low as 95% accuracy.

Instructional. This is the level at which the student should be taught because it provides enough difficulty to increase their reading skills without providing so much that it becomes to cumbersome to finish the selection. Typically, the acceptable range for accuracy is between 85-94% with 75% or greater comprehension. Some standards rely on the number of errors made instead of the accuracy percentage with no more than one error out of twenty words read being the acceptable standard.

Frustrational. Books at a student's frustrational level are too difficult for that child and should not be used. The frustrational level is any text with less than 85% word accuracy and/or less than 75% comprehension.

The use of independent, instructional and frustrational levels allow educators to provide children with texts of different ranges depending on the skills necessary to be completed. Typically, standardized or formal assessments test to the instructional level. Therefore, if reading a standardized assessment such as an Iowa Test of Basic Skills, the reported reading level would be the instructional level for that student.

Additionally, some formal and informal test results use alternate methods of reporting information. Some use the grade level and month equivalent, where a 3.2 reading level would indicate the child is reading at the third grade level second month or typically October. Still others use their own leveling system. The Developing Readers Assessment (DRA) has it's own unique method of coding book levels based on the work of Fountas and Pinnell. Regardless of the levels listed, the work can easily be translated into independent, instructional and frustrational levels, by examining the comprehension and the word reading accuracy portions of the assessment.

Skill 6.4   **Apply knowledge of how to use assessment data and information from teachers, other professionals, individuals with disabilities, and parents to determine appropriate modifications in learning environments, curriculum, and instructional strategies.**

The assessment information gathered from various sources is key to identify the strengths and the weaknesses of the student. Each test and each person will have something to offer about the child, therefore increasing the possibility of creating a well-developed plan to assist in the success of the student. The special education and general education teacher along with other professionals will use the assessment data to make appropriate instructional decisions and to modify the learning environment that it is conducive to learning.

The information gathered can be used to make some of the following instructional decisions:

I   **Classroom Organization:** The teacher can vary grouping arrangements (e.g. large group, small group, peer tutoring, or learning centers) and methods of instruction (teacher directed, student directed)

II   **Classroom Management:** The teacher can vary grading systems, vary reinforcement systems, and vary the rules (differentiate for some students).

III   **Methods of Presentation: Variation of methods include--**
    A.   Content: Amount to be learned, time to learn, and concept level
    B.   General Structure: advance organizers, immediate feedback, memory devices, and active involvement of students.
    C.   Type of presentation: verbal or written, transparencies, audiovisual

IV   **Methods of Practice:**

    A.   General Structure: amount to be practiced, time to finish, group, individual or teacher-directed, and, varied level of difficulty
    B.   Level of response: copying, recognition, or recall with and without cues
    C.   Types of materials: worksheets, audiovisual, texts

V   **Methods of Testing:**

    A   Type: Verbal, written, or demonstration
    B.   General Structure: time to complete, amount to complete, group or individual testing
    C.   Level of response: multiple choice, essay, recall of facts

Instructional Decisions
Presentation of Subject Matter
Subject Matter should be presented in a fashion that helps students organize, understand, and remember important information. Advance organizers and other instructional devices can help students to:

- Connect information to what is already known
- Make abstract ideas more concrete
- Capture students' interest in the material
- Help students to organize the information and visualize the relationships.

Organizers can be visual aids such as diagrams, tables, charts, guides, or verbal cues that alert students to the nature and content of the lesson. Organizers may be used:

- **Before the lesson** to alert the student to the main point of the lesson, establish a rationale for learning, and activate background information.
- **During the lesson** to help students organize information, keep focused on important points, and aid comprehension.
- **At the close of the lesson** to summarize and remember important points.

Examples of organizers include:

- Question and graphic-oriented study guide.
- Concept diagramming: students brainstorm a concept and organize information into three lists (always present, sometimes present, and never present).
- Semantic feature analysis: students construct a table with examples of the concept in one column and important features or characteristics in the other column opposite.
- Semantic webbing: The concept is placed in the middle of the chart or chalkboard and relevant information is placed around it. Lines show the relationships.
- Memory (mnemonic) devices. Diagrams, charts, and tables.

Instructional modifications are tried in an attempt to accommodate the student in the regular classroom. Effective instruction is geared toward individual needs and recognizes differences I how students learn. Modifications are tailored to individual student needs. some strategies for modifying regular classroom instruction shown on Table 1-1 are effective with at-risk students with disabilities, and students without learning or behavior problems.

Table 1-1 Strategies for Modifying Classroom Instruction

Strategy 1   Provide active learning experiences to teach concepts. Student motivation is increased when students can manipulate, weigh, measure, read, or write using materials and skills t hat relate to their daily lives.

Strategy 2   Provide ample opportunities for guided practice of new skills. Frequent feedback on performance is essential to overcome student feelings of inadequacy. Peer tutoring and cooperative projects provide non-threatening practice opportunities. Individual student conferences, curriculum-based tests, and small group discussions are three useful methods for checking progress.

Strategy 3   Provide multisensory learning experiences. Students with learning problems sometimes have sensory processing difficulties; for instance, an auditory discrimination problem may cause misunderstanding about teacher expectations. Lessons and directions that include visual, auditory, tactile, and kinesthetic modes are preferable to a single sensory approach.

Strategy 4   Present information in a manner that is relevant to the student. Particular attention to this strategy is needed when there is a cultural or economic gap between the lives of teachers and students. Relate instruction to a youngster's daily experience and interests.

Strategy 5   Provide students with concrete illustrations of their progress. Students with learning problems need frequent reinforcement for their efforts. Charts, graphs, and check sheets provide tangible markers of student achievement.

COMPETENCY 7.0 UNDERSTAND HOW TO INTERPRET AND COMMUNICATE ASSESSMENT RESULTS.

Skill 7.1 Apply knowledge of strategies for collaborating with families and other professionals in conducting individual assessments and reporting assessment results.

As the special educator it will often be necessary to complete individual assessments with students to determine progress or accurate skill levels. When planning on conducting assessments of this nature, it is important to keep the family and other teachers in the building informed of what you are doing and why. Sometimes, it is difficult to plan ahead and know specifically when you will have the time to work in an individual assessment. In these cases, a general information sharing may be the best strategy for informing the necessary information. For example, letting the parents know that sometime in the next few weeks you will be pulling the student out to see where they functioning in a specific subject will save misunderstandings at a later date.

It is equally important to openly communicate with the regular education teacher as to when you will be pulling certain students out of their classroom. Not only is this respectful, but the communication allows you ample opportunity to gather some informal information about the student. These informal discussions may help to guide you through the assessment process. The regular education teacher may provide insight which will give you additional areas requiring assessment or give you a more specific direction in which to take your assessments.

See skill 7.2 for strategies for sharing information gathered with parents and other school personnel.

Skill 7.2   Apply knowledge of strategies for interpreting reading diagnostic information and explaining it to classroom teachers, parents, and other specialists to plan instructional programs.

Teachers need to take the information from assessments and understand how to transfer that into instructional objectives and teachable points. This can be a confusing process. As the special educator, it is important you be able to work with teachers, other specialists and parents work through this process. Taking the time to explain the process and how you arrived at specified instructional objectives will help more than one student.

Looking at the assessment information provided to be able to determine which area of education is impacted and what skills in that area need to be taught. Keeping in mind the curriculum and state standards, the specialist can begin to categorize the information and better plan appropriate instruction.

CONCEPTS OF VALIDITY, RELIABILITY, and BIAS in Testing

Validity is how well a test measures what it is supposed to measure. Teacher made tests are therefore not generally extremely valid, although they may be an appropriate measure for the validity of the concept the teacher wants to assess for his/her own children's achievement.

Reliability is the consistency of the test. This is measured by whether the test will indicate the same score for the child who takes it twice.

Bias in testing occurs when the information within the test or the information required to respond to a multiple choice question or constructed response (essay question on the test) is information that is not available to some test takers who come from a different cultural, ethnic, linguistic or socio-economic background than do the majority of the test takers. Since they have not had the same prior linguistic, social or cultural experiences that the majority of test takers have had, these test takers are at a disadvantage in taking the test and no matter what their actual mastery of the material taught by the teacher, can not address the "biased" questions. Generally other "non-biased" questions are given to them and eventually the biased questions are removed from the examination.

To solidify what might be abstract to the reader, on a recent reading test in my school system, the grade four reading comprehension multiple choice had some questions about the well known fairy tale of the gingerbread boy. These questions were simple and accessible for most of the children in the class. But two children who were recent new arrivals from the Dominican Republic had learned English there. They were reading on grade four level, but in their Dominican grade school, the story of the Gingerbread Boy was not a major one. Therefore a question about this story on the standardized reading test did demonstrate examiner bias and was not fair to these test takers.

As a special educator within a school, part of the duties entails serving as a resource for the rest of the teachers. There are several ways that this job can be accomplished, such as:

- Working with teachers in the classroom to organize the classroom setting
- Work with small groups of students in the classroom
- Help organize professional development
- Prepare the Individual Education Plans for students needing extra assistance
- Create inclusive classrooms
- Help the teachers with learning about and employing the different learning theories and ways students learn in the classroom
- Perform the testing on students to determine their levels
- Track the progress of students
- Determine strategies to help students develop
- Identify the individual needs of students
- Analyze the assessments and evaluations to provide assistance to the teachers in reporting to parents

When administrators provide time for teachers to get together to plan instructional activities, a spirit of collaboration will exist in the school. One way to accomplish this is to provide the teachers with time to visit other schools and observe what is happening in another classroom in the district. Teachers within the same division (primary, Elementary, eg.) or teachers of one grade in the school can get together on a regular basis to discuss how they are teaching various concepts and to discuss how to best help students that are struggling. The special educator should be part of this team as well as the teacher giving support to the struggling students. It may mean after school time or shut down days for the school. Administrators can also schedule the timetable in such a way that these teachers have time off during the school day for this purpose.

As previously discussed, communicating general information about instruction is important. It is just as important to share more specific information about students with parents, other school personnel and the community.

However, once you have the reports and have gathered the information, the next step involves finding appropriate methods to share this information with the people that need the data. Again, depending on the audience the amount and type of information may change.

Some ways to share information with parents/guardians include:

- Individual parent meetings
- Small group meetings
- Regular parent updates through phone calls
- Charts and graphs of progress sent home
- Notes home

Some ways to share information with school personnel include:

- Faculty meetings
- Power point or other presentations
- Email
- Conferences
- School board presentation
- Graphs and charts

Skill 7.3   Apply knowledge of guidelines for referring students to appropriate specialists when more in-depth information about a child's needs is required for making educational decisions.

As the special educator, your primary role is to develop the academic and/or behavioral skills of the students assigned to your roster. Sometimes while working with the student, you will begin to notice specific deficits which are not of an academic or behavioral nature, or they may be out of your personal realm of expertise.   In these situations, it is important to know where to seek out further assistance.

While there are general guidelines for referring students to other specialists, specific procedures will vary from building to building and district to district. The building principal, director of special education or school psychologist can help you determine the steps to take within the building.

When you are working with a student, sometimes you will notice an awkward pencil grasp, or great difficulty manipulating small objects with their hands. These and other fine motor difficulties may require the intervention of an occupational therapist. Quite often, the therapist will voluntarily come into your class and observe the child and provide you with suggestions for further accommodations to help these skills develop. Sometimes, a more in-depth evaluation will be necessary.

If you notice a child to be having difficulty with large motor skills including, walking, running, using stairs, etc. They may benefit from the services of a physical therapist. Generally, physical therapy services are quite specific in nature. Sometimes gross motor issues can also be dealt with by a motor specialist or adaptive physical education teacher. All of these professionals can provide guidance with addressing large motor skill deficits in students.

Students who have difficulty articulating language, understanding language, or expressing themselves may benefit from the services of the speech and language pathologist. The speech and language pathologist addresses all areas of speech and language including: articulation, apraxia, expressive, receptive, pragmatic, stuttering, and other areas. As language can is pervasive in school settings as primary delivery tool for instruction and learning to occur, students with deficits in this area may have a great deal of difficulty achieving the appropriate academic skills.

There are other itinerant positions which may be beneficial when certain deficits are noticed in students. The audiologist can be provide modifications and check the students ability to hear and process language. Sometimes a room amplification system can be incorporated, where the teacher wears a microphone, and solve problems for a number of students. Hearing and vision specialists can provide guidance with children with those disabilities. There are also behavior specialists who can intervene when all school based attempts have failed to control a student's behavior. Some areas have specialists in various disabilities (autistic specialists, etc.) that can be used to provide consultation when necessary.

COMPETENCY 8.0   UNDERSTAND PROCEDURES FOR DEVELOPING AND IMPLEMENTING INDIVIDUALIZED EDUCATION PROGRAMS (IEPS), INDIVIDUAL FAMILY SERVICE PLANS (IFSPS), AND TRANSITION PLANS.

Skill 8.1   Demonstrate knowledge of issues in definition and identification procedures for individuals with disabilities, including those associated with individuals from culturally and/or linguistically diverse backgrounds.

Assessment data and information is one resource for the special educator who is writing an IEP. Such data can provide some information on the student's current level of functioning in social skills, speech, language, academics, cognitive skills, and fine and gross motor skills. (It is important to note that the student's classroom performance should also be taken into account when writing current level of performance.)

Assessment data can also generate areas of delay that should be included in the student's IEP goals and objectives. For example, a student who has tested as having a delay in rote memory skills, may have an IEP objective to rote count to 25 or to recite the alphabet. A student who demonstrates a reading delay of two years, may have IEP goals and objectives that reflect that he will demonstrate comprehension skills with material at that grade level.

Usually if there is a year or more delay in an area, the student will be eligible for special education services. (However, according to IDEA 2004 such a determination no longer must solely depend on a discrepancy in areas of achievement but may also be the result of how the student in doing in class.)This data (again, with classroom performance) can also help determine which subjects might be considered for inclusion.

The need for programming in specific therapies may also be the result of formal assessment. Such therapies might include: speech and language, physical therapy, occupational therapy, vision therapy, or music therapy.

Formal assessment and school behaviors may result in the writing of a functional behavioral plan as a part of the IEP.

The special education student with a culturally or linguistically diverse background will need additional considerations. Although special education must not be determined as needed because of a cultural or linguistic diversity, certainly some students qualify for special education services and come from a diverse background.

In the case of the ELL special education student, materials and activities must be at the student's developmental level and must, as needed, parallel skills in the child's first language and then in English. The Special Education Teacher is also reminded to foster an appreciation and respect for the student's cultural and linguistic background.

See skill 2.2 for the definitions of various disabilities

Skill 8.2   Apply knowledge of strategies for collaborating with individuals with disabilities, parents, teachers, and other school and community personnel to develop and implement individualized plans (e.g., IEPs, IFSPs, transition plans) appropriate to the age and skill level of the student.

According to IDEA 2004, the IEP team includes: the parents of a child with a disability; not less than one regular education teacher of such child (if the child is, or may be, participating in the regular education environment); not less than one Special Education Teacher, or where appropriate, not less than one special education provider of such child; a representative of the local educational agency; an individual who can interpret the instructional implications of evaluation results; at the discretion of the parent of the agency, other individuals who have knowledge or special expertise regarding the child, including related services personnel as appropriate; and whenever appropriate, the child with a disability.

Once the team is in place, it is important that they work together as a team. All parties need to understand and be clear that they have equal stake in the process and the writing of goals and objectives for the student. Sometimes emotions can become involved and this can seem a difficult process. One strategy to help all people have an active part is to ask for some input before the actual meeting. If each party provides some suggestions for items they believe need to be included in the IEP, the case coordinator can compile these suggestions ahead of time. Another suggestion is to have draft general ideas ready for discussion and review. Though in an ideal world, you would walk into an IEP meeting with blank paperwork and leave with a completed document, this is often unrealistic. By preparing a draft document and working together to make changes where necessary as a team, it can save time for all parties. Each team member has a specific function and role.

The role of the representative of the local education agency is to provide or supervise the provision of specifically designed instruction to meet the unique needs of the child. This is usually the school principal if this is the first time the child has been evaluated. If the representative is not an expert on evaluations, then one of the people who participated in the actual testing of the child must be present.

The role of the teacher is to identify the short and long term goals for the student and to give the student's current progress including strengths and weaknesses. The school must allow any other individual whom the parent wants to invite to attend the meeting. This may be a caseworker involved with the student's family, people involved with the day-to-day care of the student or any person whom the parent feels can contribute vital information to the meeting.

The parent or guardian can also bring someone to help them understand the IEP or the IEP process, such as a lawyer experienced with educational advocacy or parent advocate.

There are lists of related services that may be considered during an IEP meeting. The related services are developmental, corrective, and other supportive services that are required to help a child with special needs benefit from special education. These related services can include speech pathology and audiology, psychological services, physical and occupational therapy, recreation and extracurricular activities, counseling services, and medical services for diagnostic or evaluation purposes.

The IEP should specify the services to be provided, the extent to which they are necessary, and who will provide the services. If a specialist such as a speech teacher or occupational therapist will provide specific services, they should be included in the IEP team so they can give input on the types of services required, available, and what may be beneficial to the student in question. Information on how they are doing in particular specialist areas will also be included with an evaluation of student process with speech therapy and occupational therapy.

Support professionals are available at both the district and school-based levels, and they contribute valuable services and expertise in their respective areas. A team approach between district ancillary services and local school-based staff is essential.

1. **School Psychologist.** The school psychologist participates in the referral, identification, and program planning processes. She contributes to the multidisciplinary team by adding important observations, data, and inferences about the student's performance. As she conducts an evaluation, she observes the student in the classroom environment, takes a case history, and administers a battery of formal and informal individual tests. The psychologist is involved as a member of a professional team throughout the stages of referral, assessment, placement, and program planning.

2. **Physical Therapist.** This person works with disorders of bones, joints, muscles, and nerves following medical assessment. Under the prescription of a physician, the therapist applies treatment to the students in the form of heat, light, massage, and exercise to prevent further disability or deformity. Physical therapy includes the use of adaptive equipment, and prosthetic and orthotic devices to facilitate independent movement. This type of therapy helps individuals with disabilities to develop or recover their physical strength and endurance.

3. **Occupational Therapist.** This specialist is trained in helping students develop self-help skills (e.g., self-care, motor, perceptual, and vocational skills). The students are actively involved in the treatment process to quicken recovery and rehabilitation.

4. **Speech and Language Pathologist.** This specialist assists in the identification and diagnosis of children with speech or language disorders. In addition, she makes referrals for medical or habilitation needs, counsels family members and teachers, and works with the prevention of communicative disorders. The speech and language therapist concentrates on rehabilitative service delivery and continuing diagnosis.

5. **Administrators.** Building principals and special education directors (or coordinators) provide logistical as well as emotional support. Principals implement building policy procedures and control designation of facilities, equipment, and materials. Their support is crucial to the success of the program within the parameters of the base school. Special education directors provide information about federal, state, and local policy which is vital to the operation of a special education unit. In some districts the special education director may actually control certain services and materials. Role clarification, preferably in writing, should be accomplished to ensure effectiveness of program services.

6. **Guidance Counselors, Psychometrists, and Diagnosticians.** These persons often lead individual and group counseling sessions, and are trained in assessment, diagnostic, and observation skills, as well as personality development and functioning abilities. They can apply knowledge and skills to multidisciplinary teams, and assist in the assessment, diagnosis, placement, and program planning process.

7. **Social Worker.** The social worker is trained in interviewing and counseling skills. This person possesses knowledge of available community and school services, and makes these known to parents. She often visits homes of students, conducts intake and assessment interviews, counsels individuals and small groups, and assists in district enforcement policies.

8. **School Nurse.** This person offers valuable information about diagnostic and treatment services. She is knowledgeable about diets, medications, therapeutic services, health-related services, and care needed for specific medical conditions. Reports of communicable diseases are filed with the health department to which a health professional has access. A medical professional can sometimes obtain cooperation with the families of children with disabilities in ways that are difficult for the Special Education Teacher to achieve.

9. **Regular Teachers and Subject Matter Specialists.** These professionals are trained in general and specific instructional areas, teaching techniques, and overall child growth and development. They serve as a vital component to the referral process, as well as in the subsequent treatment program, if the student is determined eligible. They work with the students with special needs for the majority of the school day and function as a link to the children's special education and medical programs.

10. **Paraprofessional.** This staff member assists the special educator and often works in the classroom with the special needs students. She helps prepare specialized materials, tutor individual students, lead small groups, and provide feedback to students about their work.

Skill 8.3 **Apply knowledge of the continuum of placements and services within the context of the least restrictive environment when making educational recommendations for students.**

As previously stated and discussed, the ultimate goal of special education is to return the students with successful skills to complete the regular education curriculum. With this goal in mind, there are a number of possibilities for delivery of services students may be engaged in for their special education time. The law requires students to be educated in the least restrictive environment possible. This means, as close to regular education as possible with student success at the forefront.

When you think about the various levels of possible services students can receive you must keep in mind that ultimate goal. Following is a general reference to help guide thinking in regards to continuum of services. This continuum begins with the least of all environments and then progresses through various learning environments each of which is more restrictive than the prior.

- Regular education with no special education services provided
- Regular education with special education services provided only in the regular classroom setting (team teaching, inclusion, etc)
- Regular education for 95% or better of the day with a minimal support period of time in a special education classroom for services
- Regular education for 50-95% of the day with support for the remaining part of the day occurring in the special education classroom
- Regular education with 51-99% of the instruction occurring in the special education classroom
- Self contained special education classroom (no regular education time)
- Separate non regular education school (a full time special education school)
- Noneducational placement (hospitalization, detention facility, etc.)

Skill 8.4 **Demonstrate knowledge of the concept of longitudinal transition plans and considerations and procedures for using knowledge of a student's cognitive, communication, physical, cultural, social, and emotional characteristics in transition planning.**

Transition planning is mandated in the Individuals with Disabilities Education Act (IDEA). The transition planning requirements ensure that planning is begun at age 14 and continued through high school. Transition planning and services focus on a coordinated set of student-centered activities designed to facilitate the student's progression from school to post-school activities. Transition planning should be flexible and focus on the developmental and educational requirements of the student at different grades and times.

Transition planning is a student-centered event that necessitates a collaborative endeavor. In reference to secondary students, the responsibilities are shared by the student, parents, secondary personnel, and postsecondary personnel, who are all members of the transition team.

In most cases when transition is mentioned, it is referring to a child 14 or over, but in some cases children younger than 14 may need transition planning and assistance. Depending on the child's disability and its severity, a child may need assistance with transitioning to school from home, or to school from a hospital or institution or any other setting. In those cases the members of the transition team may also include doctors or nurses, social workers, speech therapist, and physical therapists.

It is important that the student play a key role in transition planning. This will entail asking the student to identify preferences and interests and to attend meetings on transition planning. The degree of success experienced by the student in postsecondary educational settings depends on the student's degree of motivation, independence, self-direction, self-advocacy, and academic abilities developed in high school. Student participation in transition activities should be implemented as early as possible, and no later than age 16.

In order to contribute to the transition planning process, the student should: Understand his learning disability and the impact it has on learning and work; implement achievable goals; present a positive self-image by emphasizing strengths, while understanding the impact of the learning disability; know how and when to discuss and ask for needed accommodations; be able to seek instructors and learning environments that are supportive and establish an ongoing personal file that consists of school and medical records, individualized education program (IEP), resume, and samples of academic work.

The primary function of parents during transition planning is to encourage and assist students in planning and achieving their educational goals. Parents also should encourage students to cultivate independent decision-making and self-advocacy skills.

Transition planning involves input from four groups: the student, parents, secondary education professionals, and postsecondary education professionals. The result of effective transition from a secondary to a postsecondary education program is a student with a learning disability who is confident, independent, self motivated, and striving to achieve career goals. This effective transition can be achieved if the team consisting of the student, parents, and professional personnel work as a group to create and implement effective transition plans. The transition team of a student entering the workforce may also include community members, organizations, company representatives, vocational education instructor, and job coaches.

Transition Services

Transition services will be different for each student. Transition services must take into account the student's interests and preferences. Evaluation of career interests, aptitudes, skills and training may be considered.

The transition activities that have to be addressed, unless the IEP team finds it uncalled for, are: (a) instruction (b) community experiences and (c) the development of objectives related to employment and other post-school areas.

a) Instruction – The instruction part of the transition plan deals with school instruction. The student should have a portfolio completed upon graduation. They should research and plan for further education and/or training after high school. Education can be in a college setting, technical school, or vocational center. Goals and objectives created for this transition domain depend upon the nature and severity of the student's disability, the students interests in further education, plans made for accommodations needed in future education and training, identification of post-secondary institutions that offer the requested training or education.

b) Community experiences – this part of the transition plan investigates how the student utilizes community resources. Resources entail places for recreation, transportation services, agencies, and advocacy services. It is essential for students to deal with the following areas:

- Recreation and leisure - examples: movies, YMCA, religious activities.
- Personal and social skills - examples: calling friends, religious groups, going out to eat.
- Mobility and transportation - examples: passing a driver's license test or utilizing Dial-A-Ride.
- Agency access - examples: utilizing a phone book and making calls.
- A system advocacy- example: have a list of advocacy groups to contact.
- Citizenship and legal issues - example: registering to vote.

c) Development of employment -This segment of the transition plan investigates becoming employed. Students should complete a career interest inventory. They should have chances to investigate different careers. Many work skill activities can take place within the classroom, home, and community. Classroom activities may concentrate on employability skills, community skills, mobility, and vocational training. Home and neighborhood activities may concentrate on personal responsibility and daily chores. Community based activities may focus on part-time work after school and in the summer, cooperative education or work-study, individualized vocational training, and volunteer work.

d) Daily living skills – This segment of the transition plan is also important although not essential to the IEP. Living away from home can be an enormous undertaking for people with disabilities. Numerous skills are needed to live and function as an adult. In order to live as independently as possible, a person should have an income, know how to cook, clean, shop, pay bills, get to a job, and have a social life. Some living situations may entail independent living, shared living with a roommate, supported living or group homes. Areas that may need to be looked into include: personal and social skills; living options; income and finances; medical needs; community resources and transportation.

Skill 8.5   Demonstrate knowledge of methods for using the characteristics of the learner, Illinois Learning Standards, general curriculum, and adaptation strategies to develop lesson plans that incorporate curriculum and instructional strategies with individualized education goals and benchmarks.

It is essential to use the school system's course of study and the student's IEP to prepare and organize materials to implement daily lesson plans. IEPs have to demonstrate that the student is working on goals as close to their general education peers as possible. Therefore the school system's course of study, including IL State Standards, curriculum and other pertinent materials should be a document used to create the annual goals of the IEP. The materials gathered should be either adapted to fit the needs of each student or specially designed materials should be purchased.

The IEP must also include any assistive technology that maybe needed for the student to be successful. The teacher must gather the necessary technology before planning a lesson.

The organization of materials should be based on the lessons plans. Assistive technology will usually be used all year long. Therefore if it needs to be purchased it should be purchased as early in the year as possible. Other materials maybe gathered and prepared a few days in advance ensuring classroom time will not be wasted while gathering materials.

<u>**SUBAREA III.**</u>   <u>**PLANNING AND DELIVERING INSTRUCTION**</u>

**COMPETENCY 9.0   UNDERSTAND STRATEGIES FOR CREATING
LEARNING EXPERIENCES THAT MAKE CONTENT
MEANINGFUL TO ALL STUDENTS.**

**Skill 9.1   Demonstrate knowledge of cognitive, thinking, and learning
processes and how these processes can be stimulated and
enhanced.**

When considering the processes of stimulating and enhancing cognition, thinking
and learning within the classroom, it is essential to have a clear understanding of
the various learning theories. These theories provide a foundational
understanding of how students learn, which when analyzed and incorporated into
the special education classroom can provide the teacher with ample supports to
increase all cognitive processes in his/her students.

There are several educational learning theories that can be applied to classroom
practices. One classic learning theory is Piaget's stages of development, which
consists of four learning stages: sensory motor stage (from birth to age 2); pre-
operation stages (ages 2 to 7 or early elementary); concrete operational (ages7
to 11 or upper elementary); and formal operational (ages 7-15 or late
elementary/high school). Piaget believed children passed through this series of
stages to develop from the most basic forms of concrete thinking to sophisticated
levels of abstract thinking.

Some of the most prominent learning theories in education today include brain-
based learning and the Multiple Intelligence Theory. Supported by recent brain
research, brain-based learning suggests that knowledge about the way the brain
retains information enables educators to design the most effective learning
environments. As a result, researchers have developed twelve principles that
relate knowledge about the brain to teaching practices. These twelve principles
are:

- The brain is a complex adaptive system
- The brain is social
- The search for meaning is innate
- We use patterns to learn more effectively
- Emotions are crucial to developing patterns
- Each brain perceives and creates parts and whole simultaneously
- Learning involves focused and peripheral attention
- Learning involves conscious and unconscious processes
- We have at least two ways of organizing memory
- Learning is developmental
- Complex learning is enhanced by challenged (and inhibited by threat)
- Every brain is unique

Educators can use these principles to help design methods and environments in their classrooms to maximize student learning.

The Multiple Intelligence Theory, developed by Howard Gardner, suggests that students learn in (at least) seven different ways. These include visually/spatially, musically, verbally, logically/mathematically, interpersonally, intrapersonally, and bodily/kinesthetically.

The most current learning theory of constructivist learning allows students to construct learning opportunities. For constructivist teachers, the belief is that students create their own reality of knowledge and how to process and observe the world around them. Students are constantly constructing new ideas, which serve as frameworks for learning and teaching. Researchers have shown that the constructivist model is comprised of the four components:

1. Learner creates knowledge
2. Learner constructs and makes meaningful new knowledge to existing knowledge
3. Learner shapes and constructs knowledge by life experiences and social interactions
4. In constructivist learning communities, the student, teacher and classmates establish knowledge cooperatively on a daily basis.

Kelly (1969) states "human beings construct knowledge systems based on their observations parallels Piaget's theory that individuals construct knowledge systems as they work with others who share a common background of thought and processes." Constructivist learning for students is dynamic and ongoing. For constructivist teachers, the classroom becomes a place where students are encouraged to interact with the instructional process by asking questions and posing new ideas to old theories. The use of cooperative learning that encourages students to work in supportive learning environments using their own ideas to stimulate questions and propose outcomes is a major aspect of a constructivist classroom.

The metacognition learning theory deals with "the study of how to help the learner gain understanding about how knowledge is constructed and about the conscious tools for constructing that knowledge" (Joyce and Weil 1996). The cognitive approach to learning involves the teacher's understanding that teaching the student to process his/her own learning and mastery of skill provides the greatest learning and retention opportunities in the classroom. Students are taught to develop concepts and teach themselves skills in problem solving and critical thinking. The student becomes an active participant in the learning process and the teacher facilitates that conceptual and cognitive learning process.

Social and behavioral theories look at the social interactions of students in the classroom that instruct or impact learning opportunities in the classroom. The psychological approaches behind both theories are subject to individual variables that are learned and applied either proactively or negatively in the classroom. The stimulus of the classroom can promote conducive learning or evoke behavior that is counterproductive for both students and teachers. Students are social beings that normally gravitate to action in the classroom, so teachers must be cognizant in planning classroom environments that are provide both focus and engagement in maximizing learning opportunities.

Designing classrooms that provide optimal academic and behavioral support for a diversity of students in the classroom can be daunting for teachers. The ultimate goal for both students and teachers is creating a safe learning environment where students can construct knowledge in an engaging and positive classroom climate of learning.

No one of these theories will work for every classroom, and a good approach is to incorporate a range of learning styles in a classroom. Still, under the guidance of any theory, good educators will differentiate their instructional practices to meet the needs of their students' abilities and interests using various instructional practices. It is through this process of building upon abilities and interests that the special educator is able to increase student thinking, learning and cognition skills.

Skill 9.2 **Demonstrate knowledge of the Illinois Learning Standards and components of effective, research-supported instructional strategies and practices for teaching the scope and sequence of the Illinois Learning Standards in the academic, social, transitional, and vocational curricular domains.**

A complete listing of the Illinois Learning Standards can be found at http://www.isbe.state.il.us/ils/. This site also has references for aligning classroom lesson plans specifically with the IL Learning Standards. It is an invaluable site and should be reviewed completely.

See also previous skills about writing IEP goals and objectives which incorporate learning standards.

Skill 9.3   Demonstrate knowledge of ways to use a variety of explanations and multiple representations of concepts that capture key ideas and help students develop conceptual understandings.

Students have various learning styles which need to be addressed through the instruction provided in the special education program. In order to meet the multitude of needs within one classroom, it is essential the teacher be equipped with a variety of tools to present information to students. The same concept should be presented in multiple formats to all the majority of students to acquire and process the information and make it a part of their knowledge base. This requires the teacher to have different methods of presentation and explanations available. Some strategies which can be used to achieve this goal are listed below.

Visual Representations: Many students need to see information presented in some visual manner in order to better understand the concept. This can involve pictures, slides, movies, or other pectoral representations. Sometimes it is helpful if the students create the visual pictures or ideas themselves. Mind mapping is a tool where the students take the concepts being presented and draw pictures which will help them better follow the ideas and connect them to their own knowledge base.

Auditory Representations: This is the most common form of presentation of information in schools today. Though it is not always the most effective for students to acquire skills, it is still used in abundance in classrooms across the country. Sometimes, it can provide additional support to other academic areas. Listening to a story on a CD after reading it, may be helpful in providing more fluent reading and thereby more comprehension of the story.

Use of Nonexamples: Students are often presented with information and many examples to support the concept being taught. Research tells us that providing them with nonexamples as well as examples is more effective at cementing the knowledge than simply providing just real examples. Showing the children pictures of triangles alone may not provide them with the understanding of what a triangle is, however, if you also show them pictures of things which are not triangles, they can begin to build a conceptual framework for the term.

Manipulatives: Often, students need to move objects to be able to develop their conceptual knowledge further. Providing them with tangible objects which they can move and explore may enhance both auditory and visual lessons to expand on their conceptual understanding.

In summary, there is no one methodology which will meet the needs of all of the students you will face in the classroom. Instead, using a mixed bag of strategies has the best shot at meeting the most needs and for the most learning to occur.

Skill 9.4   **Apply knowledge of methods for stimulating student reflection on prior knowledge, linking new ideas to already familiar ideas and experiences, and enhancing a reinforcers effectiveness in instruction.**

PRIOR KNOWLEDGE

Prior knowledge can be defined as all of an individual's prior experiences, learning, and development, which precede his/her entering a specific learning situation. Sometimes prior knowledge can be erroneous or incomplete. Obviously, if there are misconceptions in a child's prior knowledge, these must be corrected so that the child's overall comprehension skills can continue to progress. Prior knowledge, of even kindergarteners includes their accumulated positive and negative experiences both in and out of school.

These might range from wonderful family travels, watching television, visiting museums and libraries, to visiting hospitals, prisons and surviving poverty. Whatever the prior knowledge that the child brings to the school setting, the independent reading and writing the child does in school immeasurably expands his/her prior knowledge and hence broadens his/her comprehension capabilities.

The teacher must consider as he/she prepares to begin any lesson the following about the students' level of prior knowledge:

1. What prior knowledge needs to be activated for the skill to be done successfully?
2. How independent are the children in using strategies to activate their prior knowledge?

Holes and Roser (1987) have suggested five techniques for activating prior knowledge:

FREE RECALL. .. Tell us what you know about. .

UNSTRUCTURED DISCUSSION. . Let's talk about _____

STRUCTURED QUESTION. . .Who exactly was Jane Aviles in the life of the hero of the story?

WORD ASSOCIATION: When you hear these words. . hatch, elephant, who, think. . What do you think of?

RECOGNITION...Mulberry Street . . What comes to mind?

Previewing, predicting, and mapping are excellent strategies for activating prior knowledge.

It is the responsibility of the teacher to engage a student's prior knowledge for every lesson taught. Without a direct link between the new information being taught to something prior in the student's memory, new learning will not become automatic and useful for the student. It is only though these connections that the students can make sense of the new information.

In this manner, it is important to take time to provide the students with the opportunity to reflect on topics and what information they may already know about it. One way to find out what information students may already know about a topic and engage the prior knowledge is to use a strategy known as Know-Wonder-Learn.

Know	Wonder	Learn
In this column, the students list what information they already know about a topic. This is prior knowledge.	In this box, the students list information they want to learn about a topic.	At the end of a unit, the students list here what information they have learned about the topic.

Skill 9.5   Demonstrate knowledge of procedures for facilitating learning (e.g., errorless learning, teacher-delivered instruction, prompts, discrimination learning).

There are numerous methods which can be implemented to facilitate learning within the classroom. Some were previously discussed in other skills. See skills 9.1, 9.3, and 9.4. There are too many possibilities to discuss all in depth in a document such as this. However, here are a few more procedures which can be used to facilitate learning within the classroom.

Errorless Learning: The old adage practice makes perfect is good in thought and sentiment, but not quite accurate in reality. Students may practice reading the word said a million times, but if each time they read it, they say sad, they will not be correct no matter how much practicing they do. It takes about twenty repetitions of a skill before that skill is considered learned and automatic, however, if the skill is learned incorrectly, it can take up to three hundred repetitions to unlearn it and relearn it correctly. Therefore, it is important to ensure students are practicing errorlessly. Perhaps the adage should read, perfect practice makes perfection.

Teacher-Delivered Instruction: This is the typical method you will find in classrooms across the country. The teacher is responsible for providing the students with the information in a teacher led format. This is not the time for discovery or some of the other methods previously discussed, this is the traditional teacher imparting knowledge to the students.

<u>Prompts:</u> Prompting can be a very effective strategy to use in the classroom. It can be done in a subtle manner where only the teacher and student know a prompt is occurring. For example, a student who is experiencing a tendency to shout out might need to be provided with a prompt to remind him to raise his hand. The student could meet with the child individually and set up a signal (i.e. touching a shoulder) to encourage hand raising. In this scenario, when the teacher hears the student begin to shout out, she may touch her shoulder or his shoulder as a prompt to remember to raise his hand. No verbal communication need take place, yet a prompt is given which is effective at diminishing the negative behavior.

<u>Discrimination Learning:</u> In this type of learning the student is taught to only respond when specific characteristics are in place. This would be similar to the nonexample concept taught about previously. Students are taught a response based on a condition. For example when you see an addition sign you add, when you do not see an addition sign you do not add. The conditions in this example is the addition sign. The student response is to add. This is a very simplistic sample, but the concept can be used with more complex issues as well. It can also be generalized into behavioral expectations (i.e. when the teacher raises her hand, the student will be quiet).

Skill 9.6   Apply knowledge of strategies for teaching study skills and the use of technology and for integrating a study-skills curriculum and the use of technology into the delivery of academic instruction.

Content area subjects often have texts with a great deal of information. Typically, much more information than is necessary for students to know at one time. In cases like this, it is necessary for the students to develop specific study skills to help them take in the important information while weeding out the less important.

Highlighting is a difficult strategy for students to master. Even at the college level it seems students have a hard time determining what is important and necessary. Key ideas or vocabulary are a good place to start with highlighting. Teaching students to highlight less information, rather than more is also important. It is not a good study skill if a student highlights an entire page of information.
Outlining is a skill many teachers use to help students understand the important facts. Sometimes the teacher can provide the outline to the students to use as a guide when taking their own notes. In this way, the students know the important parts to key in to when reading. Developing outlines can be very difficult for some students, for those students mapping might be a more appropriate study aid.

Mapping involves using graphics, pictures, and words to represent the information in the text. The students can personalize and use colors and pictures which have meaning to them. This provides the natural bridge to prior knowledge and frames the information in a more personal way.

Note-taking skills also are something that requires direct instruction. Sometimes, in fact too often, teachers assume students understand how to take notes based on a lecture format, when in fact; the majority of students are trying to write down as much as they hear. Teachers can help in this process by taking the time to specifically teach and highlight the key factors.

Test-taking skills are another area students sometimes lag in skill development. Teaching students to eliminate automatic wrong answers first, then narrowing down the choices is a start. In open-ended questions, students need to be able to restate the question in their answer and understand they need to answer all parts of the question being asked.

Today there are numerous technological methods which can be utilized to increase the ability of students to study. Leap Frog© has study devices which are preprogrammed with text books used across the country. These computerized devices allow students to study for tests in yet a different manner. The use of word processing programs, spreadsheets, and the Internet also provide opportunities for students to use technology as part of the study process. In addition to the study process, they can also be utilized in the direct delivery of instruction as well.

Combining all of these approaches will allow the students the opportunity to read, take in new information and use that information to respond appropriately.

**COMPETENCY 10.0   UNDERSTAND THE PRINCIPLES OF
                                      INSTRUCTIONAL DESIGN AND PLANNING FOR
                                      STUDENTS WITH DISABILITIES.**

**Skill 10.1   Apply knowledge of guidelines for the evaluation, selection,
                      development, adaptation, and use of relevant, age-appropriate
                      instructional content, methods, materials, resources,
                      technologies, and strategies that respond to the context of the
                      general curriculum and to developmental, cultural, linguistic,
                      gender, and learning style differences.**

As a special educator it is important to understand and have a working
framework with the guidelines for evaluating, selecting, developing, and adapting
a variety of instructional issues in relation to the regular education
curriculum. Matching learning with the needs of the students is a complex and
sometimes overwhelming skill for teachers to develop.

Keeping in mind, the goal of helping the students to access the general
education curriculum as much as possible, the special educator can use the
district's regular education curriculum as the foundation upon which all
instructional decisions are made. In this way, the teacher can better meet the
needs of the students, yet maintain the integrity of the curriculum in place within
the district.

Whether you are evaluating, selection, or adapting pre-made materials or
developing and using materials of your own creation, if you begin by first aligning
it as much as possible with the regular education curriculum, you can see which
are closest to that end goal. It may be helpful to have the full scope and
sequence of the general education curriculum, as you may be working out of
grade level. In other words, you may have children who are in seventh grade, but
need instructional strategies and skills at a fifth grade level. When you examine
instructional content, methods, materials, resources, technologies, and
strategies, you will want to focus on the fifth grade level general curriculum to see
how well it aligns. If it meets the majority of the skills, it would be a good item to
consider.

Once you have decided upon the alignment, then it is important to look at the
students with which you will be using this material. Keep in mind the
developmental levels, cultural needs, linguistic issues, gender issues as well as
the specific learning style differences of the students themselves. It will be
difficult to find one "program" which will cover all areas. It is typically through an
eclectic approach that the special educator will find the most success.

It is also important to understand there will be some give and take involved. Making decisions about the importance of one skill or issue over another is difficult at best. In general, if you keep in mind the general education curriculum and regularly progress monitor the students using reliable and validated measures, you will be able to make the most informed decisions. Following the success or lack of success of the data gathered from the students will be the most effective method for making instructional decisions within the classroom.

No two students are alike. It follows, then, that no students *learn* alike. To apply a one dimensional instructional approach and a strict tunnel vision perspective of testing is to impose learning limits on students. All students have the right to an education, but there cannot be a singular path to that education. A teacher must acknowledge the variety of learning styles and abilities among students within a class (and, indeed, the varieties from class to class) and apply multiple instructional and assessment processes to ensure that every child has appropriate opportunities to master the subject matter, demonstrate such mastery, and improve and enhance learning skills with each lesson.

It has been traditionally assumed that a teacher will use direct instruction in the classroom. The amount of time devoted to it will vary according to the age of the class as well as other factors. Lecturing can be very valuable because it's the quickest way for transferring knowledge to students and they can also learn note-taking and information-organizing skills in this way. However, having said that, there are many cautions to using an excessive amount of lecturing in a class of any age. In the first place, attention span even of senior high-school students is short when they are using only one sense—the sense of hearing. Teachers should limit how much lecture they do as compared to other methods and how long the lectures last.

Most teachers find students enjoy the learning process when lecturing is limited and the students themselves become active in and responsible for their own learning. Students' attitudes and perceptions about learning are the most powerful factors influencing academic focus and success. When instructional objectives center on students' interests and are relevant to their lives, effective learning occurs. Learners must believe that the tasks that they are asked to perform have some value and that they have the ability and resources to perform them. If a student thinks a task is unimportant, he/she will not put forth much effort. If a student thinks he lacks the ability or resources to successfully complete a task, even attempting the task becomes too great a risk. Not only must the teacher understand the students' abilities and interests, she must also help students develop positive attitudes and perceptions about tasks and learning. Below are a few examples of instructional styles that actively involve the students.

Differentiated instruction

The effective teacher will seek to connect all students to the subject matter through multiple techniques, with the goal that each student, through their own abilities, will relate to one or more techniques and excel in the learning process. Differentiated instruction encompasses several areas:

- **Content**: What is the teacher going to teach? Or, perhaps better put, what does the teacher want the students to learn? Differentiating content means that students will have access to content that piques their interest about a topic, with a complexity that provides an appropriate challenge to their intellectual development.
- **Process**: A classroom management technique where instructional organization and delivery is maximized for the diverse student group. These techniques should include dynamic, flexible grouping activities, where instruction and learning occurs both as whole-class, teacher-led activities, as well peer learning and teaching (while teacher observes and coaches) within small groups or pairs.
- **Product**: The expectations and requirements placed on students to demonstrate their knowledge or understanding. The type of product expected from each student should reflect each student's own capabilities.

Alternative Assessments

Alternative assessment is an assessment where students create an answer or a response to a question or task, as opposed to traditional, inflexible assessments where students choose a prepared response from among a selection of responses, such as matching, multiple-choice or true/false.

When implemented effectively, an alternative assessment approach will exhibit these characteristics, among others:

- Requires higher-order thinking and problem-solving
- Provides opportunities for student self-reflection and self-assessment
- Uses real world applications to connect students to the subject
- Provides opportunities for students to learn and examine subjects on their own, as well as to collaborate with their peers.
- Encourages students to continuing learning beyond the requirements of the assignment
- Clearly defines objective and performance goals

Teachers are learning the value of giving assignments that meet the individual abilities and needs of students. After instruction, discussion, questioning, and practice have been provided, rather than assigning one task to all students— teachers are asking students to generate tasks that will show their knowledge of the information presented. Students are given choices and thereby have the opportunity to demonstrate more effectively the skills, concepts, or topics that they as individuals have learned. It has been established that student choice increases student originality, intrinsic motivation, and higher mental processes.

Below are the five basic types of grouping arrangements are typically used in the classroom:

A. Large Group with Teacher

Examples of appropriate activities include show and tell, discussions, watching plays or movies, brainstorming ideas, and playing games. Science, social studies, and most other subjects, except for reading and math are taught in large groups.

The advantage of large-group instruction is that it is time-efficient and prepares students for higher levels of secondary and post-secondary education settings. However, with large groups, instruction cannot be as easily tailored to high or low levels of students, who may become bored or frustrated. Mercer and Mercer recommend guidelines for effective large-group instruction:

- Keep instruction short, ranging from 5 to 15 minutes for first grade to seventh grade; 5 to 40 minutes, for grades 8 to 12.
- Use questions to involve all students, use lecture-pause routines, and encourage active participation among the lower-performing students.
- Incorporate visual aids to promote understanding, and maintain a lively pace
- Break up the presentation with different rates of speaking, giving students a "stretch" break", varying voice volume, etc...
- Establish rules of conduct for large groups and praise students who follow the rules

B. Small Group Instruction

Small group instruction usually includes 5 to 7 students and is recommended for teaching basic academic skills such as math facts or reading. This model is especially effective for students with learning problems. Composition of the groups should be flexible to accommodate different rates of progress through instruction. The advantages of teaching in small groups is that the teacher is better able to provide feedback, monitor student progress, and give more instruction, praise and feedback. With small groups the teacher will need make sure to provide a steady pace for the lesson, provide questions and activities that allow all to participate, and include lots of positive praise.

C. One Student with Teacher

One –to-one tutorial teaching can be used to provide extra assistance to individual students. Such tutoring may be scheduled at set times during the day or provided as the need arises. The tutoring model is typically found more in elementary and resource classrooms than secondary settings.

D. Peer Tutoring

In an effective peer tutoring arrangement, the teacher trains the peer tutors and matches them with students who need extra practice and assistance. In addition to academic skills, the arrangement can help both students work on social skills such as cooperation and self-esteem. Both students may be working on the same material or the tutee may be working to strengthen areas of weakness. The teacher determines the target goals, selects the material, sets up the guidelines, trains the student tutors, in the rules and methods of the sessions, and monitors and evaluates the sessions.

E. Cooperative Learning

Cooperative learning differs from peer tutoring in that students are grouped in teams or small groups and the methods are based on teamwork, individual accountability and team reward. Individual students are responsible for their own learning and share of the work, as well as the group's success. As with peer tutoring, the goals, target skills, materials, and guidelines, are developed by the teacher. Teamwork skills may also need to be taught, too. By focusing on team goals, all members of the team are encouraged to help each other as well as improve their individual performance.

Curriculum Design

Effective curriculum design assists the teacher from teacher demonstration to independent practice. Components of curriculum design include:

- Quizzes or reviews of the previous lesson
- Step-by-step presentations with multiple examples
- Guided practice and feedback
- Independent practice that requires the student to produce faster responses

The chosen curriculum should introduce information in a cumulative sequence and not introduce too much new information at a time. Review difficult material and practice to aid retention. New vocabulary and symbols should be introduced one at a time, and the relationships of components to the whole should be stressed. Students' background information should be recalled to connect new information to the old. Finally, teach strategies or algorithms first and then move on to tasks that are more difficult.

Course objectives may be obtained from the department head at the local school. The ESE coordinator may have copies of objectives for functional courses or applied ESE courses. District program specialists also have lists of objectives for each course provided in the local school system. Additionally, publishers of textbooks will have scope and sequence lists in the teacher's manual.

Addressing Students' Needs

There are a number of procedures teachers can use to address the varying need of the students. Some of the more common procedures are:

1. Vary assignments

A variety of assignments on the same content allows students to match learning styles and preferences with the assignment. If all assignments are writing assignments, for example, students who are hands-on or visual learners are at a disadvantage unrelated to the content base itself.

2. Cooperative learning

Cooperative learning activities allow students to share ideas, expertise, and insight with a non-threatening setting. The focus tends to remain on positive learning rather than on competition.

3. Structure environment

Some students need and benefit from clear structure that defines the expectation and goals of the teacher. The student knows what is expected and when and can work and plan accordingly.

4. Clearly stated assignments

Assignments should be clearly stated along with the expectation and criteria for completion. Reinforcement and practice activities should not be a guessing game for the students. The exception to this is, of course, those situations in which a discovery method is used.

5. Independent practice

Independent practice involving application and repetition is necessary for thorough learning. Students learn to be independent learners through practicing independent learning. These activities should always be within the student's abilities to perform successfully without assistance.

6. Repetition

Very little learning is successful with a single exposure. Learners generally require multiple exposures to the same information for learning to take place. However, this repetition does not have to be dull and monotonous. In conjunction with #1 above, varied assignments can provide repetition of content or skill practiced without repetition of specific activities. This helps keep learning fresh and exciting for the student.

7. Overlearning

As a principle of effective learning, overlearning recommends that students continue to study and review after they have achieved initial mastery. The use of repetition in the context of varied assignments and offers the means to help students pursue and achieve overlearning.

No Child Left Behind, Public Law 107-110, was signed on January 8, 2002. It addresses accountability of school personnel for student achievement with the expectation that every child will demonstrate proficiency in reading, math, and science. For example, all students should know how to read by grade three.

General education curriculum should reflect state learning standards. Because special educators are responsible for teaching students to a level of comparable proficiency as their non-disabled peers, this curriculum should also be followed closely in the special education program.

Naturally, certain modifications and accommodations will be necessary to meet learning standards. IEP goals and objectives are based on the unique needs of the child with a disability in meeting the curriculum expectations of the school (and the state/nation). Consider some of the following hypothetical cases.

Teacher in grades K-3 are mandated to teach reading to all students using scientifically-based methods with measurable outcomes. Some students (including some with disabilities) will not learn to read successfully unless taught with a phonics approach. It is the responsibility of the general education teacher and Special Education Teacher to incorporate phonics into the reading program.

Students are expected to learn mathematics. While some students will quickly grasp the mathematical concept of groupings of tens (and further skills of adding and subtracting large numbers), others will need additional practice. Research shows that many students with disabilities need a hands-on approach. Perhaps those students will need additional instruction and practice using snap-together cubes to grasp the grouping-by-tens concept.

School districts, individual general education classrooms, and special education classroom are no longer functioning independently. Learning standards set forth by the government now holds all education to the same bar and is evidenced in curriculum and related IEP goals and objectives.

Skill 10.2 **Apply knowledge of principles for designing, implementing, and evaluating instructional programs that promote successful transitions for individuals with disabilities; prepare them to live harmoniously and productively in a diverse world; and enhance their social participation in family, school, and community activities.**

Any transition in life can be overwhelming and difficult whether we are adults or children. For students with special needs, making transitions can be more than overwhelming. Specific tools and strategies need to be taught to students so they are better able to understand the issues facing them and then deal with them.

The coping skills for transitioning are similar in some respects to the same skills necessary to deal with life's stressors. One of the biggest factors that can help a student be ready to make the transition from school to work includes planning. Students that understand goal setting and building a plan that can be used to reach these goals, have a leg up on students who are not taught to look into the future. From a young age, students as young as elementary aged can be taught goal setting, it may begin with setting a goal to complete a project, but taking the students through this process several times throughout their school careers will encourage them to better be able to make generalize the process at transition time.

Furthermore, students need to understand how their voice works in the process. Being an advocate for them is a critical factor in finding a successful path. Self-advocacy requires communication skills to be well developed. Students need to use both oral and written means to express their individual hopes and dreams. Once the school personnel understand clearly the hopes and ambitions of the student, they can build a framework to help them come true.

This may by helping to provide additional course work or specific skill knowledge. It may be in providing opportunities for the students to participate in a work-study program where they can experience different work related experiences. Without the upfront knowledge of the expectations and future plans the student may have, it is difficult for the school staff to find appropriate contacts.

Outside agencies may also be a critical part of the transitioning process and should be included in all meetings and discussions. The schools do not have to be the only participants in helping students manage transitions. When all parties work together they have a better opportunity to provide the smoothest school to work experience.

It is without a doubt, collaboration is vital in order for a transition plan to be successful. On the surface, it would seem that this undeniable fact would make collaboration an easily accomplished task, however, sometimes collaborating can be quite challenging.

It has already been discussed that there are numerous outside agencies and institutions, which can be involved in the transition planning of students. Additionally, no one person can understand and be an expert at all of the available options for students with disabilities in the community. It is for this reason that collaboration is of the utmost importance.

Working with multiple service providers and outside representatives can be challenging. It is difficult to coordinate schedules and to organize the necessary parties to be able to answer questions and issues as they arise. Sometimes it happens where the special educator will receive an answer from one person, and then speak with another representative who adds an additional piece to the puzzle, which requires the first decision to be changed.

This can seem to become a never-ending chain of emails and phone calls where the wheels seem to spin and spin. One strategy for collaboration that works effectively is for each team member to complete a brief rough draft of the transition plan and ideas they may have for this student.

Having a document like this from each person in the process with invested interests allows for better use of time when all parties are brought together. As case manager, the special educator can then compile the results of these documents.

Then bringing all players to the same table to hash out any further issues and discrepancies can be a much more efficient use of time and energy for all parties. It will also lessen the amount of time spent at the table.

Good collaborative strategies rely on a strong desire to keep the needs of the student at the center of the discussion, putting aside any individual agendas should they exist. Open communication and flexibility are also fundamental skills required for effective collaboration.

In all of education, communication between school and home is paramount to providing the appropriate instruction. This is even truer when discussing students with special education needs. Often times, there are so many home related factors involved in these students, that it requires a coordinated effort to address the needs.

One crucial aspect of this home to school communication issue is highlighted at times of transition. Whether the transition is from early childhood education experiences to school age or from secondary school to post-secondary educational options, it is imperative for the special educator to have the necessary tools available to him.

The most useful skill is to be a good listener. Often times, the issues and needs will be articulated through an open dialogue between the school and parents. It is important for the special educator to be able to pull out the key components from the information shared in order to develop an appropriate transition plan.

After listening, the special educator has the responsibility to look at what services or strategies may need to be incorporated to ensure a successful transition. Having a solid understanding of all facets of transitioning and the availability of services is important, but it is just as important to know where to go to obtain the accurate information. One person cannot be expected to know and understand every contingency available in a community. It is essential that rather than setting oneself up with that expectation, instead the special educator develops a resource folder to which the can refer to gather the information needed.

Finally, taking the time to sit and explain in common everyday language the steps the student and family members need to take as part of the transition process is key. Scheduling enough time to allow for questions and provide a relaxed atmosphere will be important for all parties. It is also at this juncture that any outside agencies which may need to be involved should be included to help clarify issues as they arise.

Including parents and the student, while required by law, also helps build the ownership of the plan. After all, it is the child's plan for their entire future. It is not the school's plan or the family's plan, but the student's plan for achieving life goals. The student has the most invested and his feelings and suggestions should be considered and not discounted easily. Open, caring communication is always the key to success.

Skill 10.3   Demonstrate knowledge of short- and long-range plans that are consistent with curriculum goals, learner diversity, and learning theory.

The creation of the Individualized Education Program (IEP) is a document, which involves developing plans of instruction for students. In this way, the special educator must be very familiar with developing both short and long range plans. Since the IEP is good for one year before mandatory rewriting needs to occur, the creation needs to include short-term objectives for throughout the year as well as a year-long program. The most effective IEPs will also take into consideration the implications of learning further than one year. An example of this is with transition planning. Understanding that the transitions may occur several years down the road is still important when writing the goals and objectives so an appropriate foundation is in place for student success.

Looking down the road with the education of the students is necessary to ensure curriculum goals are being met. Though the curriculum goals may not be the exactly the same goals as they are for regular education students, they should reflect the curriculum to some degree. Supporting the curriculum should be done through the goals and objectives of the IEP and should build upon previous learning as well as take into consideration areas which need to be developed to provide a foundation for future topics as well.

In developing both short and long term plans, the Special Education Teacher needs to keep in mind appropriate learning theory and the diversity of the student's learning style and needs. Best instructional practices should be included which not only have a proven research and theoretical basis, but meet the specific needs of the student.

It is not enough to use the best math program on the market, if it is all lecture based and you have a group of students who have great difficulty learning from lectures. This balancing act requires time to complete in an effective manner. Additionally, the students will not benefit as much if delivered hands on instruction, which meets their needs, but is completed in a haphazard manner with no sequential, explicit method of skill development.

Curriculum mapping is an excellent strategy, which can be used to help the teacher develop appropriate plans. In curriculum mapping, the overriding general education curriculum, instructional tools being used to implement it, and other known factors affecting the school year (i.e. state assessment windows) are taken into consideration. A month-by-month map is then developed based on this information helping teachers to know which concepts should be taught, reviewed and mastered throughout each month of the school year. The special educator may need to refer to curriculum maps from previous grade levels, but this information can be invaluable when writing appropriate goals and objectives for the IEP. It helps to provide a clearer focus to instruction and both short- and long-range planning.

Skill 10.4   Apply knowledge of strategies for integrating in the least restrictive environment academic instruction, affective education, and behavior management for individual learners and groups of learners and for facilitating the maintenance and generalization of skills across learning environments.

The Individuals with Disabilities Education Act (1997) requires the collaboration of educational professionals in order to provide equitable opportunities for students with disabilities.

Collaboration in a school environment can take place between a variety of advocates for the students, including general educators, Special Education Teachers, School Psychologists, Speech and Language Pathologists, Interpreters, Administrators, parents, and other professionals serving students with special needs. Sporadic communication between mainstream educators and other educational professionals damages the educational experience given to students.

Students with disabilities developed greater self-images and recognized their own academic and social strengths when included in the mainstream classroom and serviced by teams of educational professionals. The staff reported professional growth, personal support, and enhanced teaching motivation. The frequent practice of creating teacher assistance teams in order to provide intervention support to the general educator, often fail due to time constraints and the lack of commitment given to collaboration.

Every member of a collaborative team has precise knowledge of his or her discipline, and transdisciplinary teams integrate these areas. For example, an ESL teacher can provide knowledge regarding the development of language skills and language instruction methodology. Counselors and psychologists can impart knowledge as human development specialists, and show their expertise in conducting small-group counseling and large-group interventions. School staff and instructors can benefit from what mainstream teachers can add in the area of performance information and knowledge of measures and benchmarks. Special Education Teachers can provide insight into designing and implementing behavior management programs and strategies for effective instruction to students with special needs. Speech pathologists can contribute their knowledge of speech and language development and provide insight into the identification of learning disabilities in language- minority students. Transdisciplinary teaming requires team members to build on the strengths and the needs of their particular populations. Therefore each professional can contribute when it comes to developing and implementing appropriate curricula.

A major focus of special education is to prepare students to become working, independent members of society. IDEA 2004 (Individuals with Disabilities Education Act) also includes preparing students for *further education*. Certain skills beyond academics are needed to attain this level of functioning.

Affective and Social Skills transcend to all areas of life. When an individual is unable to acquire information on expectations and reactions of others or misinterprets those cues, he is missing an important element needed for success as an adult in the workplace and community in general.

Special education should incorporate a level of instruction in the affective/social area as many students will not develop these skills without instruction, modeling, practice, and feedback.

Affective and social skills taught throughout the school setting might include: social greetings; eye contact with a speaker; interpretation of facial expression, body language, and personal space; ability to put feelings and questions into words; and use of words to acquire additional information as needed.

Career/Vocational Skills of responsibility for actions, a good work ethic, and independence should be incorporated into the academic setting. If students are able to regulate their overall work habits with school tasks, it is likely that the same skills will carry over into the work force. The Special Education Teacher may assess the student's level of career/vocational readiness by using the following list.

- Being prepared by showing responsibility for materials/school tools such as books, assignments, study packets, pencils, pens, assignment notebook.
- Knowing expectations by keeping an assignment notebook completed. Asking questions when unsure of the expectations.
- Use of additional checklists as needed.
- Use of needed assistive devices.
- Completing assignments on time to the best of his ability.

An additional responsibility of the special educator when teaching career/vocational skills is recognition that a variety of vocations and skills are present in the community. If academics, per se, are not an area in which students excel, other exploratory or training opportunities should be provided. Such opportunities might include art, music, culinary arts, childcare, technical, or building instruction. These skills can often be included (although not to the exclusion of additional programs) within the academic setting. For example, a student with strong vocation interest in art may be asked to create a poster to show learned information in a science or social studies unit. While addressing a career/vocational interest and skill this way, the teacher would also be establishing a program of differentiated instruction.

When considering the personal and social behavior of students with disabilities, it is important to be specific and detailed in reporting these expectations in various settings. These expectations can be included in the student's IEP or the Behavior Intervention Plan (BIP).

Students who are struggling with behavior often misread social settings and the nonverbal cues people provide to each other. In this way, their troubles can often increase due to inappropriate understanding on their part, rather than outward defiance. Children with Autism also have difficulties in reading social situations and using appropriate behavior.

It is important to clearly develop a plan where these students are taught the expectations of different settings. In this way, students can begin to make generalizations and become more functional. Understanding in detail, what may be acceptable at home in private, may not be acceptable in McDonalds, sometimes takes numerous repetitions but is invaluable for certain students.

Students may need to practice or use role playing strategies to begin to make these types of generalizations. Field trips or other practical experiences may be the most beneficial format for ensuring student success.

Developing a plan, which has been individualized for the student, can be helpful as well. Sometimes, visual aids can be used to ensure success. A note card with helpful reminders is another tool to helps students remember expectations for their personal and social behavior. A different set of reminders may need to be provided for each setting the student may be integrated into for a placement.

This type of training can begin at very young ages. Students in preschool and elementary school can begin to realize the difference in behavioral expectations depending upon the setting. Assemblies or other large group activities can provide the public setting for students. Lunch and recess are also good times to work on these types of behavioral skills.

As the child ages, mock interviews, field trips and frank, honest discussions may be strategies of more use. In any case, students often require direct teaching of these skills; most of us take for granted. Often you may hear a colleague ask why a student doesn't understand that it's inappropriate to do "that" in the classroom, the answer may be as simple as no one taught them it was wrong.

See skill 8.3 for more information on least restrictive environment

Skill 10.5   Demonstrate knowledge of issues, resources, and techniques for using instructional time effectively and efficiently while facilitating the integration of related services into the instructional program.

Teaching special education is an ever increasing balance of time, materials and instruction. If you spoke with teachers across the country, one of the items which would come up frequently is a lack of time to complete the required demands of the profession. Effective use of time is a skill unto itself and needs to be mastered, particularly by Special Education Teachers.

The Special Education Teacher needs to not only balance their own time, but to manage and keep track of the regular classroom schedule, school schedule, specialist and resource staff schedules and still manage to deliver effective instruction. Students may have needs which require the services of many different resource staff. Additionally, many of these personnel are itinerant and are only in buildings on specific days and for specific times. It is important to be flexible when building your own schedule.

It is helpful to plot into a blank weekly/cyclical calendar all of the related services and basic scheduling items before you plan which time periods you will deliver the majority of your core instruction during. In this way, you can maximize the time you have with the students to ensure they receive valuable instruction with the fewest interruptions.

Schedule development depends upon the type of class (elementary or secondary) and the setting (regular classroom or resource room). There are, however, general rules of thumb that apply to both types and settings:

1. Allow time for transitions, planning, and setups.
2. Aim for maximum instructional time by pacing the instruction quickly and allotting time for practice of the new skills.
3. Proceed from short assignments to long ones, breaking up long lessons or complex tasks into short sessions or step-by-step instruction
4. Follow a less preferred academic or activity with a highly preferred academic or activity.
5. In settings where students are working on individualized plans, do not schedule all the students at once in activities that require a great deal of teacher assistance. For example, have some students work on math or spelling while the teacher works with the students in reading, which usually requires more teacher involvement.
6. Break up a longer segment into several smaller segments with a variety of activities.

Special Considerations for Elementary Classrooms

1. Determine the amount of time that is needed for activities such as P.E., lunch, or recess.
2. Allow about 15 to 20 minutes each for opening and closing exercises. Spend this time for "housekeeping" activities such as collecting lunch money, going over the schedule, cleaning up, reviewing the day's activities, getting ready to go home.
3. Schedule academics for periods when the students are more alert and motivated, usually in the afternoon.
4. Build in time for slower students to finish their work; others may work at learning centers or other activities of interest. Allowing extra time gives the teacher time to give more attention where it is needed, conduct assessments, or for students to complete or correct work.

Special Considerations for Secondary Classes

Secondary schooldays are usually divided into five, six, or seven periods of about 50 minutes, with time for homeroom and lunch. Students cannot stay behind and finish their work, since they have to leave for a different room. Resource room time should be scheduled so that the student does not miss academic instruction in his classroom or miss desirable nonacademic activities. In schools where ESE teachers also co-teach or work with students in the regular classroom, the regular teacher will have to coordinate lesson plans with those of the Special Education Teacher. Consultation time will also have to be budgeted into the schedule.

See skill 8.2 for information on related services

Skill 10.6 **Demonstrate familiarity with the principle of partial participation as it applies to students with disabilities and its use in planning instruction for all students.**

According to IDEA 2004, students with disabilities are to participate in the general education program to the extent that it is beneficial for them. As these students are included into a variety of general education activities and classes, the need for collaboration among teachers grows.

Co-Teaching One model that is used for general education and Special Education Teachers to collaborate is co-teaching. In this model, both teachers actively teach in the general education classroom. Perhaps both teachers will conduct a small science experiment group at the same time, switching groups at some point in the lesson. Perhaps in social studies, one teacher will lecture while the other teacher writes notes on the board or points out information on a map.

In the co-teaching model, the general education teacher and special educator often switch roles back and forth within a class period or perhaps at the end of a chapter or unit.

Push-in Teaching In the push-in teaching model, the special educator is teaching parallel material in the general education classroom. When the regular education teacher is teaching word problems in math, for example, the special educator may be working with some students on setting up the initial problems and then having them complete the computation. Another example would be in science when the general education teacher is asking review questions for a test, and the special educator is working with a student who has a review study sheet to show the answer from a group of choices.

In the push-in teaching model, it may appear that two versions of the same lesson are being taught or two types of student responses / activities are being monitored on the same material. The push-in teaching model would be considered one type of differentiated instruction in which two teachers are teaching simultaneously.

Consultant Teaching In the consultant teaching model, the general education teacher conducts the class after planning with the special educator about how to differentiate activities so that the needs of the student with a disability are met.

In a social studies classroom using the consultant teaching model, both teachers may discuss what the expectations will be for a student with a learning disability and fine motor difficulty when the class does reports on states. They may decide that doing a state report is appropriate for the student, however, he may use the computer to write his report so that he can utilize the spell check feature and so that is his work is legible.

Skill 10.7   Demonstrate knowledge of the integration of students with disabilities into and out of specialized settings (e.g., psychiatric hospitals, residential treatment centers).

Sometimes students may require specialized treatment in facilities outside of the regular school setting. Transitioning students to and from various treatment centers can require much coordination to ensure successful integration.

Open, honest and consistent communication is the key to transferring students into outside treatment facilities. Many psychiatric hospitals or other residential treatment centers have an intake team of professionals as well as a discharge team. These professionals will have a wealth of information to share with the school personnel. It is important to find a coordinated time for this information sharing session to occur.   It can be an efficient use of time to conduct this session via a conference call if your school has that capability.

Sometimes, the school will be unaware of the admission of a student into a center or hospital until the student has already been placed there. There are even times when you are unaware until you receive a request for educational records. It is important to provide detailed accounts and records to the hospital, as while the student is a patient they will receive their education there as well.

Many of these facilities provided classroom activities during the daytime within the facility. The education program delivered will be based on the student's current IEP as written and input from the teacher as to specific needs, strengths and weaknesses.

Upon discharge, the hospital may contact the school to provide updated information. This may include medication changes, behavioral intervention suggestions which were successful in the inpatient setting. This will also be your opportunity to ask questions and receive clarification for a smooth transition.

As students return to your program and classroom, it is important they are treated in a similar manner as before they left. Students may have apprehensive feelings upon returning or even feelings of embarrassment. It is important to recognize these feelings and take time to talk with the student privately to provide reassurance. Involving the Guidance Counselor, school psychologist or other trained personnel can help with these issues.

It is also important to keep in mind that the student missed your instruction over a period of time. They did however receive instruction of some sort (homebound, instruction in the center, etc.). Students may need additional modifications to content or curriculum due to this period of time. It may also be necessary to revise the IEP to include findings from the hospitalization or to compensate for the differences in curriculum.

COMPETENCY 11.0 UNDERSTAND STRATEGIES AND TECHNIQUES USED TO SUPPORT THE DEVELOPMENT OF COMMUNICATION, SOCIAL COMPETENCY, AND LIFE SKILLS FOR STUDENTS WITH DISABILITIES

Skill 11.1 **Apply knowledge of effective instructional strategies that assist individuals with disabilities in developing and self-monitoring academic and social skills; self-awareness, self-control, self-reliance, self-esteem, self-determination; and the ability to manage their own behavior.**

Teachers should have a toolkit of instructional strategies, materials and technologies to encourage and teach students how to problem solve and think critically about subject content and even living skills. With each curriculum chosen by a district for school implementation, comes an expectation that students must master benchmarks and standards of learning skills. There is an established level of academic performance and proficiency in public schools that students are required to master in today's classrooms. Research of national and state standards indicate that there additional benchmarks and learning objectives in the subject areas of science, foreign language, English language arts, history, art, health, civics, economics, geography, physical education, mathematics, and social studies that students are required to master in state assessments (Marzano & Kendall, 1996).

A critical thinking skill is a skill target that teachers help students develop to sustain learning in specific areas that can be applied within other areas. For example, when learning to understand algebraic concepts in solving a math word problem on how much fencing material is needed to build a fence around a backyard area that has a 8' x 12," a math student must understand the order of numerical expression in how to simplify algebraic expressions. Teachers can provide instructional strategies that show students how to group the fencing measurements into an algebraic word problem that with minor addition, subtraction and multiplication can produce a simple number equal to the amount of fencing materials needed to build the fence.

Students use basic skills to understand things that are read such as a reading passage or a math word problem or directions for a project. However, students apply additional thinking skills to fully comprehend how what was read could be applied to their own life or how to make comparatives or choices based on the factual information given. These higher-order thinking skills are called critical thinking skills as students think about thinking and teachers are instrumental in helping students use these skills in everyday activities:

- Analyzing bills for overcharges
- Comparing shopping ads or catalogue deals
- Finding the main idea from readings
- Applying what's been learned to new situations
- Gathering information/data from a diversity of sources to plan a project
- Looking for cause and effect relationships
- Comparing and contrasting information in synthesizing information
- Following a sequence of directions

Attention to learner needs during planning is foremost and includes identification of that which the students already know or need to know; the matching of learner needs with instructional elements such as content, materials, activities, and goals; and the determination of whether or not students have performed at an acceptable level, following instruction.

The ability to create a personal and professional charting of student's academic and emotional growth found within the performance-based assessment of individualized portfolios becomes a toolkit for both students and teachers. Teachers can use semester portfolios to gauge student academic progress and personal growth of students who are constantly changing their self-images and worldviews on a daily basis. When a student is studying to master a math concept and is able to create visual of the learnings that transcend beyond the initial concept to create a bridge connecting a higher level of thinking and application of knowledge, then the teacher can share a moment of enjoyable math comprehension with the student. The idea of using art concepts as visual imagery in helping students' process conceptual learning of reading, math and science skills creates a mental mind mapping of learning for students processing new information. Using graphic organizers and concept web guides that center around a concept and the applications of the concept is an instructional strategy that teachers can use to guide students into further inquiry of the subject matter.

Imagine the research of the German chemist Fredrich August Kekule when he looked into a fire one night and solved the molecular structure of benzene and you can imagine fostering that same creativity in students. Helping students understand the art of "visualization" and the creativity of discovery may impart a student visualizing the cure for AIDS or Cancer or how to create reading programs for the next generation of readers.

Helping students become effective note-takers and stimulating a diversity of perspectives for spatial techniques that can be applied to learning is a proactive teacher strategy in creating a visual learning environment where art and visualization become natural art forms for learning. In today's computer environment, students must understand that computers cannot replace the creative thinking and skill application that comes from the greatest computer on record, the human mind.

Additionally, the teacher can look at the student's ability to monitor their own learning. Noting these self-monitoring attempts, allows the teacher to see if the student recognizes when they make a mistake. This is a very important skill for students to develop. Once they realize something does not make sense, or is wrong, they able to go back and then apply a correction strategy so as to not hinder learning.

Self-corrections by students begin to show a maturity of skills. It is an important step to begin, but as with any other learning process.

By learning to monitor their own learning and skills, the students can develop self-awareness and increase their independence. As this occurs through learning, it can also be taught and developed in the realm of behavior. Students who are able to learn to manage their own behavior have a much more realistic chance of being well integrated into society. They can become fully functioning members of society.

Skill 11.2   Apply knowledge of effective instructional strategies and behavioral interventions designed to create learning experiences and to facilitate the acquisition and development of social skills.

Teaching social skills can be rather difficult because social competence requires a repertoire of skills in a number of areas. The socially competent person must be able to get along with family and friends, function in a work environment, take care of personal needs, solve problems in daily living, and identify sources of help. A class of students with emotional disorders may present several deficits in a few areas or a few deficits in many areas. Therefore, the teacher must begin with an assessment of the skill deficits and prioritize the ones to teach first.

Type of Assessment	Description
Direct Observation	Observe student in various settings with a checklist
Role Play	Teacher observes students in structured scenarios
Teacher Ratings	Teacher rates student with a checklist or formal assessment instrument
Sociometric Measures: Peer Nomination	Student names specific classmates who meet a stated criterion (i.e., playmate). Score is the number of times a child is nominated.
Peer Rating	Students rank all their classmates on a Likert-type scale (e.g., 1-3 or 1-5 scale) on stated criterion. Individual score is the average of the total ratings of their classmates.
Paired-Comparison	Student is presented with paired classmate combinations and asked to choose who is most or least liked in the pair.
Context Observation	Student is observed to determine if the skill deficit is present in one setting, but not others
Comparison with other student	Student's social skill behavior is compared to two other students in the same situation to determine if there is a deficit, or if the behavior is not really a problem.

Social skills instruction can include teaching for conversation skills, assertiveness, play and peer interaction, problem solving and coping skills, self-help, task-related behaviors, self-concept related skills (i.e., expressing feelings, accepting consequences), and job related skills.

One advantage of schooling organizations for students is to facilitate social skills and social development. While teachers cannot take the largest role for developing such traits as honesty, fairness, and concern for others, they are extremely important in the process. The first recommendation is to be a very good role model. As we all know, actions do indeed speak louder than words. Second, teachers need to communicate expectations and be firm about them. When teachers ignore certain "infractions" and make a big deal about others, they demonstrate to students that it isn't about manners and social skills, rather discipline and favoritism. All students need to feel safe, cared about, and secure with their classmates. Teachers are the best people to ensure that students understand how to be generous, caring, considerate, and sociable individuals.

The requirements of the federal and state legislation regarding special education requires in some instances the functional living competence of students be assessed. This type of assessment generally measures the ability of a student to be able to live independently. This is an important criterion to consider as the transition out of school into the world is developed.

There are numerous tools the evaluator may use to determine the ability of student to be able to live independently. Typically, these tools involve some observation of the student and the activities he is able to complete. There are generally checklists, which other team members complete and provide as part of the full assessment protocol.

Once the assessment is completed and the data provided to the team, it must be considered as part of the transition plan. When writing the transition plan, the team must then consider what steps need to be taken to provide the necessary supports for the student after school is completed. In this way, when school is over, both the parents, students and any necessary outside agencies are prepared.

Sometimes students are unable to live independently and may require a group home setting. In this case, the school, outside agencies and/or parents may want to contact group homes to secure a visitation and availability. In this way, the student can be better prepared to make the transition when it is time. Group homes generally work well with agencies and already have prepared steps and procedures to ensure the success of this adjustment.

In other cases, there may be more or less support needed for the student. It is important to work with other professionals (i.e. social workers) to develop an appropriate transition plan. The federal law requires transition planning to begin at a somewhat early age, in order for all of the steps, which can be somewhat time consuming, to be put in place at the appropriate times. Being familiar with the local agencies, the district expectations and resources is invaluable to successfully helping students who need support with functional living skills transition to the post school environment. Working with other professional personnel is the key to success in this situation.

Social skills development is a critical to the successful integration of students with and without disabilities into society and should be treated with as much importance and support as other more traditional academic areas.

Skill 11.3 **Apply knowledge of instruction of language arts or math skills for developing curricula and instructional programs relevant to life-skill domains (i.e., domestic, recreational/leisure, vocational, and community).**

Students who have low levels of reading and math need to have familiarity with real life situations. Domestic, leisure and vocational activities often require a basic grasp of concepts, which the student should have an opportunity to learn in the classroom.

One of the best "real life" examples that can be exploited to teach basic skills in math and language arts is ordering from a restaurant menu. Here the opportunities to see life application of words like "hamburger" and "soda" being used to get what you want to order. Opportunities to learn the cost of an item on the menu and how to add them together are essential life skills. This lesson also provides an opportunity to incorporate basic money skills (identifying coins and bills; where you keep your money on your person, etc.). Advanced skills in this area would include figuring the tax and tip. When this lesson has been practiced in a classroom environment a class visit to a restaurant where the menu came from could demonstrate the actual lessons benefits. This lesson could be further developed to planning a bus trip. Students could also learn how much it costs to take public transportation, how to read a bus schedule and what buses they should take to get to the destination, if they live in an urban area.

Proper usage of the phone also provides several opportunities to teach life-skills. Number recognition, memorization of personal information are combined in a basic math lesson. Add in the proper etiquette for making and answering of a phone, and you have an excellent cross-curricular activity.

Teachers should recognize that there are several such real-life situations and they should take advantage of them when teaching basic life-skills.

It is important to recognize what is considered a basic life skill for today. This concept changes as things "modernize." Today a person needs to have the skills to use a microwave and may not need the skills to operate an oven, as was needed only 20 years ago. Ten years ago analog watches and clocks were still predominant, and today digital clocks are becoming more prevalent and questions are beginning to rise about the necessity of teaching analog clock recognition as a life skill.

Skill 11.4   Apply knowledge of strategies for increasing communication use, spontaneity, and generalization and for creating varied opportunities for all students to use effective written, verbal, nonverbal, and visual communication.

Many youngsters with disabilities have difficulty in developing social behavior that follows accepted norms. While non-disabled children learn most social behaviors from family and peers, children with disabilities are the product of a wide, complex range of different social experiences. When coupled with one or more of the disabilities, this experience adds up to a collective deficit in interpersonal relationships.

There is an irreducible philosophical issue underlying the realm of social behavior among children with disabilities. To some extent, the disability itself causes maladaptive behaviors to develop. Regardless whether social skill deficits are seminal or secondary among youth with disabilities; it is the task of the special education professional to help each child develop as normally as possible in the social-interpersonal realm.

Children with disabilities can be taught social-interpersonal skills through developing sensitivity to other people, through making behavioral choices in social situations, and through developing social maturity.

Sensitivity to Others
Central to the human communication process is the nonverbal domain. Children with disabilities may perceive facial expressions and gestures differently than their non-disabled peers, due to their impairment. There are several kinds of activities to use in developing a child's sensitivity to other people. Examples of these activities follow.

1. Offer a selection of pictures with many kinds of faces to the child. Ask the child to identify or classify the faces according to the emotion that appears in the picture. Allow the child to compare his reactions to those of the other students.
2. Compare common gestures through a mixture of acting and discussion. The teacher can demonstrate shaking her head in the negative, and then ask the students for the meaning of the gesture. Reactions can be compared, and then a game can be started in which each student performs a gesture while others tell what it means.
3. Filmstrips, videotapes, and movies are available in which famous people and cartoon characters utilize gestures. Children can be asked what a particular gesture means.
4. Tape recording with playback can be used to present social sounds. Again, a game is possible here, and the activity focuses the student's attention on one narrow issue - the sound and its precise social meaning.

5. Paris of students can be formed for exercises in reading each other's gestures and nonverbal communications. Friendships of a lasting nature are encouraged by this activity.

Social Situations

Inherent differences in appearances and motions among children with disabilities cause some of them to develop behavior problems in social situations. It is necessary to remediate this situation in order to provide as normal a life as possible in order to sustain as normal an adulthood as possible.

Here are some activities that strengthen a child's social skills, in social situations.

1. **Anticipate the consequence of social actions.** Have the students act out roles, tell stories, and discuss the consequences that flow from their actions.
2. **Gain appropriate independence.** Students can be given exercises in going places alone. For the very young, and for those with development issues, this might consist of finding a location within the room. Go on a field trip into the city. Allow older students to make purchases on their own. Using play money in the classroom for younger children would be beneficial.
3. **Make ethical and/or moral judgments.** The unfinished story, requiring the pupil to finish it at the point where a judgment is required, makes an independent critique of the choices made by the characters in the play.
4. **Plan and execute.** Children with disabilities can be allowed to plan an outing, a game, a party, or an exercise.

Having the teacher set an example is always a good way to teach social maturation. If the classroom is orderly, free of an oppressive atmosphere, and full of visibly rational judgments about what is going on, the students absorb the climate of doing things in a mature manner.

Skill 11.5 **Demonstrate knowledge of systematic instructional programs for teaching self-care skills and for facilitating mobility, including head and trunk control, sitting, crawling, standing, walking, and wheelchair use.**

Teaching self-care skills requires the ability to recognize small detailed steps that are essential to achieve a goal. For example, when the goal is that a student will independently brush his/her teeth, one of the first steps would be to have a student find the toothbrush, and then to squeeze an appropriate amount of toothpaste on the brush. Several additional steps should be listed out when attempting to teach self-care skills. Coordination between school and home is essential when teaching self-care skills.

There are two basic methods for teaching self-care skills: Forward Chaining and Backward Chaining.

Forward chaining recognizes the goal and works from the first step towards the goal and progresses forward to the goal as each new step is attained until the goal is achieved.

Backward Chaining recognizes that there may be a cognitive disability that does not normally comprehend forward chaining, looks at the goal and focuses on teaching the last step that was necessary before attaining the goal. A student who is learning the skill of putting on his/her shirt may be learning how to pull the shirt down his/her chest, before learning how to put their arms into the shirt.

Teachers working with students who are in need skills that will facilitate their mobility should consult with the school Physical Therapist and/or Occupational Therapist. The therapist should then train the teacher in the necessary methods to implement the student's learning and attaining a more independent sense of mobility.

Excellent Resource:

http://www.integratingstandards.org/

Skill 11.6 Demonstrate knowledge of the essential components of a social-skills curriculum.

Self-concept may be defined as the collective attitudes or feelings that one holds about oneself. Children with disabilities perceive, early in life, that they are deficient in skills that seem easier for their peers without disabilities. The also receive expressions of surprise or even disgust from both adults and children in response to their differing appearance and actions, again resulting in damage to the self-concept. The Special Education Teacher, for these reasons, will want to direct special and continuing effort to bettering each child's own perception of himself.

1. The poor self-concept of a child with disabilities causes that student at times to exhibit aggression or rage over inappropriate things. The teacher can ignore this behavior unless it is dangerous to others or too distracting to the total group, thereby reducing the amount of negative conditioning in the child's life. Further, the teacher can praise this child, quickly and frequently, for the correct responses he makes, remembering that these responses may require special effort on the student's part to produce. Further, correction, when needed, can be done tactfully, in private.

2. The child whose poor self-concept manifests itself in withdrawn behavior should be pulled gently into as many social situations as possible by the teacher. This child must be encouraged to share experiences with the class, to serve as teacher helper for projects, and to be part of small groups for tasks. Again, praise for performing these group and public acts is most effective if done immediately.

3. The teacher can plan, in advance, to structure the classroom experiences so that aversive situations will be avoided. Thus, settings that stimulate the aggressive child to act out can be redesigned and situations that stimulate group participation can be set up in advance for the child who acts in a withdrawn manner.

4. Frequent, positive, and immediate are the best terms to describe the teacher feedback required by children with disabilities. Praise for very small correct acts should be given immediately, and repeated when each correct act is repeated. Criticism or outright scolding should be done, whenever possible, in private. The teacher should first check the total day's interactions with students to ensure that the number and qualitative content of verbal stimuli is heavily on the positive side. While this trait is desirable in all good teaching, it is fundamental and utterly necessary to build the fragile self-concept of youngsters with disabilities.

5. The teacher must have a strategy for use with the child who persists in negative behavior outbursts. One system is to intervene immediately and break the situation down in to three components. First, the teacher requires the child to identify the worst possible outcome from the situation, the thing that he fears. To do this task, the child must be required to state the situation in the most factual way he can. Second, he is required to state what would really happen if this worst possible outcome happened, and to evaluate the likelihood of it happening. Third, he is asked to state an action or attitude that he can take, after examining the consequences in a new light. This process has been termed <u>Rational Emotive Therapy.</u>

Self-Advocacy

Learning about one's self involves the identification of learning styles, strengths and weakness, interests, and preferences. For students with mild disabilities, developing an awareness of the accommodations they need will help them ask for necessary accommodations on a job and in postsecondary education. Students can also help identify alternative ways they can learn.

Self-advocacy involves the ability to effectively communicate one's own rights, needs, and desires and to take responsibility for making decisions that impact one's life.

There are many elements in developing self-advocacy skills in students who are involved in the transition process. Helping the student to identify future goals or desired outcomes in transition planning areas is a good place to start. Self-knowledge is critical for the student in determining the direction that transition planning will take.

The role of the teacher in promoting self-advocacy should include encouraging the student to participate in the IEP process as well as other key parts of their educational development. Self-advocacy issues and lessons are effective when they are incorporated into the student's daily life. Teachers should listen to the student's problems and ask the student for input on possible changes that he may need. The teacher should talk with the student about possible solutions, discussing the pros and cons of doing something. A student who self-advocates should feel supported and encouraged. Good self-advocates know how to ask questions and get help from other people. They do not let other people do everything for them.

Students need to practice newly acquired self-advocacy skills. Teachers should have student's role play various situations, such as setting up a class schedule, moving out of the home, and asking for accommodations needed for a course.

The impact of transition planning on a student with a disability is very great. The student should be an active member of the transition team, as well as the focus of all activities. Students often think that being passive and relying on others to take care of them is the way to get things done. Students should be encouraged to express their opinions throughout the transition process. They need to learn how to express themselves so that others listen and take them seriously. These skills should be practiced within a supportive and caring environment.

A major focus of special education is to prepare students to become working, independent members of society. IDEA 2004 (Individuals with Disabilities Education Act) also includes preparing students for *further education*. Certain skills beyond academics are needed to attain this level of functioning.

Affective and Social Skills transcend to all areas of life. When an individual is unable to acquire information on expectations and reactions of others or misinterprets those cues, he is missing an important element needed for success as an adult in the workplace and community in general.

Special education should incorporate a level of instruction in the affective/social area as many students will not develop these skills without instruction, modeling, practice, and feedback.

Affective and social skills taught throughout the school setting might include: social greetings; eye contact with a speaker; interpretation of facial expression, body language, and personal space; ability to put feelings and questions into words; and use of words to acquire additional information as needed.

COMPETENCY 12.0 UNDERSTAND PRINCIPLES AND METHODS INVOLVED IN INDIVIDUALIZING INSTRUCTION FOR STUDENTS WITH DISABILITIES

Skill 12.1 Apply knowledge of principles and strategies for planning, organizing, and implementing in the least restrictive environment (LRE) educational programs appropriate to the cognitive, linguistic, and physical needs of individuals with disabilities.

When determining what is actually the least restrictive environment (LRE) for students, you must take into consideration the cognitive, linguistic and physical abilities of the student. The student's needs must drive the educational programming. It is important to look at the possible placements and break down the necessary skills which a child will need to be successful in that placement. Sometimes it is most efficient to create a table which lists the various domains of: cognitive, language, physical, social, etc.. Then under each heading, list the necessary skills a student must have to be successful in that area for each placement option. Matching the skills with the student's strengths and needs can provide a clear picture as to which placement is indeed the least restrictive for that child. Keeping in mind, the placement may vary based on different goals.

For example, a student who is to be included in a class for purely social skill development would not need to demonstrate the cognitive skills to master the academic curriculum during that time in order to achieve the goal of social skill development. All of these factors are important to consider when determining least restrictive placement.

See Skill 8.3 for more information on least restrictive environment

Skill 12.2 **Apply knowledge of methods for developing longitudinal, outcome-based curricula for individual students, prioritizing skills, choosing chronologically age-appropriate materials, emphasizing functionality, using instruction in natural settings, and promoting interactions between students with and without disabilities.**

Once you understand the general education curriculum students are asked to achieve, it is important for the special educator to look in depth at it longitudinally. As discussed in previous skills, it is important to keep in mind, that the regular curriculum, as much as is possible, should be presented to the students. However, realistically, it should be discussed that the curriculum may be delivered out of grade or age expectations. Students, who are functioning more than two years behind, may indeed be working on the skills in the regular education curriculum; however, they may be working on the skill, which are two years below the students current grade.

When a special educator has an ongoing and working knowledge of the curriculum across multiple grades, he/she is better able to provide the appropriate instruction to her students. It is also important for the teacher to utilize materials which match the student's instructional needs and their age interests. In reading, for example, students may have an instructional reading level several years below their age and will in fact need materials of that level. However, pulling out an early reader about a much younger child's cartoon, might discourage the older student from further developing his reading skill. Many publishers have realized this and have created high interest but lower level materials to meet the needs of students like this.

Throughout this process, it may be necessary to prioritize skills as well. In doing this, the special educator wants to look at the curriculum and make judgements as to which skills will provide the students with the most instructional impact in the least amount of time. Accelerating learning is challenging, but the only method available to help students catch up in their learning and return to regular education if possible. Still other times, students may be unable to complete all of the required regular education curriculum due to cognitive disabilities.

In these cases, the special educator will need to examine the general education curriculum to determine which skills are necessary for that child to be successful in life. This takes the concept behind transition planning during the IEP process to all levels. For example, a student with severe cognitive delays may be able to function in society and life without having the understanding of onomatopoeia, however, it may be a part of the regular education curriculum.

See skill 10.1 for more information on this skill

Skill 12.3   Identify considerations and procedures for evaluating, selecting, developing, and adapting instructional strategies, curricular materials, and technologies that are developmentally and functionally valid, based on an individual's age, skill level, and cognitive, communication, physical, cultural, social, and emotional characteristics.

See Skills 10.1 and 12.2 for more information on this skill

Special educators need to be able to look at assessment results provided from regular classroom teachers, school psychologists, outside evaluators or other qualified personnel and plan appropriate instruction. Often times, this will be the first line of information received on a student. Unfortunately, many times, the special educator is simply given a set of assessment results and asked to write an Individualized Education Plan (IEP) from that plan. Therefore, it is imperative that the assessment results are clearly interrupted.

When first looking at assessment results, it is most beneficial to look at those skill areas that are closest to grade level expectations. Since the student is demonstrating skills that are very close to grade level, then special educator needs to think of what simple adaptations can be made to the regular curriculum to allow the student to achieve success. There are numerous adaptations and modifications available from many different sources that could be implemented easily to provide success.

In looking at adaptations and considerations, there are numerous possibilities to be considered. Below are some general things to be considered:

- **Curriculum Adaptations** – expect mastery of less curriculum, different presentation methods of curriculum, organization of curriculum materials, provide study guides/outlines, etc.
- **Response Adaptations** – allow oral response, use of technology for responses, etc..
- **Presentation Adaptations** – provide visual with oral information, provide for review of materials using books on CD, use manipulatives when sharing new information, etc.
- **Assessment Adaptations** – read tests orally, provide word banks, limit choices, provide study guides, etc.

Once you have made all of the possible adaptations, then it is time to look deeper. In looking at skills that are significantly below grade level, the special educator needs to consider what strategy can be implemented that will help the student to make up the lost ground. It is not enough for the student to simply progress; the goal is to catch the student up to grade level in the shortest amount of time possible. This is where it is imperative to look carefully at the assessment data and through the available research based materials/skills to determine what will help the student reach this goal. For some students this may be a curriculum program (i.e. a different reading program or methodology). For still other students it may be a chill out time before a test or perhaps relaxation strategies. Either way, it is the assessment results that will drive what beginning practices the special educator puts in place to meet the needs of the students.

After the plan has been made, it is imperative that the special educator continually monitors the progress the student is making. Without this piece, the student could continue down a path far away from the goal of returning to grade level expectations. Using regular weekly or bi-weekly monitoring, the special educator can make appropriate adjustments to the students' learning curve. Thus, increasing the rate at which the student is achieving. Again, with the end goal in mind of helping the child return back to grade level curriculum in the shortest time period possible.

As we have transferred into the twenty-first century, technology has become an integral part of our day-to-day lives. In the classroom, technology levels vary greatly from state-to-state, district-to-district, and even building-to-building. There are however a variety of teaching tools that are available in today's market that truly help the educator meet the needs of all students in the classroom.

There are a large number of software programs and Internet based programs, which offer individualized instruction. These programs allow the teacher to set instructional levels, monitor ongoing progress of the student, as well as provide the individual students with a continuum of skills at their own pace and level. Additionally, some of these programs have incentive natures to encourage children. Accelerated Reader and Math$^©$ are programs that provide students with quizzes for completing work and are tied into incentives.

Other uses of technology allow students to access material they may otherwise be unable to utilize. Students, who are unable to speak, may use technology devices to communicate. These augmentative communication systems are crucial to the participation and success of these students. In other incidences, there are programs that will read text to students unable to see or read the text independently. Programs are available that will allow the student to dictate written assignments and then they will translate the spoken words into a word processing document.

Smart boards, similar to wipe boards that are connected to a computer, provide a more interactive nature to oral presentations within the classroom. Students are able to use special markers allowing them to be more active participants in lectures.

Digital cameras and digital video recorders can be wonderful enhancements to the instructional process. They allow students to add pictures to their assignments making them more personal and real. Another use is to provide the students with authenticity to daily routines. For example, a student who is in need of appropriate behavioral reminders could be photographed completing the proper task. This picture reminder can be used within the classroom to provide the student with a visual cue to the behavior the child should be exhibiting.

Whether the technology is digital clocks, computers, digital cameras, or the more complex smart boards, it is imperative that educators take full advantage of the resources available to them. Technology is a part of our daily lives and in order to prepare students, they need to feel comfortable using technology. The flexibility of the inherent nature of technology allows teachers to meet the needs of more students at an individual level than ever before.

As we have transferred into the twenty-first century, technology has become an integral part of our day-to-day lives. In the classroom, technology levels vary greatly from state-to-state, district-to-district, and even building-to-building. There are however a variety of teaching tools that are available in today's market that truly help the educator meet the needs of all students in the classroom.

There are a large number of software programs and Internet based programs, which offer individualized instruction. These programs allow the teacher to set instructional levels, monitor ongoing progress of the student, as well as provide the individual students with a continuum of skills at their own pace and level. Additionally, some of these programs have incentive natures to encourage children. Accelerated Reader and Math© are programs that provide students with quizzes for completing work and are tied into incentives.

Other uses of technology allow students to access material they may otherwise be unable to utilize. Students, who are unable to speak, may use technology devices to communicate. These augmentative communication systems are crucial to the participation and success of these students. In other incidences, there are programs that will read text to students unable to see or read the text independently. Programs are available that will allow the student to dictate written assignments and then they will translate the spoken words into a word processing document.

Smart boards, similar to wipe boards that are connected to a computer, provide a more interactive nature to oral presentations within the classroom. Students are able to use special markers allowing them to be more active participants in lectures.

Digital cameras and digital video recorders can be wonderful enhancements to the instructional process. They allow students to add pictures to their assignments making them more personal and real. Another use is to provide the students with authenticity to daily routines. For example, a student who is in need of appropriate behavioral reminders could be photographed completing the proper task. This picture reminder can be used within the classroom to provide the student with a visual cue to the behavior the child should be exhibiting.

Whether the technology is digital clocks, computers, digital cameras, or the more complex smart boards, it is imperative that educators take full advantage of the resources available to them. Technology is a part of our daily lives and in order to prepare students, they need to feel comfortable using technology. The flexibility of the inherent nature of technology allows teachers to meet the needs of more students at an individual level than ever before.

Skill 12.4   Demonstrate knowledge of the effects of second-language acquisition on communication patterns of individuals with disabilities.

One of the most important things to know about the differences between L1 (first language) and L2 (second language) acquisition is that people usually will master L1, but they will almost never be fully proficient in L2. However, if children can be trained in L2 before about the age of seven, their chances at full mastery will be much higher. Children learn language with so little effort, which is why they can be babbling one year and speaking with complete, complex ideas just a few years later. It is important to know that language is innate, meaning that our brains are ready to learn a language from birth. Yet a lot of language learning is behavioral, meaning that children imitate adults' speech.

L2 acquisition is much harder for adults. Multiple theories of L2 acquisition have come about. Some of the more notable ones come from Jim Cummins. Cummins argues that there are two types of language that usually need to be acquired by students learning English as a second language: Basic Interpersonal Communication Skills (BICS) Cognitive Academic Language Proficiency (CALP). BICS is general, everyday language used to communicate simple thoughts, whereas CALP is the more complex, academic language used in school. It is harder for students to acquire CALP, and many teachers mistakenly assume that students can learn complex academic concepts in English if they have already mastered BICS. The truth is that CALP takes much longer to master, and in some cases, particularly with little exposure in certain subjects, it may never be mastered.

Another set of theories is based on Stephen Krashen's research in L2 acquisition. Most people understand his theories based on five principles:

1. **The Acquisition-Learning Hypothesis**: This states that there is a difference between learning a language and acquiring it. Children "acquire" a first language easily—it's natural. But adults often have to "learn" a language through coursework, studying, and memorizing. One can acquire a second language, but often it requires more deliberate and natural interaction within that language.

2. **The Monitor Hypothesis**: This is when the learned language "monitors" the acquired language. In other words, this is when a person's "grammar check" kicks in and keeps awkward, incorrect language out of a person's L2 communication.

3. **The Natural Order Hpothesis**: This suggests that the learning of grammatical structures is predictable and follows a "natural order."

4. **The Input Hypothesis**: Some people call this "comprehensible input." This means that a language learner will learn best when the instruction or conversation is just above the learner's ability. That way, the learner has the foundation to understand most of the language, but still will have to figure out, often in context, what that extra more difficult element means.

5. **The Affective Filter Hypothesis**: This suggests that people will learn a second language when they are relaxed, have high levels of motivation, and have a decent level of self-confidence.

Teaching students who are learning English as a second language poses some unique challenges, particularly in a standards-based environment. The key is realizing that no matter how little English a student knows, the teacher should teach with the student's developmental level in mind. This means that instruction should not be "dumbed-down" for ESOL students. Different approaches should be used, however, to ensure that these students (a) get multiple opportunities to learn and practice English and (b) still learn content.

Many ESOL approaches are based on social learning methods. By being placed in mixed level groups or by being paired with a student of another ability level, students will get a chance to practice English in a natural, non-threatening environment. Students should not be pushed in these groups to use complex language or to experiment with words that are too difficult. They should simply get a chance to practice with simple words and phrases.

In teacher-directed instructional situations, visual aids, such as pictures, objects, and video are particularly effective at helping students make connections between words and items they are already familiar with.

ESOL students may need additional accommodations with assessments, assignments, and projects. For example, teachers may find that written tests provide little to no information about a student's understanding of the content. Therefore, an oral test may be better suited for ESOL students. When students are somewhat comfortable and capable with written tests, a shortened test may actually be preferable; take note that they will need extra time to translate.

There is wide agreement that there are generally five stages of second language development. The first stage is "pre-production." While these students may actually understand what someone says to them (for the most part), they have a much harder time talking back in the target language. Teachers must realize that if a student cannot "produce" the target language, it does not mean that they aren't learning. Most likely, they are. They are taking it in, and their brains are trying to figure out what to do with all the new language.

The second phase is early production. This is where the student can actually start to produce the target language. It is quite limited, and teachers most likely should not expect students to produce eloquent speeches during this time.

The third phase is emergent speech or speech emergence. Longer, more complex sentences are used, particularly in speech—and in social situations. But remember that students aren't fully fluent in this stage, and they cannot handle complex academic language tasks.
The fourth phase is intermediate fluency. This is where more complex language is produced. Grammatical errors are common.

The fifth stage is advanced fluency. While students may appear to be completely fluent, though, they will still need academic and language support from teachers.

Many people say that there are prescribed amounts of time by which students should reach each stage. However, keep in mind that it depends on the level at which students are exposed to the language. For example, students who get opportunities to practice with the target language outside of school may have greater ease in reaching the fifth stage quicker. In general, though, it does take years to reach the fifth stage, and students should never be expected to have complete mastery within one school year.

Factors that affect second-language acquisition

There are many factors that impact someone's ability to pick up a second or third language. Age is one common factor. It is said that after a certain age (usually seven), learning a second language becomes dramatically harder. But there are also many social factors, such as anxiety, that influence language learning. Often, informal, social settings are more conducive to second language learning. Motivation is another factor, obviously. A final important factor, particularly for teachers, is the strategies one uses to learn a language. For example, memorizing words out of context is not as effective as using words strategically for a real-life purpose.

NOTE: See www.everythingesl.net or
http://www.nwrel.org/request/2003may/overview.html for more information.

From high school and college, most of us think that learning a language strictly involves drills, memorization, and tests. While this is a common method used (some people call it a structural, grammatical, or linguistic approach). While this works for some students, it certainly does not work for all.

Although there are dozens of methods that have been developed to help people learn additional languages, we will focus on some of the more common approaches used in today's K-12 classrooms. Cognitive approaches to language learning focus on concepts. While words and grammar are important, when teachers use the cognitive approach, they focus on using language for conceptual purposes—rather than learning words and grammar for the sake of simply learning new words and grammatical structures. This approach focuses heavily on students' learning styles, and it cannot necessarily be pinned down as having specific techniques. Rather, it is more of a philosophy of instruction.

There are many approaches that are noted for their motivational purposes. In a general sense, when teachers work to motivate students to learn a language, they do things to help reduce fear and to assist students in identifying with native speakers of the target language. A very common method is often called the functional approach. In this approach, the teacher focuses on communicative elements. For example, a first grade ESOL teacher might help students learn phrases that will assist them in finding a restroom, asking for help on the playground, etc. Many functionally-based adult ESOL programs help learners with travel-related phrases and words.

Another very common motivational approach is Total Physical Response. This is a kinesthetic approach that combines language learning and physical movement. In essence, students learn new vocabulary and grammar by responding with physical motion to verbal commands. Some people say it is particularly effective because the physical actions create good brain connections with the words.

In general, the best methods do not treat students as if they have a language deficit. Rather, the best methods build upon what students already know, and they help to instill the target language as a communicative process rather than a list of vocabulary words that have to be memorized.

In addition to these methods, it is important that, particularly when second language learners have multiple teachers, such as in middle or high school, that teachers communicate and collaborate in order to provide greater consistency. It is particularly difficult for second language learners to go from one class to the next, with different sets of expectations and varied methods of instruction, to focus on the more complex elements of learning language. When students have higher levels of anxiety regarding the learning of a second language, they will be less likely to focus on the language; rather, they will be focusing on whatever it is that is creating that anxiety. This does not mean that standards and expectations should not be held for students in all classes; it just means that teachers should have common expectations so that students know what to expect in each class and don't have to think about the differences between classes.

Another hugely important reason for teachers to collaborate, particularly with the ESL specialists, is to ensure that students are showing consistent development across classes. Where there is inconsistency, teachers should work to uncover what it is that is keeping the student from excelling in a particular class.

The most important concept to remember regarding the difference between learning a first language and a second one is that if the learner is approximately age seven or older, learning a second language will occur very differently in the learner's brain than it will had the learner been younger. The reason for this is that there is a language-learning function that exists in young children that appears to go away as they mature. Learning a language prior to age seven is almost guaranteed, with relatively little effort. The mind is like a sponge, and it soaks up language very readily. Some theorists, including the famous linguist Noam Chomsky, argue that the brain has a "universal grammar" and that only vocabulary and very particular grammatical structures, related to specific languages, need to be introduced in order for a child to learn a language. What this really means is that, in essence, there are slots into which language gets filled in a child's mind. This is definitely not the case with learning a second language after about seven years old.

Learning a second language as a pre-adolescent, adolescent, or adult requires quite a bit of translation from the first language to the second. Vocabulary and grammar particulars are memorized, not necessarily internalized (at least, as readily as a first language). In fact, many (though not all) people who are immersed in a second language never fully function as fluent in the language. They may appear to be totally fluent, but often there will be small traits that are hard to pick up and internalize.

It is fairly clear that learning a second language successfully does require fluency in the first language. This is because, as stated above, the second language is translated from the first in the learner's mind. First language literacy is also a crucial factor in second language learning, particularly second language literacy.

When helping second language learners make the "cross-over" in language fluency or literacy from first language to second language, it is important to help them identify strategies they use in the first language and apply those to the second language. It is also important to note similarities and differences in phonetic principals in the two languages. Sometimes it is helpful to encourage students to translate; other times, it is helpful for them to practice production in the target language. In either case, teachers must realize that learning a second language is a slow and complicated process.

Skill 12.5 Demonstrate knowledge of cultural perspectives related to effective instruction for students with disabilities.

The mobile nature of society today provides a broader mixture of cultures around the country. Students moving from school to school may experience different curriculums and different school cultural factors. As educators expect the students to adapt, they must also remember that the schools themselves must also consider the student's individual cultural influences.

Cultural relationships, mores and values are not unique to students with disabilities. However, it is important to keep in mind that in certain cultures individual differences may be thought of very differently than perhaps the current school views them. Many cultures now accept disabilities and realize the value and functionability of students with them. However, there are still some cultures and beliefs that shield and hide anyone who are different in anyway. When discussing a child's disabilities with parents/guardians it is important to keep in mind the views on disabilities.

Additionally, acculturation is not something that occurs overnight. It takes years for students to become acculturated. Students who move from a foreign country and do not speak English can take up to seven years to become proficient in English. This is not a disability, but in fact the natural progression of language acquisition. It can be similar for other aspects of culture. When considering the identification of students who are not succeeding in school, you must take into consideration these types of cultural factors. There are a number of acculturation surveys that can be used to help guide the teacher in examining the role of culture in the academic performance of the student.

Community agencies can often times help schools bridge these cultural gaps. Reaching out to families by including appropriate translators/translations, encouraging parents to share their heritage and traditions with the school and other students, and respecting that differences of what is acceptable do exist will help all involved parties. Beyond language, it is important to respect and provide accommodations for other cultural factors. Holidays may be significantly different for certain ethnicities. Another area may even include the food served in the cafeteria, if the culture requires that foods be Kosher or a vegetarian option be offered.

The general issues that surround multiculturalism within schools are simply exasperated when dealing with disabilities. Identification of a disability naturally increases the stress level and can damage the relationships; therefore, it is more important to extend any possible method to secure positive interactions.

See Skills 1.2, 2.4, 18.2, 20.3 for additional information about cultural perspectives for instruction for students with disabilities.

Skill 12.6   Apply knowledge of methods for analyzing individual and group performance to design instruction and for adapting materials to meet learners' current needs in the cognitive, social, emotional, and physical domains at the appropriate level of development in the least restrictive environment.

See Skills 8.3, 12.2 and 12.3for additional information on least restrictive environment

COMPETENCY 13.0 UNDERSTAND THE SCOPE, SEQUENCE, AND CONCEPTS OF THE GENERAL EDUCATION PROGRAM.

Skill 13.1 Demonstrate familiarity with the scope, sequence, practices, and curricular materials used in general education.

Curriculum development today must consider many factors of alignment, scope, sequence, and design.

First, curriculum must be aligned to state standards, state and local assessments, and district and school goals. Curriculum alignment simply means that there is reflection in the curriculum to these elements. In other words, what students learn should reflect state standards. Usually, this also means that what students learn is tested on state assessments. When curriculum is aligned to district and school goals, it means that, for example, if the district wanted all students to learn how to live in a multi-cultural society, curriculum would address that theme in a variety of ways.

Second, scope is the "horizontal" aspect of curriculum. For example, if a topic of study in a biology class is invertebrate animals, the scope would define everything that must be taught for students to understand this concept. On the other hand, sequence is the outline of what should be taught before and after a particular subject. So, for example, a sequence in math might suggest that students should learn addition and subtraction before multiplication and division. Likewise, basic math topics, like those just described, should be taught prior to decimals and fractions. A sequence would line all that up.

Design considers the progression from the beginning of a unit of study to the end of a unit of study. First, curriculum should be designed with the end in mind. What do you want students to know and be able to do? And how would they prove that they know the material or have the skill? If that information has been defined, it is much easier to design a curriculum. Too often, curricula is designed only considering forward steps in a process without concern for what students should be getting out of the curriculum.

As a teacher implements a curriculum, the teacher should be familiar with three main things:

(a) The philosophy or principal aims of the curriculum—in other words, what the curriculum wants students to get out of it.

(b) The knowledge base of the curriculum. If teachers are not deeply familiar with what they are teaching to students, they will be very ineffective at getting students to learn it.

(c) The plan, scope, and sequence of the curriculum. What would students have learned prior? Where will they go next?

Skill 13.2   Apply knowledge of methods for evaluating general curricula to determine the scope and sequence of the academic content areas of language arts and math.

Becoming familiar with the general education curriculum is essential to ensuring the success of the students within the special education program. In addition to the written curriculum, the special educator should be take time to examine any adopted programs (math series, science curriculum, reading basal, etc). Often, the written curriculum is overtaken by the scope and sequence of the adopted programs.

Typically, the scope and sequence of language arts and math are laid out clearly through the written curriculum, state standards, or adopted programs. When examining the curriculum, the teacher must have in mind the beginning levels of the students entering in the subject areas. Understanding reading skills, levels as well as math skill levels will provide the educator with an appropriate starting place within the said curriculum.

Once a starting place has been established through assessment, the educator must have a clear understanding of the next steps of action. Creating an appropriate instructional design is important. The special educator needs to use both formative and summative assessments to make appropriate instructional designs and plans. At this point, the teacher can make decisions based on solid, factual information.

The progress through the rest of the scope and sequence for both language arts and math needs to be arrived at through district approved curriculum. As the district level curriculum has been aligned to state requirements, the teacher can be assured they are providing appropriate instruction to ensure the necessary levels of information are provided.

Finally, after the curriculum, assessments and scope and sequence have been reviewed in an in depth manner, the teacher can begin to determine the most educationally appropriate methods and materials to meet the unique needs of the students within their classroom. Though, as previously stated, the adopted programs sometimes seem to replace the district curriculum and drive the instruction, it is important to know and keep in mind, this should not be the case. Particularly since many programs will be reevaluated and replaced after a few years.

Skill 13.3   Demonstrate knowledge of the use and adjustment of appropriate language intervention strategies across age and skill levels.

Over the years, theories regarding language development have been very vocal and disagreed in many levels. The major disagreement can be tracked back to the 1950's where two predominant theories emerged.

Behaviorism developed and believed that language was the direct result of the situations surrounding the child. Behaviorists believed that the environment controlled all language and solely these outside forces influenced its development.

On the other hand, Nativism theorists believed that all language was similar to genetic traits. They believed that language was determined before birth and developed in a similar manner to other innate characteristics. They ruled out that any outside factors could influence the development process.

Currently, these two opposing viewpoints have been combined to form the Interactionist theories. This term indicates that children's language skills are a direct result of inherent predetermined skills and the surrounding environment.

As language develops, students begin to understand how sounds blend together to form words, how words go together to form sentences, and how sentences go together to form stories. It is through these stories and sentences that meaning is conveyed from one party to another. If a student is unable to convey that meaning or draw conclusions from the message that someone else is sending, they miss a key component of language development.

Speech pathologists, who specialize in language development, can therefore be an essential component to preventing and helping children with language disorders. In this way, these trained specialists can also help in preventing and remediating language issues.

As language is essential to all aspects of education, and is in fact how information within schools is transferred and shared, it is important to have a solid understand of the process of language development and ways to intervene when there are road blocks.

Vocabulary can be one of the biggest stumbling blocks within the school related to language. Students may have a limited bank of background knowledge related to the topics we are presenting within the classroom. Providing direct vocabulary instruction with as much real life objects and connections as possible can help to provide the students with more opportunity to interact with the activities within the classroom.

Teachers may also need to adjust their instructional "talk" to ensure the students have a complete understanding of the topics being presented. Using synonyms to provide clarification is an excellent strategy. In this way, students can make connections between new terms and others already in their knowledge base.

Skill 13.4   Demonstrate knowledge of the concepts of reading and language arts and the importance of teaching emerging literacy skills (e.g., concepts of print, phonemic awareness, fluency).

Beginning Reading Approaches
Methods of teaching beginning reading skills may be divided into two major approaches—code emphasis and meaning emphasis. Both approaches have their supporters and their critics. Advocates of code emphasis instruction point out that reading fluency depends on accurate and automatic decoding skills, while advocates of meaning emphasis favor this approach for reading comprehension. Teachers may decide to blend aspects of both approaches to meet the individual needs of their students.

Bottom-up or Code-Emphasis Approach
- Letter-sound regularity is stressed.
- Reading instruction begins with words that consist of letter or letter combinations that have the same sound in different words. Component letter-sound relationships are taught and mastered before introducing new words.
- Examples—phonics, linguistic, modified alphabet, and programmed reading series such as the Merrill Linguistic Reading Program and DISTAR Reading.

Top-down or Meaning Emphasis Model
- Reading for meaning is emphasized from the first stages of instruction.
- Programs begin with words that appear frequently, which are assumed to be familiar and easy to learn. Words are identified by examining meaning and position in context and are decoded by techniques such as context, pictures, initial letters and word configurations. Thus, a letter may not necessarily have the same sound in different words throughout the passage.
- Examples: Whole language, language experience, and individualized reading programs.

Other approaches that follow beginning reading instruction are available to help teachers design reading programs. Choice of approach will depend on the student's strengths and weaknesses. No matter what approach or combination of approaches is used, the teacher should encourage independent reading and build activities into the reading program that stimulate students to practice their skills through independent reading.

Developmental Reading Approaches
Developmental reading programs emphasize daily, sequential instruction. Instructional materials usually feature a series of books, often basal readers, as the core of the program.

Basal Reading
Basal reader series form the core of many widely used reading programs from preprimers to eighth grade. Depending on the series, basal readers may be meaning-emphasis or code-emphasis. Teacher manuals provide a highly structured and comprehensive scope and sequence, lesson plans, and objectives. Vocabulary is controlled from level to level and reading skills cover word recognition, word attack, and comprehension.

Advantages of basal readers are the structured, sequential manner in which reading is taught. The teacher manuals have teaching strategies, controlled vocabulary, assessment materials and objectives. Reading instruction is in a systematic, sequential, and comprehension-oriented manner.

Many basal reading programs recommend the <u>directed reading activity procedure,</u> for lesson presentation. Students proceed through the steps of motivation preparation for the new concepts and vocabulary, guided reading, and answering questions that give a purpose or goal for the reading, development of strengths through drills or workbook, application of skills, and evaluation.

A variation of the directed reading method is <u>direct reading-thinking,</u> where the student must generate the purposes for reading the selection, form questions, and read the selection. After reading, the teacher asks questions designed to get the group to think of answers and justify their answers.

Disadvantages of basal readers are the emphasis on teaching to a group rather than the individual. Critics of basal readers claim that the structure may limit creativity and not provide enough instruction on organizational skills and reading for secondary content levels. Basal readers, however, offer the advantage of a prepared comprehensive program, and may be supplemented with other materials to meet individual needs.

Phonics Approach
Word recognition is taught through grapheme-phoneme associations, with the goal of teaching the student to independently apply these skills to new words. Phonics instruction may be synthetic or analytic. In the synthetic method, letter sounds are learned before the student goes on to blend the sounds to form words. The analytic method teaches letter sounds letter sounds as integral parts of words.

The sounds are usually taught in the sequence: vowels, consonants, consonant blends at the beginning of words (e.g. bl and dr), and consonant blends at the end of words (e.g. ld and mp), consonant and vowel digraphs (e.g. ch and sh) and diphthongs (e.g. au and oy).

Critics of the phonics approach point out that the emphasis on pronunciation may lead to the student focusing more on decoding than comprehension. Some students may have trouble blending sounds to form words, and others may become confused with words that do not conform to the phonetic "rules". However, advocates of phonics say that the programs are useful with remedial reading and developmental reading. Examples of phonics series are *Science Research Associates, Merrill Phonics* and DML's *Cove School Reading Program.*

Linguistics Approach
In many programs, the whole-word approach is used. This means that words are taught in families as a whole (e.g. cat, hat, pat, and rat). The focus is on words instead of isolated sounds. Words are chosen on the basis of similar spelling patterns and irregular spelling words are taught as sight words. Examples of programs using this approach are *SRA Basic Reading Series* and *Miami Linguistic Readers* by D.C. Heath.

Some advantages of this approach are that the student learns that reading is talk written down, and develops a sense of sentence structure. The consistent visual patterns of the lessons guide students from familiar words to less familiar words to irregular words. Reading is taught by associating with the student's natural knowledge of his own language. Disadvantages are extremely controlled vocabulary, in which word-by-word reading is encouraged. Others criticize the programs for the emphasis on auditory memory skills and the use of nonsense words in the practice exercises.

Whole Language Approach
In the Whole Language Approach, reading is taught as a holistic, meaning-oriented activity and is not broken down into a collection of skills. This approach relies heavily on literature or printed matter selected for a particular purpose. Reading is taught as part of a total language arts program, and the curriculum seeks to develop instruction in real problems and ideas. Two examples of whole language programs are *Learning through Literature* (Dodds and Goodfellow) and *Victory!* (Brigance). Phonics is not taught in a structured, systematic way. Students are assumed to develop their phonetic awareness through exposure to print. Writing is taught as a complement to reading. Writing centers are often part of this program as students learn to write their own stories and read them back, or follow along an audiotape of a book while reading along with it.

While the integration of reading with writing is an advantage of the whole language approach, the approach has been criticized for the lack of direct instruction in specific skill strategies. When working with students with learning problems, instruction that is more direct may be needed to learn the word-recognition skills necessary for achieving comprehension of the text.

Language Experience Approach
The language experience approach is similar to the whole language in that reading is considered as a personal ac, literature is emphasized, and students are encouraged to write about their own life experiences. The major difference is that written language is considered a secondary system to oral language, while whole language treats the two as parts of the same structure. The language experience approach is used primarily with beginner readers, but can also be used with older elementary and with other older students for corrective instruction. Reading skills are developed along with listening, speaking and writing skills. The materials consist, for the most part, of the student's skills. The philosophy of language experience includes:

- What students think about, they can talk about.
- What students say, they can write, or have someone write.
- What students write or have someone write for them, they can read.

Students dictate a story to a teacher as a group activity. Ideas for stories can originate from student artwork, news items, personal experiences, or they may be creative. Topic lists, word cards, or idea lists can also be used to generate topics or ideas for a class story. The teacher writes down the story in a first draft and the students read them back. The language patterns come from the students and they read their own written thoughts. The teacher provides guidance on word choice, sentence structure and the sounds of the letters and words. The students edit and revise the story on an experience chart. The teacher provides specific instruction in grammar, sentence structure, and spelling, if the need arises, rather than using a specified schedule. As the students progress, they create their individual storybooks, adding illustrations if they wish. The storybooks are placed in folders to share with others. Progress is evaluated in terms of the changes in the oral and written expression as well as in mechanics. There is no set method of evaluating student progress. That is one disadvantage of the language experience approach. However, the emphasis on student experience and creativity stimulates interest and motivates the students.

Individualized Reading Approach
Students select their own reading materials from a variety, according to interest and ability, and they are more able to progress at their own individual rates. Word recognition and comprehension are taught, as the student needs them. The teacher's role is to diagnose errors and prescribe materials, although the final choice is made by the students. Individual work may be supplemented by group activities with basal readers and workbooks for specific reading skills. The lack of systematic check and developmental skills and emphasis on self-learning may be a disadvantage for students with learning problems.

Most reading programs conceptually separate the reading process into three major categories: sight word vocabulary, word attack skills, and comprehension. These three areas constitute the basic questions that should be asked by a teacher when assessing a student's current level of functioning. From answers obtained, the pertinent questions are:

1. How large is the student's sight word vocabulary?
2. What kinds of word attack skills does the student employ?
3. How well developed are the student's comprehension skills?

Sight words are printed words that are easily identified by the learner. The selection of words to be learned will rely to some extent on the age and abilities of the student. Primary age students will use word lists composed of high-frequency words like basal readers, Dolch Word List.

Word attack skills are those techniques that enable a student to decode an unknown word so he can pronounce and understand it in the right context. Word attack skills are included in the areas of phonics, structural analysis, contextual and configuration clues, and decoding.

Comprehension skills are categorized into levels of difficulty. The teacher should consider the following factors when analyzing a student's reading comprehension level (Schloss & Sedlak, 1986):

1. The past experience of the reader.
2. The content of the written passage.
3. The syntax of the written passage.
4. The vocabulary used in the written passage.
5. The oral language comprehension of the student.
6. The questions being asked to assess comprehension.

The major categories of reading skills, basic reading skills within these categories, and strategies for the development of each are listed. Suggestions for assisting the reader in improving silent and oral reading skills are given. Some skills overlap categories.

Comprehension involves understanding what is read regardless of purpose or thinking skills employed. Comprehension can be delineated into categories of differentiated skills. Benjamin Bloom's taxonomy includes: knowledge, comprehension, application, analysis, synthesis, and evaluation. Thomas Barrett suggests that comprehension categories be classified as: literal meaning, reorganization, inference, evaluation, and appreciation. An overview of comprehension skills is presented in Skill 4, in this section.

Strategies that might prove beneficial in strengthening a student's comprehension involve:

1. Asking questions of the student before he reads a passage. This type of directed reading activity assists the student in focusing attention on the information in the text that will help him to answer the questions.
2. Using teacher questions to assist the student in developing self-questioning skills covering all levels of comprehension.

Silent and Oral Reading Skills

Silent reading refers to the inaudible reading of words or passages. Since the reading act id one on a covert basis, the accuracy of the reading process can only be inferred through questions or activities required of the student following his reading. What may be observed is attention given to the printed material, the eye movements an indication relative pace, and body language signifying frustration, or ease of reading. Strategies that might assist the child in reading silently are:

1. Preparing activities or questions pertaining to the printed passage. Vary the activities so that some are asking specific comprehension questions and other are geared toward creative expression like art, written composition.
2. Allowing time for pleasurable reading, such as through an activity like sustained silent reading.

Concepts of Print:
As we examine the concepts of print and learn how to teach them, it is important to understand how they represent the underlying principles to other aspects of reading development.

The concepts of print provide the foundation to all other reading skills. In order for students to develop phonemic awareness skills, they must understand the difference between a word and a letter. They must understand that words are made up of smaller parts of language: phonemes (sounds). Making the transition to the written word, students need to realize that letters or letter combinations represent those smaller sounds.

Once they realize that letters and words are different, they can then begin to see how putting letters together make different sound combinations. Then, putting more and more of them together to make words and then sentences. Without this basic level of understanding, the child has no hook with which to tie the information, which will later be the root of comprehension.

Since the English language is written in a left to right format, it is essential that this concept of print be taught to the students from the very beginning. If not learned, the child will not understand how to look at a page of print and even begin. Imagine a student could have advanced skills in phonemic awareness and phonics but still be unable to read a text if they did not understand left to right progression.

Another concept of print that would directly impact a student's ability to progress is the idea of a return sweep. The child could begin to read and come to the end of the first line and without efficiently knowing to return back to the left and begin again, he would become confused by the words on the page.

Book handling skills should begin at such a young age so they will seem almost automatic by the time the child is in kindergarten. However, for some children this is not the case. The inability to master these simple concepts of print will hinder any and all further reading progress until they can be mastered. As fluent readers, we take for granted the ease with which these skills were obtained, but for some students they were quite a struggle. The key to mastery is more time spent with print, looking at books and the written word, and interacting with books

Assessment of the development of the concepts of print for students is a generally simple procedure. This can be handled in an informal basis with any book available. The easiest method for keeping track is to keep dated notes on a card or folder as to the progress students make through all of the concepts of print to report to parents or other pertinent personnel.

Simply asking the student to show you one letter on a given page will provide the teacher with the knowledge as to whether or not a student can isolate a letter and truly understands what one letter is. The same strategy works for a word and a sentence. Just asking the student to identify where one word is or where a sentence can be located on a page.

An easy method to assess left to right progression and the concept of a return sweep is to ask the students to pretend they are reading a page that they may be unable to read. Asking them to pretend to be the teacher and show you with their finger how they would read that page. Watching how the child moves his finger across the page tells the teacher whether or not the child is progressing through or has mastered these skills.

Some assessments of print concepts include a word identification portion. In this part, there are two words printed on a line for the student to see. One word is two or three letters long and the other word starts with the same letter but is significantly longer, usually eight or more letters. The teacher then says one of the two words and the child points to the word the teacher states. In this assessment, the teacher gathers some insight into whether the child has the understanding that a multisyllabic word will be longer than a single syllable word.

Concepts of print is almost always completed through informal assessment methods. It is an easy assessment to complete, but should be completed on an individual basis to ensure valuable results. For the most part, concepts of print are mastered during the kindergarten year of schooling.

Phonemic Awareness:
Since phonemic awareness is a mostly auditory skill, it can often be completed with little to no materials necessary. It can also be integrated into almost any activity you are completing during the day in any subject. The other nice thing about phonemic awareness instruction is that it is best delivered in short segments several times throughout the day. Usually, it is best worked on in less than five-minute intervals a few times during the school day.

As stated before, phonemic awareness skills are auditory skills. Some of these skills later will be combined with print as the child transitions to phonics, but in a true phonemic awareness activity, there is no print involved. Phonemic awareness skills include: rhyming, beginning sound identification, ending sound identification, syllabication, insertion of sounds, deletion of sounds, and segmentation of sounds.

In order to promote phonemic awareness in students a teacher can complete many different types of activities. One of the most powerful methods can be found in texts that contain rhyming and alliteration patterns. Using nursery rhymes or songs is an excellent way to help children begin to hear the patterns of sounds in words. Books with repetitive language also help students begin to apply these concepts. Many students also enjoy tongue twisters or the old fashion jump rope songs.

As you progress to more complex levels of phonemic awareness, introducing pictures and game formats are fun ways for the students to the move into the next level. Anytime a teacher can add some form of manipulatives to a normally auditory only skill, the students have a better chance at obtaining the skill. An example of this might be when counting syllables or sounds in a word, providing the students with blocks or cubes to connect to represent the number of sounds. The game format allows the students to receive numerous repetitions in a friendly format that they enjoy and will want to continue.

Other activities can be integrated throughout the day as opportunities arise. While waiting in the hall for a special class or students to finish at the bathroom, the teacher could ask one or several students for words that rhyme with a certain word or to name words that begin with a given sound. In math class, the teacher could test a counting skill and a phonemic awareness skill by asking students to count out the same number of blocks as a given word has syllables. In science class, clues could be given for the key concept by using phonemic awareness skills. For example, the teacher could state that he is thinking of a word that rhymes with ant and begins like please. The children would then respond with plant and a unit on plants has been introduced. These easy to implement, quick activities are indeed the most effective method for teaching phonemic awareness.

Since phonemic awareness is a mostly auditory skill, it can often be completed with little to no materials necessary. It can also be integrated into almost any activity you are completing during the day in any subject. The other nice thing about phonemic awareness instruction is that it is best delivered in short segments several times throughout the day. Usually, it is best worked on in less than five-minute intervals a few times during the school day.

As stated before, phonemic awareness skills are auditory skills. Some of these skills later will be combined with print as the child transitions to phonics, but in a true phonemic awareness activity, there is no print involved. Phonemic awareness skills include: rhyming, beginning sound identification, ending sound identification, syllabication, insertion of sounds, deletion of sounds, and segmentation of sounds.

In order to promote phonemic awareness in students a teacher can complete many different types of activities. One of the most powerful methods can be found in texts that contain rhyming and alliteration patterns. Using nursery rhymes or songs is an excellent way to help children begin to hear the patterns of sounds in words. Books with repetitive language also help students begin to apply these concepts. Many students also enjoy tongue twisters or the old fashion jump rope songs.

Fluency:
In the instruction of reading, fluent reading has often been an overlooked, undertaught skill in schools. It was with the research review from the work of the National Reading Panel, that fluency came to the forefront.

The research has indicated that there is a correlation that a child who reads fluently will be more likely to comprehend the text than a child who does not demonstrate fluent reading. Since the end result of all reading is comprehension, or the understanding of what one has read, this body of research cannot be ignored.

Reading fluency is a broad term that is used to describe reading that has a high degree of accuracy, appropriate phrasing, is smooth and is paced fittingly for the text. In order to achieve all of these areas, it requires the child to be able to decode words in a very automatic and rapid way.

As reading is a complex task, it requires many cognitive processes to occur simultaneously. Efficient and automatic decoding of text allows the student to free up some of these cognitive processes to better address other areas, particularly comprehension. The child who struggles with decoding spends so much mental energy attempting to decode words that there is not enough of a reserve to be able to adequately address the comprehension issues.

Fluency develops over time and with much repetition and practice. The analogy is often drawn to learning to drive a car. When an individual is first learning to drive a car, they must concentrate on every little aspect involved. Which foot is the accelerator, how much pressure to place on the pedal, how to keep the car within the lane, etc. Often distractions such as pedestrians or radio noise cause large over corrections or require additional time for the newer drivers to respond correctly. However, as the driver becomes more skilled, he spends less energy on those more rote tasks previously described. He now has more time to devote to anticipating events. In some cases, he can use his mental energy to think about things unrelated to driving completely. How many times have you driven somewhere and not remembered how you got there? This is because for you driving has become automatic and freed you up for other more complex cognitive thoughts.

This automatic nature in reading is essential as the amount of information in texts grows and students are required to comprehend more and more information in order to be successful. Imagine trying to proceed through a college level course or text if you had to spend time decoding every word presented. You would gain nothing from the work and time you devoted, thus it is vital that students develop automaticity with decoding.

Skill 13.5 **Demonstrate knowledge of the differences between reading skills and strategies, the role each plays in reading development, and reading intervention strategies and support systems for meeting the needs of diverse learners across age and skill levels.**

When the National Reading Panel came out with their now infamous report identifying the big ideas within reading instruction, the face of reading was changed. Now teachers have a better understanding of what skills are necessary for the appropriate development of reading in students. The big five skills for reading are:

- Phonemic Awareness
- Phonics
- Fluency
- Comprehension
- Vocabulary

These skills are the foundational areas in which instruction must be provided to ensure reading will progress and develop. Phonemic Awareness is the lowest level of skill. It is an oral understanding of the parts of language and how they will work together and later relate to reading. It involves subskills including: initial sound identification, rhyme, onset and rhyme, ending sounds, and other oral types of skills.

Phonics is the next level of development. This is where students make the connection between the sounds letters make and there written function. Sometimes referred to in the classroom as decoding, it is where students begin to apply the oral skills they understand to the print on the page.

Once students become proficient at developing this ability to decode, they must increase their skills to a fluent level. Fluency is a combination of the pace of reading and the prosody (tone, inflection, etc.) with which passages have been read. Research has proven that students who are able to read in a fluent manner usually have increased comprehension. Comprehension is the end result of reading and is the goal all should strive to attain. Comprehension is the understanding of what information has been read.

Vocabulary development is pervasive across all areas of reading and begins with a sight word reading vocabulary and progresses throughout the levels into more complex meaning based understanding of words and their purpose in text.

All of these skills need to be in place for adequate reading instruction. However, in special education, it is often necessary to provide strategies and supports in place to ensure the success. These strategies and supports should include these same reading skills, but the manner and methods in which they are presented may vary significantly. Additionally, it may be necessary to vary the order, materials or other factors to help students progress.

Strategies and supports should be increased as student levels and needs require to ensure adequate progress and success with the reading curriculum.

Skill 13.6   Demonstrate knowledge of the concepts of mathematics (e.g., numeration, geometry, measurement, statistics/probability, problem solving, algebra).

Reid, 1985, describes four processes that are directly related to an understanding of numbers. Children typically begin learning these processes in early childhood through the opportunities provided by their caretakers. Children who do not get these opportunities have difficulties when they enter school.

- <u>Describing</u> characterizing objects, sets or events in terms of their attributes such as calling all cats "kitties" whether they are tigers or house cats.
- <u>Classifying</u>: sorting objects, sets or events in terms of one or more criterion such as color, size or shape – black cats versus white cats versus tabby cats.
- <u>Comparing</u>: determining whether two objects, sets or events are similar or different on the basis of a specified attribute, such as differentiating quadrilaterals from triangles on the basis of the number of sides.
- <u>Ordering:</u> comparing two or more objects, sets or events, such as ordering children in a family on the basis of age, or on the basis of height.

Children usually begin learning these concepts during early childhood:
<u>Equalizing</u>-Making two or more objects or sets alike on an attribute, such as putting more milk into a glass so that it matches the amount of milk in another glass.

<u>Joining</u>-putting together two or more sets with a common attribute to make one set, such as buying packets of X-Men trading cards to create a complete series.

<u>Separating</u>-Dividing an object or set into two or more sets, such as passing out cookies from a bag to a group of children so that each child gets three cookies.

<u>Measuring</u>-Attaching a number to an attribute, such as three cups of flour, or ten gallons of gas.

<u>Patterns</u>-Recognizing, developing, and repeating patterns, such as secret code messages, designs in a carpet or tile floor.

However, most children are not developmentally ready to understand these concepts before they enter school:

- Understanding and working with numbers larger than ten: They may be able to recite larger numbers, but are not able to compare or add them, for example.
- Part-whole concept: The idea of one number as being a part of another number.
- Numerical notation: Place value, additive system, and zero symbol.

Children with learning problems often have difficulty with these concepts after they enter public school because they have either had not had many experiences with developing these concepts or they are not developmentally ready to understand such concepts as part-whole for example.

Sequence of Mathematics understanding

The understanding of mathematical concepts proceeds in a developmental context from concrete to semi-concrete to abstract. Children with learning difficulties may still be at the semi-concrete level when their peers are ready to work at the abstract level. This developmental sequence has implication for instruction because the teacher will need to incorporate concrete and/or semi-concrete into lessons for students who did not master these stages of development in their mathematics background. These levels may be explained as follows:

- Concrete: An example of this would be demonstrating 3 + 4 = 7 by counting out three buttons and four buttons to equal seven buttons.
- Semi-concrete: An example would be using pictures of three buttons and four buttons to illustrate 3 + 4 = 7.
- Abstract: The student solves 3 + 4 = 7 without using manipulatives or pictures.

In summary, the levels of mathematics content involve:
- Concepts such as the understanding of numbers and terms
- Development of mathematical relationships
- Development of mathematical skills such as computation and measuring
- Development of problem-solving ability not only in books, but also in the environment

The National Council of Teachers of Mathematics, in its *Principles and Standards for School Mathematics* (2000) notes that math is a "highly interconnected and cumulative subject." Accordingly, teachers should begin by steeping classrooms in mathematics awareness, examining their own attitudes and aptitudes in math and preparing themselves to be the best help they can to students. The teacher's deep understanding of math at the concrete, representational and abstract levels is important to helping students to perceive the presence of math across the curriculum and in everyday activities.

David Allsopp, Ph.D., associate professor at University of South Florida has done substantive research on best classroom practices for special needs mathematics students. He suggests that for special needs students:

- Direct instruction with significant guided practice, repetition, and support from teachers is actually more effective than student-centered instruction.

- Teaching problem-solving strategies is more effective than exclusively using rote practice.

- Concrete instruction, persistently applied throughout the levels of mathematics curriculum, is more effective in helping students develop computation and problem solving skills and to prepare for abstract mathematics work.

- Ongoing assessment of students' performance, sharing and discussing with them their progress and successes, improves learning outcomes.

- engaging students as active participants in their learning by encouraging and teaching metacognitive behaviors like goal setting, self-monitoring, and self-talk, and showing them how to apply these skills not only to their mathematics work but to general problem solving, boosts math proficiency.

- Well-planned cooperative learning activities, such as peer tutoring and work groups, can offer students opportunities for meaningful practice and skill enhancement.

Skilled teachers can apply these special needs principles to a variety of engaging approaches to instruction, which may include instructional games, use of technology, daily living activities, journaling, integration with science or literature, and cross-curricular applications in subjects such as physical education and art.

Problem Solving

The skills of analysis and interpretation are necessary for problem solving. Students with learning disabilities find problem solving difficult, with the result that they avoid problem solving activities. Skills necessary for problem solving include:

1) *Identification of the main idea*- what is the problem about?
2) *Main question of the problem*- what is the problem asking for?
3) *Identifying important facts*- what information is necessary to solve the problem?
4) *Choose a strategy and an operation* –how will the student solve the problem and with what operation?
5) *Solve the problem* – perform the computation
6) *Check accuracy of computation and compare the answer to the main question* –Does it sound reasonable?
7) *If solution is correct* –Repeat the steps.

IDENTIFY EFFECTIVE TEACHING METHODS FOR DEVELOPING THE USE OF MATH SKILLS IN PROBLEM-SOLVING

One of the main reasons for studying mathematics is to acquire the ability to perform problem-solving skills. Problem solving is the process of applying previously acquired knowledge to new and novel situations. Mathematical problem solving is generally thought of as solving word problems; however, there are more skills involved in problem solving than merely reading word problems, deciding on correct conceptual procedures, and performing the computations. Problem solving skills involve posing questions; analyzing situations; hypothesizing, translating, and illustrating results; drawing diagrams, and using trial and error. When solving mathematical problems, students need to be able to apply logic; and thus, determine which facts are relevant. Table 7-1 demonstrates this process.

Problem solving has proven to be the primary area of mathematical difficulty for students. The following methods for developing problem solving skills have been recommended.

1. Allot time for the development of successful problem solving skills. It is complex process and needs to be taught in a systematic way.
2. Be sure prerequisite skills have been adequately developed. The ability to perform the operations of addition, subtraction, multiplication, and division are necessary sub-skills.
3. Use error analysis to diagnose areas of difficulty. One error in procedure or choice of mathematical operation, once corrected, will eliminate subsequent mistakes following the initial error like the domino effect. Look for patterns of similar mistakes to prevent a series of identical errors. Instruct children on the usage of error analysis to perform self-appraisal of their own work.
4. Teach students appropriate terminology. Many words have a different meaning when used in a mathematical context than in every day life. For example "set" in mathematics refers to a grouping of objects, but it may be used as a very, such as in "set the table."
   Other words that should be defined include "order," "base," "power," and "root."
5. Have students estimate answers. Teach them how to check their computed answer, to determine how reasonable it is. For example, Teddy is asked how many hours he spent doing his homework. If he word on it two hours before dinner and one hour after dinner, and his answer came out to be 21, Teddy should be able to conclude that 21 hours is the greater part of a day, and is far too large to be reasonable.
6. Remember that development of math readiness skills enables students to acquire prerequisite concepts and to build cognitive structures. These prerequisite skills appear to be related to problem solving performance.

In a paper published by the ERIC Clearinghouse on Disabilities and Gifted Education, author Cynthia Warger writes, "...for students with disabilities to do better in math, math must be meaningful for them. Both knowing and doing mathematics must be emphasized to enhance the quality of mathematics instruction and learning for students with disabilities." (Warger 2002)

Real-world applications of mathematics abound and offer highly motivating opportunities for computational practice and the development of number sense and mathematical reasoning that can give students confidence in their mathematical ability. Finding the mathematical connections in outdoor games, planning for the purchase of lunch, comparing heights among classmates, calculating the time until recess, and figuring out which sports team is headed for the playoffs are just a few examples.

The Special Connections Project at the University of Kansas suggests a number of strategies in a paper called "Creating Authentic Mathematics Learning Contexts":

- Begin where the students are. Their ages, interests and experiences are excellent clues to the kinds of contexts that will offer the most compelling learning opportunities, whether school-, family- or community-related.

- Document interests. Comparing and contrasting them can help identify patterns and differences and assist with lesson and activity planning. Documenting and reviewing this information (student name, hobbies, interests, family activities, etc., could be an activity you share with your students.

- Model the desired concept, skill, or strategy explicitly and within the real-world context. Observing your problem-solving approach and its outcome helps ground students in the math and begins to strengthen associations between mathematics concepts and real-life situations.

- Reinforce the associations by demonstrating the relevance of the concept, skill, or strategy being taught to the "authentic context"

- Offer opportunities for guided, supported practice of the concept, skill or strategy; this includes feedback, redirection, remodeling if needed, and acknowledgement of progress and successes.

Etiologies of the learning challenges some students face can be diverse, as can their outcomes. Teachers of students with special needs are skilled at assessing, observing, implementing, reassessing and making changes to the educational environment, tools and approaches they are using with students.

To accomplish this with math instruction, teachers must begin by identifying the nature of math as a curricular area, using that information to task-analyze the concepts, skill, and strategies they want to teach. Then teachers focus on each student's observed and documented strengths and challenges, as well as the relevant information from in his/her formal assessments and individualized education plan (IEP). Such analysis may constitute an initial assessment,

In the NCTM journal article "Planning Strategies for Students with Special Needs" (*Teaching Children Mathematics*, 2004), Brodesky et al. suggest that the next step in deciding on strategies, materials and resources would be to identify the "barriers" that students' documented and observed challenges will present as they work to meet the goals and objectives of the math curriculum and their IEPs. Data-based assessments are an alternative or adjunct to such observational and record review. This information can help direct teachers' thinking about proactive solutions, including the selection and/or adaptation of the best strategies, materials and resources.

Once teachers have thus developed a clear picture of the goals and needs of their math students with learning differences, they can seek resources for best practices, including school district-based support, the federal and state departments of education, teacher training programs, and education literature. Ultimately, skilled teachers will layer creativity and keen observation with their professional skills to decide how best to individualize instruction and facilitate student achievement. Examples include:

- Varying learning modalities (visual, kinesthetic, tactile, aural)
- Integrating technology (calculators, computers, game consoles)
- Providing tools and manipulatives (Cuisinart rods, beans, protractors)
- Developing a range of engaging activities (games, music, storytelling)
- Using real world problem solving (fundraising, school-wide projects, shopping, cooking, budgeting)
- Adopting a cross-curricular approach (studying historical events strongly influenced by math, music theory)
- Developing basic skills (guided practice, pencil-and-paper computation, journaling and discussing problem solving strategies)
- Adaptations (extended wait time, recorded lessons, concept videos, ergonomic work areas, mixed-ability learning groups)

Geometry: Geometry is the understanding of shapes, properties, points, lines, angles, and figures in space. Beginning in elementary school it revolves around identifying shapes (both two dimensional and three dimensional), points, rays, and lines, as well as putting them together to form figures and defining them in space. It also is about making assumptions about objects. Through middle and high school, students use their knowledge of these items and other mathematical rules combined with their ability to make deduction of the properties to present mathematical proofs.

Measurement: Measurement is the process of finding the size, extent of coverage and assigning them numbers through a predetermined and accepted set of norms. Measurement involves distance, quantity, dimension and/or capacity.

Statistics/Probability: Statistics and Probability are the mathematical branches which help students to collect information, then classify that same information, analyze it and finally make a supposition or interpretation of the information examined. This information is referred to typically as data, which is representative of the facts gathered from presented information.

Algebra: Algebra is the area of math which helps students to see relationships between math statements and situations. Typically it uses variables where letters represent missing numbers and the students use different numerical relationships to solve or find the missing numbers.

Skill 13.7   Demonstrate knowledge of career education and Vocational/ Technical education programs.

Vocational Training
Vocational education programs prepare students for entry into occupations in the labor force. Through these programs, it is intended that they become self-sufficient, self-supporting citizens. This training has typically incorporated work-study programs at the high school and post-secondary levels. These programs include training while students are in school and on-the-job training after leaving school. Instruction focuses on particular job skills and on integral activities such as job opportunities, skill requirements for specific jobs, personal qualifications in relation to job requirements, work habits, money management, and academic skills needed for particular jobs. Such vocational training programs are based on three main ideas (Blake, 1976):

1. Students need specific training in job skills. They must acquire them prior to exiting school.
2. Students need specific training and supervision in applying skills learned in school to requirements in job situations.
3. Vocational training can provide instruction and field-based experience, which will meet these needs and help the student become able to work in specific occupations.

Career Education
Curricular aspects of career education include the phases of (1) career awareness (diversity of available jobs); (2) career exploration (skills needed for occupational groups); and (3) career preparation (specific training and preparation required for the world of work). The concept of career education (1) extended this training into all levels of public school education (i.e. elementary through high school); (2) emphasized the importance of acquiring skills in the areas of daily living and personal-social interaction, as well as occupational training and preparation; and (3) focused upon integrating these skills into numerous areas of academic and vocational curricula. In general, career education attempts to prepare the individual for all facets of life.

Vocational Training in Special Education

Vocational training in special education has typically focused upon the exceptionality area if intellectual disabilities. Special guidance and training services have more recently been directed toward students with learning disabilities, emotional behavior disorders, physically disabled, visually impaired, and hearing impaired. Individuals with disabilities are mainstreamed with non-disabled students in vocational training programs when possible. Special sites provide training for those persons with more severe disabilities who are unable to be successfully taught in an integrated setting. Specially trained vocational counselors monitor and supervise student work sites.

Regardless of the disabling condition, aptitude testing is considered an important component in vocational training for the students in a mild or moderate setting. This assessment is necessary in order to identify areas of interest and capability. Attitudes and work habits are deemed important by many prospective employers, and so these competencies are included in the training.

Training provisions for individuals with severe intellectual disabilities have expanded. They include special programs for school-aged children and secondary-level adolescents, and sheltered workshop programs for adults. Instruction focuses upon self-help skills, social-interpersonal skills, motor skills, rudimentary academic skills, simple occupational skills, and lifetime leisure and recreational skills. In addition, secondary-level programs offer on-the-job supervision, and sheltered workshop programs provide work supervision and pay a small wage for contract labor. Some persons with moderate to severe intellectual disabilities can be trained for employment in supervised unskilled occupations, while others are only able to perform chores and other simple tasks in sheltered workshops.

SUBAREA IV.   MANAGING THE LEARNING ENVIRONMENT AND PROMOTING STUDENTS' SOCIAL INTERACTION AND COMMUNICATION SKILLS

COMPETENCY 14.0   UNDERSTAND HOW TO CREATE A POSITIVE LEARNING ENVIRONMENT THAT PROMOTES AND SUPPORTS THE PARTICIPATION OF ALL LEARNERS.

Skill 14.1   Demonstrate knowledge of the effects of teacher attitudes and behaviors on all students.

As the teacher in the classroom, students will look to you as a role model. In this way, it is important to consider how your attitude, behavior and actions will affect the students you are responsible for teaching.

Setting the tone of the classroom is an important part of the instructional process. Creating a warm, positive and safe environment allows the students to feel more able to take risks. Since many special education students have struggled for years, they may be very hesitant to take educational risks. Having and using regularly a positive attitude can go a long way in helping these students.

In addition to attitude, it is important that the special educator model the behavior she expects from her students. Demonstrating respect for the students by not demeaning, listening with an open mind and truly valuing their responses and opinions on topics that arise in the classroom can go a long way to building a relationship with the students.

Being optimistic and providing positive encouragement to always strive for better are good steps to take within the classroom. Having open communication and taking an active interest in the lives of your students can also help to build the trust zone. If students do not trust the teacher, they will be less likely to work with that educator through difficult educational assignments.

Here are numerous ways to have a positive attitude and build acceptable behavior within the classroom. Some of these include:

- Engage in discussions with your students about events in your life as well as things happening in their lives
- Teach and model social skills
- Share cultural differences and embrace the uniqueness of all people
- Use cooperative learning models and teach strategies for cooperation
- Build on intrinsic motivation
- Encourage inquiry and discovery
- Provide time for sharing
- Involve families in the classroom on a regular basis
- Build classroom rules with the students
- Discuss and allow natural, logical consequences to occur and regularly discuss them
- Look at the furniture and overall organization of the classroom and try to make it a warm and welcoming environment

See Skill 25.2 for additional information on teacher attitudes

Skill 14.2   Demonstrate knowledge of the process for inventorying instructional environments to determine whether adaptations to the environment must be made to meet a student's individual needs.

See Skills 1.1, 8.3, 10.4, 23.1, and 24.4

Skill 14.3   Demonstrate knowledge of common environmental barriers that hinder accessibility and learning.

There are a number of environmental barriers which may impact the accessibility in order for learning to occur in the school setting. The Americans with Disabilities Act (ADA) was passed in 1990 to help reduce the amount of barriers those with disabilities would be faced with.

Today, more than ten years later, most schools have made many physical changes to the structures to allow students with disabilities more access to the educational process. Many schools include elevators, accessible restrooms, wider hallways, ramps and other structural changes to better address the needs of those with disabilities.

As the special educator, it will be necessary to work with other specialists to examine the environment of your school, including the cafeteria, playground (if appropriate), gym, locker rooms, etc. This examination should be completed with regards to specific students to ensure there are no environmental barriers which prevent the student from being able to access an appropriate education.

Some things to consider include:

- Are walkways within classrooms wide enough to accommodate the needs of the student?
- Does the playground have equipment the student can use to allow for socialization?
- Can the student manage to buy lunch from the cafeteria with no difficulties (manage their food tray, get their food from the line to a table, etc..)?
- Is there a bathroom the student can use with no help?
- Is there a person available to assist the student as necessary?
- Are the outside doors accessible to the student (i.e. does the student have enough strength to open and close the doors independently)?
- Is there appropriate equipment available to allow the student to access the learning being presented?

Keeping in mind these types of questions in addition to others, the IEP team can better ensure the student is able to fully access the information presented within the school, which includes socialization with peers. The district may need to make some specific changes in order to meet the needs of the students. Keeping in mind, the student needs to have access free from environmental barriers whenever possible.

Skill 14.4 Apply knowledge of strategies for facilitating a learning community in which individual differences are respected.

Within the classroom, it is important the students respect each other and celebrate their individual differences. This is also true throughout the school as a whole. It is important teachers respect various teachers' different teaching styles and learning styles. It is through this mutual respect upon which strong learning communities can be built.

Sometimes it may be helpful for students to complete some small exercises to increase awareness of the struggles a person with disabilities may face. Keep in mind the age and maturity level of your students when explaining individual differences. An example might include having the children try to complete a worksheet while wearing a "blindfold" of wax paper to simulate a visual disability. This type of activity can build their awareness and respect for the students within the classroom.

It is also necessary to explain that each of us are individuals and because it is the responsibility of the teacher to reach each student, not everyone will complete the same work at the same time. Having this frank discussion with the students at the beginning of the year, and reviewing it periodically as necessary can eliminate the challenges of "it's not fair", which will sometimes arise in the classroom.

Making your classroom into a learning community where each individual has something productive to contribute is an ongoing task throughout the year. It is important to celebrate some successes for each student. This will help to demonstrate to the entire class how each member of the community is important to the group as a whole.

The techniques from the research of *The Responsive Classroom* provide numerous ideas and suggestions for building a classroom community. You can find information about the Responsive Classroom at www.responsiveclassroom.org.

Skill 14.5   Recognize personal attitudes and biases that affect the acceptance of individuals with disabilities.

As a special educator, you will see various demonstrations of attitudes and biases which relate to the students you serve. It is important to recognize these personal opinions and have strategies with which to deal with them throughout your career.

One of the most common attitudes/biases you will hear within the school system deals with fairness. It seems the less visible the disability the more unaccepting some people are of the differences. Many times when it comes to adaptations and modifications for students with learning disabilities you will receive comments about the fairness to other students.

As the Special Education Teacher, it may be necessary to provide instruction to parents, peers, or administrators as to the nature of disability of a specific child and why it is necessary these changes be made. Explaining it in a non-demeaning manner which clarifies how it is actually leveling the playing field for the child with the learning disability requires specialized communication skills.

As more and more students are included in regular education, these attitudes and biases have generally decreased. Additionally, many teachers have benefited greatly as have regular education students. Large quantities of teachers have incorporated simple modifications into their daily teaching allowing many more children to benefit.

As with any negative attitude or personal biases someone faces, it is difficult to put emotions aside but it is necessary. Listening and responding in a dispassionate and logical manner helps to diffuse these situations. Being matter of fact and providing clear explanations is the most effective method for handling these situations. If after doing this, there still remain significant issues; you may need to involve the administration as a very last resort.

Skill 14.6   Demonstrate knowledge of the effects cultural and gender differences can have on communication in the classroom.

The diversity in classrooms today continues to grow. As it does so do the cultural impacts. As previously discussed in other skills (14.1, 14.2, 14.3, 14.4 and 14.5) there are numerous strategies for dealing with individual differences within the classroom. It is important to keep these in mind when dealing with cultural differences as well.

Cultural differences sometimes have the added component of language and communication barriers. Sometimes students for whom English is not their primary language may have great difficulty participating in class discussions or sharing their feelings in a manner others can understand.

It can be quite intimidating to be in a room where you do not understand most of what is being said and then also not being able to share any information yourself. Sometimes this can lead to behavioral issues or other methods of handling frustrations. For still some other students, they become very shy and reserved.

As they begin to become more familiar with English, there may still be impacts on the communication as misunderstandings arise. Colloquial phrases sometimes provide a great deal of difficult. It is important for the teacher to ensure all of the students are understanding what is happening within the classroom and have the opportunity to participate.

Gender differences are often discussed when it comes to boys and reading and girls with sciences and math. These are broader generalities, but certainly things to consider and keep in mind, without stereotyping either gender. Suffice to say, each student in your classroom regardless of gender needs to have equal learning experiences.

In order to provide these types of experiences it may be necessary to do more research and gather more materials. For example, you may need to find different more interesting reading materials to engage the boys in specific reading assignments. For girls, you may need to search out role models in the math and science disciplines.

No matter the subject, students will become as engaged and enthusiastic as you are. In the end, it is the teacher and his influence which helps improve the communication within the classroom.

Skill 14.7 Demonstrate knowledge of universal design and its application to accommodate a diverse student population.

Universal design describes an approach whereby everything is accessible by everyone. In the case of schools, it means that all activities, materials, educational opportunities, environments, etc. are free from barriers and are able to be used by all students. Universal design goes beyond the instruction into the physical space.

Typically, universal design for the environment has seven principles which are broad and considered for all. They are:

1. Equal use for all
2. Flexible use for all
3. Simple and intuitive
4. Perceptible information
5. Tolerance for error (we all make mistakes)
6. Low physical effort
7. Size, space for approach and use

In addition, we in schools also want a universal design approach to all teaching and educational opportunities. This might include:

- Providing many different ways to acquire information
- Providing many different ways for students to demonstrate what they know
- Providing many different ways to engage the students in the learning

Universal design approaches align very well with differentiated teaching descriptions. It is through a variety of methods both with the tangible environment surrounding students and with the intangible learning of information that we will be able to meet the needs of the most students.

It is through a varied curriculum with multiple goals and objectives that the teacher is able to provide each student with a customized learning experiences which will bring them in with challenges and interests. Then once they are engaged, provide them with a variety of methods to acquire the new learning like: media, visual, auditory, kinesthetic, etc. Finally, when asked to show the teacher what they learned, the students will have multiple methods from which to choose.

COMPETENCY 15.0 UNDERSTAND PROCEDURES FOR STRUCTURING AND MANAGING THE LEARNING ENVIRONMENT

Skill 15.1 **Demonstrate knowledge of basic classroom management theories and methods and ways in which technology can assist with creating and managing the learning environment.**

Classroom management plans should be in place when the school year begins. Developing a management plan takes a proactive approach—that is, decide what behaviors will be expected of the class as a whole, anticipate possible problems, and teach the behaviors early in the school year.

Behavior management techniques should focus on positive procedures that can be used at home as well as at school. Involving the students in the development of the classroom rules lets the students know the rationale for the rules, and allows them to assume responsibility in the rules because they had a part in developing them. When students get involved in helping establish the rules, they will be more likely to assume responsibility for following them. Once the rules are established, enforcement and reinforcement for following the rules should begin right away.

Consequences should be introduced when the rules are introduced, clearly stated, and understood by all of the students. The severity of the consequence should match the severity of the offense and must be enforceable. The teacher must apply the consequence consistently and fairly; so the students will know what to expect when they choose to break a rule.

Like consequences, students should understand what rewards to expect for following the rules. The teacher should never promise a reward that cannot be delivered, and follow through with the reward as soon as possible. Consistency and fairness is also necessary for rewards to be effective. Students will become frustrated and give up if they see that rewards and consequences are not delivered timely and fairly.

About four to six classroom rules should be posted where students can easily see and read them. These rules should be stated positively, and describe specific behaviors so they are easy to understand. Certain rules may also be tailored to meet target goals and IEP requirements of individual students. (For example, a new student who has had problems with leaving the classroom may need an individual behavior contract to assist him or her with adjusting to the class rule about remaining in the assigned area.) As the students demonstrate the behaviors, the teacher should provide reinforcement and corrective feedback. Periodic "refresher" practice can be done as needed, for example, after a long holiday or if students begin to "slack off." A copy of the classroom plan should be readily available for substitute use, and the classroom aide should also be familiar with the plan and procedures.

The teacher should clarify and model the expected behavior for the students. In addition to the classroom management plan, a management plan should be developed for special situations, (i.e., fire drills) and transitions (i.e., going to and from the cafeteria). Periodic review of the rules, as well as modeling and practice, may be conducted as needed, such as after an extended school holiday.

Procedures that use social humiliation, withholding of basic needs, pain, or extreme discomfort should never be used in a behavior management plan. Emergency intervention procedures used when the student is a danger to himself or others are not considered behavior management procedures. Throughout the year, the teacher should periodically review the types of interventions being used; assess the effectiveness of the interventions used in the management plan, and make revisions as needed for the best interests of the child.

Motivation
Before the teacher begins instruction, he or she should choose activities that are at the appropriate level of student difficulty, are meaningful, and relevant. Teacher behaviors that motivate students include:

- Maintain Success Expectations through teaching, goal setting, establishing connections between effort and outcome, and self-appraisal and reinforcement.
- Have a supply of intrinsic incentives such as rewards, appropriate competition between students, and the value of the academic activities.
- Focus on students' intrinsic motivation through adapting the tasks to students' interests, providing opportunities for active response, including a variety of tasks, providing rapid feedback, incorporating games into the lesson, allowing students the opportunity to make choices, create, and interact with peers.
- Stimulate students' learning by modeling positive expectations and attributions. Project enthusiasm and personalize abstract concepts. Students will be better motivated if they know what they will be learning about. The teacher should also model problem-solving and task-related thinking so students can see how the process is done.

For adolescents, motivation strategies are usually aimed at getting the student actively involved in the learning process. Since the adolescent has the opportunity to get involved in a wider range of activities outside the classroom (job, car, being with friends), stimulating motivation may be the focus even more than academics.

Motivation may be achieved through extrinsic reinforcers or intrinsic reinforcers. This is accomplished by allowing the student a degree of choice in what is being taught or how it will be taught. The teacher will, if possible, obtain a commitment either through a verbal or written contract between the student and the teacher. Adolescents also respond to regular feedback, especially when that feedback shows that they are making progress.

Rewards for adolescents often include free time for listening to music, recreation or games. They may like extra time for a break or exemption from a homework assignment. They may receive rewards at home for satisfactory performance at school. Other rewards include self-charting progress, and tangible reinforcers. In summary, motivational activities may be used for goal setting, self-recording of academic progress, self-evaluation, and self-reinforcement.

Classroom Interventions
Classroom interventions anticipate student disruptions and nullify potential discipline problems. Every student is different and each situation is unique; therefore, student behavior cannot be matched to specific interventions. Good classroom management requires the ability to select appropriate interventions strategies from an array of alternatives. The following non-verbal and verbal interventions were explained in Henley, Ramsey, and Algonzzine (1993).

Nonverbal Intervention - The use of nonverbal interventions allows classroom activities to proceed without interruption. These interventions also enable students to avoid "power struggles" with students.

Body Language - Teachers can convey authority and command respect through body language. Posture, eye contact, facial expressions, and gestures are examples of body components that signal leadership to students.

Planned Ignoring - Many minor classroom disturbances are best handled through planned ignoring. When teachers ignore attention-seeking behaviors, often students do likewise.

Signal Interference - There are numerous non-verbal signals that teachers can use to quiet a class. Some of these are eye contact, snapping fingers, a frown, shaking the head, or making a quieting gesture with the hand. A few teachers present signs like flicking the lights, putting her finger over her lips, or wink at a selective student.

Proximity Control - Teachers who move around the room merely need to stand near a student or small group of students, or gently place a hand on a student's shoulder to stop a disturbing behavior. Teachers who stand or sit as if rooted are compelled to issue verbal directions in order to deal with student disruptions.

Removal of Seductive Objects - some students become distracted by objects. Removing seductive objects eliminates the need some students have to handle, grab, or touch objects that distract their attention.

Verbal Interventions-Because non-verbal interventions are the least intrusive, they are generally preferred. Verbal Interventions are useful after it is clear that non-verbal interventions have been unsuccessful in preventing or stopping disruptive behavior.

Humor - Some teachers have been successful in dispelling discipline problems with a quip or an easy comment that produces smiles or gentle laughter from students. This does not include sarcasm, cynicism, or teasing, which increase tension and often creates resentment.

Sane Messages. Sane messages are descriptive and model appropriate behavior. They help students understand how their behavior affects others. "Karol, when you talk during silent reading, you disturb everyone in your group," is an example of a sane message.

Restructuring. When confronted with student disinterest, the teacher makes the decision to change activities. This is an example of an occasion when restructuring could be used by the teacher to regenerate student interest.

Hypodermic Affection. Sometimes students get frustrated, discouraged, and anxious in school. Hypodermic affection lets students know they are valued. Saying a kind word, giving a smile, or just showing interest in a child gives the encouragement that is needed.

Praise and Encouragement. Effective praise is directed at student behavior rather than at the student personally. "Catching a child being good," is an example of an effective use of praise that reinforces positive classroom behavior. Comments like, "you are really trying hard," encourages student effort.

Alerting. Make abrupt changes from one activity to another can bring on behavior problems. Alerting helps students to make smooth transitioning by giving them time to make emotional adjustments to change.

Accepting Student Feelings. Provide opportunities for students to express their feelings, even those that are distressful, helps them to learn to do so in appropriate ways. Role playing, class meetings or discussions, life space interviews, journal writings, and other creative modes help students to channel difficult feelings into constructive outlets.

Transfer between classes and subjects
Effective teachers use class time efficiently. This results in higher student subject engagement and will likely result in more subject matter retention. One way teachers use class time efficiently is through a smooth transition from one activity to another; this activity is also known as "management transition." Management transition is defined as "teacher shifts from one activity to another in a systemic, academically oriented way." One factor that contributes to efficient management transition is the teacher's management of instructional material. Effective teachers gather their materials during the planning stage of instruction. Doing this, a teacher avoids flipping through things looking for the items necessary for the current lesson. Momentum is lost and student concentration is broken when this occurs.

Additionally, teachers who keep students informed of the sequencing of instructional activities maintain systematic transitions because the students are prepared to move on to the next activity. For example, the teacher says, "When we finish with this guided practice together, we will turn to page twenty-three and each student will do the exercises. I will then circulate throughout the classroom helping on an individual basis. Okay, let's begin." Following an example such as this will lead to systematic smooth transitions between activities because the students will be turning to page twenty-three when the class finishes the practice without a break in concentration.

Another method that leads to smooth transitions is to move students in groups and clusters rather than one by one. This is called "group fragmentation." For example, if some students do seat work while other students gather for a reading group, the teacher moves the students in pre-determined groups. Instead of calling the individual names of the reading group, which would be time consuming and laborious, the teacher simply says, "Will the blue reading group please assemble at the reading station. The red and yellow groups will quietly do the vocabulary assignment I am now passing out." As a result of this activity, the classroom is ready to move on in a matter of seconds rather than minutes.

Additionally, the teacher may employ academic transition signals, defined as academic transition signals— "teacher utterance that indicate[s] movement of the lesson from one topic or activity to another by indicating where the lesson is and where it is going." For example, the teacher may say, "That completes our description of clouds, now we will examine weather fronts." Like the sequencing of instructional materials, this keeps the student informed on what is coming next so they will move to the next activity with little or no break in concentration.

Therefore, effective teachers manage transitions from one activity to another in a systematically oriented way through efficient management of instructional matter, sequencing of instructional activities, moving students in groups and by employing academic transition signals. Through an efficient use of class time, achievement is increased because students spend more class time engaged in on-task behavior.

Transition refers to changes in class activities that involve movement. Examples are:

(a) Breaking up from large group instruction into small groups for learning centers and small-group instructions
(b) Classroom to lunch, to the playground, or to elective classes
(c) Finishing reading at the end of one period and getting ready for math the next period
(d) Emergency situations such as fire drills

Successful transitions are achieved by using proactive strategies. Early in the year, the teacher pinpoints the transition periods in the day and anticipates possible behavior problems, such as students habitually returning late from lunch. After identifying possible problems with the environment or the schedule, the teacher plans proactive strategies to minimize or eliminate those problems. Proactive planning also gives the teacher the advantage of being prepared, addressing behaviors before they become problems, and incorporating strategies into the classroom management plan right away. Transition plans can be developed for each type of transition and the expected behaviors for each situation taught directly to the students.

Technology can be helpful with classroom management. You can use technology to keep grade books, seating charts, behavior charts, progress monitoring data, and many other items. Using technology can save the teacher tremendous time and energy in keeping record keeping and other things under control, freeing up time for the teacher to improve and provide instruction.

Skill 15.2   **Apply knowledge of strategies and techniques for arranging and modifying the learning environment (e.g., materials, equipment, spatial arrangements, daily routines, transitions) to facilitate development, interaction, and learning according to students' needs.**

Learning styles refer to the ways in which individuals learn best. Physical settings, instructional arrangements, materials available, techniques, and individual preferences are all factors in the teacher's choice of instructional strategies and materials. Information about the student's preference can be done through a direct interview or a Likert-style checklist where the student rates his preferences.

Physical Environment (Spatial Arrangements)
The physical setting of the classroom contributes a great deal toward the propensity for students to learn. An adequate, well-built, and well-equipped classroom will invite students to learn. This has been called "invitational learning." Among the important factors to consider in the physical setting of the classroom are the following:

a) Adequate physical space
b) Repair status
c) Lighting adequacy
d) Adequate entry/exit access (including handicap accessibility)
e) Ventilation/climate control
f) Coloration

A classroom must have adequate physical space so students can conduct themselves comfortably. Some students are distracted by windows, pencil sharpeners, doors, etc. Some students prefer the front, middle, or back rows.

The teacher has the responsibility to report any items of classroom disrepair to maintenance staff. Broken windows, falling plaster, exposed sharp surfaces, leaks in ceiling or walls, and other items of disrepair present hazards to students.

Another factor which must be considered is adequate lighting. Report any inadequacies in classroom illumination. Florescent lights placed at acute angles often burn out faster. A healthy supply of spare tubes is a sound investment.

Local fire and safety codes dictate entry and exit standards. In addition, all corridors and classrooms should be wheelchair accessible for students and others who use them. Older schools may not have this accessibility.

Another consideration is adequate ventilation and climate control. Some classrooms in some states use air conditioning extensively. Sometimes it is so cold as to be considered a distraction. Specialty classes such as science require specialized hoods for ventilation. Physical Education classes have the added responsibility for shower areas and specialized environments that must be heated such as pool or athletic training rooms.

Classrooms with warmer subdued colors contribute to students' concentration on task items. Neutral hues for coloration of walls, ceiling, and carpet or tile are generally used in classrooms so distraction due to classroom coloration may be minimized.

In the modern classroom, there is a great deal of furniture, equipment, supplies, appliances, and learning aids to help the teacher teach and students learn. The classroom should be provided with furnishings that fit the purpose of the classroom. The kindergarten classroom may have a reading center, a playhouse, a puzzle table, student work desks/tables, a sandbox, and any other relevant learning/interest areas.

Whatever the arrangement of furniture and equipment may be the teacher must provide for adequate traffic flow. Rows of desks must have adequate space between them for students to move and for the teacher to circulate. All areas must be open to line-of-sight supervision by the teacher.

In all cases, proper care must be taken to ensure student safety. Furniture and equipment should be situated safely at all times. No equipment, materials, boxes, etc. should be placed where there is danger of falling over. Doors must have entry and exit accessibility at all times.

Noise level should also be considered as part of the physical environment. Students vary in the degree of quiet that they need and the amount of background noise or talking that they can tolerate without getting distracted or frustrated. So a teacher must maintain an environment that is conducive to the learning of each child.

The major emergency responses include two categories for student movement: tornado warning response; and building evacuation, which includes most other emergencies (fire, bomb threat, etc.). For tornadoes, the prescribed response is to evacuate all students and personnel to the first floor of multi-story buildings, and to place students along walls away from windows. All persons, including the teacher, should then crouch on the floor and cover their heads with their hands. These are standard procedures for severe weather, particularly tornadoes.

Most other emergency situations require evacuation of the school building. Teachers should be thoroughly familiar with evacuation routes established for each classroom in which they teach. Teachers should accompany and supervise students throughout the evacuation procedure, and check to see that all students under their supervision are accounted for. Teachers should then continue to supervise students until the building may be reoccupied (upon proper school or community authority), or until other procedures are followed for students to officially leave the school area and cease to be the supervisory responsibility of the school. Elementary students evacuated to another school can wear nametags and parents or guardians should sign them out at a central location.

Instructional Arrangements
Some students work well in large groups; others prefer small groups or one-to-one instruction with the teacher, aide or volunteer. Instructional arrangements also involve peer-tutoring situations with the student as tutor or tutee. The teacher also needs to consider how well the student works independently with seatwork.

The physical set up of your classroom is exceedingly important to support the effective development of all your children. (Of course your room must "coordinate" with the other classrooms in what ever school you are currently working or hope to work in—so if the "home decoration" below piece won't fly, copy the room layout and style of a veteran teacher on your floor who has a parallel grade and skip the rest of this, except to review it for a possible constructed response question.)

Understanding Our Role and Goals

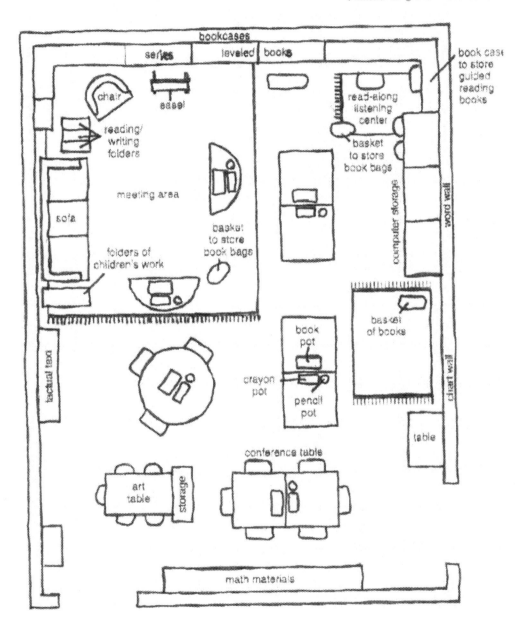

The homey look of the classroom belies its deliberate design as a space where children can experience, practice, share and learn. Some teachers have done away with the large desk and use smaller tables instead. Sharon Taberski advocates for young children K-3 adjusting the height of the table legs so the children can use the tables as writing spaces and sit on the floor. Sharon gives each of her children a personal 12"x 9"x 2" tray on which they place their home possessions, books, homework, folder, etc. This is kept in a small storage unit near the coat closet during the day.

Children put their completed homework in a wire basket and notes from parents or the office in a second wire basket.

Supplies such as pencils, markers, crayons, scissors, and erasers are not brought from home, but rather available for all in the class from "community "pots at the center of each of the children's tables.

All the children's reading, writing, and individual math folders are stored together in plastic bins in the meeting area. Every child has an individual book bag which is kept in one of two large wicker baskets set in different areas of the room.

This storing of materials away from children decreases their "fiddling with " their belongings during class, makes the room look much neater, and frees the children to focus on their learning experiences, rather than where their belongings are at any given time of day.

As you can see on the accompanying diagram the 10'x10' meeting area is the center of classroom learning. This is where the whole class is gathered at the beginning of the reading and the writing workshop and for share sessions. It is also the demonstration and modeling center for both the teacher and for children.

In a high school or middle school classroom, you should also consider trying to make the classroom homey to the students. Putting desks together in small groups will encourage cooperative learning and help the students to form relationships with each other. Many of the other materials ideas mentioned above work with students of any age.

Finding strategies to help students transition between activities can be sometimes difficult. The more engaged the students are with the activities provided; the less likely there will be difficulties, except when it is time to end an activity. There are novel ways (whistles, bells, playing a song, etc.) to let the students know it's time to wrap up an activity. It is usually helpful to provide the students with some warning prior to ending an activity (you have three more minutes before we must stop). Using timers in the classroom is a great strategy for keeping both you and the students on task.

Skill 15.3 **Apply knowledge of theories of individual and group motivation and behavior, and methods for monitoring and analyzing changes in behavior and performance across settings, curricular areas, and activities.**

Lesson Plan Collaboration

According to Walther-Thomas et al (2000), "Collaboration for Inclusive Education," ongoing professional development that provides teachers with opportunities to create effective instructional practice is vital and necessary, "A comprehensive approach to professional development is perhaps the most critical dimension of sustained support for successful program implementation." The inclusive approach incorporates learning programs that include all stakeholders in defining and developing high quality programs for students. Figure 1 below shows how an integrated approach of stakeholders can provide the optimal learning opportunity for all students.

Figure 1-Integrated Approach to Learning

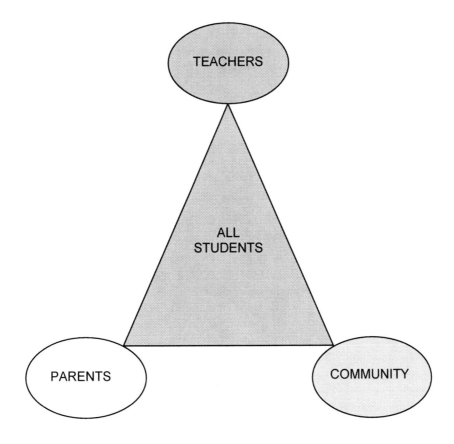

In the integrated approach to learning, teachers, parents, and community support become the integral apexes to student learning. The focus and central core of the school community is triangular as a representation of how effective collaboration can work in creating success for student learners. The goal of student learning and achievement now become the heart of the school community. The direction of teacher professional development in constructing effective instruction is clearly articulated in a greater understanding of facilitating learning strategies that develop skills and education equity for students.

Teachers need diversity in their instructional toolkits, which can provide students with clear instruction, mentoring, inquiry, challenge, performance-based assessment, and journal reflections on their learning processes. For teachers, having a collaborative approach to instruction fosters for students a deeper appreciation of learning, subject matter and knowledge acquisition. Implementing a consistent approach to learning from all stakeholders will create equitable educational opportunities for all learners.

Research has shown that educators who collaborate become more diversified and effective in implementation of curriculum and assessment of effective instructional practices. The ability to gain additional insight into how students learn and modalities of differing learning styles can increase a teacher's capacity to develop proactive instruction methods. Teachers who team teach or have daily networking opportunities can create a portfolio of curriculum articulation and inclusion for students.

People in business are always encouraged to network in order to further their careers. The same can be said for teaching. If English teachers get together and discuss what is going on in their classrooms, those discussions make the "whole" much stronger than the parts. Even if there are not formal opportunities for such networking, it's wise for schools or even individual teachers to develop them and seek them out.

In general terms, motivation is the student finding a way to meet their needs. The cycle looks something like this:

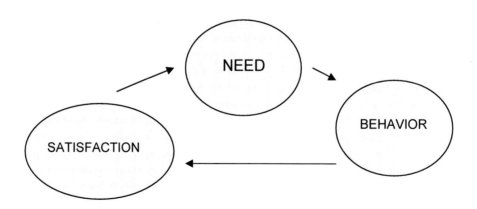

The needs referred to in this diagram have been classified many different ways by different theorists. Maslow used five categories in a hierarchical nature to describe the needs. They are (from lowest to highest):

1. Physiological
2. Safety
3. Belongingness
4. Esteem
5. Self-actualization

Alderfer developed his own theory known as ERG. He classified needs in three ways.

1. Growth Needs
2. Relatedness Needs
3. Existence Needs

Cognitive Evaluation Theory talks about motivation as being intrinsic (from within themselves) or extrinsic (from the outside).

Skinner was most famous for the operant conditioning theory. He described four types of conditions:

- Positive Reinforcement (get a reward)
- Negative Reinforcement (something taken away)
- Extinction (do nothing to eliminate behavior)
- Punishment

Skinner also explored various schedules for delivering motivators and rewards.

- Fixed Interval Schedule (every day say time)
- Fixed Ratio Schedule (after every ___ number of responses)
- Variable Interval Schedule (random times with no set pattern)
- Variable Ratio Schedule (number of response varies with no set pattern)

See also skill 15.1

Skill 15.4 **Demonstrate knowledge of ways to identify expectations for student behavior in various settings and to select specific management techniques for individuals with disabilities.**

Setting behavioral expectations across settings can provide a challenge to educators. The first step is to have an accurate description and baseline of the inappropriate behavior. Typically, this is completed through a series of classroom observations. Data from at least three different observations should be used to obtain an accurate baseline of the inappropriate behavior.

Once the baseline is determined, the educator must then work with other professional to determine an adequate goal for reducing the behavior. Realistic and attainable goals should be set. If calling out was the behavior you wanted to reduce, and the child is calling out 100 times a day, it would be unrealistic to expect that child to completely extinguish that behavior immediately. It might be more appropriate to have them reduce it by half first, then work on the other half.

Appropriate expectations will come from the school and class rules as defined by the teacher. Additionally, it is sometimes necessary to consider tolerance levels of all parties involved. A child who moves from teacher to teacher throughout the day may not understand that different teachers may have different tolerance levels of specific behaviors. It is important as the special educator to find some common ground so that the student receives a common behavioral goal across all settings.

Selecting the strategy to use with the student will rely on your understanding of the student's needs, triggers and available strategies within the classrooms and building. See skill 15.3 for more clarification on student's levels of needs.

Finding the specific strategy which will work for a student may require several different attempts. It can be helpful to provide the students with a menu of possible motivators to use at the beginning to find incentives they may be interested in receiving. Sometimes a more 'grab bag' approach may be a great motivator for the student. In this approach the student has no idea what may be in the hidden bag which he will earn. The surprising nature can be of great enticement to the children.

At older grades, free homework passes, are sometimes the most motivating things available. The idea that they are 'getting out' of some work is of great incentive and will sometimes work.

There will always be students who are challenging and require many different attempts to find something which works. The key is perseverance and to keep trying. Sometimes, a motivator will work for a short period of time, and then another will have to be put in place. Alternating motivators as well as the frequency with which they are given can be a beneficial strategy.

Skill 15.5 **Demonstrate knowledge of ways to identify expectations for student behavior in various settings and to select specific management techniques for individuals with disabilities.**

Setting behavioral expectations across settings can provide a challenge to educators. The first step is to have an accurate description and baseline of the inappropriate behavior. Typically, this is completed through a series of classroom observations. Data from at least three different observations should be used to obtain an accurate baseline of the inappropriate behavior.

Once the baseline is determined, the educator must then work with other professional to determine an adequate goal for reducing the behavior. Realistic and attainable goals should be set. If calling out was the behavior you wanted to reduce, and the child is calling out 100 times a day, it would be unrealistic to expect that child to completely extinguish that behavior immediately. It might be more appropriate to have them reduce it by half first, then work on the other half.

Appropriate expectations will come from the school and class rules as defined by the teacher. Additionally, it is sometimes necessary to consider tolerance levels of all parties involved. A child who moves from teacher to teacher throughout the day may not understand that different teachers may have different tolerance levels of specific behaviors. It is important as the special educator to find some common ground so that the student receives a common behavioral goal across all settings.

Selecting the strategy to use with the student will rely on your understanding of the student's needs, triggers and available strategies within the classrooms and building. See skill 15.3 for more clarification on student's levels of needs.

Finding the specific strategy which will work for a student may require several different attempts. It can be helpful to provide the students with a menu of possible motivators to use at the beginning to find incentives they may be interested in receiving. Sometimes a more 'grab bag' approach may be a great motivator for the student. In this approach the student has no idea what may be in the hidden bag which he will earn. The surprising nature can be of great enticement to the children.

At older grades, free homework passes, are sometimes the most motivating things available. The idea that they are 'getting out' of some work is of great incentive and will sometimes work.

There will always be students who are challenging and require many different attempts to find something which works. The key is perseverance and to keep trying. Sometimes, a motivator will work for a short period of time, and then another will have to be put in place. Alternating motivators as well as the frequency with which they are given can be a beneficial strategy.

Remember a motivator is found to be effective when it provides the desired response (a decrease in the inappropriate behavior). Regular data and observations should be used to ensure the motivators are having the desired effect.

See also Skill 15.1 and 15.3

Skill 15.6   Apply knowledge of methods for identifying, using, and evaluating a hierarchy of appropriate reinforcers and evaluating their effectiveness for individuals with disabilities.

See Skill 15.4

Skill 15.7   Apply knowledge of correct uses of transfers (e.g., floor to sitting, sitting to floor, chair to chair) and procedures for handling and positioning and of methods for managing specialized health care needs at school (e.g., gastrostomies, ventilator-assisted breathing, blood glucose testing).

Transitioning children from the floor to chairs and all positions in between require specialized training and procedures which will vary for each child. Speaking to the appropriate therapist or medical personal and receiving training is imperative to ensure the safety of both yourself and the child.

Skill 15.8   Demonstrate knowledge of scientifically valid procedures for helping individuals achieve bowel and bladder control.

Strategies for encouraging/helping individuals to achieve bowel and bladder control include scheduling, remolding/restructuring the environment, select assistive devices and/or methods towards independence. This all must be done while insuring that the child's privacy is respected.

One of the most important components of achieving bladder and bowel control is a recognition of the times voiding is occurring. When these times are recognized and a regular schedule to meet those times is implemented. The probability of accidents lessens. However, not all bladder and bowel needs can be scheduled. The goal here is to get an understanding that this is how you feel around the time you go to the bathroom, and this is what you should do when you have that feeling. Should the timing component be achieved it is likely that the person will recognize their needs to use the bathroom at other times than those scheduled.

At times a student may be enrolled in your class who has a catheter and can take care of his/her needs. The student must be given the opportunities to use the health office and/or a private bathroom stall, or a time when the other students are not using the bathroom to allow their privacy to be respected. Therapists who work in with children with this disability will share with you daily routines and health habits that will lessen/ eliminate possible odors.

It is also possible that the bathroom environment may need to be adapted to meet the needs of a student. Tactile stimulation and odors may interfere with a student's ability to toilet and need to be adjusted accordingly. The toilet seat should allow the student to feel physically secure, enabling his/her feet to rest on the floor which will aid in defecation. Students with smaller bodies may need reducer rings to improve their support when using the toilet.

Commodes can be used for students who are to big for training potties. These can be purchased by families and schools with a variety of adaptation devices.

COMPETENCY 16.0   UNDERSTAND THE DEVELOPMENT AND IMPLEMENTATION OF BEHAVIOR INTERVENTIONS FOR STUDENTS WITH DISABILITIES.

Skill 16.1   Apply knowledge of principles for developing, implementing, and evaluating the effects of positive behavior intervention techniques and individual behavior intervention plans for individuals with disabilities.

A Functional Behavior Assessment (FBA) is a method of gathering information. The information that is collected is utilized to assess why problem behaviors occur. The data will also help pinpoint things to do that will help alleviate the behaviors. The data from a functional behavioral assessment is used to create a positive behavioral intervention plan.

The Individuals with Disabilities Education Act (IDEA) specifically calls for a functional behavior assessment when a child with a disability has their present placement modified for disciplinary reasons. IDEA does not elaborate on how an FBA should be conducted as the procedures may vary dependent on the specific child. Even so, there are several specific elements that should be a part of any functional behavior assessment.

The first step is to identify the particular behavior that must be modified. If the child has numerous problem behaviors then it is important to assess which behaviors are the primary one's that should be addressed. This should be narrowed down to one or two primary behaviors. The primary behavior is then described so that everyone is clear as to what the behaviors consist of. The most typical order of procedures is as follows:

Identify and come to an agreement about the behaviors that need to be modified. Find out where the behaviors are most likely to happen and where they are not likely to happen. Identify what may trigger the behavior to occur.

The team will ask these types of questions: What is unique about the surroundings where behaviors are not an issue? What is different in the locations where the problem conduct occurs? Could they be linked to how the child and teacher get along? Does the amount of other students or the work a child is requested to do trigger the difficulty? Could the time of day or a child's frame of mind affect the behaviors? Was there a bus problem or an argument in the hallway? Are the behaviors likely to happen in a precise set of conditions or a specific location? What events seem to encourage the difficult behaviors?

Assemble data on the child's performance from as many resources as feasible. Develop a hypothesis about why difficult behaviors transpire (the function of the behaviors). A hypothesis is an educated deduction, based on data. It helps foretell in which location and for what reason problem behaviors are most likely to take place, and in which location and for what reason they are least likely to take place. Single out other behaviors that can be taught that will fulfill the same purpose for the child.

Test the hypothesis. The team develops and utilizes positive behavioral interventions that are written into the child's IEP or behavior intervention plan. Assess the success of the interventions. Modify or fine-tune as required.

If children have behaviors that place them or others at risk, they may require a crisis intervention plan. Crisis interventions should be developed before they are required. The team should determine what behaviors are crises and what they (and the child) will do in a crisis. By having a plan that guides actions, teachers can assist children through difficult emotional circumstances.

Essential Elements of Behavior Intervention Plan

A Behavior Intervention Plan is utilized to reinforce or teach positive behavior skills. It is also known as a behavior support plan or a positive intervention plan. The child's team normally develops the Behavior Intervention Plan. The essential elements of a behavior intervention plan are as follows:

- Skills training to increase the likelihood of appropriate behavior
- Modifications that will be made in classrooms or other
- Environments to decrease or remove problem
- Behaviors
- Strategies to take the place of problem behaviors and institute
- Appropriate behaviors that serve the same function for the child
- Support mechanisms for the child to utilize the most appropriate
- Behaviors

The IEP team determines whether the school discipline procedures need to be modified for a child, or whether the penalties need to be different from those written into the policy. This decision should be based on an assessment and a review of the records, including the discipline records or any Manifestation Determination review(s) that have been concluded by the school. A child's IEP or behavior intervention plan should concentrate on teaching skills. Sometimes school discipline policies are not successful in rectifying problem behaviors. That is, the child does not learn what the school staff intended through the use of punishments such as suspension. The child may learn instead that problem behaviors are useful in meeting a need, such as being noticed by peers. When this is true; it is difficult to defend punishment, by itself, as effective in changing problem behaviors. One of the most useful questions parents can ask when they have concerns about the discipline recommendations for their child is "Where are the data that support the recommendations?" Special education decisions are based on data. If school staff wants to use a specific discipline procedure, they should check for data that support the use of the procedure.

While educational literature and studies may suggest best practices in fostering appropriate classroom behavior, teachers must rely on their assessment skills including observation and data collection to help them identify the most effective and constructive interventions for their students. Using data they collect through permanent product, observational and anecdotal recording, and teachers can document individual and group behaviors and preempt or redirect behavior what might be of concern. Because data collection, by definition, requires tracking information regularly over time, patterns, trends and anomalies are easier to identify and evaluate than through undocumented impressions of behavior.

Teachers may collect information on an individual student, either to establish a baseline or to document areas of interest. For example, it may seem that Susan is constantly kicking the back of her classmate's chair during class, but data collection on Susan's kicking behavior may reveal many more or many fewer such kicks, or that it happens only when Susan has missed breakfast, etc. Data collection that centers on the group may reveal that her classmates don't seem to notice her kicking, or it may show that her kicking, if left unchecked, precipitates disruptive behaviors in others throughout the class period. Teachers can use information revealed through such data analysis to inform their intervention choices.

Before selecting behavioral interventions, teachers should first evaluate the environment and culture in their classrooms. Research conducted by the Northwest Regional Educational Library (Cotton, 1990) agrees that prevention of inappropriate behavior in classrooms is far preferable to remediation, but further suggests that certain baseline practices should be exercised in effective classrooms from the *first day of school*, including:

- Providing a functional and organized learning environment and well organized instruction;
- Presenting clear rules and routines and supporting students in adhering to them;
- Making plain consequences for inappropriate behavior;
- Ensuring consistent and timely enforcement of those rules; and
- Fostering a sense of personal responsibility in students, and engendering a culture of shared responsibility for classroom management.

Once those fundamental supports are in place, teachers can examine data for clues about adjustments and tools that may help foster appropriate behavior. They then can implement those changes one at a time or in well considered clusters, keeping in mind that the effects of their interventions should be documented through continued data collection.

So based on the data he'd recorded, Susan's teacher might decide to try adjusting the position of Susan's chair to make it less likely that her swinging leg will hit other students' chairs, *and* to assure that Susan ate breakfast or had access to a snack during morning recess. He might help Susan become more aware of respecting the personal space of other students. He might engage the class in a discussion about things that distract them from their schoolwork and ways classmates can help one another concentrate, which might include keeping feet near one's own desk. Whatever his choices, the teacher's proactive adjustments and interventions will likely be best informed by his analysis of the data collected on Susan and her classmates.

See Skills 6.2 and 8.1 for further information

Skill 16.2   Apply knowledge of principles for selecting target behaviors to be changed and conducting a functional assessment of the target behavior.

See Skills 16.1, 6.2 and 8.1 for further information

Skill 16.3 **Demonstrate knowledge of strategies for managing a range of behavior problems, decreasing self-abusive behaviors and promoting conflict resolution and strategies for crisis prevention and crisis intervention.**

Self-Injurious Behavior. One area of maladaptive behavior that teachers find in schools is self-injurious behavior. Students exhibiting this in some way harm themselves. The types of behaviors these students demonstrate vary greatly. They can include: banging their head, using an eraser to rub away skin, cutting themselves, picking at scabs or skin until it bleeds.

Eating Disorders. Sometimes student's maladaptive behavior manifests itself in an eating disorder. The two most common include: anorexia and bulimia. Students exhibiting eating disorders generally binge and purge food or refrain from eating totally. Students may begin exercising to extreme and people will notice significant weight loss.

Reducing these behaviors should follow the same strategies as described earlier for reducing any inappropriate behavior, however, it may be necessary and critical to involve a counselor of some sort to help in providing alternative activities the student can complete rather than harming themselves.

In schools today, students sometimes have difficulty relating to each other and working through troubling situations. In some cases, it is necessary for professionals such as the Guidance Counselor or school psychologist may need to be involved and work with specific students. However, research has found that when peers work with each other instead of having to work with adults, a much better result is achieved. From this, peer mediation was born. Peer mediation involves using specially trained students to work with the two students having the problem. There is a specific set of procedures and questions those trained use to guide the troubled students to develop a workable plan where they are better able to address the underlying difficulties.

All schools, across the country, are now required to have in place a specific procedure and set of steps to follow in the event of a crisis. The level and detail of the plans needs to be very specific, depending on the circumstances. Crisis's can vary in level and intensity. Small specific crisis might involve students unable to control themselves to a student who unfortunately has taken her own life. The steps that occur within a district are laid out to provide the necessary level of support to all those members of faculty, staff and students. More involved crises would involve something as the school shootings, which have become a regrettable part of our society today.

There is specific behavioral intervention training available to help prevent and deescalate behavior before it reaches crisis levels. Crisis Prevention Training (CPT) provides the teachers with specific strategies to help resolve situations before they become out of control.

Skill16.4 **Apply knowledge of appropriate, nonaversive, least intrusive management procedures that can effectively address spontaneous behavioral problems.**

Sometimes behavioral issues will arise unexpectedly. As the teacher, you need to have at your disposal strategies for handling these in a positive manner. For the most part, these behavioral issues will be minor and require little time to address if handled properly.

It is important to use nonaversive and less intrusive procedures than you would for behavior which is ongoing and severe. The teacher should also keep in mind the needs of the student exhibiting the behavior.

When addressing the behavior specifically, it should be done in a private nonembarrassing way. This shows respect to the student and allows you to address things in a more personal manner. This might involve a private discussion or some other private method of communication (a look, a touch on the shoulder, etc).

Keeping in mind the severity of the behavior with the manner in which you address it. It is important to maintain your own professionalism and to not overreact to the situation. Staying calm and factual will help to keep things on an even keel and may prevent the situation from escalading.

Behavior support plans should only be implemented for ongoing, uncontrollable behavior. The majority of behavior should be dealt with individually as it arises. Using a good set of classroom rules with natural consequences the students will be able to tell you the consequence for the behavior they displayed, which helps provide structure and continuity for the students.

Some additional strategies which are helpful with dealing with minor misbehavior in the classroom:

- Private discussion with the student
- Natural consequences following your class/school rules
- Loss of privilege
- Make eye contact with the student
- Touch the student on the shoulder to indicate your disapproval
- Class meetings to involve all students in solving the problem
- Creating class rules (have students help create) which are posted
- Creating a discipline plan (lists consequences clearly) you share with the students
- Individual behavior contracts
- Praise those not displaying inappropriate behaviors
- Planned ignoring
- Reward the students showing appropriate behavior with a fun activity

Skill 16.5 **Apply knowledge of appropriate ways to collaborate with other educators and parents in the use of specific academic or behavior management strategies and counseling techniques.**

As a specialist of any kind within a school building, it is imperative that collaboration among all staff be of top priority. It is not enough to simply service the students who are assigned through whatever means the district or building uses. Current educational trends place collaboration at a high priority.

In some cases special educators are becoming coaches and then become responsible for working closely with regular educators to increase the skills of the students across the building. This collaborative model has the specialist working in the classroom beside the teacher in a team teaching model. At times, lessons may be modeled to demonstrate new or innovative ideas or different ways to structure lessons. Still other times, the two professionals would work together to provide instruction to groups of students.

This coaching model also provides out of the classroom time where professional development activities may occur. These may take the form of study groups, individual discussion sessions, or workshop offerings for different strategies. For this to be a successful implementation, it is important for all parties to realize this is a learning session for everyone and one party is not evaluating another.

Another less formal collaboration model simply involves regular meetings where children and their needs are discussed. These meetings may be formal or informal. Usually they revolve around the assessment data gathered on the students, but may not. As the data and needs of the students are reviewed, the teachers present will discuss items indicating various needs. This allows for the most appropriate professional development to occur.

As it is directly related to an immediate need for the teacher with his current students, the skills learned are more likely to be implemented. In an informal setting, anyone with knowledge can share his or her ideas, suggestions, strategies or skills. It is in this format that all parties feel less threatened and comfortable sharing.

As the special educator, it is vital to collaborate with other special educators as much as possible. Today's use of technology and the availability of email can make this a much less cumbersome task. Collaboration is a vital part of growth for all teachers and should not be seen as a negative. It should instead be viewed as a team; a team of professionals working together to ensure that all students receive the most appropriate educational experience possible.

Special educators need to also be responsible for bringing parents into the collaborative process as they are a part of the IEP team responsible for writing and implementing all of the goals and objectives. Keeping parents and other teachers involved and up-to-date with the strategies being utilized will make for a smoother school to home transition daily.

Skill 16.6   Demonstrate knowledge of the relationship between communicative intent and problem behavior.

The communicative intent of the student is the information that child is trying to tell others by the manner in which he is acting. It can also refer to what other students understand about each other from their behavior.

It is important to formulate a hypothesis as to the communicative intent of the behavior exhibited by the student. This is typically completed during the FBA process described earlier in this document.

This hypothesis generally needs to be the best guess of the professionals involved, as the student himself is rarely able to articulate their communicative intent. However, it can be very important to determine. If the intent can be clearly defined, the team can provide the student with other more acceptable ways in which to convey the information and thus limit or eliminate the problematic behavior.

See skills See Skills 16.1, 16.2, 6.2 and 8.1 for further information

COMPETENCY 17.0   UNDERSTAND PRINCIPLES FOR SELECTING, CREATING, AND USING SPECIALIZED MATERIALS, EQUIPMENT, AND ASSISTIVE TECHNOLOGY FOR INDIVIDUALS WITH DISABILITIES.

Skill 17.1   Apply knowledge of the guidelines involved in the selection and use of augmentative or alternative communication devices and systems (i.e., sign language, electronic devices, picture and symbol systems, language boards) for use with students with disabilities.

Determination of Student Need for Assistive Technology Often the special educator will identify the need for consultation or testing in an area that a student is having difficulty. Testing or other professional evaluation may result in the trial or ongoing use of some form of assistive technology as listed on the student's IEP.

Development of Student Skill Using Specific Assistive Technology Students who have been identified as needing assistive technology require training in the use of the equipment. Sometimes a therapist or consultant will "push in" to the classroom providing training for the student in the classroom setting. Other times the student will practice using the assistive technology in a separate setting until a level of experience/expertise is reached. Then the assistive technology may be used in the special education or inclusion classroom.

Communication of Expected Skill Level in Classroom As students begin to use assistive technology in the classroom, the desired use (Including activity, location, and time) should be outlined for the special educator so that misunderstanding does not result in a student misusing or under using the technology. The student, then, will have a level of accountability and be functioning to the best of his abilities.

Training of School Personnel on Use of Assistive Technology Although special educators are often trained in using a variety of assistive devices, advances in technology make it necessary for professionals to participate in ongoing training for new or unfamiliar equipment. This training may be conducted by a knowledgeable therapist or consultant in the school district, or school personnel may need to attend a workshop off campus.

Evaluation of Student Independent Management of Assistive Technology in Various Settings On going evaluation of the student's use of the equipment is vital. This may be monitored through observation by the therapist or consultant, anecdotal records of the special educator, or some type of checklist. Often an IEP goal will address how the use and evaluation of the student's performance with the equipment will be implemented.

Skill 17.2 **Apply knowledge of sources for and uses of basic adaptive equipment and assistive technology, when applicable, to create, arrange, and maintain a positive environment that facilitates learning and interaction.**

ASSISTIVE DEVICES

Sensory Impairments

The use of electronic devices is nothing new to persons with vision and hearing impairments. For many years, people with sensory impairments have utilized various kinds of technologies to help them learn and function in society (Smith & Luckasson, 1992).

Other technology users who have, and continue to benefit from modern scientific advances, are those with physical and health impairments, and speech/communication disorders. Though the assistive devices are presented in categories, overlap occurs. For example, communication boards can be used to facilitate sound and communication, physical conditions, and when in raised symbols, can facilitate visually impaired persons. Computers and television screens can be adapted to assist persons with visual, auditory, physical, and speech /communication problems.

Visual Impairment

Visual Aids. For those with visual disorders, the Laser Cane and Sonicguide are two examples of electronic devices that have been in use for some time. These devices operate on the principle that people can learn to locate objects by hearing their echoes. For instance, the Laser Cane emits three beams of infrared light (one up, one down, and one straight ahead) that are converted into sound when they strike objects in the path of the person. The Sonicguide functions as an ultrasonic aid that helps youngsters born blind to gain an awareness of their environment and objects in it. The device is worn on the head, emits ultrasound, and converts reflections from objects into audible sounds.

A newly developed machine, the Personal Companion, can respond to human voice and answer with synthesized voice. It can look up someone's telephone number from an internal directory and dial the telephone. Even though it cannot write a check, it can balance someone's checkbook. The Personal Companion can "read" aloud sections from a morning newspaper delivered through telecommunications over telephone lines. This machine can maintain a daily appointment book, and turn on and off appliances such as radio or lights.

Advances in computer technology are providing access to printed information for many people with visual impairments. Book will soon be available on computer disks, allowing for a variety of outputs: voice, enlarge print, Braille.

Organizations such as the Visually Impaired and Blind User Group (VIBUG) of the Boston Computer Society are exchanging information to expand computer literacy among persons with visual impairments (Smith & Luckasson, 1992). Personal computers with special printers can transform print to Braille. By attaching a specially designed Braille printer to a computer, standard text can be converted into Braille, allowing teachers to produce copies of handouts, worksheets, tests, maps, charts, and other class materials in Braille.

Closed-circuit television (CCTV) can be used to enlarge the print found in printed texts and books. By using a small television camera with a zoom lens and a sliding reading stand upon which the printed materials are placed, the greatly enlarged printed material can be viewed on a television monitor. All types of printed materials can be enlarged, such as magazines, textbooks, and photocopied handouts.

Computers with special word processing programs can produce large print displays that enable persons to adjust the size of the print with their visual capabilities. Not only can different size print be selected for individual students on the viewing monitor, but hard copy printouts can be printed in different sizes for individual uses.

Audio Aids. Talking books have been available through the Library of Congress since 1934, using specially designed record players and tape cassette machines developed by the American Printing House for the Blind. Regional resource and materials centers disseminate these records, tapes, and machines. Audiotape versions of many classic books and current best-sellers are available in most bookstores.

Newly devised systems that allow printed materials to be synthesized into speech are available. They can be purchased at a much lesser cost and with higher quality sound than older devices such as the Kurzwell Reader. One of these newer systems uses a small sensor attached to a computer. When the sensor is moved along a line of type, information is passed to the computer, which in turn translates the print to speech. The person listening can select how fast they want the speech to be delivered (rate), the pitch, and the gender of the voice/sound the computer generates. This enables students with visual impairments to use the same books and materials as their regular classmates. They do not have to wait for orders to be prepared or mailed to them.

For those who listen to television, but cannot see what is happening, new technology is being piloted at the present time which adds a sound track. By using the added sound track available in stereo televisions, descriptive videos tell the listener the nonverbal messages others see on the screen.

Hearing Impairments

Visual Aids. Telecommunications and alerting devices are two types of assistive devices that use sight and touch. Captions are like subtitles that appear at the bottom of a television screen that can be read. Open captions appear on the screen for all viewers to see (e.g., foreign films translations), and have been available for some time. Closed captions are relatively new, and are somewhat expensive. In this system, captions can be seen on the screen, only if a decoder is accessible.

The Telecommunication Device for the Deaf (TDD) enables persons who have hearing impairments to make and receive telephone calls. A teletypewriter connected to the telephone prints out a voice message. The teletypewriter can also print out messages, but the receiver must have a teletypewriter as well in order to do this. A TDD can be used in a relay system, where the operator places the call on a voice line and reads the typed message to the non-TDD user. A full conversation can be made using a relay system (Smith & Luckasson, 1992).

DeafNet and Disabilities Forum are computer networks that provide electronic mail for persons with hearing impairments. These network systems function like other kinds of electronic mail where individuals or groups can subscribe to a communication system that transfers printed messages to subscribers. Electronic mail enables individuals and groups with common interests to communicate by using computers and information sent by telephone lines.

Audio Aids. Hearing aids and other equipment that help people make better use of their residual hearing are referred to as assistive listening devices (ALDs). For those with hearing impairments, the hearing aid is the most commonly used electronic device. Other types of ALDs help individuals with hearing impairments use their residual hearing.

Hearing aids differ in size, cost, and efficiency. Types range from wearable hearing aids to group auditory training units that can be used by several children at the same time. Wearable hearing aids can be inserted into the external auditory canal, built into glasses, and worn behind glasses, behind the ear, and on clothing.

FM (frequency-modulated) transmission deices (auditory trainers) are used in some classrooms by teachers and students. To use an auditory trainer, the teacher speaks into a microphone, and the sound is received directly by each student's receiver or hearing aid. This system reduces background noise, allows teachers to move freely around the room, and helps students benefit more from lectures.

The audio loop is an ALD that directs sound from its source directly to the listener's ear through a specially equipped hearing aid or earphone. Sound travels through a wire connection or by radio waves. Audio loops can be built into the walls of a classroom or some smaller area like a conference room.

Physical and Health Impairments

Technology has helped individuals with physical and health impairments to gain access to and control of the environment around them, communicate with others, and take advantage of health care. There are high-tech devices such as computers, but also low-tech devices like built-up spoons and crutches. Computers, spell checkers, and automated language boards provide means for communication to occur.

Mobility has been assisted by use of lightweight or electric specialized wheelchairs. These include motorized chairs, computerized chairs, chairs in which it is possible to rise, wilderness sports chairs, and racing chairs (Smith & Luckasson, 1992). Electronic switches allow persons with only partial movement (e.g., head, neck, fingers, toes) to be more mobile. Even driving a car is possible.

Mobility is also enhanced by use of artificial limbs, personalized equipped vans, and electrical walking machines. Myoelectric (or bionic) limbs contain a sensor that picks up electric signals transmitted from the person's brain through the limb. Robotic arms can manipulate objects by at least three directional movements: extension/retraction, swinging/rotating, and elevation/depression. Manipulator robots can assist by dialing a telephone, turning book pages, and drinking from a cup.

Speech/Communication

A communication board is a flat surface on which words, pictures, or both can be placed. The student is encouraged to point to the symbols of what he or she wants to communicate. Simple boards can be made from magazine or newspaper pictures. Others can be written on to display messages. More sophisticated boards incorporate an attachment that synthesizes a "voice." Communication books function like a board and assist communication.

Media Equipment
Many types of media equipment are available for use in the classroom. Multidimensional teaching approaches are possible with machines that provide instruction through various sensory modality channels. Individual receptive strengths can be matched with equipment directing learning through visual, auditory, haptic, or multidimensional input channels.

The <u>CD Player</u> is particularly of benefit to students who learn best by auditory input. Both frequently accompany commercial instructional programs (e.g., reading kits, programmed workbooks) and can be operated by students trained to do so. Both can accommodate earphones or headsets for single or group listening opportunities.

CD players offer the additional benefit of being lightweight for transporting relatively inexpensive, and adaptable for recording information or responses by teachers or students. Teacher recorded CDs offer the opportunity for students to read along with or follow story sequences with accompanying pictures, listen to stories for pleasure, practice spelling words, and learn to follow instructions. They can also be used to answer comprehension questions, discriminate auditory sounds, perform word study exercises, and in general, maintain and motivate student interest.

Media such as <u>VCRs. DVDs, and Television</u> provide unlimited opportunities for visual and auditory input. Equipment of this type offer the capability of presenting instructional content to individuals or groups of students in a format that readers and nonreaders alike can understand. Special effects (e.g., flashbacks, fades, close-ups, quick and slow pans) can be obtained by use of videocassettes. Selected pauses and review of material are easily achieved by means of filmstrips and videocassettes.

CCTV, a special television programs, and VHS and DVDs are often used to supplement and to enhance instructional material already introduced. On occasion, instructional material is introduced by these means. Reinforcement may also be delivered through the showing of entertaining visual material.

Dependent on your schools policies, students may be allowed to go to a media center and view a video for pleasure. Another alternative is to show a part of a selected video and ask students to hypothesize what preceded the viewed portion, or what followed the action they saw. Students can be asked to write a narrative for a film which they have only seen in silence. A videocassette dealing with a social problem can be stopped before the solutions are offered; students may offer their own solutions. A videocassette portraying a dramatic story can be ended prematurely. Students are directed to write endings and act them out.

The <u>Overhead Projector (OVH)</u> is an easy-to-use and maintain visual communication device. A bright lamp source transmits light through the translucent material to a screen close to the machine. Transparencies can be purchased commercially or made from clear photocopies of materials.

Computers and Software

PCs and Macs are valuable teaching tools. Software programs and adaptations enable learners with disabilities (i.e., physical, cognitive, and sensory) to profit from instruction in the classroom which they might not be able to receive otherwise. For example, tutorial programs simulate the teaching function of presentations, questions, and feedback. By this means, children are provided learning exercises on an appropriate level of difficulty, and in an interesting manner. Other programs can be used which allow drill and practice (with correct answers shown) over previously learned material. Games are effective as motivators and reinforcers. In addition, use of computer software provides a way of testing students that is more appealing to many than a written test.

Teachers can acquire the skills needed to program the computer so that tasks provided by software correspond with students' individualized education programs. Teaching students to program will develop problem-solving and discovery skills, and also foster reasoning comprehension skills.

Computer Assisted Instruction

Stages of Learning

Suggestions about selecting and using software were given by Male (1994). First, make sure there is a curriculum correspondence between what students are working on at their desks and what they do at the computers. This should follow what he calls stages of learning. Then, make certain the students proceed through the five stages of learning. Software should be selected with these stages in mind:

1. Acquisition.   Introduction of a new skill.
2. Proficiency.   Practice under supervision to achieve accuracy and speed.
3. Maintenance.   Continued practice without further instruction.
4. Generalization.   Application of the new skills in new settings and situations.
5. Adaptation.   Modifications of the task to meet new needs and demands of varying situations.

Learning Environment

Computers are used to provide a safe, stimulating learning environment for many youth. The computer does not evaluate or offer subjective opinions about the student's work. It merely provides feedback about the correctness or incorrectness of each answer in a series. The computer is like an effective teacher by the way in which it:

1. Provides immediate attention and feedback.
2. Individualizes to the particular skill level.
3. Allows students to work at their own pace.
4. Makes corrections quickly.
5. Produces a professional looking product.
6. Keeps accurate records on correct and error rates.
7. Ignores inappropriate behavior.
8. Focuses on the particular response.
9. Is nonjudgmental. (Smith & Luckasson, 1992)

Computers are useful in helping to teach traditional academic subjects like math, reading, spelling, geography, and science. Effective teachers allow for drill and practice on the computer, monitor student progress, and reinforce appropriately. When students have mastered a particular level, these teachers help them to progress to another level. Reasoning and problem-solving are other skill areas which teachers have discovered can be taught using computers.

One type of newly developed computer software is the program Hypertext. It enables further explanation of textbook material. This is accessed by a simple press of a key while the student is working on the learning material. For example, by a single press of a key, students can access definitions of difficult vocabulary words, reworded complicated text, additional detailed maps, and further information about concepts being introduced in the text. By using this, teachers can help students by creating individualized lessons. Students with learning disabilities can benefit especially.

Computer games can enhance learning skills and provide a highly desired reinforcement opportunity. When played alone, the games serve as leisure activities for the individual. When played with classmates, the games can help develop interpersonal relationships. This is particularly applicable to youngsters with behavioral disorders, and learning and intellectual disabilities, as well as those without any identified disability.

Word Processors

Word processors are used to assist students with written composition. Students with learning disabilities often have difficulty organizing thoughts. Problems with writing are compounded by handwriting difficulties. Many teachers report that use of a word processor has enabled them to motivate students to write. Most are less resistant to rewriting texts when they can do it on a word processing program that erases and replaces text quickly. Printed texts in typewritten form are easier to read. Spelling checkers, built into many word processing programs, assist those who may not be able to spell words correctly. Another option is a thesaurus which provided synonyms and in so doing helps to build vocabulary. The overall quantity and quality of written work improves when word processing programs are used in conjunction with computers.

When working on the word processor, each student needs a storage disc, preferably a jump drive. so that his work can be evaluated over time and stored electronically. Having a portfolio of printouts enables students to take work home to show parents.

Process Approach

The process approach to writing is encouraged, especially when using a word processor (Male, 1994). These stages include planning/prewriting, drafting, revising/editing, and sharing/publication. Progressing through these stages is particularly helpful to developing writers.

The planning stage is characterized by written outlines, brainstorming, clustering or mind mapping, and lists of ideas, themes, or key words. These activities are ideally suited to a classroom that has a large television monitor or a computer projection device that will allow the teacher to list, group, revise, and expand ideas as students share them. Printed copies of what was generated by the group can be distributed at the end of the class session.

In the **drafting stage**, individuals can do draft work at a computer by themselves, or they can collaborate as a group on the work. Some students may choose to use pencil and paper to do initial draft work, or they may want to dictate stories to the teacher or another student who writes it down for them.

Students share their work during the **revising/editing stage**. Students read their stories aloud to a partner, a small group, or the whole class. Classmates are instructed to ask questions and give feedback that will help the writer make revisions to his work. After the story has been completed as far as content, attention is given to mechanics and writing conventions.

The **sharing/publication stage** enables students to experience being authors responding to an audience. Students are encouraged to share their work by reading it aloud and in printed form. They can do this with or without graphics or illustrations.

The **sharing/publication stage** enables students to experience being authors responding to an audience. Students are encouraged to share their work by reading it aloud and in printed form. They can do this with or without graphics or illustrations.

There are numerous sources for obtaining basic adaptive equipment and assistive technology in Illinois. You should always start with your building administrator and district personnel. They will know of what is locally available. Another source to consider includes any support professionals working with you and the student in need (occupational therapist, physical therapist, speech pathologist, etc.).

Another excellent source is the Illinois Assistive Technology Program. They can provide you with information, assistance, loans of devices, demonstrate how devices work, low interest loans, on-site workshops and many other services. They can be reached at:

1 West Old State Capitol Plaza
Suite 100
Springfield, IL 62701
(271) 522-7985
http://www.iltech.org/index.asp

See Skill 15.2 for classroom arrangement suggestions

Skill 17.3   Demonstrate knowledge of approaches to adapting environments to meet the specific learning and developmental needs of individuals.

The ultimate goal of all environments and instruction is to have students transfer their learning and begin to make generalizations.

Transfer of Learning
Transfer of learning occurs when experience with one task influences performance on another task. Positive transfer occurs when the required responses are about the same and the stimuli are similar, such as moving from baseball, handball, to racquetball, or field hockey to soccer. Negative transfer occurs when the stimuli remain similar, but the required responses change, such as shifting from soccer to football, tennis to racquetball, and boxing to sports karate. Instructional procedures should stress the similar features between the activities and the dimensions that are transferable. Specific information should emphasize when stimuli in the old and new situations are the same as or similar, and when responses used in the old situation apply to the new.

To facilitate learning, instructional objectives should be arranged in order according to their patterns of similarity. Objectives involving similar responses should be closely sequenced; thus, the possibility for positive transfer is stressed. Likewise, learning objectives that involve different responses should be programmed within instructional procedures in the most appropriate way possible. For example, students should have little difficulty transferring handwriting instruction to writing in other areas; however, there might be some negative transfer when moving from manuscript to cursive writing. By using transitional methods and focusing upon the similarities between manuscript and cursive writing, negative transfer can be reduced.

Generalization
Generalization is the occurrence of a learned behavior in the presence of a stimulus other than the one that produced the initial response (e.g. novel stimulus). It is the expansion of a student's performance beyond conditions initially anticipated. Students must be able to generalize what is learned to other settings (e.g. reading to math, word problems; resource room to regular classroom).

Generalization training is a procedure in which a behavior is reinforced in each of al series of situations until it generalizes to other members of the same stimulus class. Stimulus generalization occurs when responses, which have been reinforced in the presence of a specific stimulus, the discriminative stimulus (SD), occur in the presence of related stimuli (e.g. bathrooms labeled women, ladies, dames). In fact, the more similar the stimuli, the more likely it is that stimulus generalization will occur. This concept applies to intertask similarity, in that the more one task resembles another; the greater the probability the student will be able to master it. For example, if Johnny has learned the initial consonant sounds of "b" and "d," and he has been taught to read the word "dad," it is likely that when he is shown the word "bad," he will be able to pronounce this formerly unknown word upon presentation. (Refer to Skills 2 in this section).

Generalization may be enhanced by the following:

1. Use many examples in teaching to deepen application of learned skills.
2. Use consistency in initial teaching situations, and later introduce variety in format, procedure, and use of examples.
3. Have the same information presented by different teachers, in different settings, and under varying conditions.
4. Include a continuous reinforcement schedule at first, later changing to delayed, and intermittent schedules as instruction progresses.
5. Teach students to record instances of generalization and to reward themselves at that time.
6. Associate naturally occurring stimuli when possible.

It is the responsibility of the special educator to ensure the appropriate modifications and adaptations have been made to ensure that transfer and generalization occur.

See various other skills throughout this text for ideas on making modifications and adaptations.

Skill 17.4 Demonstrate knowledge of strategies for integrating assistive and instructional technology to facilitate students' individual needs (e.g., eating, dressing, grooming, bowel and bladder control, independent living, mobility).

Many students with disabilities require assistive technologies in order to be successful within the regular curriculum or environment. As with any form of technology, assistive device are constantly being changed and updated, therefore it is important to stay as up-to-date as possible. It is also essential to search out within your district, who to contact to provide help in finding the necessary technologies to allow student success.

When considering adding technology for students with special needs it is important to conduct a multi-disciplinary evaluation to ensure the specific student strengths are utilized in providing appropriate technology. This might include people such as: an Assistive Technology Specialist, an Occupational Therapist, a Physical Therapist, a Speech Pathologist, or other designated people with specific training.

Consider the needs of the student and those working with the device. For instance, an augmentative communication device is only as good as it is easy for the student to use and access and for the person in school and at home to program. If the device is so complicated to program with phrases or to make changes to when necessary, it will be less than ideal in the school setting.

Also, always start with the least restrictive device. If, for example a student requires information to be visually presented at the same time it is orally presented, an overhead/ smart board might be your best bet. There are also other students in the classroom who will benefit from this type of modification as well, and the student with special needs will not have to be isolated or pointed out to his classmates.

If any form of assistive technology, even simply typing assignments instead of handwriting them, is required it is essential to include it in the child's IEP. While many teachers and parents will follow the special educator's word and implement what is best for the child with no difficulties, it can provide future teachers with beneficial information. While the IEP is legally binding and therefore mandates the users to implement what is written in it, it is also a wealth of information for people who are working with that child.

Teachers in future years can look back and see what worked in previous years, or if the student moves, the new personnel will understand what specific devices and needs the student has and better service those needs from the beginning. In the end, the IEP is an important document where all information pertaining to the student, including assistive technology needs should be conveyed.

As you are thinking of assistive technology devices, remember there is a very broad range of possible items including those which help with:

- **Eating** – Such as spoons and forks with thicker handles, plates and bowls with suction cups to prevent them from moving, etc.
- **Dressing** – Such as adaptive equipment to help with closures like snaps and buttons, shoe horns with extended handles, etc.
- **Grooming** – Such as brushes with thicker handles, electric razors, etc.
- Bowel and bladder control - Such as Depends, adaptive seating to access the toilets, etc.
- **Independent living** – Such as jar openers, sticks with a grasper at the end to reach higher things, etc.
- **Mobility** – Such as wheelchairs, scooters, etc.

Skill 17.5 Demonstrate knowledge of assistive technologies that facilitate the acquisition of academic knowledge and/or the completion of academic tasks.

There are too many different types of assistive technologies available to include a comprehensive and complete list. Here are some general academic issues for which there is assistive technology available to increase academic knowledge and the completion of assigned academic tasks.

- Adaptive keyboards
- Books and publications recorded on CD/tapes
- Math (or other subject area) worksheets online or in an electronic format
- Database software
- Graphic organizers and outlining
- Information/data managers
- Optical character recognition
- Personal iPods and FM Listening Systems
- Portable word processors
- Proofreading programs
- Speech recognition programs
- Speech synthesizers/Screen Readers
- Calculators which speak
- Talking spell-checkers and electronic dictionaries
- Variable speed tape recorders
- Word processors with word prediction programs

See also Skills 17, 17.2 and 17.4

SUBAREA V.   WORKING IN A COLLABORATIVE
                                          EARNING COMMUNITY

COMPETENCY 18.0   UNDERSTAND THE ROLE OF THE SPECIAL
                  EDUCATION TEACHER IN THE COLLABORATIVE
                  LEARNING COMMUNITY.

Skill 18.1   Demonstrate knowledge of the collaborative and consultative
              roles of special educators working with parents, general
              educators, other professionals, and paraprofessionals to
              integrate individuals with disabilities into general education
              and community settings.

See Skills 10.2, 10.4, 15.3, 18.3, and 18.4

Skill 18.2   Apply knowledge of strategies for collaborating with others
              and creating situations in which that collaboration will
              enhance student learning.

Effective collaboration among teachers and other professionals allows them to
feel supported by other teachers in their mission to better meet the needs of their
students. When collaboration is done successfully, teachers feel comfortable
admitting what they do not know without feeling embarrassed as it is assumed
that everyone is faced with challenges and has knowledge to bring to the
situation. When teachers are able to share challenges and difficulties, as well as
successful teaching strategies, teachers can effectively evaluate teaching
practices in school and provide a variety of resources for teachers to use in their
classroom.

In collaborating, teachers can discuss effective techniques in dealing with
transition time so that what is done effectively in one class can be shared and
tried in other settings.

When teachers are sharing ideas for successful teaching practices with one
another, they will have a wider base of knowledge to bring to the classroom. A
variety of pedagogical approaches will be available, and the teacher will have a
resource to rely on when they need additional input or advice in effectively
teaching students. Additionally, if a teacher is part of a community of sharing, that
teacher is more likely to value the benefits of the support and knowledge that is
created in such a community. The teacher who places importance on
collaboration, sharing, and peer-oriented learning will attempt to create a similar
community in their class. A community of sharing within the classroom permits
students to feel safe sharing ideas, challenges, and achievements with peers.

Depending on a student's disability and the school setting, Special Education Teachers need to work with speech pathologists, school psychologists, occupational therapists, social workers, general education teachers, and community workers to plan the most optimal education program for each student. Special Education Teachers who work in inclusive settings or who co-teach or team-teach with general education teachers must spend enough time to sufficiently plan, develop, and put into practice an educational situation that is stimulating and suitable for all the students in the class.

Parents are also a significant part of the collaboration team. They are the experts on their child. Both parents and teachers have a lot to give in the educational planning for students with disabilities. If they work together, they can be a strong team.

Collaboration and working together requires time, which is in short supply in the educational setting. Educators never have enough time to do everything that they want to do. In order to work effectively, Special Education Teachers need the time to work and plan with parents and other professionals.

Effective communication strategies are required when dealing with families with student's with disabilities. The communication strategies should be flexible and respond to the individual needs of the families.

Teachers traditionally communicate their educational philosophies to families through parent workshops or newsletters. These methods have their drawbacks; however as in many cases workshops may have low attendance as parents may have problems with work schedules or with getting outside help to take care of a student with disability.

Newsletters may be thrown away or not read thoroughly; and those that are only written in English distance parents for whom English is not their first language.

Family school partnerships are developed when families are encouraged to spend more time in the classroom and when they are offered more information about their child's education. When families are in the classroom they have a chance to observe teacher student interactions, ask the teacher questions, and give feedback on curriculum or development. They also have an opportunity to meet other families.

As the structure of families in today's societies continue to change, teachers may need to try different family outreach strategies that target the new family structure as what was done in the past may not be effective.

Teachers need to have a range of strategies for contacting parents such as using the telephone, email, letters, newsletters, classroom bulletin boards, and parent teacher conferences.

Teachers also need to be familiar with the student's home culture and have an appreciation for diversity by planning lessons and activities that are inclusive of the multi-cultural classroom. Through effective communication, teachers can involve parents as leaders and decision makers in the school. As more students with disabilities are included in the general education curriculum, both special and regular educators will need training that focuses on effectively interacting with parents of children with disabilities to involve them as equal partners in the educational planning and decision-making process for their child.

UNDERSTAND WHAT CONSTITUTES EFFECTIVE COMMUNICATION SKILLS BETWEEN THE SENDER AND THE RECEIVER

Communication occurs when one person sends a message and gets a response from another person. In fact, whenever two people can see or hear each other they are communicating. The receiver changes roles and becomes the sender, once the response is given. The communication process may break down if the receiver's interpretation differs from that of the sender.

Effective teaching depends on communication. By using good sending skills, the teacher has more assurance that she is getting her message across to her students. By being a model of a good listener, a teacher can help her students learn to listen and respond appropriately to others.

Attending Skills: The sender is the person who communicates the message; the receiver is the person who ultimately responds to the message.

Attending skills are used to receive a message. Some task-related attending skills that have been identified include: (1) looking at the teacher when information or instructions are being presented, (2) listening to assignment directions, (3) listening for answers to questions, (4) looking at the chalkboard, (5) listening to others speak when appropriate.

For some students, special techniques must be employed to gain and hold attention. For example, the teacher might first call the student by name when asking a question to assure attending by that individual, or she may ask the question before calling the name of a student to create greater interest. Selecting students at random to answer questions helps to keep them alert and listening. Being enthusiastic and keeping lessons short and interactive assists in maintaining the attention of those students who have shorter attention spans. Some students may be better able to focus their attention when environmental distraction are eliminated or at least reduced, and non-verbal signals can be used to draw students' attention to the task. Finally, arranging the classroom so that all students can see the teacher helps direct attention to the appropriate location.

Clarity of Expression

Unclear communication between the teacher and special needs students sometimes contributes to problems in academic and behavioral situations. In the learning environment, unclear communication can add to the student's confusion about certain processes or skills he is attempting to master.

There are many ways in which the teacher can improve the clarity of her communication. Giving clear, precise directions is one. Verbal directions can be simplified by using shorter sentences, familiar words, and relevant explanations. Asking a student to repeat directions or to demonstrate understanding of them by carrying out the instructions is an effective way of monitoring the clarity of expression. In addition, clarification can be achieved by the use of concrete objects, multidimensional teaching aids, and by modeling or demonstrating what should be done in a practice situation.

Finally, a teacher can clarify her communication by using a variety of vocal inflections. The use of intonation juncture can help make the message clearer, as can pauses at significant points in the communication. For example, verbal praise should be spoken with inflection that communicates sincerity. Pausing before starting key words, or stressing those that convey meanings, helps students learn concepts being taught.

Paraphrasing

Paraphrasing, that is, restating what the student says using one's own words, can improve communication between the teacher and that student. First, in restating what the students has communicated, the teacher is not judging the content - she is simply relating what she understands the message to be. If the message has been interpreted differently from the way intended, the student is asked to clarify. Clarification should continue until both parties are satisfied that the message has been understood.

The act of paraphrasing sends the message that the teacher is trying to better understand the student. Restating the student's message as fairly and accurately as possible assists the teacher in seeing things from the student's perspective.

Paraphrasing if often a simple restatement of what has been said. Lead-ins such as "Your position is..." or "it seems to you that..." are helpful in paraphrasing a student's messages. A student's statement, "I am not going to do my math today" might be paraphrased by the teacher as, "Did I understand you to say that you are not going to do your math today?" By mirroring what the student has just said, the teacher has telegraphed a caring attitude for that student and a desire to respond accurately to his message.

To paraphrase effectively a student's message, the teacher should:

(1)   Restate the student's message in her own words;
(2)   Preface her paraphrasing with such remarks as, "You feel..." or "I hear you say that..."
(3)   Avoid indicating any approval or disapproval of the student's statements.

Johnson (1978) states the following as a rule to remember when paraphrasing: "Before you can reply to a statement, restate what the sender says, feels, and means correctly and to the sender's satisfaction." (p.139)

Descriptive feedback is a factual, objective (i.e. unemotional) recounting of a behavioral situation or message sent by a student. Descriptive feedback has the same effect as paraphrasing, in that: (1) when responding to a student's statement, the teacher restates (i.e. paraphrases) what the student has said, or factually describes what she has seen, and (2) it allows the teacher to check her perceptions of the student and his message. A student may do or say something but because of the teacher's feelings or state of mind, the student's message or behavior might be totally misunderstood. The teacher's descriptive feedback, which Johnson (1972) refers to as "understanding," indicates that the teacher's intent is to respond only to ask the student whether his statement has been understood, how he feels about the problem, and how he perceives the problem. The intent of the teacher is to more clearly "understand" what the student is saying, feeling, or perceiving, in relation to a stated message or a behavioral event.

Evaluative feedback is verbalized perception by the teacher that judges, evaluates, approves, or disapproves of the statements made by the student. Evaluative feedback occurs when the student makes a statement and the teacher responds openly with "I think you're wrong," "That was a dumb thing to do," or "I agree with you entirely." The tendency to give evaluative responses is heightened in situations where feelings and emotions are deeply involved. The stronger the feelings, the more likely it is that two persons will each evaluate the other's statements solely from their own point of view.

Since evaluative feedback intones a judgmental approval or disapproval of the student's remark or behavior in most instances, it can be a major barrier to mutual understanding and effective communication. It is a necessary mechanism for providing feedback of a quantitative (and sometimes qualitative) instructional nature (e.g. test scores, homework results, classroom performance). In order to be effective, evaluative feedback must be offered in a factual, constructive manner. Descriptive feedback tends to reduce defensiveness and feelings of being threatened because it will most likely communicate that the teacher is interested in the student as a person, has an accurate understanding of the student and what he is saying, and encourages the students to elaborate and further discuss his problems.

To summarize, in the learning environment, as in all situations, effective communication depends upon good sending and receiving skills. Teaching and managing students involves good communication. By using clear, non-threatening feedback, the teacher can provide students with information that helps them to understand themselves better, at the same time providing a clearer understanding of each student on the teacher's part.

Skill 18.3 Demonstrate knowledge of the types and importance of information generally available from family, school officials, the legal system, and community service agencies.

The best resource a teacher has in reaching a student is having contact with his/her parents/guardians. Good teaching recognizes this fact and seeks to strengthen this bound through communication.

The first contact a teacher has with parents should be before the school year starts. While the teacher may be required to send a letter out stating the required supplies for the class, this does not count as an initial contact.

Parents are used to hearing that their child has done something bad/wrong when they receive a phone call from a teacher. Parents should be contacted whenever possible to give positive feedback. When you call John's mother and say, "John got an A on the test today," you have just encouraged her to maintain open communication lines with you. Try to give 3 positive calls for every negative call you must give.

Parent-Teacher Conferences are scheduled at regular intervals throughout the school year. These provide excellent opportunities to discuss their children's progress, what they are learning and how it may relate to your future plans for their academic growth. It is not unusual for the parent or teacher to ask for a conference outside of the scheduled Parent-Teacher Conference days. These meetings should be looked at as opportunities to provide assistance to that student's success.

Modern technology has opened 2 more venues for communicating with parents. School/ Classroom websites are written with the intent of sharing regularly with parents/guardians. Many teachers now post their plans for the marking period and provide extra-credit/homework from these websites. Email is now when of the major modes of communication in the world today. Most parents now have Email accounts and are more than willing to give you their email address to be kept appraised of their child's academic progress.

Special events also provide opportunities for parental contact. Poetry readings, science fairs, ice-cream socials, etc. are such events.

Role of the Family
The discovery at birth or initial diagnosis of a child's disabling condition(s) has a strong impact upon the family unit. Though reactions are unique to individuals, the first emotion generally felt by a parent of a child with disabilities is chock, followed by disbelief, guilt, rejection, shame, denial, and helplessness. As parents finally accept the realization of their child's condition, many report feelings of anxiety or fearfulness about their personal ability to care for and rear exceptional child. Many parents will doctor shop, hoping to find answers, while others will reject of deny information given them by health care professionals.

The presence of a child with a disability within the family unit creates changes and possible stresses that will need addressing. Many will feel parenting demands greatly in excess of a non-disabled child's requirements. "A child (with a disability) frequently needs more time, energy, attention, patience, and money than the child (without a disability), and frequently returns less success, achievement, parent pride-inducing behavior, privacy, feelings of security and well-being" (Paul, 1981, p.6).

The family as a microcosmic unit is a society plays a vital role in many ways. The family assumes a protective and nurturing function, is the primary unit for social control, and plays a major role in the transmission of cultural values and mores. This role is enacted concurrently with changes in our social system at large. Paradoxically, the parents were formerly viewed as the cause of their children's disability who is now depended upon to enact positive changes in their children's lives.

Siblings play an important role in fostering the social and emotional developments of a brother or sister with a disability. A wide range of feelings and reactions will evolve as siblings interact. Some experience guilt over being the normal child, and try to over compensate by being the successful, perfect child for their parents. Others react in a hostile, resentful manner toward the amount of time and care the disabled sibling receives, and frequently creates disruption as a way of obtaining parental attention.

The extended family, especially grandparents, can provide support and assistance to the nuclear family unit if they live within a manageable proximity, childcare services for an evening or a few days can provide a means of reprieve for heavily involved parents.

Parents as Advocates

Ironically, the possibility for establishing the partnership, which is now sought by educators with parents of children with disabilities, came about largely through the advocacy efforts of parents. The state compulsory education laws began in 1918 and were adopted across the nation with small variances in agricultural regions. However, due to the fact that these children did not fit in with the general school curriculum, most continued to be turned away at the schoolhouse door, leaving the custodial services at state or private institutions as the primary alternative placement site for parents.

Educational policies reflected the litigation and legislation of the times, which overwhelmingly sided with the educational system and not with the family. After all, the educational policies reflected the prevailing philosophies of the times, such as Social Darwinism (i.e. survival of the fittest). Thus, persons with disabilities were set apart from the rest of society - literally out of sight, out of mind. Those with severe disabilities were placed in institutions, and those with moderate disabilities were kept at home to do family or farm chores.

Following the two world wars, the realization that disabling conditions could be incurred by a member of any family came to the forefront. Several celebrity families allow stories to be published in national magazines about a family member with an identified disability, thus taking the entire plight of this family syndrome out of the closet. The 1950s brought about the founding of many parent and professional organization, and the movement continued into the next decade. Learning groups included the National Association of Parents and Friends of Mentally Retarded Children founded in 1950, later called the National Association for Retarded Children, and now named the National Association of Retarded Citizens; the International Parents Organization in 1957, as the parents' branch of the Alexander Graham Bell Association for Parents of the Deaf in 1965. The Epilepsy Foundation of America was founded in 1967. The International Council for Exceptional Children had been established by faculty and students at Columbia University as early as 1922, and the Council for Exceptional Children recognized small parent organizations in the late 1940s.

During the 1950s, Public Law 85-926 brought about support for the preparation of teachers to work with children with disabilities so that these children might receive educational services.

The 1960s was the first period in time during which parents received tangible support from the executive branch of the national government in 1960, the White House Conference on Children and Youth made the declaration that a child should only be separated from his family as a last resort. This gave vital support to parents' efforts toward securing a public education for their youngsters with disabilities.

Parent as Partners
Parent groups are a major component in assuring appropriate services for children with disabilities, co-equal with special education and community service agencies. Their role is individual and political advocacy, and socio-psychological support. Great advances in services for children with disabilities have been made through the efforts of parent advocacy groups, which have been formed to represent almost every type of disabling condition.

In addition to the family, there are many other places where information may be obtained which is pertinent to the education of the student. School officials will have a wealth of information to provide. Sometimes this may mean contacting previous year's teachers, the school psychologist/Guidance Counselor who worked previously with the student, or other appropriate personnel. The information gathered should provide a historical nature of what has been tried and worked in the past which is invaluable as a time saver to new staff working with that student.

There may be other officials outside of the school and family systems who may have some information which could be used by the teacher to incorporate into the IEP or BIP. Community services agencies, such as social services or mental health agencies could help with diagnostic and support arrangements. The legal system may have become involved and documents which could clarify issues or stressors in the child's life might need to be shared and reviewed.

It is necessary for the school based team to gather all information from all sources so informed decisions can be made in regards to a student's education.

Skill 18.4   Demonstrate knowledge of factors that promote effective communication and collaboration with individuals, parents, families, and school and community personnel in a culturally responsive program.

Teachers of exceptional students are expected to manage many roles and responsibilities, not only as concern their students, but also with respect to students' caregivers and other involved educational, medical, therapeutic and administrative professionals. Because the needs of exceptional students are by definition multidisciplinary, a teacher of exceptional children often serves as the hub of a many-pronged wheel, communicating, consulting and collaborating with the various stakeholders in a child's educational life. Managing these relationships effectively can be a challenge, but is central to successful work in exceptional education.

Students

Useful standards have been developed by the Council for Exceptional Children (2003) that outline best practices in communicating and relating to children and

their families. For example, CEC guidelines suggest that effective teachers:

- Offer students a safe and supportive learning environment, including clearly expressed and reasonable expectations for behavior;
- Create learning environments that encourage self-advocacy and developmentally appropriate independence; and
- Offer learning environments that promote active participation in independent or group activities.

Such an environment is an excellent foundation for building rapport and trust with students, and communicating a teacher's respect for and expectation that they take a measure of responsibility for their educational development. Ideally, mutual trust and respect will afford teachers opportunities to learn of and engage students' ideas, preferences and abilities.

Parents and Families

Families know students better than almost anyone, and are a valuable resource for teachers of exceptional students. Often, an insight or observation from a family member, or his or her reinforcement of school standards or activities, mean the difference between success and frustration in a teacher's work with children. Suggestions for relationship building and collaboration with parents and families include:

- Using laypersons' terms when communicating with families, and make the communication available in the language of the home;
- Searching out and engage family members' knowledge and skills in providing services, educational and therapeutic, to student;

- Exploring and discussing the concerns of families and helping them find tactics for addressing those concerns;
- Planning collaborative meetings with children and their families, and assisting them to become active contributors to their educational team
- Ensuring that communications with and about families is confidential and conducted with respect for their privacy;
- Offering parents accurate and professionally presented information about the pedagogical and therapeutic work being done with their child;
- Keeping parents abreast of their rights, of the kinds of practices that might violate them, and of available recourse if needed; and
- Acknowledging and respect cultural differences.

Paraprofessionals and General Education Teachers

Paraprofessionals and general education teachers are also important collaborators with teachers of exceptional students. Although they may have daily exposure to exceptional students, they may not have the theoretical or experience to assure their effective interaction with such students. They do bring valuable perspective to and opportunities for breadth and variety in, an exceptional child's educational experience. General education teachers also offer curriculum and subject matter expertise and a high level of professional support, while paraprofessionals may provide insights born of their particular familiarity with individual students. CEC suggests that teachers can best collaborate with general education teachers and paraprofessionals by:

- Offering information about the characteristics and needs of children with exceptional learning needs
- Discussing and brainstorming ways to integrate children with exceptionalities into various settings within the school community
- Modeling best practices and instructional techniques and accommodations, and coaching others in their use
- Keeping communication about children with exceptional learning needs and their families confidential
- Consulting with these colleagues in the assessment of individuals with exceptional learning needs.
- Engaging them in group problem-solving and in developing, executing, and assessing collaborative activities.
- Offer support to paraprofessionals by observing their work with students, and offering feedback and suggestions

Related Service Providers and Administrators

Related service providers and administrators offer specialized skills and abilities that are critical to an exceptional education teacher's ability to advocate for his or her student and meet a school's legal obligations to the student and his or her family. Related service providers—like Speech, Occupational and Language Therapists, Psychologists, and Physicians—offer expertise and resources unparalleled in meeting a child's developmental needs. Administrators are often experts in the resources available at the school and local education agency levels, the culture and politics of a school system, and can be powerful partners in meeting the needs of exceptional education teachers and students.

A teacher's most effective approach to collaborating with these professional includes:

- Confirming mutual understanding of the accepted goals and objectives of the student with exceptional learning needs as documented in his or her IEP;
- Soliciting input about ways to support related service goals in classroom settings;
- Understanding the needs and motivations of each and acting in support whenever possible;
- Facilitating respectful and beneficial relationships between families and professionals; and regularly and accurately communicating observations and data about the child's progress or challenges.

All parents share some basic goals for their children. They want their children to grow up to be healthy, happy members of society who lead independent lives with productive employment. Parents of students with disabilities are no different, although the path that their children take may have additional turns and obstacles along the way.

Health Many children with disabilities have associated health problems or are at risk for health problems. Many also take medication(s) routinely for health or behavioral conditions.

Parents of students with disabilities are concerned with their children's long range health, the cost of health care (as children as later as adults), and the effects of medication on their child's behavior, health, and school work.

It is not uncommon for special education students to take some medication while at school. Providing the school with the needed medication may be a financial strain for the family. Just the fact that others will be aware of the child's health and medications can also be a parental concern.

Parents are often concerned because many of these students have difficulty identifying changes in their health and in communicating possible changes in medication reactions. IEPs often include objectives for the child to communicate changes in his health and effects of medication.

Happiness The quality of life for more severely disabled children is different than that of the general population. Even students with less severe physical conditions (for example, a learning disability) may have lower self-esteem because they feel "stupid" or "different" because they leave the inclusion classroom for some special education services. Students with disabilities often have difficulty making friends which can also impact happiness.

Parents of students with disabilities (as all parents) feel the emotional impact of the disability on their children. Parents are anxious to help their children feel good about themselves and fit in to the general population of their peers.

Social goals may be included on the IEP. Some students (particularly those on the autism spectrum) may have a time (per the IEP minutes) to meet with a speech and language pathologist to work on social language. Other students may meet regularly (again, per IEP minutes) with the social worker to discuss situations from the classroom or general school setting.

Independence Initially, parents of students with disabilities may be somewhat overprotective of their child. Soon after, however, parents begin to focus on ways to help their child function independently.

Young children with disabilities may be working on self-care types of independence such as dressing, feeding, and toilet use. Elementary students may be working on asking for assistance as needed, completing work, being prepared for class with materials (books, papers, etc.) High school students may be working on driving, future job skills, or preparation for post-secondary education.

Job Training IDEA 2004 addresses the need for students with a disability to be prepared for a job or post-secondary education in order to be independent, productive members of society.

Job training goals and objectives for the student with a disability may be vocational such as food service, mechanical, carpentry, etc. Job training goals for other students may include appropriate high school coursework to prepare for a college program.

Productivity Ultimately, the goal of parent and school is for the student to become a productive member of society who can support himself financially and live independently. This type of productivity happens when the student becomes an adult with a measure of good health, positive self-esteem and ability to interact positively with others, independent personal and work skills, and job training.

Particular Stages of Concern Parents of students with special needs deal with increased concerned at times when the child is going into a new stage of development or age. Some of these times include: when the child is first identified as having a disability, entrance into an early childhood special education program, kindergarten (when it is evident that the disability remains despite services received thus far), third grade (when the student is expected to use more skills independently), junior high school, and entrance into high school. Additional IEP goals and objectives may be warranted at these times as the student is expected to use a new set of skills or may be entering a new educational setting.

It should be noted that parents are often more concerned when a younger, non-disabled sibling surpasses the child with the disability in some skill (such as feeding or reading). Previously, the parents may not have fully been aware of what most children can do at a particular age.

Skill 18.5   Apply knowledge of the social, intellectual, political, and cultural influences on language use (e.g., jargon, second language).

In special education, there is more specialized jargon and abbreviations used than in numerous other fields of education. It is important to consider your audience and be sure to utilize clear language when communicating. Be sure to speak in clear understandable language and avoid assuming the party with which you are communicating understands the terminology you are using.

This is also important to consider when working with families and students for whom English is not the primary language. Although a translator may be present, it is still necessary to use common language as some of the terms may not exist in the native language in the same manner as is used in the American Educational System.

Here is a brief list of some of the abbreviations used commonly in special education and what they refer to:

- **ADD (ADHD)** – Attention Deficit Disorder (Attention Deficit with Hyperactivity Disorder)
- **APE** – Adaptive Physical Education
- **ARD** – Admission, Review and Dismissal Committee
- **ASL** – American Sign Language
- **AT** – Assistive Technology
- **AU** – Autism
- **AYP** – Annual Yearly Progress
- **BD** – Behavior Disorders
- **BIP** – Behavior Intervention Plan
- **CAPD** – Central Auditory Processing Disorder
- **CD** – Communication Disorder
- **CF** – Cystic Fibrosis
- **CM** – Case Manager
- **COTA** – Certified Occupational Therapy Assistant
- **CP** – Cerebral Palsy
- **CPS** – Child Protective Services
- **CST** – Child Study Team
- **D/B** – Deaf and Blind
- **DD** – Developmental Disorder
- **EC** – Early Childhood
- **ED** – Emotional Disorders
- **EI** – Early Intervention
- **ESD** – Extended School Day
- **ESY** – Extended School Year
- **FAPE** – Free Appropriate Public Education
- **FBA** – Functional Behavior Assessment
- **FERPA** – Family Educational Rights to Privacy Act
- **GT** – Gifted and Talented
- **HI** – Hearing Impaired
- **IA** – Instructional Assistant
- **IDEA** – Individuals with Disabilities Education Act
- **IEP** – Individualized Education Plan
- **IFSP** – Individual Family Service Plan
- **IQ** – Intelligent Quotient
- **LD** – Learning Disability
- **LEA** – Local Education Agency
- **LEP** – Limited English Proficient
- **LRE** – Least Restrictive Environment
- **LSW** – Licensed Social Worker
- **MA** – Medical Assistance

- **MBD** - Minimal Brain Damage
- **MD** – Multiple Disabilities
- **MD** – Muscular Dystrophy
- **MH** –Mental Health
- **OCD** – Obsessive-Compulsive Disorder
- **ODD** – Oppositional Defiant Disorder
- **OHI** – Other Health Impaired
- **OI** – Orthopedic Impairment
- **OSEP** – Office of Special Education
- **OSERS** – Office of Special Education and Rehabilitative Services
- **OT** – Occupational Therapist
- **PAC** – Parent Advisory Council
- **PDD** – Pervasive Developmental Disorder
- **PI** – Physically Impaired
- **PT** – Physical Therapy
- **SB** – Spina Bifida
- **SEA** – State Education Agency
- **SED** – Serious Emotionally Disturbed
- **TBI** – Traumatic Brain Injury
- **VI** – Visually Impaired

Skill 18.6 Demonstrate knowledge of collaborative skills and conflict-resolution strategies.

See Skills 15.1, 15.3, and 16.3

COMPETENCY 19.0 UNDERSTAND HOW TO ESTABLISH PARTNERSHIPS WITH OTHER MEMBERS OF THE SCHOOL COMMUNITY TO ENHANCE LEARNING OPPORTUNITIES FOR STUDENTS WITH DISABILITIES.

Skill 19.1 Apply knowledge of strategies for collaborating with classroom teachers (e.g., co-teaching, teaming, co-planning), para-educators, and other school personnel to integrate individuals with disabilities into various social and learning environments.

Sometimes it is necessary to include paraprofessionals in the instruction of students. This provides the students with more opportunity to work with an adult to improve their skills and continues to allow the teacher to direct the instruction.

It is necessary for the teacher to plan all lessons or activities for the paraprofessional to implement. As the paraprofessional is not a trained educator, the teacher is responsible for making sure the necessary curriculum objectives are included and that the activities planned. As the teacher, all responsibility for progression and skill growth is placed in your hands. The paraprofessional is responsible for implementing your plans and objectives.

Therefore, it is imperative that the teacher provides clear plans and activities and at the beginning takes the time necessary to train and ensure a complete understanding of what is to be completed. A little time of clear explanations at the beginning can provide misunderstandings at a later time.

The paraprofessional should understand clearly how and what the teacher wants implemented. In this way, it is important that the teacher writes lesson plans, which can be easily interpreted with no misunderstandings. Clear language should used and all necessary materials provided. Highlighting is a good strategy for indicating which parts of the lesson the paraprofessional is responsible for within one set of lesson plans.

Communication is probably the most important factor when working with a paraprofessional. Open dialogue can prevent miscommunications and provide valuable input and ideas as to how the student is progressing. Gathering data from another person working with the child can help to reaffirm ideas or thoughts as well as provide the next steps in the instructional process. Teaching the paraprofessional how to keep notes and documentation on students can help note progress.

As discussed it is important to work closely with any paraprofessionals involved in providing instruction or support to students. Occasionally, it is important to touch base with the paraprofessional to ensure the lesson plans asked to be implemented are being implemented as described.

This can be a sensitive area for both the teacher and paraprofessional. It is important to provide feedback without being punitive or seeming judgmental. With proper training and the open communication previously discussed, a great working relationship with give and take can be achieved. When providing feedback it can help to follow the following suggestions:

- Observe informally first – this can be achieved by working in the same room as when the instruction is being delivered and seems less threatening than a formal observation
- Provide the feedback in the form of additional instruction into the manner in which lessons should be delivered. In this way, there is no blame, it simply becomes a new lesson, not something someone did wrong
- Provide praise frequently
- Use open communication to ask the paraprofessional for their suggestions as well, indicating their opinions are valuable to you
- Provide professional training for paraprofessionals
- Schedule a regular meeting to discuss the students being worked with and keep it
- Listen carefully and make time for any questions the paraprofessional may have even if it interrupts your schedule
- Encourage leadership and decision making by the paraprofessional as their skills increase.

The paraprofessional may also accompany students into the regular education environment to ensure student success. Again as previously discussed, it is essential clear expectations are explained and discussed so the paraprofessional understands her responsibilities when in the classroom. The regular education teacher should be a part of discussing the responsibilities and role of the paraprofessional within his classroom.

See Skill 10.6 for information on co-teaching and teaming.

Skill 19.2 **Apply knowledge of considerations (e.g., privacy, confidentiality), approaches, and ethical practices for communicating with general educators, administrators, paraeducators, and other school personnel, as appropriate, about characteristics and needs of individuals with disabilities and the effects of disabilities on learning, and ways to use that knowledge to develop an effective learning climate within the school.**

One of the most important professional practices a teacher must maintain is student confidentiality. This extends far beyond paper records, and goes into the realm of oral discussions. Teachers are expected not to mention the names of students and often the specifics of their character in conversations with those who are not directly involved with them, inside and outside of school.

In the school environment, teacher record keeping comes in three main formats with specific confidentiality rules. All of the records stated below should be kept in a locked place within the classroom or an office within the school:

1) *Teacher's personal notes on a student* - When a teacher takes notes on a student's actions including behaviors and/or grade performance that are not intended to be placed in a school recorded format, such as a report card, the teacher may keep this information private and confidential to his/her own files. Teachers may elect to share this information or not.

2) *Teacher daily recorded grades and attendance of the student* - Teacher's grade books and attendance records are to be open to the parent/guardian of that child who wishes to check on their child. Only that child's information may be shared not that of others.

3) *Teacher recorded/notation on records that appear in the student cumulative file.* - there are specific rules regarding the sharing of the Cumulative Records of students.

   a) Cumulative files will follow a student that transfers within the school district, from school to school.
   b) All information placed in a cumulative file may be examined by a parent at any time it is requested. If a parent shows up to review their child's cumulative file the file should be shown as it is in its current state. (This includes IEPs.)
   c) When information from a cumulative file is requested by another person/entity outside of the parent/guardian the information may not be released without the express written consent of the parent/guardian. The parental consent must specify which records may be shared with the other party of interest.

d) A school which a student may intend to enroll may receive the student's educational record without parental consent. However, the school sending that information must make a reasonable attempt to notify the parent/guardian of the request. (FERPA)

Today's world is quickly becoming a digital environment. Teacher's now communicate often with Email and are keeping records in digital formats, often within a district mandated program. Teachers should keep in mind that Emails and other electronic formats can be forwarded and are as "indelible" as permanent ink and should maintain a professional decorum just as when they are writing their own records that will be seen outside of their personal notations.

The special educator is expected to demonstrate ethical practice in all areas of his teaching responsibilities. With regards to interaction with students, teaching and discipline practices should reflect practices that are respectful of the student as a person. Researched-based methods should be employed that will provide measurable outcomes.

The ethics of special education goes beyond methods to materials. With students of a variety of age and/or ability levels and often limited funding, appropriate materials can become difficult to obtain. If possible, students should be included in the head count for ordering general education materials. When alternative materials are needed, it is important to secure those through special education funding sources in the school. Teaching materials that are copyrighted may no be photocopied unless they are specifically intended for such use as printed on the book. The same is true for musical materials that have a copyright. If materials are intended for reproduction it will be stated.

Information technology brings a world of information to the special educator and student's classroom. Careful consideration should be given, however, to the validity of the information before it is incorporated into practice or curricular material. Reputable sources for education practices will have connection to recognized organizations for special educators such as the Council for Exceptional Children or to teacher training programs. Likewise, students should be guided in the finding and use of valid sites for research and learning. It is important to teach the philosophy that not everything on the internet is true.

Ethical practice in communication is an additional expectation of all educators but especially of those teaching students with disabilities. Confidentiality is crucial. Specific information regarding a student's disability and IEP (Individualized Education Program) should be discussed only with the team of professionals working with the student and his family. When an exchange of information is needed with another school district, physician, therapist, or other professional outside of the school district, it is necessary to get written permission from the student's parent. Often, forms for such are available from the school district.

Skill 19.3 **Apply knowledge of strategies for coordinating activities of related service personnel to maximize instructional time for individuals with disabilities and to ensure that related services are integrated into individuals' daily activities and schedule.**

See Skill 10.5

Skill 19.4 **Demonstrate knowledge of techniques and strategies for training, planning, and directing activities for and monitoring, evaluating, and providing feedback to paraeducators, volunteers, and peer tutors.**

Schools, particularly at the elementary level, have a wealth of adults who want to be an active part of the child's education. Parent volunteers and other adults want to come into the schools and are often times willing to help with a broad range of activities the teacher needs completed. These may include: copying, giving individual assessments, reading with children, tutoring, gathering and making materials, and many others.

Putting these adults to use in the classroom can be a tremendous benefit. However, it is important to guide and train both tutors and volunteers. Taking a few minutes at the onset can save time and effort later. This can be done on an individual basis or school wide tutoring training sessions can be offered.

It can be a time saving device to train all adults interested in providing tutoring services at one time. They can work in small groups to develop their skills, and as a specialist, your time is only taken once for the training. It is important to provide the materials for the tutors, to maximize their time with the students. This involves organization and a lot of fore thought before the actual tutoring begins. There are various resources available to obtain the materials for tutoring, but it is a time-consuming process the first year of set up.

Finding a communication method between the tutors and yourself is also important. One strategy that works well and is rather inexpensive involves a bagged book system. In this strategy, the book and activities to complete with the student are kept in a Zip-lock type storage bag with the child and tutor's name on it. Inside the bag, a communication notebook with some general questions can be left. The tutor writes the answers to the guided questions about the activity completed with the student. In this way, the teacher can review the answers as they are changing materials in the bag for the next tutoring session.

Overall, it is important to take the time and effort to be organized for volunteers and tutors before inviting them in to the classroom to maximize the use and benefits.

See skill 19.1 for paraeducators

Skill 19.5 **Demonstrate knowledge of roles and responsibilities of school-based medical and related service personnel in identifying, assessing, and providing services to individuals with disabilities.**

Some things will be the responsibility of the school-based medical and related service persons to determine. These have been previously discussed under previous skills about related services. See those skills for details.

COMPETENCY 20.0 UNDERSTAND HOW TO PROMOTE POSITIVE SCHOOL-HOME RELATIONSHIPS

Skill 20.1 **Demonstrate knowledge of typical concerns of families of individuals with disabilities, including families transitioning into and out of the special education system, and of appropriate strategies for planning and conducting collaborative conferences with families to address these concerns and to encourage and support families' active involvement in their children's programs and educational teams.**

Any transition in life can be overwhelming and difficult whether we are adults or children. For students with special needs, making transitions can be more than overwhelming. Specific tools and strategies need to be taught to students so they are better able to understand the issues facing them and then deal with them.

The coping skills for transitioning are similar in some respects to the same skills necessary to deal with life's stressors. One of the biggest factors that can help a student be ready to make the transition from school to work includes planning. Students that understand goal setting and building a plan that can be used to reach these goals, have a leg up on students who are not taught to look into the future. From a young age, students as young as elementary aged can be taught goal setting, it may begin with setting a goal to complete a project, but taking the students through this process several times throughout their school careers will encourage them to better be able to make generalize the process at transition time.

Furthermore, students need to understand how their voice works in the process. Being an advocate for them is a critical factor in finding a successful path. Self-advocacy requires communication skills to be well developed. Students need to use both oral and written means to express their individual hopes and dreams. Once the school personnel understand clearly the hopes and ambitions of the student, they can build a framework to help them come true.

This may by helping to provide additional course work or specific skill knowledge. It may be in providing opportunities for the students to participate in a work-study program where they can experience different work related experiences. Without the upfront knowledge of the expectations and future plans the student may have, it is difficult for the school staff to find appropriate contacts. Outside agencies may also be a critical part of the transitioning process and should be included in all meetings and discussions. The schools do not have to be the only participants in helping students manage transitions. When all parties work together they have a better opportunity to provide the smoothest school to work experience.

Skill 20.2 **Apply knowledge of strategies for collaborating with parents to integrate individuals with disabilities into various social and learning environments.**

Schools today must continually respond and interact with the parents and family of the students they service. These relationships are essential to building a firm academic basis upon which all future learning throughout life will be based. Family support encourages a life-long value to education and learning. It also provides support in areas of behavior and social skill development for the students involved. Additionally, there is a great body of research demonstrating the higher test scores, better emotional development and overall improved life of students for whom family is an active participant in the educational process. In the elementary grades having fathers come in and participate by reading to the class or eating lunch with their children can provide tremendous benefits.

As previously discussed, there are many different factors which can provide barriers to the learning in students. It is important schools understand these situations and develop appropriate strategies to provide support for the family and student.

A family in crisis (caused by economic difficulties, divorce, substance abuse, physical abuse, etc.) creates a negative environment which may profoundly impact all aspects of a student's life, and particularly his or her ability to function academically. The situation may require professional intervention. It is often the classroom teacher who will recognize a family in crisis situation and instigate an intervention by reporting on this to school or civil authorities.

This disruption in what we consider a normal childhood can make it difficult or impossible for a student to cope in the regular classroom environment. Professional assessment is most often necessary to determine the most effective means of meeting the child's needs, behaviorally, emotionally, physically and socially. There are many different places a classroom teacher can turn to find support to help a student and family who may be struggling. The teacher can turn to the Administrator, Guidance Counselor, School Psychologist, or other community agencies to begin to find support. All schools also have a pre-referral team of experts within the school system who are available to meet and discuss issues specific to a student and help support the classroom teacher develop strategies to provide the necessary support.

Administrators can pull this team of intervention specialists together who can meet regularly to address the needs of the students in the school setting. This team of specialists will usually include: special educators, reading specialists, literacy coaches, math coaches, Guidance Counselors etc.

Additionally, classroom teachers often deal with numerous outside of the school setting agencies, due to the needs of the students they serve. Becoming familiar with support services available to students and helping parents sort through the maze of paperwork usually required to receive these services, helps not only the student and family but in the end provides additional assistance to the school. It is important to keep a file of counseling agencies, local pediatricians, local psychologists, social services, and mental health services available. This becomes a place for the educator to turn when asked by parents. It is important, however, to simply report the names as possible contacts.

Some possible long term effects of situational problems which go unrecognized and unaltered or unresolved may include:

Impairment of cognitive development: A mind that is stressed by the child's need to cope with situations he or she can not fully comprehend, let-alone resolve, is unlikely to develop the capacity to think abstractly, synthesize and evaluate information and solve complex problems.

Restriction in the Affective Domain: Inability to concentrate, focus on classroom activities, the teachers instructions; lack of interest or participation in activities or discussions; inconsistent behavior; inability to express himself or herself coherently; inconsistent behavior.

Psychomotor Skills: Normal functioning within the physical domain can also be reduced through a reaction to emotional stress and/or intellectual bewilderment.

No one can predict the effects familial relationships will have on the school work of students. The same can be said for cultural issues left unresolved. It is also important to understand, the school system cannot solve all of the outside issues which may be affecting the learning of a student. There will always be some factors outside of the schools control. What is most important is to be empathetic, compassionate, and provide the most appropriate support available to educate the student. In some cases, school may be the most structured and safest place for a student, keeping this in mind when delivering instruction will not only make you a better teacher, but will ensure your students learn more information.

Skill 20.3   Demonstrate knowledge of family systems theory; variations in beliefs, traditions, values, family dynamics, and family structures across cultures; and the effects of the relationships among child, family, and schooling.

When considering the family as part of the educational process, it is imperative to consider multiple factors. Understanding how families work together, the dynamics which make up families, and the diversity within families we service in the school systems.

Family Systems Theory developed and popularized by Murray Bowen, MD uses the psychological and psychiatric information gained about human behavior to help people work through problems in their life. The focus differs from traditional psychological therapy in that Family Systems Theory works with people to think of their problems in broader terms as related to the entire family system, across multiple generations. It is a problem solving approach used to improve the relationships people have in their lives by shifting away from blaming others and into accepting the responsibility for their own actions. There are eight factors discussed in Family Systems Theory; they include:

- Triangles
- Differentiation of Self
- Nuclear Family Emotional System
- Multigenerational Transmission Process
- Emotional Cutoff
- Sibling Position
- Family Projection Process
- Societal Emotional Process

The mobile nature of society today provides a broader mixture of cultures around the country. Students moving from school to school may experience different curriculums and different school cultural factors. As educators expect the students to adapt, they must also remember that the schools themselves must also consider the student's individual cultural influences.

Cultural relationships, mores and values are a continual part of what we must consider when educating students. It is important to keep in mind that in certain cultures individual differences may be thought of very differently than perhaps the current school views them. Many cultures have different views on education and the implications of various factors which may affect schooling, such as disabilities.

Additionally, acculturation is not something that occurs overnight. It takes years for students to become acculturated. Students who move from a foreign country and do not speak English can take up to seven years to become proficient in English. This is not a disability, but in fact the natural progression of language acquisition. It can be similar for other aspects of culture. When considering students who are not succeeding in school, you must take into consideration these types of cultural factors. There are a number of acculturation surveys that can be used to help guide the teacher in examining the role of culture in the academic performance of the student.

Community agencies can often times help schools bridge these cultural gaps. Reaching out to families by including appropriate translators/translations, encouraging parents to share their heritage and traditions with the school and other students, and respecting that differences of what is acceptable do exist will help all involved parties. Beyond language, it is important to respect and provide accommodations for other cultural factors. Holidays may be significantly different for certain ethnicities. Another area may even include the food served in the cafeteria, if the culture requires that foods be Kosher or a vegetarian option may need to be offered.

As cultures place varying value on education or on the role of genders, different views may be taken of individuals with disabilities, appropriate education, career goals, and the individual's role in society. The special educator must first become familiar with the cultural representations of her students and the community in which she teaches. As she demonstrates respect for the individual student's culture, she will build the rapport necessary to work with the student, family, and community to prepare him for future, productive work, independence, and possible post-secondary education or training (IDEA 2004).

While society has "progressed" and many things are acceptable today than they were yesterday, having a disability still carries a stigma. Historically, people with disabilities have been ostracized from their communities. Up until the 1970s a large number of people with special needs were institutionalized at birth because the relatives either did not know what to do, they felt embarrassed to admit they had a child with a disability, or they gave into the cultural peer pressure to put their "problem" away. Sometimes this meant hiding a child's disability, which may even have meant locking a child in a room in the house. Perhaps the worst viewpoint society had expressed up to the 1970s and still prevails today is that the person with "special needs" is unable to contribute to society.

Today, American society has left the "must institutionalize" method for a "normalcy" concept. Houses in local communities have been purchased for the purpose of providing supervision and/or nursing care that allows for people with disabilities to have "normal" social living arrangements. Congress passed laws that have allowed those with disabilities to access public facilities. American society has widened doorways, added special bathrooms, etc. The regular education classroom teacher is now learning to accept and teach students with special needs. America's media today has provided education and frequent exposure of people with special needs. The concept of acceptance appears to be occurring for those with physically noticeable handicaps.

But the appearance of those with special needs in media such as television and movies generally are those who rise above their "label" as disabled, because of an extraordinary skill. Most people in the community are portrayed as accepting the "disabled" person when that special skill is noted. In addition, those who continue to express revulsion or prejudice towards the person with a disability often express remorse when the special skill is noted of peer pressure becomes too intense. This portrayal often ignores those who appear normal by appearance with learning and emotional disabilities, who often feel and suffer from the prejudices.

The most significant group any individual faces is their peers. Pressure to appear normal and not "needy" in any area is still intense from early childhood to adulthood. During teen years when young people are beginning to "express their individuality," the very appearance of walking into a Special Education classroom often brings feelings of inadequacy, and labeling by peers that the student is "special." Being considered normal is the desire of all individuals with disabilities regardless of the age or disability. People with disabilities today, as many years ago, still measure their successes by how their achievements mask/hide their disabilities.

The most difficult cultural/community outlook on those who are disabled comes in the adult work world where disabilities of persons can become highly evident often causing those with special needs difficulty in finding work and keeping their jobs. This is a particularly difficult place for those who have not learned to self advocate or accommodate for their area/s of special needs.

Skill 20.4   Apply knowledge of considerations (e.g., privacy, confidentiality), approaches, and ethical practices for providing parents/guardians/ surrogates with information about students with disabilities.

See Skill 21.5

Skill 20.5 **Demonstrate knowledge of effective strategies and practices to facilitate good working relationships with families (e.g., regular communication, trust, respect).**

See previous skills

COMPETENCY 21.0   UNDERSTAND HOW TO ENCOURAGE SCHOOL-COMMUNITY INTERACTIONS THAT ENHANCE LEARNING OPPORTUNITIES FOR STUDENTS WITH DISABILITIES.

Skill 21.1   Apply knowledge of strategies for collaborating with community members to integrate individuals with disabilities into various social and learning environments.

A consideration of IDEA 2004 is for inclusion of students with disabilities into activities and educational settings with their non-disabled peers. Furthermore, it specifies that they will become adults with productive employment and independent living skills to the fullest extent possible. To this end, training or post-secondary education will often be necessary and appropriate. The role of the special educator is to facilitate this transition into the community, and indeed, the transition begins when the student is of a very young age.

Social Environments in the Community

The special educator is an advocate for her students and her programs at school and in the community. The following are ways to promote awareness and subsequently influence opportunities for students with disabilities.

- The special educator may be asked to speak to various community groups that provide social opportunities for students.
- It is also not uncommon for special educators to serve on advisory boards.
- Community groups which may contact the special educator for the above involvement may include scouts, church youth activities, recreational sports leagues, and camps.
- Many special educators become natural advocates as they choose some of the previously mentioned routes for additional summer employment.
- In addition, special educators may have opportunities for planning input and feedback as their own children participate in such events and they serve as coaches and leaders.

Community Learning Environments

- The special educator may be asked to speak to a board, a group of employees, or volunteers for libraries, museums, or educational camps.
- The special educator may serve one of the above capacities and therefore have input for planning and decision-making.
- The special educator may be involved in community educational opportunities as a parent and have spontaneous opportunity for input.

Creating Collaboration with the Community

- The special educator may plan programs, tours, or luncheons during which members of community groups have the opportunity to observe the needs of the students and strategies that work well. In this situation, the special educator should take care to guard confidential information about specific students.
- Media coverage of special events can promote community awareness.
- Moore / Illinois Special Education Skill 21.1 / Void / Page 2
- The special educator may be involved in events, such as Special Olympics, that recruit scouts and other youth to volunteer. As the members and leaders of these groups have more experience with students with disabilities, opportunities for and reception of the student with a disability's involvement in community activities increase.

Skill 21.2 Demonstrate awareness of resources, strategies, networks, organizations, and unique services, including possible local, state, and federal funding agencies and financial sources for secondary aged students, that work with individuals with disabilities and their families to provide career, vocational, and transition support.

A smooth transition from high school to a training program, post-secondary education program, or employment is the goal of students with disabilities, their parents, school, and the community. Independent living skills are also important. The following are some resources available to the student for that end.

Community Social Service Agencies
- Housing assistance programs and offices
- Medical assistance programs and offices
- Medicare
- Women Infants and Children (WIC)
-

Other Community Resources for Individuals with Disabilities
- Audiologists
- Adaptive equipment sources
- Physical and occupational therapy practices
- Medical supply sources

Educational/Vocational Institutions, Offices, and Resources
- Job coaching programs
- Vocational training programs
- Vocational Rehabilitation Services (VR)
- Postsecondary programs
- Postsecondary funding sources

1. The Heath Resource Center of George Washington University has published a number of papers that outline various considerations and types of funding available for postsecondary education of the student with a disability.
2. The National Center on Secondary Education and Transition
3. (http://www.ncset.org/) is another source of information.

Government Offices Related to Disability
- Social Security (SSI)
- Social Security Administration

Disability Related Offices and Organizations
- Community advocacy programs
- Illinois Association of the Deaf – IAD (http://www.iadeaf.org/)

Moore / Illinois Special Education Skill 21.2 / Void / Page 2
- Illinois Council of the Blind (http://www.icbonline.org/)
- Learning Disabilities Association of Illinois (http://www.ldail.org/)

Often the special educator's community involvement as a speaker, board member, or volunteer leads to natural networking with individuals and organizations that can provide assistance to students with special needs who are transitioning out of high school. (Skill 21.1 outlines ways for the special educator to be involved in such networking.)

Skill 21.3   Demonstrate knowledge of roles and responsibilities of professional groups and community organizations in identifying, assessing, and providing services to individuals with disabilities.

IDEA 2004 states that it is the responsibility of the school district to identify children with disabilities at an early age. Newborn hearing screenings are performed in hospitals with follow up testing available as needed. Pediatricians are educated to screen for certain physical, hearing, and vision difficulties. When a concern shows up in one of these areas, parents are referred to a specialist for further evaluation. In the cases of the child aged birth to three, the state of Illinois provides in home services that include developmental therapy, speech and language, occupational and physical therapy, and social work services.

Local school districts (including special education departments or cooperatives) provide preschool screenings to check for disabilities. Children with a disability who are age three to six are eligible for early childhood special education services. These services may be housed in a local school district building or in a specialized educational setting such as the state school for the deaf or the state school for the blind.

As Early Intervention Services (EIS) are utilized, the possibility of the students needing ongoing special education services decreases. (See also Skill 21.4.)

Skill 21.4 Demonstrate knowledge of the roles of schools, early childhood settings, and other agencies relative to young children and families within the larger community context.

Educational institutions (including public schools and preschools), birth to three early intervention programs, daycare facilities, government agencies that provide resources for the well-being of young children (such and Women, Infants, and Children – WIC), health clinics, and medical offices share the responsibility of finding and identifying children with disabilities.

IDEA 2004 stresses this responsibility and the positive impact of early intervention services. Many students who receive intervention services and developmentally appropriate and stimulating programs early will not need ongoing special education services. (Naturally, there will be some who will continue to need such services.)

The identification of infants and young children with disabilities involves newborn hearing screenings, routine medical checkups, preschool screenings usually coordinated by local school districts, and daily observation by trained professionals who work with infants and young children.

When a child is suspected of having a delay or disability in the area of hearing, vision, fine or gross motor skills, or cognitive ability, it is important to refer the family to an appropriate source for further evaluation. An infant who does not pass the hospital hearing screening should be seen at a later date by an audiologist who is equipped to test the hearing of infants. Sometimes, the initial screening results will be unfounded.

Sometimes, the suspected delay will be treatable with medication or other medical intervention. Many young children have problems with reoccurring ear infections. A build up of fluid in the ears, can cause a temporary (if treated) hearing loss. Medication or the placement of tubes in the child's ears may be necessary to treat the problem. This condition, in and of itself, does not mean that the child has a permanent hearing loss.

When all professionals working with infants and young children are aware of the typical progression of development, the chances increased that children with disabilities will be identified early.

Skill 21.5 **Apply knowledge of considerations (e.g., privacy, confidentiality), approaches, and ethical practices for providing community members with information about students with disabilities.**

The special educator is charged with guarding the confidentiality of her students with disabilities. When engaging in community networking, specific students and their individual needs and the details of their IEPs should not be discussed. Rather, the special educator can address more general considerations of students with disabilities and disability awareness. Specifics of certain disabilities may be necessary for the discussion. (For example, communication, language, and deaf cultural considerations might be presented, but not the specific language strengths and weaknesses of a given student.)

Privacy should also be a consideration of the special educator as she functions in her professional role at school and in the community as an advocate. In particular, a student with disabilities who has physical needs (assistance in toileting or using a feeding tube) should receive assistance in a manner and location that does not cause observance by others. This is a consideration of special educators as they plan field trips and outings as well as in the day to day logistics of the special education program at school. Students who use special equipment should also be given consideration when changing equipment. This would be the case of a student who may be putting on leg braces that are used primarily at school, or hearing impaired students who may be putting on auditory processors.

Again, whether in the school or in the community, the student with the disability should be respected with regards to privacy and confidentiality. This is not to be confused with the positive self esteem that educators hope to foster. When, where, and how personal information is shared should always be the decision of the student or his family with the exception of transition meetings and the sharing of information with professionals in the field.

At times, teachers are asked to provide or obtain information regarding a student with disabilities from another professional, school, or organization in the community. This may be in the form of classroom performance evaluation and observation – often as a questionnaire or inventory. Prior to such exchange of information, written permission must be received from the parent. Usually the special education department of the school will have a form to be used.

Transition meetings are another time that it may be acceptable if confidential information regarding a particular student is shared. In this case, the parent (or student, if 18 years of age or older) has granted permission for a professional from outside of the school district to attend the meeting. This is often the case at meetings for children who will be turning three and entering the school district's early childhood special education program. Then representatives from the state birth to three intervention program or professionals from a specialized school such as the Moog School for the Deaf may attend.

Another time when transition meetings are used is as the student prepares to leave the high school and post high school planning is needed. Then representatives from a post secondary institution or a Vocational Rehabilitation counselor (as examples) may attend.

COMPETENCY 22.0 UNDERSTAND THE PRINCIPLES AND PROCEDURES FOR PROVIDING COMMUNITY-BASED EDUCATIONAL EXPERIENCES

Skill 22.1 Apply knowledge of methods and strategies for providing community-referenced instruction, identifying and prioritizing objectives for skills training within the community, and identifying available community recreational/leisure activities.

As IDEA calls for preparing students with disabilities for productive personal and work lives and independent living skills to the fullest extent possible, the special educator must be knowledgeable of the offerings and expectations of the local community.

Community-referenced instruction involves a community awareness and inclusion of necessary knowledge and skills into the special education curriculum. Community referenced instruction might include transportation, shopping, leisure activities, work expectations, and independent living skills.

Using transportation as an example, the special educator will evaluate commonly used forms of transportation in the community: bus, commuter train, car, taxi, bike, and walking. Then, in the classroom, she will introduce her students to the skills needed to access the transportation. If she is teaching her students how to use the bus, she will teach money skills, purchasing a ticket or a pass, reading a schedule, and appropriate bus behavior (including how to ask for assistance). After students have learned the basic skills associated with riding a bus, the class will use these skills on a bus outing to key community location (store, recreation, etc.).

While community skills training might involve transportation, shopping, leisure activities, work expectations, and independent living skills as listed above, not all skills are appropriate for the individual needs of the student. For example, a severely physically disabled student may not need to know how to get to the local gym that has only workout equipment, but he may benefit from learning how to use facilities at the local YMCA where he can use the swimming pool and participate in outings and clubs. Because time is limited and each student has unique needs, the special educator chooses the most beneficial experiences and prioritizes their introduction to her students.

Leisure/recreational activities as mentioned above (gym/YMCA) vary greatly in offering and in availability in various communities. Again, the special educator will seek a variety of appropriate leisure and recreational activities in the community to include in her program. Knowledge of and experience in using these activities will assist the student with a disability in becoming a well-rounded, happy adult. Some leisure/recreational activities and locations that may be considered include swimming, bowling, skating, YMCA, gym, parks, restaurants, movies, museums, live performances, sporting events, and festivals.

Skill 22.2   Apply knowledge of methods for identifying vocational and community options and placements, including supported and competitive employment, appropriate to the age and skill level of an individual student.

To provide students with the educational experiences and exposure to appropriate vocational and community opportunities, the special educator must be aware of the offerings of the community. Her program may include instruction, experience, or referral to a combination of some of the following as appropriate for her students.

- Communication skills (including ability to describe one's disability and to request assistance, modifications, and accommodations)
- Independent living skills
- Housing assistance offices
- Assisted living facilities
- Group homes
- Living facilities

To the end of becoming productive citizens who are as financially independent as possible, the special educator may also include an appropriate combination of the following vocational instruction, experience, or referral. (For additional information in this area see Skill 21.2.).

- Job search/application skills
- High school job coaching programs
- High school vocational training
- Postsecondary job coaching programs
- Postsecondary vocational training programs
- Postsecondary educational programs (including community college and/or four year college programs)

Representatives from the above programs can assist in transition planning for the high school student with a disability. In fact, planning for transition into the community begins as the student progresses through elementary school and vocational interests are documented on Individualized Education Plan (IEP) forms and at more formal transition planning meetings beginning at age 14 and throughout high school. In addition, a representative from Vocational rehabilitation Services is often involved in planning for postsecondary training, education, and work.

Skill 22.3   Apply knowledge of a variety of ways of assessing entrance-level skill requirements of a potential site for a vocational placement and matching individual needs with appropriate community placements, including supported and competitive employment models.

See previous skills on transitioning

Skill 22.4   Demonstrate familiarity with the rationale for career education across the preschool to postsecondary age span.

See previous skills on transitioning

SUBAREA VI.   **PROFESSIONAL CONDUCT, LEADERSHIP, AND GROWTH**

COMPETENCY 23.0   UNDERSTAND THE ROLES OF TEACHERS AS PROFESSIONALS AND LEADERS.

Skill 23.1   Demonstrate knowledge of the importance of the teacher's serving as a role model and of the ethical responsibility to advocate for the least restrictive environment and appropriate services for students.

Because of the unique needs of each student with disabilities, Special Education Teachers are frequently advocates for their students and the special education program in general.

In order to be an effective advocate, the teacher must be knowledgeable in a number of areas. First, the special educator must understand the general education program that is the counterpart of her program. Factors such as student expectations (learning standards), materials used, and teacher training and inservice provide a starting point. If the special educator is familiar with the goals and overall program for all students at her grade level, she will have a clear picture of the direction she should be working with her students with disabilities.

The special educator should also have a clear understanding of each student's strengths and needs. She must consider how each student can participate in the general education curriculum to the extent that it is beneficial for that student (IDEA 2004). When should services and instruction take place outside of the general education classroom?

In addition, special educators should have an understanding of alternate materials that would be useful or necessary for her students and what resources for materials are available to her.

Knowledge of the Individual's with Disabilities Education Act (IDEA 2004) and NCLB (No Child Left Behind) provides an outline of legislative mandates for special education.

A clear understanding of the above points will allow the special educator to most effectively advocate for the most appropriate placement, programming, and materials for each student. She will be able to advocate for research-based methods with measurable outcomes.

Often advocacy happens between regular and Special Education Teachers. A special educator may see modification or accommodation possibilities that could take place in the general education classroom. It is her responsibility to advocate those practices. The Special Education Teacher may also offer to make supplementary materials or to work with a group of students in the general education setting to achieve that goal. When students with disabilities are in an inclusion classroom, give and take on the part of both teachers as a team is crucial.

The Special Education Teacher may need to be an advocate for her program (or the needs of an individual student) with the administration. Although success for all students is important to administration, often the teacher must explain the need for comparable materials written at the different reading level, the need for assistance in the classroom, or the offering of specific classes or therapies.

Occasionally, the local school district cannot provide an appropriate educational setting. The special educator must advocate with the school district for appropriate placement of the child in another, more suitable environment.

Skill 23.2　　**Apply knowledge of opportunities for and the benefits of engaging in professional activities, including participation in professional organizations, that benefit professional colleagues as well as individuals with disabilities and their families.**

The special educator is expected to use accepted teaching practices with measurable outcomes. She is expected to use professionalism and confidentiality in her role as a teacher. Professional organizations provide a structure for understanding those expectations.

The Council for Exceptional Children (CEC) is a national professional organization (with state chapters) that encompasses teaching in of all areas of disability. The CEC has established a *Code of Ethics for Educators of Persons with Exceptionalities.* In brief, the code charges educators with continuing to learn best practices in the education of students with disabilities, providing a quality educational program that will best meet the needs of their students and their families, and abiding by legal and ethical guidelines of the profession.

The CEC has a number of *Special Interest Divisions* such as the Council for Children with Behavioral Disorders (CCBD) and the Division for Culturally and Linguistically Diverse Exceptional Learners (DDEL).

In addition to the Council for Exceptional Children, there are other organizations specific to particular disabilities. The Learning Disabilities Association of American (LDA) and the National Center for Learning Disabilities (NCLD) provide guidance in best practices and conduct for teachers of students with learning disabilities.

ASHA (the American Speech and Hearing Association) is one professional organization for speech therapists. CED (Council on the Education of the Deaf) is a professional organization for educators of deaf children.

The National Institute of Mental Health also provides information on emotional disabilities, autism, and ADD/ADHD.

Membership in a reputable organization for educators of children with disabilities (such as the above examples) provides ongoing education through workshops and conventions, professional literature and communication with other professionals in the field. It is the educator's checkpoint for implementation of professional standards and policies.

Skill 23.3   Recognize the scope of the teacher's practice and the benefits of seeking additional resources and assistance, as needed, to meet the needs of individual students.

See previous skills on related services

Skill 23.4   Demonstrate knowledge of consumer and professional organizations, publications, and journals relevant to individuals with disabilities.

A number of resources are available for educators as resources for working with students with disabilities. Some resources are professional or parent organizations that require membership. Others are agencies that provide information without membership.

The benefits of these organizations may include websites, message boards, newsletters, journals, workshops, and conferences.

Resource organizations may be in the field of special education; social services; legal assistance; housing information and assistance; employment training and job search; or health (including mental health).

The professional associations representing the spectrum of services for individuals with disabilities are listed here as Table 9-2. Some of these organizations date from the pioneer times of special education and are still in active service. Divisional organizations under the Council for Exceptional Children (CEC) are included and are listed separately along with information about their professional publications in Skill 9.6 of this section. In addition, the following organizations are specific to the state of Illinois.

1. **Organization:** Illinois Teachers of Hard of Hearing/Deaf Individuals
   http://www.ithi.org/index.html

2. **Organization:** Illinois Council for Exceptional Children
   http://www.illinoiscec.org/

Table 23-1

Organization	Members	Mission
Alexander Graham Bell Association for the Deaf and Hard of Hearing 3417 Volta Place, N.W. Washington, D.C. 20007 http://www.agbell.org	Teachers of the deaf, speech-language pathologists, audiologists, physicians, hearing aid dealers	To promote the teaching of speech, lip reading, and use of residual hearing to persons who are deaf; encourage research; and work to further better education of persons who are deaf.
Alliance for Technology Access 1304 Southpoint Blvd., Suite 240, Petaluma, CA 94954 Phone (707) 778-3011 Fax (707) 765-2080 TTY (707) 778-3015 Email: ATAinfo@ATAccess.org http://ww.Ataccess.org	People with disabilities, family members, and professionals in related fields, and organizations with work in their own communities and ways to support our mission.	**To** increase the use of technology **by** children and adults with disabilities and functional limitations**.**

Organization	Members	Mission
American Council of the Blind 1155 15th Street, NW, Suite 1004, Washington, DC 20005 Phone: (202) 467-5081 (800) 424-8666 FAX: (202) 467-5085 http://Acb.org		To improve the well-being of all blind and visually impaired people by: serving as a representative national organization of blind people and conducting a public education program to promote greater understanding of blindness and the capabilities of blind people.
American Council on Rural Special Education (ACRES) Utah State University 2865 Old Main Hill Logan, Utah 84322 Phone: (435) 797 3728 E-mail: inquiries at acres-sped.org	Open to anyone interested in supporting their mission	To provide leadership and support that will enhance services for individuals with exceptional needs, their families, and the professionals who work with them, and for the rural communities in which they live
American Society for Deaf Children 3820 Hartzdale Drive, Camp Hill, PA 17011 Phone: (717) 703-0073 (866) 895-4206 FAX: (717) 909-5599 Email: asdc@deafchildren.org www.deafchildren.org	Open to all who support the mission of THE association	To provide support, encouragement and information to families raising children who are deaf or hard of hearing.
American Speech-Language-Hearing Association 10801 Rockville Pike Rockville, MD 20852	Specialists in speech-language pathology and audiology	To advocate for provision of speech-language and hearing services in school and clinic settings; advocate for legislation relative to the profession; and work to promote effective services and development of the profession.

Organization	Members	Mission
Asperger Syndrome Education Network (ASPEN) 9 Aspen Circle Edison, NJ 08820 Phone: (732) 321-0880 Email: info@AspenNJ.org http://www.aspennj.org		Provides families and individuals whose lives are affected by Autism Spectrum Disorders and Nonverbal Learning Disabilities with education, support and advocacy.
Attention Deficit Disorder Association 15000 Commerce Pkwy, Suite C Mount Laurel, NJ 08054 Phone: (856) 439-9099 FAX: (856) 439-0525 http://www.add.org/	Open to all who support the mission of ADDA	Provides information, resources and networking to adults with AD/HD and to the professionals who work with them.
Autism Society of America 7910 Woodmont Avenue, Suite 300 Bethesda, Maryland 20814 Phone: (800) 328-8476 http://www.autism-society.org	Open to all who support the mission of ASA	To increase public awareness about autism and the day-to-day issues faced by individuals with autism, their families and the professionals with whom they interact. The Society and its chapters share a common mission of providing information and education, and supporting research and advocating for programs and services for the autism community.
Brain Injury Association of America 8201 Greensboro Drive Suite 611 McLean, VA 22102 Phone: (703) 761-0750 http://www.biausa.org	Open to all	Provides information, education and support to assist the 5.3 million Americans currently living with traumatic brain injury and their families.

Organization	Members	Mission
Child and Adolescent Bipolar Association (CABF) 1187 Wilmette Ave. P.M.B. #331 Wilmette, IL 60091 **http://www.bpkids.org**	Physicians, scientific researchers, and allied professionals (therapists, social workers, educators, attorneys, and others) who provide services to children and adolescents with bipolar disorder or do research on the topic	**educates** families, professionals, and the public about pediatric bipolar disorder; **connects** families with resources and support; **advocates** for and **empowers** affected families; and **supports research** on pediatric bipolar disorder and its cure.
Children and Adults with Attention Deficit/ Hyperactive Disorder (CHADD) 8181 Professional Place - Suite 150 Landover, MD 20785 Phone: (301) 306-7070 Fax: (301) 306-7090 Email: national@chadd.org http://www.chadd.org	Open to all	providing resources and encouragement to parents, educators and professionals on a grassroots level through CHADD chapters
Council for Exceptional Children (CEC) 1110 N. Glebe Road Suite 300 Arlington, VA 22201 Phone: (888) 232-7733 TTY: (866) 915-5000 FAX: (703) 264-9494 http://www.cec.sped.org	Teachers, administrators, teacher educators, and related service personnel	Advocate for services for [disabled] and gifted individuals. A professional organization that addresses service, training, and research relative to exceptional persons.
Epilepsy Foundation of America (EFA) 8301 Professional Place Landover, MD 20785 Phone: (800) 332-1000 http://www.epilepsyfoundation.org	A non-membership organization	Works to ensure that people with seizures are able to participate in all life experiences; and to prevent, control and cure epilepsy through research, education, advocacy and services

Organization	Members	Mission
Family Center on Technology and Disability (FCTD) 1825 Connecticut Avenue, NW 7th Floor Washington, DC 20009 Phone: (202) 884-8068 fax: (202) 884-8441 Email: fctd@aed.org http://www.fctd.info/	Non member association	A resource designed to support organizations and programs that work with families of children and youth with disabilities.
Hands and Voices P.O. Box 371926 Denver CO 80237 Phone: (866) 422-0422 Email: parentadvocate@handsandvoices.org http://www.handsandvoices.org	Families, professionals, other organizations, pre-service students, and deaf and hard of hearing adults who are all working towards ensuring successful outcomes for children who are deaf and hard of hearing.	To support families and their children who are deaf or hard of hearing, as well as the professionals who serve them.
The International Dyslexia Association Chester Building, Suite 382 8600 LaSalle Road Baltimore, Maryland 21286 Phone: (410) 296-0232 Fax: (410) 321-5069 http://www.interdys.org	Anyone interested in IDA and its mission can become a member	Provides information and referral services, research, advocacy and direct services to professionals in the field of learning disabilities.
Learning Disabilities Association of America (LDA) 4156 Library Road Pittsburgh, PA 15234 Phone: (412) 341-1515 Fax: (412) 344-0224 http://www.ldanatl.org	Anyone interested in LDA and its mission can become a member	• Provides cutting edge information on learning disabilities, practical solutions, and a comprehensive network of resources. • Provides support to people with learning disabilities, their families, teachers and other professionals.

Organization	Members	Mission
National Association of the Deaf (NAD) 8630 Fenton Street, Suite 820, Silver Spring, MD Phone: (209) 210-3819 TTY: (301) 587-1789, , FAX: (301) 587-1791 Email: NADinfo@nad.org http://nad.org	Anyone interested in NAD and its mission can become a member	To promote, protect, and preserve the rights and quality of life of deaf and hard of hearing individuals in the United States of America.
National Mental Health Information Center P.O. Box 42557 Washington, DC 20015 Phone: (800) 789-2647 http://www.mentalhealth.samhsa.gov	Government Agency	Developed for users of mental health services and their families, the general public, policy makers, providers, and the media.
National Dissemination Center for Children with Disabilities (NIHCY) P.O. Box 1492 Washington, DC 20013 Phone: (800) 695-0285 · Fax: (202) 884-8441 Email: nichcy@aed.org http://www.mentalhealth.samhsa.gov	Non membership association	A central source of information on: • disabilities in infants, toddlers, children, and youth, • IDEA, which is the law authorizing special education, • No Child Left Behind (as it relates to children with disabilities), and • research-based information on effective educational practices.
US Department of Education Office of Special Education and Rehabilitative Services http://www.ed.gov/about/offices/list/osers/index.html	Government Resource	Committed to improving results and outcomes for people with disabilities of all ages.

Organization	Members	Mission
Wrights Law Email: webmaster@wrightslaw.com http://wrightslaw.com	Non membership organization	Parents, educators, advocates, and attorneys come to Wrightslaw for accurate, reliable information about special education law, education law, and advocacy for children with disabilities. Provides parent Advocacy training and updates on the law through out the country.
TASH (Formerly The Association for Persons with Severe Handicaps) 29 W. Susquehanna Ave., Suite 210 Baltimore, MD 21204 Phone: (410) 828-8274 Fax: (410) 828-6706 http:// www.tash.org	Anyone interested in TASH and its mission can become a member	To create change and build capacity so that all people, no matter their perceived level of disability, are included in all aspects of society.
American Psychological Association 750 First Street, NE, Washington, DC 20002-4242 Phone: (800) 374-2721; FAX: (202) 336-5500. TTY: (202) 336-6123 http://www.apa.org	Psychologists and professors of Psychology	Scientific and professional society working to improve mental health services and to advocate for legislation and programs that will promote mental health; facilitate research and professional development.
Association for Children and Adults with Learning Disabilities 4156 Library Road Pittsburgh, PA 15234 http://www.acldonline.org/	Parents of children with learning disabilities and interested professionals	Advanced the education and general well-being of children with adequate intelligence who have learning disabilities arising from perceptual, conceptual, or subtle coordinative problems, sometimes accompanied by behavior difficulties.

Organization	Members	Mission
The Arc of the United States 1010 Wayne Avenue Suite 650 Silver Springs, MD 20910 Phone: (301) 565-3842 FAX: (301) 565-3843 http://www.the arc.org	Parents, professionals, and others interested in individuals with mental retardation	Work on local, state, and national levels to promote treatment, research, public understanding, and legislation for persons with mental retardation; provide counseling for parents of students with mental retardation.
National Association for Gifted Children 1707 L Street, NW Suite 550 Washington, DC 20036 Phone: (202) 785-4368 FAX: (202) 785-4248 Email: nagc@nagc.org http://nagc.org	Parents, educators, community leaders and, other professionals who work with Gifted children.	To address the unique needs of children and youth with demonstrated gifts and talents.
Council for Children with Behavioral Disorders Two Ballston Plaza 1110 N. Glebe Road Arlington, VA 22201 Phone: (800) 224-6830 FAX: (703) 264-9494	Members of the Council for Exceptional Children who teach children with behavior disorders or who train teachers to work with those children	Promote education and general welfare of children and youth with behavior disorders or serious emotional disturbances. Promote professional growth and research on students with behavior disorders and severe emotional disturbances.
Council for Educational Diagnostic Services Two Ballston Plaza 1110 N. Glebe Road Arlington, VA 22201	Members of the Council for Exceptional Children who are school psychologists, educational diagnosticians, [and] social workers who are involved in diagnosing educational difficulties	Promote the most appropriate education of children and youth through appraisal, diagnosis, educational intervention, implementation, and evaluation of a prescribed educational program. Work to facilitate the professional development of those who assess students. Work to further development of better diagnostic techniques and procedures.

Organization	Members	Mission
Council for Exceptional Children Two Ballston Plaza 1110 N. Glebe Road Arlington, VA 22201	Teachers, administrators, teacher educators, and related service personnel	Advocate for services for [disabled] and gifted individuals. A professional organization that addresses service, training, and research relative to exceptional persons.
Council of Administrators of Special Education Two Ballston Plaza 1110 N. Glebe Road Arlington, VA 22201	Members of the Council for Exceptional Children who are administrators, directors, coordinators, or supervisors of programs, schools, or classes for exceptional children; college faculty who train administrators	Promote professional leadership; provide opportunities for the study of problems common to its members; communicate through discussion and publications information that will facilitate improved services for children with exceptional needs.
Division for Children with Communication Disorders Two Ballston Plaza 1110 N. Glebe Road Arlington, VA 22201	Members of the Council for Exceptional Children who are speech-language pathologists, audiologists, teachers of children with communication disorders, or educators of professionals who plan to work with children who have communication disorders	Promote the education of children with communication disorders. Promote professional growth and research.
Division for Early Childhood Two Ballston Plaza 1110 N. Glebe Road Arlington, VA 22201	Members of the Council for Exceptional Children who teach preschool children and infants or educate teachers to work with young children	Promote effective education for young children and infants. Promote professional development of those who work with young children and infants. Promote legislation and research.

Organization	Members	Mission
Division for the Physically Handicapped Two Ballston Plaza 1110 N. Glebe Road Arlington, VA 22201	Members of the Council for Exceptional Children who work with individuals who have physical disabilities or educate professionals to work with those individuals	Promote closer relationships among educators of students who have physical impairments or are homebound. Facilitate research and encourage development of new ideas, practices, and techniques through professional meetings, workshops, and publications.
Division for the Visually Handicapped Two Ballston Plaza 1110 N. Glebe Road Arlington, VA 22201	Members of the Council for Exceptional Children who work with individuals who have visual disabilities or educate professionals to work with those individuals	Work to advance the education and training of individuals with visual impairments. Work to bring about better understanding of educational, emotional, or other problems associated with visual impairment. Facilitate research and development of new techniques or ideas in education and training of individuals with visual problems.
Division on Career Development Two Ballston Plaza 1110 N. Glebe Road Arlington, VA 22201	Members of the Council for Exceptional Children who teach or in other ways work toward career development and vocational education of exceptional children	Promote and encourage professional growth of all those concerned with career development and vocational education. Promote research, legislation, information dissemination, and technical assistance relevant to career development and vocational education.
Division on Mental Retardation Two Ballston Plaza 1110 N. Glebe Road Arlington, VA 22201	Members of the Council for Exceptional Children who work with students with mental retardation or educate professionals to work with those students	Work to advance the education of individuals with mental retardation, research mental retardation, and the training o professionals to work with individuals with mental retardation. Promote public understanding of mental retardation and professional development of those who work with persons with mental retardation.

Organization	Members	Mission
Gifted Child Society P.O. Box 120 Oakland, NJ 07436	Parents and educators of children who are gifted	Train educators to meet the needs of students with gifted abilities, offer assistance to parents facing special problems in raising children who are gifted, and seek public recognition of the needs of these children.
National Association for the Education of Young Children 1313 L St. N.W. Suite 500, Washington DC 20005 Phone: (800) 424-2460 Email: webmaster@naeyc.org http://www.naeyc.org		Promote service and action on behalf of the needs and rights of young children, with emphasis on provision of educational services and resources.
National Asociation for Retarded Citizens 5101 Washington Ave., N.W. Washington, D.C http://www.thearc.org		Work to promote the general welfare of persons with mental retardation; facilitate research and information dissemination relative to causes, treatment, and prevention of mental retardation.
National Easter Seal Society 230 West Monroe Street, Suite 1800 Chicago, IL 60606 Phone: (800) 221-6827 TTY: (312) 726-1494 http://www.easterseals.com	State units (49) and local societies (951); no individual members	Establish and run programs for individuals with physical impairments, usually including diagnostic services, speech therapy, preschool services, physical therapy, and occupational therapy.
The National Association of Special Education Teachers 1201 Pennsylvania Avenue, N.W., Suite 300Washington D.C. 20004 Phone: (800) 754-4421 FAX: 800-424-0371 Email: contactus@naset.org	Special Education Teachers	To render all possible support and assistance to professionals who teach children with special needs. to promote standards of excellence and innovation in special education research, practice, and policy in order to foster exceptional teaching for exceptional children.

Skill 23.5 Apply knowledge of attitudes and behaviors that demonstrate a commitment to developing the highest educational and quality-of-life potential for individuals with disabilities.

The special educator is often the strongest advocate for a student apart from parents. IDEA 2004 calls for preparing students for optimum quality-of-life as well as continued education past the high school level. The special educator can foster these potentials by the following.

Attitude The special educator should demonstrate a belief in the potential of her students by her attitude. Because she is often the individual who introduces the student to new educational settings (such as the inclusion classroom) it is vital that her attitude be positive and realistic.

Modeling As the special educator works with parents, support staff, general educators, and administration she has many opportunities to model appropriate communication with and education of her students. As others see strategies in action for working with a child with disabilities, they are more willing to try such and become more confident in their own efforts.

Communication regarding student abilities and individual needs for modifications and accommodations must come from the special educator and her knowledge of the child's disability as well as her perception of the individual child and his personality and temperament.

Education The special educator is often the educator of the child with a disability as well as the educator of parents, family members, and school personnel. She may provide print materials to this end such as newsletters and handouts. She may organize the availability of published materials such as pamphlets, magazines and journals, books, and website links. The special educator may also provide training (workshop, inservice, presentation) regarding the needs of a particular student or the needs represented in a special education program. At times the special educator may be called upon to teach group of students about these needs.

Coaching As the special educator works in the general education setting she has many opportunities to provide feedback or coaching for general education teachers, other school personnel, general education students, and family members. As other gain awareness and skills they become coaches to yet others, and the supportive environment that assists the child with a disability in reaching his fullest potential grows.

Involvement The special educator gains respect and has increased opportunity to educate and coach as she becomes more involved in the general education classroom (team teaching), activities of the school (clubs, sports, and other extracurriculars), and the community as a whole. When all individuals are working together as a team to meet the needs of all students, everyone is open to suggestions. The overall task is lightened. All students become more productive and empathetic members of society.

Representation works hand and hand with involvement. As the special educator is involved in more educational settings within the school (inclusion classroom, committees, extracurriculars) and in the community (civic groups, churches, professional organizations, and post-secondary institutions) the opportunity for influence widens. As a member of a number of groups, the special educator has the ability to represent the needs of students and individuals who have a disability.

COMPETENCY 24.0 UNDERSTAND THE PRACTICES AND PURPOSES OF REFLECTION, SELF-EVALUATION, AND CONTINUING EDUCATION.

Skill 24.1 Demonstrate familiarity with the continuum of lifelong professional development activities that can help one's methods remain current regarding research-validated practice.

Ongoing professional development is required in the state of Illinois with each teacher developing a personal, five year plan for such. A system of CPDUs (Continuing Professional Development Units) is used to monitor activities. A total of 120 CPDUs must be obtained in each five year period. These activities may include a combination of the following as defined by the Illinois State Board of Education:

- Completion of a master's degree or doctorate in the field of education.
- Eight semester hours of college/university coursework

Each semester hour of coursework is equal to 15 CPDUs.

- Continuing education
- Addition of a teaching endorsement or certification
- Evidence of *Highly Qualified Teacher* status
- Participation in the National Board Certification Process
- Completion of CPDUs (activity may include professional workshop
- attendance)

In addition to completion of the above requirement, the special educator should be involved in professional organizations that represent general education and special education. Workshop attendance and review of professional publications of these organizations assist the special educator in staying current with research-based practice.

Networking with other professionals in the education, community service, and medical areas is another way for special educator to maintain a broader understanding of current, research-based practice that impacts the field of special education.

Experienced special educators find having a field student or student teacher is beneficial to both parties. While the host teacher provides an experience base, the student teacher offers fresh ideas that represent ways to gather data and implement current research-based techniques. Many colleges and universities offer free tuition for a course to teachers who participate in mentoring teachers-in-training.

Skill 24.2 **Demonstrate familiarity with concepts and methods of inquiry for reflecting on one's own practice to improve instruction and guide professional growth.**

In providing services to students with disabilities and their families, teachers need to be involved in a wide range of professional activities that will help improve their instruction and their effectiveness in the classroom. This should include self-reflection and self-assessment. Self-reflection involves reflecting on one's practice to improve instruction and guide professional growth. In the area of special education, this would entail evaluating how successful one is in ensuring that student's are meeting their short and long-term goals in the classroom. When teacher's reflects on their own performance then they can evaluate what they are doing right and where improvements should be made.

The teacher should participate in professional activities and organizations that benefit individuals with exceptional needs, their families, and their colleagues. This will ensure that they are on the cutting edge of any new legislation that applies to Special Education Teachers, as well as ensuring that they are aware of the best practices that are being implemented in teaching students with disabilities. They should also ensure that they incorporate the research into their daily teaching practice.

Other activities that improve teacher effectiveness include using available and innovative resources and technologies to enhance personal productivity and efficiency; using methods to remain current regarding evidence-based practices; and maintaining student, familial, and collegial confidentiality.

The Special Education Teacher needs to be aware of how personal cultural biases and differences impact one's teaching and learning. They should also be aware of professional organizations relevant to practice.

The self-assessment and reflection process should form the basis for decisions about programs and instructional strategies. After the teacher has reflected and assessed his performance in the classroom, he should work to improve his teaching practice, as professional growth is the practitioner's responsibility.

Skill 24.3   **Apply knowledge of the benefits of and strategies for mentoring and self-evaluation methods for making ongoing adjustments to assessment and intervention techniques, as needed, to improve services to students.**

The special educator often fills the role of mentor to parents, other family members, teachers-in-training, general educators, support staff, administrators, and members of the community. Strategies for such mentoring (as outlined in Skill 23.5) provide ongoing instruction and feedback which is often referred to as coaching. As in any educational setting (formal or informal) the person who is instructing often learns as much or more than those she is guiding.

Self-evaluation is another critical, professional practice of the special educator. Because the special educator is often on her own so to speak or working with a small group of special educators, she must have means of self-evaluation. It is her responsibility to keep up with current, researched-based techniques of assessment and intervention and to evaluate the effectiveness of those with regards to the students on her caseload.

Skill 24.1 outlines the criteria of the state of Illinois for ongoing professional development. In order to evaluate for needed adjustments in practice, the special educator must also evaluate the methods and materials she uses for instruction and evaluation. The following is a list for such consideration.

- Are the methods, materials, and assessments reflective of current, researched-based study?
- Do practices address Early Intervention Service and Response to Intervention models?
- Do the materials and strategies consider the unique needs of the student including his ethnicity and culture?
- Do the methods and practices provide a means for collecting data of student progress?
- If the resulting data does not support student progress, what other materials, strategies, and assessment will be considered?

Skill 24.4 **Apply knowledge of how to formulate and communicate a personal philosophy of special education, including its relationship to the general education curriculum and the concept of least restrictive environment.**

As reflected in Skill 23.5, a major role of the special educator is mentor and advocate. Before one can effectively serve in those roles, it is necessary to have a well-developed and perpetually evolving philosophy of special education.

Education The field of special education is rapidly changing. Current trends in special education are for Early Intervention Services with a strong emphasis on Response to Intervention. Researched-based methods and data-driven decisions are necessary to provide students with disabilities programs that place them in inclusion settings to the fullest extent that is beneficial for them. A focus is on the individual's quality of life and the possibility of education or training beyond high school. A solid education that reflects coursework and teacher preparatory experiences in important to develop a well-grounded personal philosophy of special education.

Experience The focus of special education is education of the student with a disability largely in the general education setting. The special educator is charged with being a team member who is knowledgeable of the learning standards set forth for all students by the state of Illinois. As she becomes more experienced in working with students (general education or disabled) she is better able to establish appropriate programming that includes the least restrictive environment for the student.

Communication As the special educator grows in experience as a team member with general educators, she is better able to offer input on programming decisions for students as a whole. Communication between trusted teammates is valued and given careful consideration.

Teamwork The willingness of the special educator to work with parents, family members, support staff, general educators, and administrators demonstrates a commitment to the student with a disability, general education students, and the current and future educational program. As family members and professionals work as a team over time, the quality of the working relationship and the demonstrated possibilities for the student in educational inclusion and in the community become broader and more accepted.

Ongoing Professional Development The state of Illinois requires ongoing professional development for all educators. (See Skill 24.1.) Regardless of this requirement, it is obviously beneficial

Skill 24.5 **Demonstrate knowledge of personal and cultural biases and differences that affect one's teaching and interactions with others.**

Your job as an educator allows your personality to reflect upon your students. They will pick up on your prejudicial tendencies should you communicate them. Some may even begin to adapt them.

Teachers are professionals and must at all times be able to view others through the eyes of a professional, going beyond their small world. Your previous impressions of a group of people must be tested for inaccuracies. Did you think all White people had money? Did you think all Black people were poor? Both of these things are not true and when tested prove false. At the same time it is wise to learn of cultural differences, note the differing language, food, clothing, concept of time, concepts of personal space, values, religion, and their roles in their families. Recognizing these differences will allow you to reach out to a child or colleague and receive their trust and respect.

With your new knowledge of cultural differences you will now be able to pick out pieces of curriculum that may be deemed offensive or provide assessments that can be misunderstood due to cultural differences. Professionalism requires the educator to share this information with their colleagues so that they too will be able to avoid cultural misunderstandings.

A good way to teach your students tolerance is to present your own cultural differences. This will open the door for a teaching moment both for you and your students as you lean about the differences and similarities of the different cultures of your students. Your colleagues of different colors, creeds, and ethnicity will recognize your attempts to "break barriers" as an earnest attempt to improve yourself and open the eyes of those with prejudicial misunderstandings.

COMPETENCY 25.1 UNDERSTAND HISTORICAL, LEGAL, AND ETHICAL ISSUES RELEVANT TO SPECIAL EDUCATION.

Skill 25.1   Apply knowledge of techniques for promoting and maintaining a high level of integrity and exercising objective professional judgment in the practice of the profession consistent with the requirements of the law, rules and regulations, local district policies and procedures, and professional ethical standards.

The rights and responsibilities of individuals as they relate to ensuring that the individual learning needs of students with disabilities are met are multi-faceted.

Teacher of students with disabilities have a wide range of responsibilities. They are responsible for understanding and implementing appropriate instruction and strategies incorporating relevant curriculum frameworks; providing developmentally appropriate learning experiences; and preparing and implementing individual education plans (IEPs).

Parents and students have rights under the No Child Left Behind (NCLB) Act of 2001. The purpose of the NCLB is to ensure that all children have a fair, equal and significant opportunity to obtain a high-quality education. The act has several parental involvement provisions which reflect shared accountability between schools and parents for high student achievement, including expanded public school choice and supplemental educational services for eligible children in low performing schools, local development of parental involvement plans with sufficient flexibility to address local needs, and building parents' capacity for using effective practices to improve their own children's academic achievement.

Parental involvement is important as research has shown that families have a major influence on their children's achievement in school and through life. When schools, families, and community groups work together to support learning, children do better in school, stay in school longer, and enjoy school more.

Initially parents need to fully understand their child's disabilities and consider how their disability will impact their self-help skills, communication, discipline, play and independence. Parents should be encouraged to take advantage of their daily routines to foster the development of certain concepts and skills that appear to be weak. Whatever parents decide to do, however, should be done in the context of a social relationship that is pleasant and non-threatening. Emphasis should be placed on the child's strengths, not just the weaknesses.

IDEA requires schools to establish performance goals and indicators for children with disabilities--consistent to the maximum extent appropriate with other goals and standards for all children established by the state--and to report on progress toward meeting those goals.

The IEP team determines how the student will participate in state and district-wide assessments of student achievement. They also determine if any individual modifications in administration are needed in order for the student to participate in the assessment. Alternate assessments need to be aligned with the general curriculum standards set for all students and should not be assumed appropriate only for those students with significant cognitive impairments.

The CEC Code of Ethics below addresses this skill:

CEC Code of Ethics for Educators of Persons with Exceptionalities

We declare the following principles to be the Code of Ethics for educators of persons with exceptionalities. Members of the special education profession are responsible for upholding and advancing these principles. Members of The Council for Exceptional Children agree to judge and be judged by them in accordance with the spirit and provisions of this Code.

1. Special education professionals are committed to developing the highest educational and quality of life potential of individuals with exceptionalities.
2. Special education professionals promote and maintain a high level of competence and integrity in practicing their profession.
3. Special education professionals engage in professional activities which benefit individuals with exceptionalities, their families, other colleagues, students, or research subjects.
4. Special education professionals exercise objective professional judgment in the practice of their profession.
5. Special education professionals strive to advance their knowledge and skills regarding the education of individuals with exceptionalities.
6. Special education professionals work within the standards and policies of their profession.
7. Special education professionals seek to uphold and improve where necessary the laws, regulations, and policies governing the delivery of special education and related services and the practice of their profession.
8. Special education professionals do not condone or participate in unethical or illegal acts, nor violate professional standards adopted by the Delegate Assembly of CEC.

The Council for Exceptional Children. (1993). CEC Policy Manual, Section Three, part 2
(p. 4). Reston, VA: Author.Originally adopted by the Delegate Assembly of The Council for Exceptional Children in April 1983.

Skill 25.2 **Apply knowledge of attitudes and actions that demonstrate positive regard for the culture, religion, gender, and sexual orientation of individual students and their families.**

The role of the Special Education Teacher is to advocate for the most appropriate education for her students and to guide them in discovering new knowledge and developing new skills to the best of their potential. According to IDEA 2004 (Individual's with Disabilities Education Act) she is to prepare them for future, purposeful work in the society with the possibility of post-secondary education or training.

Although each special educator is also a person with a set of experiences, opinions and beliefs, it is important the she remain unbiased and positive in her professional role with students, parents, administration and the community. Differences in culture, religion, gender, or sexual orientation should not influence the teacher's approach to instruction, student goals or expectations, or advocacy.

In order to remain unbiased, the special educator should avail herself of opportunities to learn about various cultures, religions, genders, and sexual orientations. This can be accomplished through reading, classroom awareness activities as appropriate, and teacher inservice.

Reading to increase awareness and acceptance of cultural differences may be done through professional, adult literature as well as through books to be read with the class.

Cultural activities in the classroom are especially well-received as foods, dress, and games are easily added to curriculum and often address learning standards.

The special educator is charged with academic, social, communicative, and independent skills instruction. Education or influence in other areas is not appropriate.

When the special educator remains unbiased, she is better able to meet the needs of her students and not react to additional factors. The students and their families are also more open to school-related suggestions.

The teacher's reaction to differences with her students and their families models the commonly taught character education trait of respect. When she demonstrates respect for all individuals in her program, it is likely that respect will also be practiced by students, parents, and administration.

Skill 25.3 **Apply knowledge of signs of emotional distress, child abuse, and neglect and procedures for reporting known or suspected abuse or neglect to appropriate authorities.**

Teachers are mandated reporters of Child Abuse/Neglect. It is your responsibility to recognize signs of possible abuse and to report on those situations where you believe child neglect/abuse has or is currently occurring.

The following graphs provide possible indicators/symptoms of children who have been or are currently being abused.

Possible Symptoms of Emotional Abuse	
Child	• Shows extremes in behavior, such as overly compliant or demanding behavior, extreme passivity, or aggression. • Is either inappropriately adult (parenting other children, for example) or inappropriately infantile (frequently rocking or head-banging, for example). • Is delayed in physical or emotional development. • Has attempted suicide. • Reports a lack of attachment to the parent.
Parent or Other Adult	• Constantly blames, belittles, or berates the child. • Is unconcerned about the child and refuses to consider offers of help for the child's problems. • Overtly rejects the child.

Information provided by the Child Welfare Information Gateway. (childwelfare.gov).

Possible Symptoms of Physical Abuse	
Child	• Has unexplained burns, bites, bruises, broken bones, or black eyes. • Has fading bruises or other marks noticeable after an absence from school. • Seems frightened of the parents and protests or cries when it is time to go home. • Shrinks at the approach of adults. • Reports injury by a parent or another adult caregiver.
Parent or Other Adult	• Offers conflicting, unconvincing, or no explanation for the child's injury. • Describes the child as "evil," or in some other very negative way. • Uses harsh physical discipline with the child. • Has a history of abuse as a child.

Information provided by the Child Welfare Information Gateway. (childwelfare.gov).

Possible Symptoms of Sexual Abuse

Child	<ul><li>Has difficulty walking or sitting.</li><li>Suddenly refuses to change for gym or to participate in physical activities.</li><li>Reports nightmares or bed wetting.</li><li>Experiences a sudden change in appetite.</li><li>Demonstrates bizarre, sophisticated, or unusual sexual knowledge or behavior.</li><li>Becomes pregnant or contracts a venereal disease, particularly if under age 14.</li><li>Runs away.</li><li>Reports sexual abuse by a parent or another adult caregiver.</li></ul>
Parent or Other Adult	<ul><li>Is unduly protective of the child or severely limits the child's contact with other children, especially of the opposite sex.</li><li>Is secretive and isolated.</li><li>Is jealous or controlling with family members.</li></ul>

Information provided by the Child Welfare Information Gateway. (childwelfare.gov).

Possible Symptoms of Neglect

Child	<ul><li>Is frequently absent from school.</li><li>Begs or steals food or money.</li><li>Lacks needed medical or dental care, immunizations, or glasses.</li><li>Is consistently dirty and has severe body odor.</li><li>Lacks sufficient clothing for the weather.</li><li>Abuses alcohol or other drugs.</li><li>States that there is no one at home to provide care.</li></ul>
Parent or Other Adult	<ul><li>Appears to be indifferent to the child.</li><li>Seems apathetic or depressed.</li><li>Behaves irrationally or in a bizarre manner.</li><li>Is abusing alcohol or other drugs.</li></ul>

Information provided by the Child Welfare Information Gateway. (childwelfare.gov).

It is your responsibility as a teacher to know the Child/Abuse reporting procedures of your school. Your principal may want you to call the Child Abuse Hotline in their presence; they also may want to have a Child Protective's Worker or Police Officer physically present when you report the abuse. Regardless of thee procedures in your individual schools, it is our professional responsibility to both report the abuse to the authorities, and to your administrator.

Skill 25.4 **Demonstrate understanding of historical, legal, and philosophical foundations of and historical and current issues and trends in special education.**

LEGAL MANDATES AND HISTORICAL ASPECTS

Special education is precisely what the term denotes: education of a special nature for students who have special needs. The academic and behavioral techniques that are used today in special education are a culmination of "best practices" and evolved from a number of disciplines (e.g. medicine, psychology, sociology, language, ophthalmology, otology) to include education. Each of these disciplines contributed uniquely to their field so that the needs of special students might be better met in the educational arena.

Unfortunately, during the earlier part of the 1900s and mid-1950s, too many educators placed in positions of responsibility, refused to recognize their professional obligation for assuring all children a free, appropriate, public education. Today, door can no longer be shut, eyes cannot be closed, and heads cannot be turned since due process rights have established for special needs students and their caregivers. Specific mandates are now stated in national laws, state regulations, and local policies. These mandates are the result of many years of successful litigation and politically advocacy, and they govern the delivery of special education.

What special educators do is one thing; how services are delivered is yet another. The concept if **inclusion** stresses the need for educators to rethink the continuum of services, which was designed by Evelyn Deno and has been in existence since the early 1970s. Many school districts developed educational placement sites, which contain options listed on this continuum. These traditional options extend from the least restrictive to the most restrictive special education settings. The least restrictive environment is the regular education classroom. The present trend is to team special education and regular classroom teachers in regular classrooms. This avoids pulling out students for resource room services, and provides services by specialists for students who may be showing difficulties similar to those of special education students.

The competencies in this section include the mandates (i.e. laws, regulations, policies) that apply to or have a bearing upon the respective states and local districts, as well as the major provisions of federal laws implemented twenty or more years ago, such as Public Laws 94-142 (1975), 93-112 (1973) and 101-476 (1990). These laws culminated into the comprehensive statute, IDEA (Individuals with Disabilities Education Act), which requires the states to offer comprehensive special education service programs to students with disabilities, and to plan for their transition into the work world. Most local districts have elaborately articulated delivery systems, which are an extension of national or state Department of Education of Department of Public Instruction. Any inquires should be directed to the unit that administers programs for exceptional children.

THE MAJOR DEVELOPMENTS IN THE HISTORY OF SPECIAL EDUCATION

Although the origin of special education services for youngsters with disabilities is relatively recent, the history of public attitude toward people with disabling conditions was recorded as early as 1552. The Spartans practiced infanticide, the killing of abandonment of malformed or sickly babies. The ancient Greeks and Romans thought people with disabilities were cursed and forced them to beg for food and shelter. Those who could who could not fend for themselves were allowed to perish. Some with mantel disabilities were employed as fools for the entertainment of the Roman royalty.

In the time of Christ, people with disabilities were thought to be suffering the punishment of God. Those with emotional disturbances were considered to be possessed by the devil, and although early Christianity advocated humane treatment of those who were not normal physically or mentally, many remained outcasts of society, sometimes pitied and sometimes scorned.
During the Middle Ages, persons with disabilities were viewed within the aura of the unknown, and were treated with a mixture of fear and reverence. Some were wandering beggars, while others were used as jesters in the courts. The Reformation brought about a change of attitude, however. Individuals with disabilities were accused of being possessed by the devil, and exorcism flourished. Many innocent people were put in chains and cast into dungeons.

The early seventeenth century was marked by a softening of public attitude toward persons with disabilities. Hospitals began to provide treatment for those with emotional disturbances and mental retardation. A manual alphabet for those with deafness was developed, and John Locke became the first person differentiate between persons who were mentally retarded and those who were emotionally disturbed.

In America, however, the colonists treated people with severe mental disorders as criminals, while those who were harmless were left to beg or were treated as paupers. At one time, it was common practice to sell them to the person who would provide for them at the least cost to the public. When this practice was stopped, persons with mental retardation were put into poorhouses, where conditions were often extremely squalid.

The Nineteenth Century: The Beginning of Training

In 1799, Jean Marc Itard, a French physician, found a 12-year old boy who had been abandoned in the woods of Averyron, France. His attempts to civilized and educate the boy, Victor, established many of the educational principles presently in use in the field of special education, including developmental and multi-sensory approaches, sequencing of tasks, individualized instruction, and a curriculum geared toward functional life skills.

Itard's work had an enormous impact upon public attitude toward individuals with disabilities. They began to be seen as educable. During the late 1700s, rudimentary procedures were devised by which those with sensory impairments (i.e. deaf, blind) could be taught, closely followed in the early 1800s by attempts to teach students with mild intellectual disabilities and emotional disorders (i.e. at that time to as the "idiotic" and "insane"). Throughout Europe, schools for students with visual and hearing impairments were erected, paralleled by the founding of similar institutions in the United States. In 1817, Thomas Hopkins Galluder founded the first American school for students who were deaf, known today as Galluder College in Washington, D.C., one of the world's best institutions of higher learning for those with deafness. Galluder's work was followed closely by that of Samuel Gridley However, who was instrumental in the founding of the Perkins Institute for students who were blind in 1829.

The mid-1800s saw the further development of Itard's philosophy of education of students with mental disabilities. Around that time, his student, Edward Seguin, immigrated to the United States, where he established his philosophy of education for persons with mental retardation in a publication entitles Idiocy and Its Treatment by the Physiological Method in 1866. Seguin was instrumental in the establishment of the first residential school for individuals with retardation in the United States.

State legislatures began to assume the responsibility for housing people with physical and mental disabilities - the institutional care was largely custodial. Institutions were often referred to as warehouses due to the deplorable conditions of many. Humanitarians like Dorthea Dix helped to relieve anguish and suffering to institutions for persons with mental illnesses.

1900 - 1919: Specific Programs
The early twentieth century saw the publication of the first standardized test of intelligence by Alfred Binet of France. The test was designed to identify educationally sub-standard children, but by 1916, the test was revised by an American Louis Terman, and the concept of the intelligence quotient (IQ) was introduced. Since then the IQ test has come to be used as a predictor of both retarded (delayed) and advanced intellectual development.

At approximately the same time, Italian physician Maria Montessori was concerned with the development of effective techniques for early childhood education. Although she is known primarily for her contributions to this field, her work included methods of education for children with mental retardation as well, and the approach she developed is used in preschool programs today.

Ironically, it was the advancement of science and the scientific method that led special education to its worst setback in modern times. In 1912, psychologist Henry Goddard published a study based on the Killikak family, in which he traced five generations of the descendants of a man who had one legitimate child and one illegitimate child. Among the descendants of the legitimate child were numerous mental defectives and social deviates. This led Goddard to conclude that mental retardation and social deviation were inherited traits, and therefore that mental and social deviates were a threat to society, an observation that he called the Eugenics Theory. Reinforcing the concept of retardation as hereditary deviance was a popular philosophy called positivism, under which these unscientific conclusions were believed to be fixed, mechanical laws that were carrying mankind to inevitable improvement. Falling by the wayside was seen as the natural, scientific outcome for the defective person in society. Consequently, during this time mass institutionalization and sterilization of person with mental retardation and criminals were practiced.

Nevertheless, public school programs for persons with retardation gradually increased during this same period. Furthermore, the first college programs for the preparation of Special Education Teachers were established between 1900 and 1920.

1919 - 1949: Professional and Expansion of Services
As awareness of the need for medical and mental health treatment in the community, was evidenced during the 1920s. Halfway houses became a means for monitoring the transition from institution to community living; outpatient clinics were established to provide increased medical care. Social workers and other support personnel were dispensed into the community to coordinate services for the needy. The thrust toward humane treatment within the community came to an abrupt halt during the 1930s and 1940s, primarily due to economic depression and widespread dissatisfaction toward the recently enacted social programs.

Two factors related to the Word Wars I and II helped to improve public opinion toward persons with disabilities. First, the intensive screening of the population of young men with physical and mental disabilities that were in the United States. Second, patriotism caused people to regard the enormous number of young men who returned from the wars with physical and emotional disabilities in a different light than they would have been regarded before that time. People became more sensitive to the problems of the veterans with disabilities, and this acceptance generalized to other groups in the special needs population.

With increased public concern for people with disabilities came new research. John B. Watson introduced behaviorism, which shifted the treatment emphasis from psychoanalysis to learned behavior. He demonstrated in 1920 that maladaptive (or abnormal) behavior was learned by Albert, an 11-month old boy, through conditioning. B.F. Skinner followed with a book entitled the Behavior of Organisms, which outlined principles of operant behavior (i.e. voluntary) behavior.

In 1922, the Council for Exceptional Children (first called the International Council for Exceptional Children) was founded. During the 1920s, many comprehensive statewide programs were initiated. The number of special education programs in public schools increased at a rapid rate until the 1930s, when the push for humane and effective treatment of people with disabilities began to diminish once again. The period of the Depression was marked by large-scale institutionalization and lack of treatment. Part of the cause was inadequately planned programs and poorly trained teachers. WW II did much to swing the pendulum back in the other direction, however, and inaugurated the most active period in the history of the development of special education.

1950 - 1969: The Parents, the Legislators, and the Courts Become Involved

The first two decades of the second half of this century was characterized by increased federal involvement in general education, gradually extending to special education. In 1950, came the establishment of the National Association of Retarded Children, later renamed the National Association of Retarded Citizens (NARC). It was the result of the efforts among concerned parents who felt the need of an appropriated public education. Increased media coverage exposed the miserable conditions in some of the institutions devoted to caring for people with disabilities, especially those with intellectual and emotional disabilities, and treatment consequently became more humane.

It was at about this time that parents of children with disabilities discovered the federal courts as a powerful agent on behalf of their children. The 1954 decision in the Brown v. the Topeka Board of Education case guaranteed equal opportunity rights to a free public education for all citizens, and the parents of children and youth with disabilities insisted that their children be included in that decision. From this point on, the court cases and public laws enacted[11] as a result of court decisions, are too numerous to include in their entirety. Only those few, which had the greatest impact on the development of special education, as we know it today, are listed. Collectively, they are part of a movement in U.S. Supreme Court history known as the Doctrine of Selective Incorporation, under which the states are compelled to honor various substantive rights under procedural authority of the 14th Amendment.

1954: **The Cooperative Research Act** was passed, the first designation of general funds for the use of students with disabilities.
1958: **Public Law 85-926** provided grants to intuitions of higher learning \ and to state education agencies for training professional personnel
who would, in turn, train teachers of students with mental retardation.

1963: **Public Law 88-164** (Amendment to Public Law 85-926) extended support to the training of personnel for teaching those with other disabling conditions (i.e. hard of hearing, speech impaired, visually impaired, seriously emotionally disturbed, crippled and other health impaired.

1965: **Elementary and Secondary Education Act** provided funds for the education of children who were disadvantaged and disabled (Public Law 89-10).

1965: **Educational Consolidation and Improvement Act** (Public Law 89-313-State Operated Programs) provided funds for children with disabilities who are or have been in state-operated or state-supported schools.

1966: **Public Law 89-750** authorized the establishment of the Bureau Education for the Handicapped (BEH) and a National Advisory Committee on the Handicapped.

1967: **Hanson v. Hobson** ruled that ability grouping (tracking) based on student performance on standardized tests is unconstitutional.

1968: **Handicapped Children's Early Education Assistance Act** (Public Law 80-538) funded model demonstration programs for preschool students with disabilities.

---

[1] The first cluster of two digits of each public law represents the congressional session during which the law, numbered by the last three digits, was passed.. Congressional sessions begin every two years on the odd numbered year. The first biennial session sat in 1787-88. Bills may be passed and signed into law during either of the two years during which the congressional session is being held. For example, Public Law 94-142 was the 142nd law passed by the Ninety-fourth Congress, which was in session in 1975-76 and was passed and signed in 1975.

1968: **Public Law 90-247** included provisions for deaf-blind centers, resource centers and expansion of media services for students with disabilities.

1968: **Public Law 90-576** specified that 10 percent of vocational education funds be earmarked for youth with disabilities.

1969: **Public Law 91-230** (Amendments to Public Law 89-10). Previous Enactment relating to children with disabilities was consolidated into one act: Education of the Handicapped.

1970-Present: Federal Involvement in the Education of Children and Youth with Disabilities

During early involvement of the government in the education of individuals with disabilities, states were encouraged to establish programs, and they were rewarded with monetary assistance for compliance. Unfortunately, this assistance as often abused by those in control of services and funds. Therefore, a more dogmatic attitude arose, and the states were mandated to provide education for those with disabilities, or else experience the cutoff of education funds from the federal government. Federal legal authority for this action was the 14th Amendment due process denial, paralleling enforcement of the 1954 Brown v. Topeka desegregation decision. High proportions of minority students in programs for mental retardation resulted in a mandatory reexamination of placement procedures, which in turn brought about a rigid legal framework for the provision of educational services for students with disabilities.

1970: **Diana v. the State Board of Education** resulted in the decision that all children must be tested in their native language.

1971: **Wyatt v. Stickney** established the right to adequate treatment (education) for institutionalized persons with mental retardation.

1971: The decision in **Pennsylvania Association for Retarded Children (PARC) v. the Commonwealth of Pennsylvania** prohibited the exclusion of students with mental retardation from educational treatment at state schools.

1972: **Mills v. the Board of Education of the District of Columbia** asserted the right of children and youth with disabilities to a constructive education, which includes appropriate specialized instruction.

1973: **Rehabilitation Amendments of 1973** (Public Law 93-112) was the first comprehensive federal statute to address specifically the rights of disabled youth. It prohibited illegal discrimination in education, employment, or housing on the basis of a disability.

1974: **Public Law 93-380 (Education Amendments of 1974**. Public Law 94-142 is the funding portion of this act). It requires the states to provide full educational opportunities for children with disabilities. It addressed identification, fair evaluation, alternative placements, due process procedures, and free, appropriate public education.

1975: **Education for all Handicapped Children Act** (Public Law 94-142) provided for a free, appropriate public education for all children with disabilities, defined special education and related services, and imposed rigid guidelines on the provisions of those services. It paralleled the provision for a free and appropriate public education in Section in 504 of Public Law 94-142, and extended these services to preschool children with disabilities (ages 3-5) through provisions to preschool incentive grants.

1975: **Goss v. Lopez** ruled that the state could not deny a student: education without following due process. While this decision is not based on a special education issue, the process of school suspension and expulsion is obviously critical in assuring an appropriate public education to children with disabilities.

1978: **Gifted and Talented Children's Act** (Public Law 95-56) defined the gifted and talented population, and focused upon this exceptionally category, which was not included in Public Law 94-142.

1979: **Larry P. v. Riles** ordered the reevaluation of black students enrolled in classes for educable mental retardation (EMR) and enjoined the California State department of Education from the use of intelligence tests in subsequent EMR placement decisions.

1980: **Parents in Action on Special Education (PASE) v. Hannon** ruled that IQ tests are necessarily biased against ethnic and racial subcultures.

1982: The appeal for services of an interpreter during the school day for a deaf girl was denied by the Supreme Court in **Hendrick Hudson Board of Education v. Rowley**. Established that an "appropriate" education does not mean the "best" education has to be provided. What is required is that individuals benefit and those due process procedures are followed in developing the educational program.

1983: Public Law 98-199 (**Education of the Handicapped Act [EHA] Amendments**). Public Law 94-142 was amended to provide added emphasis on parental education and preschool, secondary, and post-secondary programs for children and youth with disabilities.

1984: **Irving Independent School District v. Tarro** (468 U.S. 883) established that catheterization and similar health-type services are "related services" when they are relatively simple to provide and medical assistance is not needed in providing them.

1985: **Public Law 99-457** mandated service systems for infants and young children.

1986: Public Law 99-372 (**Handicapped Children's Protection Act of 1985**). This law allowed parents who are unsuccessful in due process hearings or reviews to seek recovery of attorney's fees.

1986: **Public Law 99-457** (Education of the Handicapped Act Amendments of 1986). It re-authorized existing EHA, amended Public Law 94-142 to include financial incentives for states to educate children 3 to 5 years old by the 1990-1991 school years, and established incentive grants to promote programs serving infants with disabilities (birth to 2 years of age).

1986: Public Law 99-506 (**Rehabilitation Act Amendments of 1986**). It authorized formula grant funds for the development of supported employment demonstration projects.

1987: **School Board of Nassau County v. Arline** Established that contagious diseases are a disability under Section 504 of the Rehabilitation Act and that people with them are protected from discrimination, if otherwise qualified (actual risk to health and safety to others may persons unqualified).

1988: **Honig v. Doe** established that expulsion from school programs for more than ten days constitutes a change in placement for which all due process provisions must be met; temporary removals permitted in emergencies.

1990: **American with Disabilities Act (ADA)** (Public Law 101-336) gives civil rights protection to individuals with disabilities in private sector employment, all public services, public accommodations, transportation, and telecommunications. Patterned after Section 504 of the Rehabilitation Act of 1973.

1990: The U.S. House of Representatives opened for citizen comment the issue of a separate exceptionality category for students with attention deficit disorders. The issue was tabled without legislative action.

1990: **Public Law 101-476 (Individuals with Disabilities Education Act IDEA)** reauthorized and renamed existing EHA. This amendment to EHA changed the term "handicapped" to "disability," expanded related services, and required individual education programs (IEPs) to contain transitional goals and objectives for adolescents (ages 16 and above, special situations).

1993 **Florence County School Dist Four v. Shannon Carter** established that when a school district does not provide FAPE for a student with disability, the parents may seek reimbursement for private schooling. This decision has encouraged districts to be more inclusive of students with Autism who receive ABA/Lovaas therapy.

1994 **Goals 2000: Educate America Act**, Pub. L. 103-227, established national education goals to help guide state and local education systems

1997 **Reauthorization of IDEA**—required involvement of a regular education teacher as part of the IEP team. Provided additional strength to school administrators for the discipline of students with special needs.

2002 **No Child Left Behind Act (NCLB)**

2004 **M.L. v. Federal Way School District** (WA) in the Ninth Circuit Court of Appeals ruled that absence of a regular education teacher on an IEP team was a serious procedural error.

2004 **Reauthorization of IDEA**—Required all Special Education Teachers on a Secondary Level to be no less qualified than other teachers of the subject areas.

Present and Future Perspectives-What is the state of special education today? What can we anticipate as far as changes that might occur in the near future? It has been two decades since the passage of the initial Individuals with Disabilities Education Act as Public Law 93-142 in 1975.

So far, mandates stand with funding intact. The clients are still here, and in greater numbers to improved identification procedures and to medical advances that has left many, who might have died in the past, with conditions considered disabling. Among the disabling conditions afflicting the population with recently discovered lifesaving techniques are blindness, deafness, amputation, central nervous system or neurological impairments, brain dysfunction, and mental retardation from environmental, genetic, traumatic, infectious, and unknown etiologies.

Despite challenges to the principles underlying PL 94-142 in the early 1980s, total federal funding for the concept increased as new amendments were passed throughout the decade. These amendments expanded services to infants, preschoolers, and secondary students. (Rothstein, 1995).

Following public hearings, Congress voted in 1990 not to include Attention Deficit Disorders (ADD) as a new exceptionality area. Determining factors included the alleged ambiguity of the definition and eligibility criteria for students with ADD, the large number of students who might be identified if it became a service delivery area, the subsequent cost of serving such a large population, and the fact that many of these students are already served in the exceptionality areas of learning disabilities and behavior disorders.

The revision of the original law that we now call IDEA included some other changes. These changes were primarily in language (terminology), procedures (especially transition), and addition of new categories (autism and traumatic brain injury). Read Objective 4 in this section for these specific changes.

Thus, we can see that despite challenges to federal services and mandates in special education as an extension of the Fourteenth Amendment since 1980, there has actually been growth in mandated categories and net funding. The Doctrine of Selective Incorporation is the name for one major set of challenges to this process.

While the 1994 conservative turnover in the Congress might seem to undercut the force of PL 94-132, two decades of recent history show strong bi-partisan support for special education, and consequently, IDEA, or a joint federal-state replacement, will most likely remain strong. Lobbyists and activists representing coalition and advocacy groups for those with disabilities have combined with bi-partisan congressional support to avert the proposed changes, which would have meant drastic setbacks in services for persons with disabilities.

Nevertheless, there remain several philosophical controversies in special education for the late 1990s. The need for labels for categories continues to be questioned. Many states are serving special needs students by severity level rather than by the exceptionality category.

Presently, special educators are faced with possible changes in what is considered to be the least restrictive environment (LRE) for educating students with special needs. Following upon the heels of the Regular Education Initiative, the concept of **inclusion** has come to the forefront. Both of these movements were, and are, an attempt to educate special needs students in the mainstream of the regular classroom. Both would eliminate pulling out students from regular classroom instructional activities, and both would incorporate the services of Special Education Teachers in the regular classroom in collaboration with general classroom teachers.

Skill 25.5 **Demonstrate knowledge of current legislation, regulations, policies, litigation, and ethical issues (e.g., due process, assessment, behavior management, discipline, transition, supplemental services and supports, specialized health care, assistive technology) related to the provision of educational services to individuals with all types of disabilities across the age range.**

The Family Educational Rights and Privacy Act (1974), also known as the Buckley Amendment, assures confidentiality of student records. Parents are afforded the right to examine, review, request changes in information deemed inaccurate, and stipulate persons who might access their child's records.

Due Process
"Due process is a set of procedures designed to ensure the fairness of educational decisions and the accountability of both professionals and parents in making these decisions" (Kirk and Gallagher, 1986, p. 24). These procedures serve as a mechanism by which the child and his family can voice their opinions or concerns, as sometimes dissents. Due process safeguards exist in all matters pertaining to identification, evaluation, and educational placement.

Due process occurs in two realms, substantive and procedural. Substantive due process is the content of the law (e.g. appropriate placement for special education students). Procedural due process is the form through which substantive due process is carried out (i.e. parental permission for testing). Public Law 101-476 contains many items of both substantive and procedural due process.

1. A due process hearing may be initiated by parents of the LEA as an impartial forum for challenging decisions about identification, evaluation, or placement. Either party may present evidence, cross-examine witnesses, obtain a record of the hearing, and be advised by counsel or by individuals having expertise in the education of individuals with disabilities. Findings may be appealed to the state education agency (SEA) and if still dissatisfied, either party may bring civil action in a state of federal district court. Hearing timelines are set by legislation.

2. Parents may obtain an independent evaluation if there is disagreement about the education evaluation performed by the LEA. The results of such an evaluation: (1) must be considered in any decision made with respect to the provision of a free, appropriate public education for the child, and (2) may be presented as evidence at a hearing. Further, the parents may request this evaluation at public expense: (1) if a hearing officer requests an independent educational evaluation, (2) if the decision from a due process hearing is that the LEA's evaluation was inappropriate. If the final decision holds that, the evaluation performed is appropriate, the parent still ahs the right to an independent educational evaluation, but not as public expense.

3. Written notice must be provided to parents prior to a proposal or refusal to initiate or make a change in the child's identification, evaluation, or educational placement.

   a. A listing of parental due process safeguards.
   b. A description and a rationale for the chosen action.
   c. A detailed listing of components (e.g. tests, records, reports) which was the basis for the decision.
   d. Assurance that the language and content of notices were understood by the parents.

4. Parental consent must be obtained before evaluation procedures can occur, unless there is a state law specifying otherwise.

5. Sometimes parents or guardians cannot be identified to function in the due process role. When this occurs, a suitable person must be assigned to act as a surrogate. This is done by the LEA in full accordance with legislation.

As the due process procedure is followed, a series of major decisions are made by multidisciplinary teams. A typical chain of events that occur as decisions are made is outlined in the figure below. Multidisciplinary teams are composed of persons from various disciplines. Team members include teachers (regular and special education), building and district administrators, school psychologists, school social workers, parents, and medical experts.

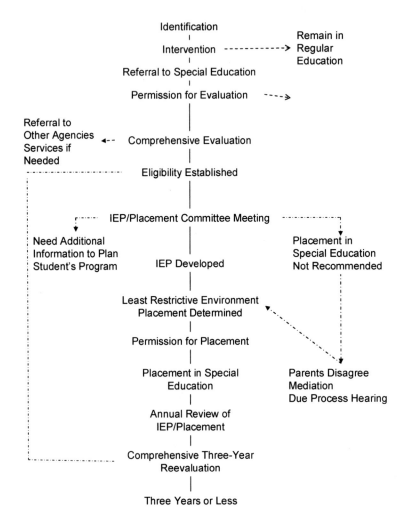

From: Georgia Department of Education

Irving Independent School District v. Tatro 1984. IDEA lists health services as one of the "related services" that schools are mandated to provide to exceptional students. Amber Tatro, who had spina bifida, required the insertion of a catheter on a regular schedule in order to empty her bladder. The issue was specifically over the classification of clean, intermittent catheterization (CIC) as a medical service (not covered under IDEA) or a "related health service", which would be covered. In this instance, the catheterization was not declared a medical service, but a "related service" necessary for the student to have in order to benefit from special education. The school district was obliged to provide the service. The Tatro case has implications for students with other medical impairments who may need services to allow them to attend classes at the school.

School Board of Nassau County v. Arline, 1987. Established that contagious diseases are a disability under Section 504 of the Rehabilitation Act and that people with them are protected from discrimination, if otherwise qualified (actual risk to health and safety to others may persons unqualified).

Skill 25.6 **Demonstrate knowledge of the rights and responsibilities of parents, students, teachers, other professionals, and schools as they relate to an individual's learning needs and educational program.**

The following Material was taken from your Illinois's Parents Rights Guide:

Written consent

Parents have the right to be given written consent before the school conducts any new tests to determine whether their child is, or continues to be, eligible for special education

- To give your written consent before your child first receives special education or related services
- To revoke your consent for evaluation any time before the school completes new tests and measures (Any tests or measures the school has already completed become part of your child's education record.)
- To revoke your consent for special education services before those services first begin. Although you have the right to withhold written consent for your child's first evaluation, the school has the right to ask for a due process hearing to find out whether your child should be evaluated. If you fail to respond to the school's request for a reevaluation, the school may conduct the reevaluation if it can show it took reasonable steps to obtain your consent.

Notice

As parents you have the right

- To be notified by the school before it begins (or refuses) to provide special education services to your child and before it plans (or refuses) to change your child's identification, evaluation, special education services, or education placement
- To be notified in writing by the school in your native language (or other type of communication, such as sign language) and in a way that can be understood by the general public.
- To notice from the school describing what it is planning to do and why it is planning to do it *clear understanding of your rights can help you make special education work for a child. Here is a summary of state and federal regulations that apply to children ages three through 21.*
- To notice from the school of options that were considered and why those options were not chosen
- To be notified of other reasons why those options were refused
- To be notified of each evaluation procedure, test, record or report the school uses to decide whether your child is eligible for special education
- To be notified of your rights, including the right to file an administrative complaint or request mediation or a due process hearing if you disagree with the school about your child's identification, evaluation, education program or placement

Education records and confidentiality

As parents, you have the right:

- To review your child's education records "without unreasonable delay" (within 45 days) or anytime before a meeting to discuss your child's identification, evaluation, placement in special education, or Individualized Education Program (IEP)
- To request copies of your child's records. You may be asked to pay for the copies themselves (not the time it took to make them) unless the charge would prevent you from having copies.
- To know where your child's records are kept.
- To know what information your child's records contain and to have information in the records explained to you.
- To request that the records be changed if you believe they are wrong misleading or violate your privacy.
- To ask for a hearing if the school refuses to change the records as you have requested.

- To have information in your child's records changed, if as the result of a hearing it is determined that the information is wrong, misleading or violates your privacy.
- To see information only about your child if records include information about other children as well
- To add to your child's records a written statement describing any disagreement you have with any of the information
- To know when the school plans to destroy information in your child's records

Independent evaluation

As parents you have the right

- To an independent evaluation of your child if you disagree with the school's evaluation
- To an independent evaluation of your child conducted by a qualified evaluator who is not a school employee.
- To payment by the school of independent evaluation and related expenses if you disagree with the school's evaluation
- To information from the school about where to get an independent evaluation
- To an independent evaluation at your own expense if the school's evaluation is considered appropriate as the result of a due process hearing. The school must ask for a due process hearing to show that its evaluation is appropriate.
- To have independent evaluation results considered by the Evaluation and Planning Team when a decision is being made about your child's special education eligibility, program or placement.
- To have independent evaluation results considered during mediation or a due process hearing.
- To have a hearing officer order an independent evaluation at no cost to you as part of a due process hearing Although you have the right to an independent evaluation at public expense, that evaluation must meet the school's guidelines for such an evaluation unless those guidelines make it impossible for you to get an appropriate evaluation.

Individualized Education Program (IEP)

As parents you have the right

- To participate in meetings to develop your child's Individualized Education Program (IEP)
- To be notified of the IEP meeting early enough to make arrangements to attend.
- To be notified about the time and place of the IEP meeting and who will attend.
- To have the meeting held at a time and place that is convenient for you and your child's team.
- To participate in the IEP meeting by other means, such as the telephone or video conference, if you cannot attend in person.
- To receive a copy of your child's written evaluation report and to review your child's records before the IEP meeting.
- To bring a friend, advocate or someone else with you to your child's IEP meeting.
- To be informed regularly of your child's progress toward annual goals.

Least restrictive environment (LRE)

As parents you have the right:

- To have your child educated to the greatest degree possible with nondisabled peers.
- To a variety of education placements for your child, such as preschool or day care settings, regular classes and special education classes.
- To a variety of support services to assure that your child will do well in the regular classroom, such as one-to-one tutoring and adjustments in homework assignments and/or grading procedures.
- To an education for your child in the same school he or she would attend if not disabled, unless your child's IEP requires another placement.
- To an equal opportunity for your child to participate in in-school and after-school activities with nondisabled children.

Private school placement

If your child receives special education services in a private or independent school as part of his or her IEP, you have the same rights as though your child attended public school.

If the local school district offered your child a free appropriate public education (FAPE) and you decide to place your child in a private school on your own, the school district does not have to pay the cost of special education and related services. If you disagree with the school, you have the right to request a due process hearing.

A school district may have to pay the cost of special education and related services at a private school if you remove your child from his or her IEP placement and a hearing officer decides that the school district did not offer your child a free appropriate public education.

Reimbursement for private school placement may be reduced or denied if:

- You fail to tell the school that you are rejecting the IEP placement and enrolling your child in private school.
- You fail to notify the school in writing within 10 days of your decision to remove your child from the public school.
- The school notified you before you enrolled your child in a private school that it wanted to evaluate your child and you did not make your child available for the evaluation.

Transferring Rights at 18

One year in advance, the school must notify you and your child of the transfer of special education rights to your child at age 18. If the court has appointed you or someone else as legal guardian, special education rights will not transfer to your child at age 18.

As the parent of an 18-year-old child with a disability, you will continue to be informed of meetings. But you may attend meetings only with your son's or daughter's permission. If you claim your child as a dependent on your federal income tax return, or if your child gives written permission, you will continue to have the right to review and request copies of his or her education records.

Skill 25.7   Demonstrate knowledge of types of student records (e.g., medical, academic, progress monitoring data) and their appropriate use and maintenance (e.g., storage, transfer, destruction).

Electronic Records

Today's world is quickly becoming a digital environment. Teacher's now communicate often with Email (Federal law mandate school districts to keep copies for 5 years) and are keeping records in digital formats, often within a district mandated program. Teachers should keep in mind that Emails and other electronic formats can be forwarded and are as "indelible" as permanent ink and should maintain a professional decorum just as when they are writing their own records that will be seen outside of their personal notations.

Storage of Records

While information on students that is not of a personal nature such as a grade book, it is best to treat all student information as confidential. When student information is confidential, that material must be stored in a locked cabinet, desk, etc.

CAUTION: Do not blend student files. This could cause a potential breech in confidentiality should a parent/guardian, etc. accidentally stumble onto the misplaced items.

Destruction of Records

It is important to maintain the confidentiality of your students. This is the reason for the destruction of any school records. Records that are deemed confidential and are able to be destroyed according to state, district, and school policies should be shredded to maintain confidentiality.

See also Skill 19.2

Sample Test

1. One technique that has proven especially effective in reducing self-stimulation and repetitive movements in autistic or severely retarded children is:

A. Shaping
B. Overcorrection
C. Fading
D. Response cost

2. In math class, Mary talked out without raising her hand. Her teacher gave her a warning and asked her to state the rule for being recognized to speak. However, Mary was soon talking out again and lost a point from her daily point sheet. This is an example of:

A. Shaping
B. Overcorrection
C. Fading
D. Response cost

3. Which body language would not likely be interpreted as a sign of defensiveness, aggression, or hostility?

A. Pointing
B. Direct eye contact
C. Hands on hips
D. Arms crossed

4. The minimum number of IEP meetings required per year is:

A. As many as necessary
B. One
C. Two
D. Three

5. Satisfaction of the LRE requirement means that:

A. A school is providing the best services it can offer there.
B. The school is providing the best services the district has to offer.
C. The student is being educated in the least restrictive setting that meets his or her needs.
a. The student is being educated with the fewest special education services necessary.

6. A review of a student's eligibility for an exceptional student program must be done:

A. At least once every 3 years.
B. At least once a year.
C. Only if a major change occurs in academic or behavioral performance.
D. When a student transfers to a new school.

7. Crisis intervention methods are above all concerned with:

A. Safety and well-being of the staff and students.
B. Stopping the inappropriate behavior.
C. preventing the behavior from occurring again.
D. The student learning that outbursts are inappropriate.

8. Ricky, a third grade student, runs out of the classroom and onto the roof of the school. He paces around the roof, looks around to see who is watching, and laughs at the people on the ground. He appears to be in control of his behavior. What should the teacher do?

A. Go back inside and leave him up there until he decides he is ready to come down.
B. Climb up to get Ricky so he doesn't fall off and get hurt.
C. Notify the crisis teacher and arrange to have someone monitor Ricky.
D. Call the police.

9. Mike was caught marking graffiti on the walls of the bathroom. His consequence was to clean all the walls of the bathroom. This type of overcorrection would be:

A. Response cost
B. Restitution
C. Positive Practice
D. Negative Practice

10. Judy, a fourth grader, is often looking around the room or out of the window. She does not disturb anyone, but has to ask for directions to be repeated and does not finish her work. Her teacher decides to reinforce Judy when she is on task. This would be an example of which method of reinforcement?

A. Fading
B. DRO
C. DRI
D. Shaping

11. An appropriate time out for a ten-year-old would be:

A. Ten minutes
B. Twenty minutes
C. No more than one-half hour.
D. Whatever time it takes for the disruptive behavior to stop.

12. During the science lesson Rudy makes remarks from time to time but his classmates are not attending to them. The teacher reinforces the students who are raising their hand to speak, but ignores Rudy. The teacher reinforces Rudy when he raises his hand. This technique is an example of:

A. Fading
B. Response Cost
C. Extinction
D. Differential Reinforcement of Incompatible behavior

13. Which of these would probably not be a result of implementing an extinction strategy?

A. Maladaptive behavior gets worse before it gets better.
B. Maladaptive behavior stops, then starts up again for a brief time.
C. Aggression may occur for a brief period following implementation of extinction.
D. The length of time and patience involved to implement the strategy might tempt the teacher to give up.

14. Withholding or removing a stimulus that reinforces a maladaptive behavior is:

A. Extinction
B. Overcorrection
C. Punishment
D. Reinforcing an incompatible Behavior.

15. Which of these would not be used to strengthen a desired behavior?

A. Contingency contracting
B. Tokens
C. Chaining
D. Overcorrection

16. If the arrangement in a fixed-ratio schedule of reinforcement is 3, when will the student receive the reinforcer?

A. After every third correct response.
B. After every third correct response in a row.
C. After the third correct response in the time interval of the behavior sample.
D. After the third correct response even if the undesired behavior occurs in between correct responses.

17. Wesley is having trouble ignoring distractions. At first you have him seated at a carrel which is located in a corner of the room. He does well so, you eventually move him out of the carrel for increasing portions of the day. Eventually he is able to sit in a seat with the rest of his classmates. This is an example of:

A. Shaping
B. Extinction
C. Fading
D. Chaining

18. Laura is beginning to raise her hand first instead of talking out. An effective schedule of reinforcement would be:

A. Continuous
B. Variable
C. Intermittent
D. Fixed

19. As Laura continues to raise her hand to speak, the teacher would want to change this schedule of reinforcement on order to wean her from reinforcement:

A. Continuous
B. Variable
C. Intermittent
D. Fixed

20. Laura has demonstrated that she has mastered the goal of raising her hand to speak, reinforcement during the maintenance phase should be:

A. Continuous
B. Variable
C. Intermittent
D. Fixed

21. An integral part of ecological interventions are consequences that:

A. Are natural and logical.
B. Include extinction and Overcorrection.
C. Are immediate and consistent.
D. Involve fading and shaping.

22. Examples of behaviors that are appropriate to be measured for their duration, include all EXCEPT:

A. Thumb-sucking
B. Hitting
C. Temper tantrums
D. Maintaining eye contact

23. Examples of behaviors that are appropriate to be monitored by measuring frequency include all EXCEPT:

A. Teasing
B. Talking out
C. Being on time for class
D. Daydreaming

24. Criteria for choosing behaviors to measure by frequency include all but those that:

A. Have an observable beginning.
B. Last a long time.
C. Last a short time.
D. Occur often.

25. Criteria for choosing behaviors to measure by duration include all but those that:

A. Last a short time.
B. Last a long time.
C. Have no readily observable beginning or end.
D. Do not happen often.

26. Data on quiet behaviors (e.g. nail biting or daydreaming) are best measured using a:

A. Interval or time sample.
B. Continuous sample.
C. Variable sample.
D. Fixed-ratio sample.

27. Mr. Jones wants to design an intervention for reducing Jason's sarcastic remarks. He wants to find out who or what is reinforcing Jason's remarks, so he records data on Jason's behavior as well as the attending behavior of his peers. This is an example of collecting data on:

A. Reciprocal behaviors
B. Multiple behaviors for single subjects
C. Single behaviors for multiple subjects
D. Qualitative data on Jason

28. Ms. Beekman has a class of students who frequently talk out. She wishes to begin interventions with the students who are talking out the most. She monitors the talking behavior of the entire class for 1 minute samples every half hour. This is an example of collecting data on:

A. Multiple behaviors for single subjects
B. Reciprocal behaviors
C. Single behaviors for multiple subjects
D. Continuous behaviors for fixed intervals

29. Mark got a B on his social studies test. Mr. Wilner praised him for his good grade but he replies, "I was lucky this time. It must have been an easy test." Mark's statement is an example of:

A. External locus of control
B. Internal locus of control
C. Rationalization of his performance
D. Modesty

30. Mr. Smith is on a field trip with a group of high school EH students. On the way they stop at a fast food restaurant for lunch, and Warren and Raul get into a disagreement After some heated words, Warren stalks out of the restaurant and refuses to return to the group. He leaves the parking lot, continues walking away from the group, and ignores Mr. Smith's directions to come back. What would be the best course of action for Mr. Smith?

A. Leave the group with the class aide and follow Warren to try to talk him into coming back.
B. Wait a little while and see if Warren cools off and returns .
C. Telephone the school and let the crisis teacher notify the police in accordance with school policy.
D. Call the police himself.

31. Which is the least effective of reinforcers in programs for mildly to moderately handicapped learners?

A. Tokens
B. Social
C. Food
D. Activity

32. Tyrone likes to throw paper towards the trash can instead of getting up to throw it away. After several attempts of positive interventions, Tyrone has to serve a detention and continue to throw balls of paper at the trash can for the entire detention period. This would be an example of:

A. Negative practice
B. Overcorrection
C. Extinction
D. Response cost

33. A student may have great difficulty in meeting a target goal if the teacher has not first considered:

A. If the student has external or internal locus of control.
B. If the student is motivated to attain the goal.
C. If the student has the essential prerequisite skills to perform the goal.
D. If the student has had previous success or failure meeting the goal in other classes.

34. The Premack principle of increasing the performance of a less-preferred activity by immediately following it with a highly-preferred activity is the basis of:

A. Response cost
B. Token systems
C Contingency contracting
D. Self-recording management

35. Mr. Brown finds that his chosen consequence doe s not seem to be having the desired effect of reducing the target misbehavior. Which of these would LEAST LIKELY account for Mr. Brown's lack of success with the consequence?

A. The consequence was aversive in Mr. Brown's opinion, but not the students'.
B. The students were not developmentally ready to understand the connection between the behavior and the consequence.
C. Mr. Brown was inconsistent in applying the consequence.
D. The intervention had not previously been shown to be effective in studies.

36. Teaching techniques that stimulate active participation and understanding in the mathematics class include all but which of the following?

A. Having students copy computation facts for a set number of times.
B. Asking students to find the error in an algorithm.
C. Giving immediate feedback to Students.
D. Having students chart their Progress.

37. Justin, a second grader, is reinforced if he is on task at the end of each 10-minute block of time that the teacher observes him. This is an example of what type of reinforcement schedule?

A. Continuous
B. Fixed-interval
C. Fixed ratio
D. Variable ratio

38. Addressing a student's maladaptive behavior right away with a "time out" should be reserved for situations where:

A. The student has engaged in the behavior continuously throughout the day.
B. Harm might come to the student or others.
C. Lesser interventions have not been effective.
D. The student displayed the behavior the day before.

39. At the beginning of the school year, Annette had a problem with being late to class. Her teacher reinforced her each time she was in her seat when the bell rang. In October, her teacher decided to reward her every other day when she was not tardy to class. The reinforcement schedule appropriate for making the transition to maintenance phase would be:

A. Continuous
B. Fixed interval
C. Variable ratio
D. Fixed ratio

40. By November, Annette's teacher is satisfied with her record of being on time and decides to change the schedule of reinforcement. The best type of reinforcement schedule for maintenance of behavior is:

A Continuous
B. Fixed interval
C. Variable ratio
D. Fixed Ratio

41. Which of these groups is not comprehensively covered by IDEA?

A. Gifted and talented
B. Mentally retarded
C. Specific learning disabilities
D. Speech and language impaired

42. Organizing ideas by use of a web or outline is an example of which writing activity?

A. Revision
B. Drafting
C. Prewriting
D. Final Draft

43. When a teacher is choosing behaviors to modify, the issue of social validity must be considered. Social validity refers to:

A. The need for the behavior to be performed in public.
B. Whether the new behavior will be considered significant by those who deal with the child.
C. Whether there will be opportunities to practice the new behavior in public.
D. Society's standards of behavior.

44. Dena, a second grader, is a messy eater who leaves her lunch are messy as well. Dena's teacher models correct use of eating utensils and napkins for her. As Dena approximates the target behavior of eating neatly and leaving her area clean, she receives praise and a token. Finally, Dena reaches her target behavior goal and redeems her tokens. Dena's teacher used the strategy of:

A. Chaining
B. Extinction
C. Overcorrection
D. Shaping

45. Educators who advocate educating all children in their neighborhood classrooms and schools, propose the end of labeling and segregation of special needs students in special classes, and call for the delivery of special supports and services directly in the classroom may be said to support the:

A. Full Service Model
B. Regular Education Initiative
C. Full Inclusion Model
D. Mainstream Model

46. In Ellis's ABC model, maladaptive behavior in response to a situation results from:

A. Antecedent events
B. Stimulus events
C. Thinking about the consequences
D. Irrational beliefs about the event

47. Section 504 differs from the scope of IDEA because its main focus is on:

A. Prohibition of discrimination on the basis of disability.
B. A basis for additional support services and accommodations in a special education setting.
C. Procedural rights and safeguards for the individual.
D. Federal funding for educational Services.

48. Public Law-457 amended the IDEA to make provisions for:

A. Education services for "uneducable" children.
B. Education al services for children in jail settings.
C. Procedural rights and safeguards for the individual.
D. Federal funding for educational services

49. A holistic approach to stress management should include all of the following EXCEPT:

A. Teaching a variety of coping Methods.
B. Cognitive modification of Feelings.
C. Teaching the flight or fight Response.
D. Cognitive modification of Behaviors.

50. Marisol has been mainstreamed into a ninth grade language arts class. Although her behavior is satisfactory and she likes the class, Marisol's reading level is about two years below grade level. The class has been assigned to read "Great Expectations" and write a report. What intervention would be LEAST successful in helping Marisol complete this assignment?

A. Having Marisol listen to a taped recording while following the story in the regular text.
B. Giving her a modified version of the story.
C. Telling her a modified version of the story.
D. Showing a film to the entire class and comparing and contrasting it to the book.

51. Fractions may be thought of in each of these ways EXCEPT:

A. Part of a whole
B. Part of a parent set
C. Ratio
D. An exponent

52. Many special education students may have trouble with the skills necessary to be successful in algebra and geometry for all but one of these reasons:

A. Prior instruction focused on computation rather than understanding.
B Unwillingness to problem solve.
C. Lack of instruction in prerequisite skills.
D. Large amount of new vocabulary.

53. Which of these processes is NOT directly related to the meaningful development of number concepts in young children:

A. Describing
B. Classifying
C. Grouping
D. Ordering

54. Mr. Ward wants to assess Jennifer's problem-solving skills in mathematics. Which question would not address her use of strategies?

A. Does Jennifer check for mistakes in computation?
B. Does Jennifer use trial and error to solve problems?
C. Does Jennifer have an alternative strategy if the first one fails?
D. Does Jennifer become easily frustrated if she doesn't immediately get an answer?

55. Ryan is working on a report about dogs. He uses scissors and tape to cut and rearrange sections and paragraphs, then photocopies the paper so he can continue writing. Ryan is in which stage of the writing process?

A. Final Draft
B. Prewriting
C. Revision
D. Drafting

56. Talking into a tape reorder is an example of which writing activity?

A. Prewriting
B. Drafting
C. Final Draft
D. Revision

57. Publishing a class newsletter, looking through catalogues and filling out order forms and playing the role of secretaries and executives are activities designed to teach:

A. Expressive writing
B. Transactional writing
C. Poetic writing
D. Creative writing

58. Under the provisions of IDEA, the student is entitled to all of these EXCEPT:

A.   Placement in the best environment
B.   Placement in the least restrictive environment
C.   Provision of educational needs at no cost
D.   Provision of individualized, appropriate educational program

59. Teacher modeling, student-teacher dialogues, and peer interactions are part of which teaching technique designed to provide support during the initial phases of instruction?

A.   Reciprocal teaching
B.   Scaffolding
C.   Peer tutoring
D.   Cooperative learning

60. Modeling of a behavior by an adult who verbalizes the thinking process, overt self-instruction, and covert self-instruction are components of:

A.   Rational-Emotive Therapy
B.   Reality Therapy
C.   Cognitive Behavior Modification
D.   Reciprocal Teaching

61. Standards of accuracy for a student's spelling should be based on the student's:

A.   Grade level spelling list
B.   Present reading book level
C.   Level of spelling development
D.   Performance on an informal assessment

62. Which of these techniques is least effective in helping children correct spelling problems?

A.   The teacher models the correct spelling in a context.
B.   Student sees the incorrect and the correct spelling together in order to visualize the correct spelling.
C.   Positive reinforcement as the child tests the rules and tries to approximate the correct spelling.
D.   Copying the correct word 5 times

63. The single most important activity for eventual reading success of young children is:

A.   Giving them books.
B.   Watching animated stories.
C.   Reading aloud to them.
D.   Talking about pictures in books.

64. Skilled readers use all but which one of these knowledge sources to construct meanings beyond the literal text:

A.   Text Knowledge
B.   Syntactic Knowledge
C.   Morphological Knowledge
D.   Semantic Knowledge

65. The cooperative nature of Glasser's Reality Therapy in which the problem-solving approach is used to correct misbehavior is best signified by:

A. Minimal punishment
B. Its similar approach to methods that teach students how to deal with academic mistakes.
C. Students' promises to use the alternative behavior plan to help them reach their goals.
D. Procedure sheets used during conflict situations.

66. Diaphragmatic breathing, progressive relaxation training, and exercises are examples of which type of stress coping skills?

A. Rational-emotive
B. Cognitive-psychological
C. Somatic-physiological
D. Stress inoculation

67. The stress that we experience when we win a race or accomplish a difficult task is called:

A. Stressor
B. Stresses
C. Eustress
D. Distress

68. Jane is so intimidated by a classmate's teasing that she breaks down in tears and cannot stand up for herself. The feelings she is experiencing is:

A. Stressors
B. Stresses
C. Eustress
D. Distress

69. The movement towards serving as many children with disabilities as possible in the regular classroom with supports and services is known as:

A. Full service Model
B. Regular Education Initiative
C. Full Inclusion Model
D. Mainstream Model

70. Which of the following is NOT a feature of effective classroom rules?

A. They are about 4 to 6 in number.
B. They are negatively stated.
C. Consequences for infraction are consistent and immediate.
D. They can be tailored to individual classroom goals and teaching styles.

71. A suggested amount of time for large-group instruction lesson for a sixth or seventh grade group would be:

A. 5 to 40 minutes
B. 5 to 50 minutes
C. 5 to 30 minutes
D. 5 to 15 minutes

72. Sam is working to earn half an hour of basketball time with his favorite P E teacher. At the end of each half-hour Sam marks his point sheet with an X if he reached his goal of no call-outs. When he has received 25 marks, he will receive his basketball free time. This behavior management strategy is an example of:

A. Self-recording
B. Self-evaluation
C. Self-reinforcement
D. Self-regulation

73. Mark has been working on his target goal of completing his mathematics class work. Each day he records on a scale of 0 to 3 how well he has done his work and his teacher provides feedback. This self-management technique is an example of:

A. Self-recording
B. Self-reinforcement
C. Self-regulation
D. Self-evaluation

74. When Barbara reached her target goal, she chose her reinforcer and softly said to herself, "I worked hard and I deserve this reward." This self-management technique is an example of:

A. Self-reinforcement
B. Self-recording
C. Self-regulation
D. Self-evaluation

75. Grading should be based on all of the following EXCEPT:

A. Clearly defined mastery of course objectives
B. A variety of evaluation methods
C. Performance of the student in relation to other students
D. Assigning points for activities and basing grades on a point total

76. The following words describe an IEP objective EXCEPT:

A. Specific
B. Observable
C. Measurable
D. Criterion-referenced

77. Teacher feedback, task completion, and a sense of pride over mastery or accomplishment of a skill are examples of:

A. Extrinsic reinforcers
B. Behavior modifiers
C. Intrinsic reinforces
D. Positive feedback

78. Social approval, token reinforcers, and rewards such as pencils or stickers are examples of:

A. Extrinsic reinforcers
B. Behavior modifiers
C. Intrinsic reinforcers
D. Positive feedback

79. Aggression, escape, and avoidance are unpleasant side effects which can be avoided by using:

A. Time out
B. Response cost
C. Overcorrection
D. Negative practice

80. Josie forgot that it was school picture day and did not dress up for the pictures. In the media center, Josie notices some girls in the line waiting to have their pictures taken. They appear to be looking over at her and whispering. Josie feels certain that they are making fun of the way her hair and clothes look and gets so upset that she leaves the line and hides out in the bathroom. Josie did not think to ask when the makeup day for pictures would be. According to Ellis's ABC Model, Jodie's source of stress is:

A. Her forgetting to dress appropriately for picture day.
B. The girls in the library who appear to be whispering about her.
C. Her belief that they are making fun of her appearance.
D. The girls' insensitive behavior.

81. Token systems are popular for all of these advantages EXCEPT:

A. The number needed for rewards may be adjusted as needed.
B. Rewards are easy to maintain.
C. They are effective for students who generally do not respond to social reinforcers.
D. Tokens reinforce the relationship of desirable behavior and reinforcement.

82. Which would not be an advantage of using a criterion-referenced test?

A. Information about an individual's ability level is too specific for the purposes of the assessment.
B. It can pinpoint exact areas of weaknesses and strengths.
C. You can design them yourself.
D. You do not get comparative Information.

83. Which is NOT an example of a standard score?

A. T Score
B. Z Score
C. Standard deviation
D. Stanine

84. The most direct method of obtaining assessment data and perhaps the most objective is:

A. Testing
B. Self-recording
C. Observation
D. Experimenting

85. The basic tools necessary to observe and record behavior include all BUT:

A. Cameras
B. Timers
C. Counters
D. Graphs or charts

86. Which of these characteristics is NOT included in the P.L. 94-142 definition of emotional disturbance:

A. General pervasive mood of unhappiness or depression
B. Social maladjustment manifested in a number of settings
C. Tendency to develop physical symptoms, pains, or fear associated with school or personal problems
D. Inability to learn which is not attributed to intellectual, sensory, or health factors

87. Of the various factors that contribute to delinquency and antisocial behavior, which has been found to be the weakest?

A. Criminal behavior and/or alcoholism in the father
B. Lax mother and punishing father
C. Socioeconomic disadvantage
D. Long history of broken home or marital discord among parents

88. Poor moral development, lack of empathy, and behavioral excesses such as aggression are the most obvious characteristics of which behavioral disorder?

A. Autism
B. ADD-H
C. Conduct disorder
D. Pervasive development disorder

89. School refusal, obsessive-compulsive disorders, psychosis, and separation anxiety are also frequently accompanied by:

A. Conduct disorder
B. ADD-H
C. Depression
D. Autism

90. Signs of depression do not typically include:

A. Hyperactivity
B. Changes in sleep patterns
C. Recurring thoughts of death or suicide
D. Significant changes in weight or appetite

91. Children who are characterized by impulsivity, generally:

A. Do not feel sorry for their actions.
B. Blame others for their actions.
C. Do not weigh alternatives before Acting.
D. Do not out grow their problem.

92. Which of these is listed as only a minor scale on the Behavior Problem Checklist?

A. Motor Excess
B. Conduct Disorder
C. Socialized Aggression
D. Anxiety Withdrawal

93. The extent that a test measure what it claims to measure is called:

A. Reliability
B. Validity
C. Factor Analysis
D. Chi Square

94. Which is not a goal of collaborative consultation?

A. Prevent learning and behavior problems with mainstreamed students.
B. Coordinate the instructional programs between mainstream and ESE classes,
C. Facilitate solutions to learning and behavior problems.
D. Function as an ESE service Model.

95. An important goal of collaborative consultation is:

A. Mainstream as many ESE students as possible
B. Guidance on how to handle ESE students from the ESE teacher
C. Mutual empowerment of both the mainstream and the ESE teacher.
D. Document progress of mainstreamed students.

96. Knowledge of evaluation strategies, program interventions, and types of data are examples of which variable for a successful consultation program?

A. People
B. Process
C. Procedural implementation
D. Academic preparation

97. Skills as an administrator, and background in client, consulter, and consultation skills are examples of which variable in a successful consultation program?

A. People
B. Process
C. Procedural implementation
D. Academic preparation

98. The ability to identify problems, generate solutions, and knowledge of theoretical perspectives of consultation are examples of which variable in a successful consultation program?

A. People
B. Process
C. Procedural implementation
D. Academic preparation

99. A serious hindrance to successful mainstreaming is:

A. Lack of adapted materials
B. Lack of funding
C. Lack of communication among teachers
D. Lack of support from administration

100. Which of the following statements was not offered as a rationale for the REI?

A. Special education students are not usually identified until their learning problems have become severe.
B. Lack of funding will mean that support for the special needs children will not be available in the regular classroom.
C. Putting children in segregated special education placements is stigmatizing.
D. There are students with learning or behavior problems who do not meet special education requirements but who still need special services.

101. The key to success for the exceptional student placed in a regular classroom is:

A. Access to the special aids and Materials.
B. Support from the ESE teacher.
C. Modifications in the curriculum.
D The mainstream teacher's belief that the student will profit from the placement.

102. Lack of regular follow-up, difficulty in transporting materials, and lack of consistent support for students who need more assistance are disadvantages of which type of service model?

A. Regular classroom
B. Consultant with Regular Teacher
C. Itinerant
D. Resource Room

103. Ability to supply specific instructional materials, programs, and methods, and to influence environmental learning variables are advantages of which service model for exceptional students?

A. Regular Classroom
B. Consultant Teacher
C. Itinerant Teacher
D. Resource Room

104. An emphasis on instructional remediation and individualized instruction in problem areas, and a focus on mainstreaming students are characteristics of which model of service delivery?

A. Regular Classroom
B. Consultant Teacher
C. Itinerant Teacher
D. Resource Room

105. Which of these would not be considered a valid attempt to contact a parent for an IEP meeting?

A. Telephone
B. Copy of correspondence
C. Message left on an answering machine
D. Record of home visits

106. A best practice for evaluation student performance and progress on IEP is:

A. Formal assessment
B. Curriculum based assessment
C. Criterion based assessment
D. Norm-referenced evaluation

107. Guidelines for an Individualized Family Service Plan (IFSP) would be described in which legislation?

A. PL 94-142
B. PL 99-457
C. PL 101-476
D. ADA

108. In a positive classroom environment, errors are viewed as:

A. Symptoms of deficiencies
B. Lack of attention or ability
C. A natural part of the learning process
D. The result of going too fast

109. Recess, attending school social or sporting events, and eating lunch with peers are examples of:

A. Privileges
B. Allowances
C. Rights
D. Entitlements

110. Free time, shopping at the school store, and candy are examples of:

A. Privileges
B. Allowances
C. Rights
D. Entitlements

111. Eating lunch, access to a bathroom, and privacy are examples of:

A. Privileges
B. Allowances
C. Rights
D. Entitlements

112. Cheryl is a 15-year-old student receiving educational services in a full-time EH classroom. The date for her IEP review will take place two months before her 16th birthday. According to the requirements of IDEA, what must ADDITIONALLY be included in this review?

A. Graduation plan
B. Individualized transition plan
C. Individualized Family Service Plan
D. Transportation planning

113. Hector is a 10th grader in a program for the severely emotionally handicapped. After a classmate taunted him about his mother, Hector threw a desk at the other boy and attacked him. As a crisis intervention team attempted to break up the fight, one teacher hurt his knee. The other boy received a concussion. Hector now faces disciplinary measures. How long can he be suspended without the suspension constituting a "change of placement"?

A. 5 days
B. 10 days
C. 10 + 30 days
D. 60 days

114. The concept that a handicapped student cannot be expelled for misconduct which is a manifestation of the handicap itself is not limited to students which was labeled "seriously emotionally disturbed." Which reason does NOT explain this concept?

A. Emphasis on individualized Evaluation.
B. Consideration of the problems and needs of handicapped students.
C. Right to a free and appropriate public education.
D. Putting these students out of school will just leave them on the streets to commit crimes.

115. An effective classroom behavior management plan includes all but which of the following?

A. Transition procedures for changing activities
B. Clear consequences for rule infractions
C. Concise teacher expectations for student behavior
D. Copies of lesson plans

116. Statements like "Darrien is lazy," are not helpful in describing his behavior for all but which of these reasons?

A. There is no way to determine if any change occurs from the information given.
B. The student and not the behavior becomes labeled.
C. Darrien's behavior will manifest itself clearly enough without any written description.
D. Constructs are open to various interpretations among the people who are asked to define them.

117. Mercie often is not in her seat when the bell rings. She may be found at the pencil sharpener, throwing paper away, or fumbling through her notebook. Which of these descriptions of her behavior can be described as a "pinpoint"?

A. Is tardy a lot
B. Is out of seat
C. Is not in seat when late bell rings
D. Is disorganized

118. When choosing behaviors for change, the teacher should ask if there is any evidence that the behavior is presently or potentially harmful to the student or others. This is an example of which test?

A. Fair-Pair
B. "Stranger" Test
C. Premack Principle
D. "So-What Test

119. Ms. Taylor takes her students to a special gymnastics presentation that the P.E. coach has arranged in the gym. She has a rule against talk-outs and reminds the students that they will lose 5 points on their daily point sheet for talking out. The students get a chance to perform some of the simple stunts. They all easily go through the movements except for Sam, who is known as the class klutz. Sam does not give up, and finally completes the stunts. His classmates cheer him on with comments like "Way to go!" their teacher, however, reminds them that they broke the no talking rule and will lose the points. What mistake was made here?

A. The students forgot the no-talking rule.
B. The teacher considered talk-outs to be maladaptive in all school Settings.
C. The other students could have distracted Sam with talk-outs and caused him to get hurt.
D. The teacher should have let the P. E. coach handle the discipline in the gym.

120. Which of the following should be avoided when writing objectives for social behavior?

A. Nonspecific adverbs
B. Behaviors stated as verbs
C. Criteria for acceptable performance
D. Conditions where the behavior is expected to be performed

121. Criteria for choosing behaviors that are in the most need of change involve all but the following:

A. Observations across settings to rule out certain interventions.
B. Pinpointing the behavior that is the poorest fit in the child's environment.
C. the teacher's concern about what is the most important behavior to target.
D. Analysis of the environmental Reinforcers.

122. Ms. Wright is planning an analysis of Audrey's out-of-seat behavior. Her initial data would be called:

A. Pre-referral phase
B. Intervention phase
C. Baseline phase
D. Observation phase

123. To reinforce Audrey each time she is on-task and in her seat, Ms. Wright decides to deliver specific praise and stickers which Audrey may collect and redeem for a reward. The data collected during the time Ms. Wright is using this intervention is called:

A. Referral phase
B. Intervention phase
C. Baseline phase
D. Observation phase

124. Indirect requests and attempts to influence or control others through one's use of language is an example of:

A. Morphology
B. Syntax
C. Pragmatics
D. Semantics

125. Kenny, a fourth grader, has trouble comprehending analogies, using comparative, spatial, and temporal words, and multiple meanings. Language interventions for Kenny would focus on:

A. Morphology
B. Syntax
C. Pragmatics
D. Semantics

126. Celia, who is in fourth grade, asked, "Where are my ball?" She also has trouble with passive sentences. Language interventions for Celia would target:

A. Morphology
B. Syntax
C. Pragmatics
D. Semantics

127. Scott is in middle school, but still says statements like "I gotted new high-tops yesterday," and, "I saw three mans in the front office." Language interventions for Scott would target:

A. Morphology
B. Syntax
C. Pragmatics
D. Semantics

128. Which is not indicative of a handwriting problem?

A. Errors persist over time.
B. Little improvement on simple handwriting tasks.
C. Fatigue after writing for a short Time.
D. Occasional letter reversals, word omissions, and poor spacing.

129. All of these are effective in teaching written expression EXCEPT:

A. exposure to various styles and direct instruction in those styles.
B. Immediate feedback from the teacher with all mistakes clearly marked.
C. Goal setting and peer evaluation of written products according to a set criteria.
D. Incorporating writing with other academic subjects.

130. Mr. Mendez is assessing his student's written expression. Which of these is not a component of written expression?

A. Vocabulary
B. Morphology
C. Content
D. Sentence Structure

131. Ms. Tolbert is teaching spelling to her students. The approach stresses phoneme-grapheme relationships within parts of words. Spelling rules, generalizations, and patterns are taught. A typical spelling list for her third graders might include light, bright, night, fright, and slight. Which approach is Ms. Tolbert using?

A. Rule-based instruction
B. Fernald Method
C. Gillingham Method
D. Test-Study-Test

132. At the beginning of the year, Mr. Johnson wants to gain an understanding of his class' social structure in order to help him assess social skills and related problems. The technique that would best help Mr. Johnson accomplish this is:

A. Personal interviews with each student
B. Parent rating form
C. Sociometric techniques
D. Self-reports

133. In assessing a group's social structure, asking a student to list the classmates whom he or she would choose to be his or her best friend, and preferred play partners is an example of:

A. Peer nomination
B. Peer rating
C. Peer assessment
D. Sociogram

134. Naming classmates who fit certain behavioral descriptions such as smart, disruptive, or quiet, is an example of which type of sociometric assessment?

A. Peer nomination
B. Peer rating
C. Peer assessment
D. Sociogram

135. Mr. Johnson asks his students to score each of their classmates in areas such as who they would prefer to play with and work with. A Likert-type scale with non-behavioral criteria is used. This is an example of:

A. Peer nomination
B. Peer rating
C. Peer assessment
D. Sociogram

136. Which of these explanations would not likely account for the lack of a clear definition of behavior disorders?

A. Problems with measurement
B. Cultural and/or social influences and views of what is acceptable
C. The numerous types of manifestations of behavior disorders
D. Differing theories that use their own terminology and definitions

137. Ryan is 3, and her temper tantrums last for an hour. Bryan is 8, and he does not stay on task for more than 10 minutes without teacher prompts. These behavior differ form normal children in terms of their:

A. Rate
B. Topography
C. Duration
D. Magnitude

138. All children cry, hit, fight, and play alone at different times. Children with behavior disorders will perform these behaviors at a higher than normal:

A. Rate
B. Topography
C. Duration
D. Magnitude

139. The exhibition of two or more types of problem behaviors across different areas of functioning is known as:

A. Multiple maladaptive behaviors
B. Clustering
C. Social maladjustment
D. Conduct disorder

140. Children with behavior disorders often do not exhibit stimulus control. This means that they have not learned:

A. The right things to do
B. Where and when certain behaviors are appropriate
C. Right from wrong
D. Listening skills

141. Social withdrawal, anxiety, depression, shyness, and guilt are indicative of:

A. Conduct disorder
B. Personality disorders
C. Immaturity
D. Socialized aggression

142. Short attention span, daydreaming, clumsiness, and preference for younger playmates are associated with:

A. Conduct disorder
B. Personality disorders
C. Immaturity
D. Socialized aggression

143. Truancy, gang membership, and feeling of pride in belonging to a delinquent subculture are indicative of:

A.   Conduct disorder
B.   Personality disorders
C.   Immaturity
D.   Socialized aggression

144. Temper tantrums, disruption of class, disobedience, and bossiness are associated with:

A.   Conduct disorder
B.   Personality disorders
C.   Immaturity
D.   Socialized aggression

145. Which of these is not true for most children with behavior disorders?

A.   Many score in the "slow learner" or "mildly retarded" range on IQ tests.
B.   They are frequently behind their classmates in terms of academic achievement.
C.   They are bright, but bored with their surroundings.
D.   A large amount of time is spent in nonproductive, nonacademic behaviors.

146. Echolalia, repetitive stereotype actions, and a severe disorder of thinking and communication are indicative of:

A.   Psychosis
B.   schizophrenia
C.   Autism
D.   Paranoia

147. Teaching children functional skills that will be useful in their home life and neighborhoods is the basis of:

A.   Curriculum-based instruction
B.   Community-based instruction
C.   Transition planning
D.   Functional curriculum

148. Disabilities caused by fetal alcohol syndrome are many times higher for which ethnic group?

A.   Native Americans
B.   Asian Americans
C.   Hispanic Americans
D.   African Americans

149. Which of these would be the least effective measure of behavioral disorders?

A.   Projective test
B.   Ecological assessment
C.   Standardized test
D.   Psychodynamic analysis

150. Which behavioral disorder is difficult to diagnose in children because the symptoms are manifested quite differently than in adults?

A.   Anorexia
B.   Schizophrenia
C.   paranoia
D.   Depression

Answer Key

1. B	45. C	89. C	133. A
2. D	46. D	90. A	134. C
3. B	47. A	91. C	135. A
4. B	48. C	92. A	136. C
5. D	49. C	93. B	137. C
6. A	50. C	94. D	138. A
7. A	51. D	95. C	139. B
8. C	52. A	96. B	140. B
9. C	53. C	97. A	141. B
10. A	54. D	98. C	142. C
11. C	55. C	99. C	143. D
12. C	56. C	100. B	144. A
13. B	57. B	101. D	145. C
14. A	58. A	102. C	146. C
15. D	59. B	103. B	147. B
16. B	60. C	104. D	148. A
17. A	61. C	105. C	149. C
18. A	62. D	106. B	150. D
19. D	63. C	107. B	
20. B	64. C	108. C	
21. A	65. C	109. D	
22. B	66. C	110. A	
23. D	67. C	111. C	
24. B	68. D	112. B	
25. A	69. C	113. B	
26. A	70. B	114. D	
27. A	71. C	115. D	
28. C	72. A	116. C	
29. A	73. D	117. C	
30. C	74. A	118. D	
31. C	75. C	119. D	
32. A	76. D	120. A	
33. C	77. C	121. C	
34. C	78. A	122. C	
35. D	79. B	123. B	
36. A	80. C	124. C	
37. B	81. B	125. D	
38. B	82. D	126. B	
39. B	83. C	127. A	
40. C	84. C	128. D	
41. C	85. A	129. B	
42. C	86. B	130. B	
43. D	87. C	131. A	
44. A	88. C	132. C	

Sample Questions with Rationale

1. One technique that has proven especially affective in reducing self-stimulation and repetitive movements in autistic or severely retarded children is:
   a. Shaping
   b. Overcorrection
   c. Fading
   d. Response Cost

A Shaping: To change a person's behavior gradually using rewards as the person comes closer to the desired behavior, or punishment for moving away from it.
B Overcorrection: a form of punishment, e.g. cleaning of a marked surface.
C Fading: gradual lessening of a reward or punishment.
D Response cost a form of punishment, e.g. loss of privileges

b. is correct.
Rationale: All behavior is learned

2. In math class, Mary talked out without raising her hand. Her teacher gave her a warning and asked her to state the rule for being recognized to speak. However, Mary was soon talking again, and lost a point from her daily point sheet. This is an example of:
   a. Shaping
   b. Overcorrection
   c. Fading
   d. Response cost

d. is correct.
Rationale: Mary lost a point in response to the undesirable behavior.

3. Which body language would not likely be interpreted as a sign of defensiveness, aggression, or hostility?
   a. Pointing
   b. Direct eye contact
   c. Hands on hips
   d. Arms

b. is correct.
Rationale: In our culture, A, C, and D are considered nonverbal acts of defiance. Direct eye contact is not considered an act of defiance.

4. The minimum number of IEP meetings required per year is:
   a. as many as necessary
   b. one
   c. two
   d. three

b. is correct.
Rationale: P. L. 99-457 (1986) grants an annual IEP

5. Satisfaction of the LRE requirement means:
   a. The school is providing the best services it can offer
   b. The school is providing the best services the district has to offer
   c. The student is being educated with the fewest special education services necessary
   d. The student is being educated in the least restrictive setting that meets his or her needs

d. is correct.
Rationale: The legislation mandates **LRE** Least Restrictive Environment

6. A review of a student's eligibility for an exceptional student program must be done:
   a. At least once every three years
   b. At least once a year
   c. Only if a major change occurs in academic or behavioral performance
   d. When a student transfers to a new school

a. is correct.
Rationale: P. L. 95-56 1978, (Gifted and Talented Children's Act)

7. Crisis intervention methods are above all concerned with:
   a. Safety and well-being of the staff and students
   b. Stopping the inappropriate behavior
   c. Preventing the behavior from occurring again
   d. The student learning that out bursts are inappropriate

a. is correct.
Rationale: It encompasses B, C, and D.

8. Ricky, a third grade student, runs out of the classroom and onto the roof of the school. He paces around the roof, looks around to see who is watching, and laughs at the person standing on the ground. He appears to be in control of his behavior. What should the teacher do?
   a. Go back inside and leave him up there until he decides he is ready to come down
   b. Climb up to get Ricky so he does not fall off and get hurt
   c. Notify the crisis teacher and arrange to have someone monitor Ricky
   d. Call the police

c. is correct.
Rationale: The teacher cannot be responsible for both Ricky and his or her class. He must pass the responsibility to the appropriate person.

9. Judy, a fourth grader, is often looking around the room or out the window. She does not disturb anyone, but has to ask for directions to be repeated and does not finish her work. Her teacher decides to reinforce Judy when she is on task. Which method of reinforcement is she using?
    a. Fading
    b. DRO
    c. DRI
    d. Shaping

c. is correct.
Rationale: This is an example of Direct Reinforcement (Individual)

10. An appropriate time out for a ten-year old would be:
    a. Ten minutes
    b. Twenty minutes
    c. No more than one half-hour
    d. Whatever time it takes for the disruptive behavior to stop

a. is correct.
Rationale: An appropriate time-out is no more than 10 minutes.

11. During the science lesson Rudy makes remarks from time to time, but his classmates are not attending to them. the teacher reinforces the students who are raising their hand to speak, but ignores Rudy. The teacher reinforces Rudy when he raises his hand. This technique is an example of:
    a. Fading
    b. Response cost
    c. Extinction
    d. Differential reinforcement of incompatible behavior

c. is correct.
Rationale: By ignoring the behavior, the teacher hopes it will become extinct.

12. Mike was caught marking up the walls of the bathroom with graffiti. His consequence was to clean all the walls of the bathroom. This type of overcorrection would be:
    a. Response cost
    b. Restitution
    c. Positive practice
    d. Negative practice

c. is correct.
Rationale: This is a positive form of over correction in which the student is learning another skill.

13. Which of these would probably not be a result of implementing an extinction strategy?
    a. Maladaptive behavior gets worse before it gets better
    b. Maladaptive behavior stops, then starts up again for a brief time
    c. Aggression may occur for a brief period following implementation of extinction
    d. The length of time and patience involved to implement the strategy might tempt the teacher to give up

b. is correct.
Rationale: The student responds in A, B, and C. In B, he ignores the teacher's action.

14. Withholding or removing a stimulus that reinforces a maladaptive behavior is:
    a. Extinction
    b. Overcorrection
    c. Punishment
    d. Reinforcing an incompatible behavior

a. is correct.
Rationale: There is no stimulus involved in this strategy.

15. Which of these would not be used to strengthen a desired behavior?
    a. Contingency contracting
    b. Tokens
    c. Chaining
    d. Overcorrection

d. is correct.
Rationale: A, B, and C are all used to strengthen a desired behavior. D is punishment.

16. If the arrangement in a fixed-ratio schedule of reinforcement is 3, when will the student receive the reinforcer?
    a. After every third correct response
    b. After every third correct response in a row
    c. After the third correct response in the time interval of the behavior sample
    d. After the third correct response even if the undesired behavior occurs in be between correct responses

b. is correct.
Rationale: This is the only one that follows a pattern. A fixed ratio is a pattern.

17. Wesley is having difficulty ignoring distractions. At first you have him seated at a carrel which is located in a corner of the room. He does well, so you eventually move him out of the carrel for increasing portions of the day. Eventually, he is able to sit in a seat with the rest of his classmates. This is an example of:
    a. Shaping
    b. Extinction
    c. Fading
    d. Chaining

a. is correct.
Rationale: The teacher is <u>shaping</u> a desired behavior.

18. Laura is beginning to raise her hand first instead of talking out. An effective schedule of reinforcement should be:
   a. Continuous
   b. Variable
   c. Intermittent
   d. Fixed

a. is correct.
Rationale: The pattern of reinforcement should not be variable, intermittent or fixed. It should be continuous.

19. As Laura continues to raise her hand to speak, the teacher would want to change to this schedule of reinforcement in order to wean her from the reinforcement:
   a. Continuous
   b. Variable
   c. Intermittent
   d. Fixed

d. is correct.
Rationale: The pattern should be in a fixed ratio.

20. Laura has demonstrated that she has mastered the goal of raising her hand to speak; reinforcement during the maintenance phase should be:
   a. Continuous
   b. Variable
   c. Intermittent
   d. Fixed

b. is correct.
Rationale: Reinforcement should be intermittent, as the behavior should occur infrequently.

21. An integral part of ecological interventions are consequences that:
    a. Are natural and logical
    b. Include extinction and overcorrection
    c. Care immediate and consistent
    d. Involve fading and shaping

a. is correct.
Rationale: The student must understand both the behavior and the consequence. The consequence should fit the infraction.

22. Examples of behaviors that are appropriate to be monitored by measuring frequency include all EXCEPT:
    a. Thumb sucking
    b. Hitting
    c. Temper tantrums
    d. Maintaining eye contact

b. is correct.
Rationale: Hitting takes place in an instant. This should be measured by frequency.

23. Examples of behaviors that are appropriate to be monitored by measuring frequency include all EXCEPT:
    a. Teasing
    b. Talking out
    c. Being on time for class
    d. Daydreaming

d. is correct.
Rationale: Daydreaming cannot be measured by frequency. It should be measured by duration.

24. Criteria for choosing behaviors to measure by frequency include all but those that:
    a. Have an observable beginning
    b. Last a long time
    c. Last a short time
    d. Occur often

b. is correct.
Rationale: We use frequency to measure behaviors that do not last a long time.

25. Criteria for choosing behaviors to measure by duration include all but those that:
    a. Last a short time
    b. Last a long time
    c. Have no readily observable beginning or end
    d. Don't happen often

a. is correct.
Rationale: We use duration to measure behavior that do not last a short time.

26. Data on quiet behaviors e.g.nailbiting or daydreaming, are best measured using a (an):
    a. Interval or time sample
    b. Continuous sample
    c. Variable sample
    d. Fixed-ratio sample

a. is correct.
Rationale: An interval or time sample is best to measure the duration of the behavior.

27. Mr. Jones wants to design an intervention for reducing Jason's sarcastic remarks. He wants to find out who or what is reinforcing Jason's remarks, so he records data on Jason's behavior as well as the attending behavior of his peers. This is an example of collecting data on:
    a. Reciprocal behaviors
    b. Multiple behaviors for single subjects
    c. Single behaviors for multiple subjects
    d. Qualitative data on Jason

a. is correct.
Rationale: Jason's peers' behaviors are in response to Jason's disruptive behaviors.

28. Ms Beekman has a class of students who frequently talk out. She wishes to begin interventions with the students who are talking out the most. She monitors the talking behavior of the entire class for 1-minute samples every half-hour. this is an example of collecting data on:
    a. Multiple behavior for single subjects
    b. Reciprocal behaviors
    c. Single behaviors for multiple subjects
    d. Continuous behaviors for fixed intervals

c. is correct.
Rationale: Talking out is the only behavior being observed.

29. Mark got a B on his social studies test. Mr. Wilner praised him for his good grade but he replies, "I was lucky this time. It must have been an easy test." Mark's statement is an example of:
    a. External locus of control
    b. Internal locus of control
    c. Rationalization of his performance
    d. Modesty

a. is correct.
Rationale: Locus of control refers to the way a person perceives the relation between his or her efforts and the outcome of an event. A person who has an external orientation anticipates no relation between his or her efforts and the outcome of an event.

30. Mr. Smith is on a field trip with a group of high school EH students. On the way, they stop at a fast-food restaurant for lunch, and Warren and Raul get into an argument. After some heated words, Warren stalks out of the restaurant and refuses to return to the group. He leaves the parking lot, continues walking away from the group, and ignores Mr. Smith's directions to come back. What would be the best course of action for Mr. Smith?
    a. Leave the group with the class aide and follow Warren to try to talk him into coming back.
    b. Wait a little while and see if Warren cools off and returns.
    c. Telephone the school and let the crisis teacher notify the police in accordance with school policy.
    d. Call the police himself.

c. is correct.
Rationale: Mr. Smith is still responsible for his class. This is his only option.

31. Which is the least effective of reinforcers in programs for mildly to moderately handicapped learners?
    a. Tokens
    b. Social
    c. Food
    d. Activity

c. is correct.
Rationale: Food is the least effective reinforcer for most handicapped children. Tokens, social interaction or activity is more desirable. Food may have reached satiation.

32. Tyrone likes to throw paper towards the trashcan instead of getting up to throw it away. After several attempts at positive interventions, Tyrone has to serve a detention and continue to throw balls of paper at the trashcan for the entire detention period. This would be an example of:
    a. Negative practice
    b. Overcorrection
    c. Extinction
    d. Response cost

a. is correct.
Rationale: Tyrone has to continue to practice the negative behavior.

33. A student may have great difficulty in meeting a target goal if the teacher has not first considered:
    a. If the student has external or internal locus of control.
    b. If the student is motivated to attain the goal.
    c. If the student has the essential prerequisite skills to perform the goal.
    d. If the student has had previous success or failure meeting the goal in other classes.

c. is correct.
Rationale: Prerequisite skills are essential in both setting goals and attaining goals.

34. The Premack Principle of increasing the performance of a less-preferred activity by immediately following it with a highly preferred activity is the basis of:
    a. response cost
    b. token systems
    c. contingency contracting
    d. self-recording management

c. is correct.
Rationale: The student eagerly completes the less desirable activity, to obtain the reward of the more desirable activity, in an unwritten contract.

35. Mr. Brown finds that his chosen consequence does not seem to be having the desired effect of reducing the target misbehavior. Which of these would LEAST LIKELY account for Mr. Brown's lack of success with the consequence?
    a. The consequence was aversive in Mr. Brown's opinion but not the students'.
    b. The students were not developmentally ready to understand the connection.
    c. Mr. Brown was inconsistent in applying the consequence.
    d. The intervention had not previously been shown to be effective in studies.

d. is correct.
Rationale: A, B, and C, might work if applied in the classroom, but research, it is the least of Mr. Brown's options.

36. Teaching techniques that stimulate active participation and understanding in the mathematics class include all but which of the following?
    a. Having students copy computation facts for a set number of times.
    b. Asking students to find the error in an algorithm.
    c. Giving immediate feedback to students.
    d. Having students chart their progress.

a. is correct.
Rationale: Copying does not stimulate participation or understanding.

37. Justin, a second grader, is reinforced if he is on task at the end of each 10-minute block of time that the teacher observes him. This is an example of what type of schedule?
    a. Continuous
    b. Fixed interval
    c. Fixed-ratio
    d. Variable ratio

b. is correct.
Rationale: 10 minutes is a fixed interval of time.

38. Addressing a student's maladaptive behavior right away with a "time out" should be reserved for situations where:
    a. The student has engaged in the behavior continuously throughout the day.
    b. Harm might come to the student or others.
    c. Lesser interventions have not been effective.
    d. The student displayed the behavior the day before.

b. is correct.
Rationale: The best intervention is to move the student away from the harmful environment.

39. At the beginning of the school year, Annette had a problem with being late for class. Her teacher reinforced here each time she was in her seat when the bell rang. In October, her teacher decided to reward her every other day when she was not tardy to class. The reinforcement schedule appropriate for making the transition to maintenance phase would be:
    a. Continuous
    b. Fixed interval
    c. Variable ratio
    d. Fixed ratio

b. is correct.
Rationale: Every other day is a fixed interval of time.

40. By November, Annette's teacher is satisfied with her record of being on time and decides to change the schedule of reinforcement. The best type of reinforcement schedule for maintenance or behavior is:
    a. Continuous
    b. Fixed interval
    c. Variable ratio
    d. Fixed ratio

c. is correct.
Rationale: The behavior will occur infrequently. Variable Ratio is the best schedule.

41. Which of these groups is not comprehensively covered by IDEA?
    a. Gifted and talented
    b. Mentally retarded
    c. Specific learning disabilities
    d. Speech and language impaired

c. is correct.
Rationale: IDEA: Individuals with Disabilities Education Act 101-476 (1990) did not cover all exceptional children. The Gifted and Talented Children's Act, P. L. 95-56 was passed in 1978.

42. Organizing ideas by use of a web or outline is an example of which writing activity?
    a. Revision
    b. Drafting
    c. Prewriting
    d. Final draft

c. is correct.
Rationale: Organizing ideas come before Drafting, Final Draft and Revision.

43. When a teacher is choosing behaviors to modify, the issue of social validity must be considered. Social validity refers to:
    a. The need for the behavior to be performed in public.
    b. Whether the new behavior will be considered significant by those who deal with the child.
    c. Whether there will be opportunities to practice the new behavior in public.
    d. Society's standards of behavior.

d. is correct.
Rationale: Validity has to do with the appropriateness of the behavior. Is it age appropriate? Is it culturally appropriate?

44. Dena, a second grader, is a messy eater who leaves her lunch area messy as well. Dena's teacher models correct use of eating utensils, and napkins for her. As Dena approximates the target behavior of neatly and leaving her area clean, she receives praise and a token. Finally, Dena reaches her target behavior goal and redeems her tokens. Dena's teacher used the strategy of:
a. Chaining
b. Extinction
c. Overcorrection
d. Shaping

a. is correct.
Rationale: Chaining is a procedure in which individual responses are reinforced when occurring in sequence to form a complex behavior. Shaping, however, targets single behaviors.

45. Educators who advocate educating all children in their neighborhood classrooms and schools, propose the end of labeling and segregation of special needs students in special classes, and call for the delivery of special supports and services directly in the classroom may be said to support the:
a. Full service model
b. Regular education initiative
c. Full inclusion model
d. Mainstream model

c. is correct.
Rationale: All students must be included in the regular classroom.

46. In Ellis' ABC model, maladaptive behavior in response to a situation results from:
a. Antecedent events
b. Stimulus events
c. Thinking about the consequences
d. Irrational beliefs about the event

d. is correct.
Rationale: All behavior is learned. This behavior is different from the norm. It is different because of something the child has experienced or learned.

47. Section 504 differs from the scope of IDEA because its main focus is on:
    a. Prohibition of discrimination on the basis of disability.
    b. A basis for additional support services and accommodations in a special education setting.
    c. Procedural rights and safeguards for the individual.
    d. Federal funding for educational services.

a. is correct.
Rationale: Section 504 prohibits discrimination on the basis of disability.

48. Public Law 99-457 amended the EHA to make provisions for:
    a. Education services for "uneducable" children
    b. Education services for children in jail settings
    c. Special education benefits for children birth to five years
    d. Education services for medically fragile children

c. is correct.
Rationale: P.L. 99-457 amended EHA to provide Special Education programs for children 3-5 years, with most states offering outreach programs to identify children with special needs from birth to age 3.

49. A holistic approach to stress management should include all of the following EXCEPT:
    a. Teaching a variety of coping methods
    b. Cognitive modification of feelings
    c. Teaching the fight or flight response
    d. Cognitive modification of behaviors

c. is correct.
Rationale: A, B, and D are coping interventions. C is not.

50. Marisol has been mainstreamed into a ninth grade language arts class. Although her behavior is satisfactory and she likes the class, Marisol's reading level is about two years below grade level. The class has been assigned to read "Great Expectations" and write a report. What intervention would be LEAST successful in helping Marisol complete this assignment?
    a. Having Marisol listen to a taped recording while following the story in the regular text.
    b. Giving her a modified version of the story.
    c. Telling her to choose a different book that she can read.
    d. Showing a film to the entire class and comparing and contrasting it with the book.

c. is correct.
Rationale: A, B, and D, are positive interventions. C is not an intervention.

51. Fractions may be thought of in each of these ways EXCEPT:
    a. Part of a whole
    b. Part of a parent set
    c. Ratio
    d. An exponent

d. is correct.
Rationale: An exponent can never be a fraction

52. Many special education students may have trouble with the skills necessary to be successful in algebra and geometry for all but one of these reasons:
    a. Prior instruction focused on computation rather than understanding
    b. Unwillingness to problem solve
    c. Lack of instruction in prerequisite skills
    d. Large amount of new vocabulary

a. is correct.
Rationale: In order to build skills in math, students must be able to understand math concepts.

53. Which of these processes is NOT directly related to the meaningful development of number concepts in younger children?
    a. Describing
    b. Classifying
    c. Grouping
    d. Ordering

c. is correct.
Rationale: Grouping does not involve the meaningful development of number concepts.

54. Mr. Ward wants to assess Jennifer's problem-solving skills in mathematics. Which question would not address her use of strategies?
    a. Does Jennifer check for mistakes in computation?
    b. Does Jennifer use trial and error to solve problems?
    c. Does Jennifer have an alternative strategy if the first one fails?
    d. Does Jennifer become easily frustrated if she doesn't get an answer immediately?

d. is correct.
Rationale: A, B, and C, are problem-solving skills Jennifer needs to develop.

55. Ryan is working on a report about dogs. He uses scissors and tape to cut and rearrange sections and paragraphs, then photocopies the paper so he can continue writing. In which stage of the writing process is Ryan?
    a. Final draft
    b. Prewriting
    c. Revision
    d. Drafting

c. is correct.
 Rationale: Ryan is Revising and reordering before final editing.

56. Talking into a tape recorder is an example of which writing activity?
    a. Prewriting
    b. Drafting
    c. Final Draft
    d. Revision

c. is correct.
Rationale: Ryan is preparing his final draft.

57. publishing a class newsletter, looking through catalogues, and filling out order forms and playing the role of secretaries are activities designed to teach:
    a. Expressive writing
    b. Transactional writing
    c. Poetic writing
    d. Creative writing

b. is correct.
Rationale: Transactional writing includes expository writing, descriptive writing and persuasive writing. It does not include any of the other three types of writing listed.

58. Under the provisions of IDEA, the student is entitled to all of these EXCEPT:
    a. Placement in the best environment
    b. Placement in the least restricive environment (LRE)
    c. Provision of educational needs at no cost
    d. Provision of individualized, appropriate educational program

a. is correct.
Rationale: IDEA mandates a **least restricive environment (LRE), an IEP, (individual education plan) and a free public education.**

59. Teacher modeling, student-teacher dialogues, and peer interactions are part of which teaching technique designed to provide support during the initial stages of instruction?
    a. Reciprocal teaching
    b. Scaffolding
    c. Peer tutoring
    d. Cooperative learning

b. is correct.
Rationale: Scaffolding provides support.

60. Modeling of a behavior by an adult who verbalizes the thinking process, overt self-instruction, and covert self-instruction are components of:
    a. Rational-emotive therapy
    b. Reality therapy
    c. Cognitive behavior modification
    d. Reciprocal teaching

c. is correct.
Rationale: Neither A, B, nor D, involves modification or change of behavior.

61. Standards of accuracy for a student's spelling should be based on the student's:
    a. Grade level spelling list
    b. Present reading book level
    c. Level of spelling development
    d. Performance on an informal assessment

c. is correct.
Rationale: Spelling instruction should include words misspelled in daily writing, generalizing spelling knowledge and mastering objectives in progressive stages of development.

62. Which of these techniques is least effective in helping children correct spelling problems?
    a. The teacher models the correct spelling in a context
    b. Student sees the incorrect and the correct spelling together in order to visualize the correct spelling
    c. Positive reinforcement as the child tests the rules and tries to approximate the correct spelling
    d. Copying the correct word five times

d. is correct.
Rationale: Copying the word is least effective.

63. The single most important activity for eventual reading success of young children is:
    a. Giving them books
    b. Watching animated stories
    c. Reading aloud to them
    d. Talking about pictures in books

C. is correct.
Rationale: Reading aloud exposes them to language.

64. Skilled readers use all but which one of these knowledge sources to construct meanings beyond the literal text:
    a. Text knowledge
    b. Syntactic knowledge
    c. Morphological knowledge
    d. Semantic knowledge

c. is correct.
Rationale: The student is already skilled so morphological knowledge is already in place.

65. The cooperative nature of Glasser's Reality Therapy, in which problem-solving approach is used to correct misbehavior, is best signified by:
    a. Minimal punishment
    b. It's similar approach to methods that teach students how to deal with academic mistakes
    c. Student's promises to use the alternative behavior plan to help them reach their goals
    d. Procedure sheets used during conflict situations

c. is correct.
Rationale: Glasser's Reality Therapy makes use of an alternative behavior plan, a form of group therapy.

66. Diaphragmatic breathing, progressive relaxation training, and exercises are examples of which type of stress coping skills?
    a. Rational-emotive
    b. Cognitive-psychological
    c. Somatic-physiological
    d. Stress inoculation

C. is correct.
Rationale: When we analyze the expression, somatic-physiological, we find, somatic: relating to the body physiological: relating to nature and natural phenomena.

67. The stress that we experience when we win a race or experience a difficult task is called:
    a. Stressor
    b. Stresses
    c. Eustress
    d. Distress

c. is correct.
Rationale: Eustress is a sort of elation, or release of anxiety. It is the opposite of distress.

68. Jane is so intimidated by a classmate's teasing that she breaks down in tears and cannot stand up for herself.
    a. Stressors
    b. Stresses
    c. Eustress
    d. Distress

d. is correct.
Rationale: Jane is in a state of distress.

69. The movement towards serving as many children with disabilities as possible in the regular classroom with supports and services is known as:
    a. Full service model
    b. Regular education initiative
    c. Full inclusion model
    d. Mainstream model

c. is correct.
Rationale: It is the movement to include all students in the regular classroom.

70. Which of the following is NOT a feature of effective classroom rules?
    a. They are about 4to 6 in number
    b. They are negatively stated
    c. Consequences are consistent and immediate
    d. They can be tailored to individual teaching goals and teaching styles

b. is correct.
Rationale: Rules should be positively stated and they should follow the other three features listed.

71. A suggested amount of time for large-group instruction lesson for a sixth or seventh grade group would be:
    a. 5 to 40 minutes
    b. 5 to 20 minutes
    c. 5 to 30 minutes
    d. 5 to 15 minutes

c. is correct.
Rationale: The recommended time for large group instruction is 5 - 15 minutes for grades 1-5 and 5 – 40 minutes for grades 8-12.

72. Sam is working to earn half an hour of basketball time with his favorite PE teacher. At the end of each half-hour, Sam marks his point sheet with an X, if he reached his goal of no call-outs. When he has received 25 marks, he will receive his basketball free time. This behavior management strategy is an example of:
    a. Self-recording
    b. Self-evaluation
    c. Self-reinforcement
    d. Self-regulation

Self-Management-This is an important part of social skills training, especially for older students preparing for employment. Components for self-management include:

1. *Self-Monitoring:* choosing behaviors and alternatives and monitoring those actions.
2. *Self-Evaluation:* deciding the effectiveness of the behavior in solving the problem.
3. *Self-Reinforcement:* telling oneself that one is capable of achieving success.

a. is correct.
Rationale: Sam is recording his behavior.

73. Mark has been working on his target goal of completing his mathematics class work. Each day he records on a scale of 0 to 3 how well he has done his work and his teacher provides feedback. This self-management technique is an example of:
    a. Self-recording
    b. Self reinforcement
    c. Self-regulation
    d. Self-evaluation

d. is correct.

Rationale: Sam is evaluating his behavior, not merely recording it.

74. When Barbara reached her target goal, she chose her reinforcer and said softly to herself, "I worked hard and I deserve this reward". This self-management technique is an example of:
    a. Self-reinforcement
    b. Self recording
    c. Self-regulation
    d. Self-evaluation

a. is correct.

Rationale: Barbara is reinforcing her behavior.

75. Grading should be based on all of the following EXCEPT:
    a. Clearly defined mastery of course objectives
    b. A variety of evaluation methods
    c. Performance of the student in relation to other students
    d. Assigning points for activities and basing grades on a point total

c. is correct.

Rationale: Grading should never be based on the comparison of performance of other students. It should always be based on the student's mastery of course objectives, the methods of evaluation and the grading rubric (how points are assigned).

76. The following words describe an IEP objective EXCEPT:
a. Specific
b. Observable
c. Measurable
d. Criterion-referenced

D. is correct.
Rationale: An Individual Education Plan should be specific, observable, and measurable.

77. Teacher feedback, task completion, and a sense of pride over mastery or accomplishment of a skill are examples of:
a. Extrinsic reinforcers
b. Behavior modifiers
c. Intrinsic reinforcers
d. Positive feedback

Motivation may be achieved through intrinsic reinforcers or extrinsic reinforcers. Intrinsic rieinforcers are usually intangible and extrinsic reinforcers are usually tangible rewards and from an external source.

c. is correct.
Rationale: These are intangibles.

78. Social approval, token reinforcers, and rewards such as pencils or stickers are examples of:
    a. Extrinsic reinforcers
    b. Behavior modifiers
    c. Intrinsic reinforcers
    d. Positive feedback reinforcers

a. is correct.
Rationale: These are rewards from external sources

79. Aggression, escape and avoidance are unpleasant side effects, which can be avoided by using:
    a. Time-out
    b. Response cost
    c. Overcorrection
    d. Negative practice

b. is correct.
Rationale: In response cost, students know that there will be consequences for these undesirable behaviors.

80. Josie forgot that it was school picture day and did not dress up for the pictures. In the media center, Josie notices some girls in the line waiting to have their pictures taken. They appear to be looking over at her and whispering. Josie feels certain that they are making fun of the way her hair and clothes look and gets so upset that she leaves the line and hides out in the bathroom. Josie did not think of asking when the make-up day for pictures would be. According to Ellis' ABC model, Josie's source of stress is:
    a. Her forgetting to dress appropriately for picture day
    b. The girls in the library who appear to be whispering about her
    c. Her belief that they are making fun of her appearance
    d. The girls' insensitive behavior

c. is correct.
Rationale: Josie is responding to her belief.

81. Token systems are popular for all of these advantages EXCEPT:
    a. The number needed for rewards may be adjusted as needed
    b. Rewards are easy to maintain
    c. They are effective for students who generally do not respond to social reinforcers
    d. Tokens reinforce the relationship between desirable behavior and reinforcement

b. is correct.
Rationale: The ease of maintenance is not a valid reason for developing a token system.

82. Which would not be an advantage of using a criterion-referenced test?
    a. Information about an individual's ability level is too specific for the purposes of the assessment
    b. It can pinpoint exact areas of weaknesses and strengths
    c. You can design them yourself
    d. You do not get comparative information

d. is correct.
Rationale: Criterion-referenced tests measure mastery of content rather than performance compared to others. Test items are usually prepared from specific educational objectives and may be teacher-made or commercially prepared. Scores are measured by the percentage of correct items for a skill (e.g. adding and subtracting fractions with like denominators).

83. Which is NOT an example of a standard score?
     T score
     Z score
     Standard deviation
     Stanine

c. is correct.
Rationale: A, B, and D, are all standardized scores. Stanines are whole number scores from 1 to 9, each representing a wide range of raw scores. Standard deviation is **not a score.** It measures how widely scores vary from the mean.

84. The most direct method of obtaining assessment data and perhaps the most objective is:
     a. Testing
     b. Self-recording
     c. Observation
     d. Experimenting

c. is correct.
Rationale: Observation is often better than testing, due to language, culture or other factors.

85. The basic tools necessary to observe and record behavior include all BUT:
     a. Cameras
     b. Timers
     c. Counters
     d. Graphs or charts

a. is correct.
Rationale: The camera gives a snapshot. It does not record behavior.

86. Which of these characteristics is NOT included in the P.L. 94-142 definition of emotional disturbance?
    a. General pervasive mood of unhappiness or depression
    b. Social maladjustment manifested in a number of settings
    c. Tendency to develop physical symptoms, pains, or fear associated with school or personal problems
    d. Inability to learn which is not attributed to intellectual, sensory, or health factors

b. is correct.
Rationale: Social maladjustment is not considered a disability.

87. Of the various factors that contribute to delinquency, and anti-social behavior, which has been found to be the weakest?
    a. Criminal behavior and/or alcoholism in the father
    b. Lax mother and punishing father
    c. Socioeconomic disadvantage
    d. Long history of broken home and marital discord among parents

c. is correct.
Rationale: There are many examples of A, B, and C, where there is socio-economic advantage.

88. Poor moral development, lack of empathy, and behavioral excesses such as aggression are the most obvious characteristics of which behavioral disorder?
    a. Autism
    b. ADD-H
    c. Conduct disorder
    d. Pervasive developmental disorder

c. is correct.
Rationale: A student with conduct disorder or social maladjustment displays behaviors/values that are in conflict with the school, home, or community. The characteristics listed are all behavioral/social.

89. School refusal, obsessive-compulsive disorders, psychosis, and separation anxiety are also frequently accompanied by:
    a. Conduct disorder
    b. ADD-H
    c. depression
    d. autism

c. is correct.
Rationale: These behaviors are usually accompanied by depression in ADD-H.

90. Signs of depression do not typically include:
    a. Hyperactivity
    b. Changes in sleep patterns
    c. Recurring thoughts of death or suicide
    d. Significant changes in weight or appetite

a. is correct.
Rationale: depression is usually characterized by listlessness, brooding, low anxiety, and little activity. Hyperactivity, conversely is over activity.

91. Children who are characterized by impulsivity generally:
    a. Do not feel sorry for their actions
    b. Blame others for their actions
    c. Do not weigh alternatives before acting
    d. Do not outgrow their problem

c. is correct.
Rationale: They act without thinking, so they either cannot think or do not think before they act.

92. Which of these is listed as only a minor scale on the Behavior Problem Checklist?
    a. Motor Excess
    b. Conduct Disorder
    c. Socialized Aggression
    d. Anxiety/Withdrawal

a. is correct.
Rationale: Motor Excess has to do with over activity, or hyperactivity, physical movement. The other three items are disorders, all of which may be characterized by excessive activity.

93. The extent that a test measures what it claims to measure is called:
    a. Reliability
    b. Validity
    c. Factor analysis
    d. Chi Square

b. is correct.
Rationale: The degree to which a test measures what it claims to measure.

94. Which is not a goal of collaborative consultation?
    a. Prevent learning and behavior problems with mainstreamed students
    b. Coordinate the instructional programs between mainstream and ESE classes
    c. Facilitate solutions to learning and behavior problems
    d. Function as an ESE service model

d. is correct.
Rationale: A, B, and C are goals. Functioning as an Exceptional Student Education model is not a goal. Collaborative consultation is necessary for the classification of students with disabilities and provision of services to satisfy their needs.

95. An important goal of collaborative consultation is:
    a. Mainstream as many ESE students as possible
    b. Guidance on how to handle ESE students from the ESE teacher
    c. Mutual empowerment of both the mainstream and the ESE teacher
    d. Document progress of mainstreamed students

C. is correct.
Rationale: Empowerment of these service providers is extremely important.

96. Knowledge of evaluation strategies, program interventions, and types of data are examples of which variable for a successful consultation program?
    a. People
    b. Process
    c. Procedural implementation
    d. Academic preparation

b. is correct.
Rationale: Consultation programs cannot be successful without knowledge of the process.

97. Skills as an administrator and background in client, consulter, and consultation skills are examples of which variable in a successful consultation program?
    a. people
    b. Process
    c. Procedural implementation
    d. Academic preparation

a. is correct.
Rationale: Consultation programs cannot be successful without people skills.

98. The ability to identify problems, generate solutions, and knowledge of theoretical perspectives of consultation are examples of which variable in a successful consultation program?
    a. People
    b. Process
    c. Procedural implementation
    d. Academic preparation

c. is correct.
Rationale: Consultation programs cannot be successful without implementation skills.

99. A serious hindrance to successful mainstreaming is:
    a. Lack of adapted materials
    b. Lack of funding
    c. Lack of communication among teachers
    d. Lack of support from administration

c. is correct.
Rationale: All 4 choices are hindrances but lack of communication and consultation between the service providers is serious.

100. Which of the following statements was not offered as a rationale for REI?
    a. Special education students are not usually identified until their learning problems have become severe
    b. Lack of funding will mean that support for the special needs children will not be available in the regular classroom.
    c. Putting children in segregated special education placements is stigmatizing
    d. There are students with learning or behavior problems who do not meet special education requirements but who still need special services

b. is correct.
Rationale: All except lack of funding were offered in support of Regular Education Intervention or Inclusion.

101. The key to success for the exceptional student placed in a regular classroom is:
    a. Access to the special aids and materials
    b. Support from the ESE teacher
    c. Modification in the curriculum
    d. The mainstream teacher's belief that the student will profit from the placement

d. is correct.
Rationale: Without the regular teacher's belief that the student can benefit, no special accommodations will be provided.

102. Lack of regular follow-up, difficulty in transporting materials, and lack of consistent support for students who need more assistance are disadvantages of which type of service model?
    a. Regular classroom
    b. Consultant with regular teacher
    c. Itinerant
    d. Resource room

c. is correct.
Rationale: The itinerant model, as the name implies, is not regular.

103. Ability to supply specific instructional materials, programs, and methods and to influence environmental learning variables are advantages of which service model for exceptional students?
    a. Regular classroom
    b. Consultant teacher
    c. Itinerant teacher
    d. Resource room

b. is correct.
Rationale: Consultation is usually done by specialists.

104. An emphasis on instructional remediation and individualized instruction in problem areas, and a focus on mainstreaming are characteristics of which model of service delivery?
    a. Regular classroom
    b. Consultant teacher
    c. Itinerant teacher
    d. Resource room

d. is correct.
Rationale: The Resource room is usually a bridge to mainstreaming.

105. Which of these would not be considered a valid attempt to contact a parent for an IEP meeting?
    a. Telephone
    b. Copy of correspondence
    c. Message left on answering machine
    d. Record of home visits

c. is correct.
Rationale: A message left on an answering machine is not direct contact.

106. A best practice for evaluating student performance and progress on IEPs is:
    a. Formal assessment
    b. Curriculum based assessment
    c. Criterion based assessment
    d. Norm-referenced evaluation

b. is correct.
Rationale: This is a teacher-prepared test that measures the student's progress, but at the same time shows the teacher whether or not the accommodations are effective.

107. Guidelines for an Individualized Family Service Plan (IFSP) would be described in which legislation?
    a. P.L. 94-142
    b. P. L. 99 – 457
    c. P.L. 101 – 476
    d. ADA

B. is correct.
Rationale: P. L. 99-457, 1986 provides services for children of ages 3-5 and their families; P.L. 101 – 476 is IDEA; P.L. 94 – 142 Education for All Handicapped Children Act, was passed in the Civil Rights era. ADA is the Americans with Disabilities Act.

108. In a positive classroom environment, errors are viewed as:
    a. Symptoms of deficiencies
    b. Lack of attention or ability
    c. A natural part of the learning process
    d. The result of going too fast

c. is correct.
Rationale: We often learn a great deal from our mistakes and shortcomings. It is normal. Where it is not normal, fear develops. This fear of failure, inhibits children from working and achieving. Copying and other types of cheating, results.

109. Recess, attending school social or sporting events, and eating lunch with peers are examples of:
    a. Privileges
    b. Allowances
    c. Rights
    d. Entitlements

d. is correct.
Rationale: These are entitlements. They may be used as consequences.

110. Free time, shopping at the school store, and candy are examples of:
    a. Privileges
    b. Allowances
    c. Rights
    d. Entitlements

a. is correct.
Rationale: These are privileges, or positive consequences.

111. Eating lunch, access to a bathroom, and privacy are examples of:
    a. Privileges
    b. Allowances
    c. Rights
    d. Entitlements

c. is correct.
Rationale: These are rights. They may not be used as consequences.

112. Cheryl is a 15-year old student receiving educational services in a full-time EH classroom. The date for her IEP review is planned for two months before her 16th birthday. According to the requirements of IDEA, what must ADDITIONALLY be included in this review?
    a. Graduation plan
    b. Individualized transition plan
    c. Individualized family service plan
    d. Transportation planning

b. is correct.
Rationale: This is necessary, as the student should be transitioning from school to work.

113. Hector is 10th grader in a program for the severely emotionally handicapped. After a classmate taunted him about his mother, Hector threw a desk at the other boy and attacked him. A crisis intervention team tried to break up the fight, one teacher hurt his knee. The other boy received a concussion. Hector now faces disciplinary measures. How long can he be suspended without the suspension constituting a "change of placement?"
    a. 5 days
    b. 10 days
    c. 10 + 30 days
    d. 60 days

b. is correct.
Rationale: According to ***Honig versus Doe,*** 1988, _Where the student has presented an immediate threat to others, that student may be temporarily suspended for up to 10 school days to give the school and the parents time to review the IEP and discuss possible alternatives to the current placement._

114. The concept that a handicapped student cannot be expelled for misconduct which is a manifestation of the handicap itself, is not limited to students which are labeled "seriously emotionally disturbed". Which reason does not explain this concept?
    a. Emphasis on individualized evaluation
    b. Consideration of the problems and needs of handicapped students
    c. Right to a free and appropriate public education
    d. Putting these students out of school will just leave them on the streets to commit crimes

d. is correct.
Rationale: A, B, and C are tenets of IDEA, and should take place in the least restrictive environment. D does not explain this concept.

115. An effective classroom behavior management plan includes all but which of the following?
    a. Transition procedures for changing activities
    b. Clear consequences for rule infractions
    c. Concise teacher expectations for student behavior
    d. Copies of lesson plans

d. is correct.
Rationale: D is not a part of any behavior management plan. A, B, and C are.

116. Statements like "Darren is lazy" are not helpful in describing his behavior for all but which of these reasons?
    a. There is no way to determine if any change occurs from the information given
    b. The student and not the behavior becomes labeled
    c. Darren's behavior will manifest itself clearly enough without any written description
    d. Constructs are open to various interpretations among the people who are asked to define them

c. is correct.
Rationale: 'Darren is lazy' is a label. It can be interpreted in a variety of ways and there is no way to measure this description for change. A description should be measurable.

117. Often, Marcie is not in her seat when the bell rings. She may be found at the pencil sharpener, throwing paper away, or fumbling through her notebook. Which of these descriptions of her behavior can be described as a pinpoint?
    a. Is tardy a lot
    b. Is out of seat
    c. Is not in seat when late bell rings
    d. Is disorganized

c. is correct.
Rationale: Even though A, B, and D describe the behavior, C is most precise.

118. When choosing behaviors for change, the teacher should ask if there is any evidence that the behavior is presently or potentially harmful to the student or others. This is an example of which test?
    a. Fair-Pair
    b. "Stranger" Test
    c. Premack Principle
    d. "So – What?" Test

D. is correct.

119. Mrs. Taylor takes her students to a special gymnastics presentation that the P.E. coach has arranged in the gym. She has a rule against talk-outs and reminds the students that they will lose 5 points on their daily point sheet for talking out. The students get a chance to perform some of the simple stunts. They all easily go through the movements except for Sam, who is known as the class klutz. Sam does not give up and finally completes the stunts. His classmates cheer him on with comments like "Way to go". Their teacher, however, reminds them that they broke the no talking rule and will lose the points. What mistake was made here?
    a. The students forgot the no talking rule
    b. The teacher considered talk outs to be maladaptive in all school settings
    c. The other students could have distracted Sam with talk-outs and caused him to get hurt
    d. The teacher should have let the P.E. coach handle the discipline in the gym

d. is correct.
The gym environment is different from a classroom environment. The gym teacher should have been in control of a possibly hazardous environment.

120. Which of the following should be avoided when writing objectives for social behavior?
- a. Non-specific adverbs
- b. Behaviors stated as verbs
- c. Criteria for acceptable performance
- d. Conditions where the behavior is expected to be performed

a. is correct.
Behaviors should be specific. The more clearly the behavior is described, the less the chance for error.

121. Criteria for choosing behaviors that are in the most need of change involve all but the following:
- a. Observations across settings to rule out certain interventions
- b. Pinpointing the behavior that is the poorest fit in the child's environment
- c. The teacher's concern about what is the most important behavior to target
- d. Analysis of the environmental reinforcers

c. is correct.
Rationale: The teacher must take care of the criteria in A, B, and D. Her concerns are of the least importance.

122. Ms. Wright is planning an analysis of Audrey's out of seat behavior. Her initial data would be called:
- a. Pre-referral phase
- b. Intervention phase
- c. Baseline phase
- d. Observation phase

c. is correct.
Rationale: Ms Wright is a teacher. She should begin at the Baseline phase.

123. To reinforce Audrey each time she is on task and in her seat, Ms. Wright delivers specific praise and stickers, which Audrey may collect and redeem for a reward. The data collected during the time Ms. Wright is using this intervention is called:
    a. Referral phase
    b. Intervention phase
    c. Baseline phase
    d. Observation phase

b. is correct.
Rationale: Ms Wright is involved in behavior modification. This is the intervention phase.

124. Indirect requests and attempts to influence or control others through one's use of language is an example of:
    a. Morphology
    b. Syntax
    c. Pragmatics
    d. Semantics

c. is correct.
Rationale: Pragmatics involves the way that language is used to communicate and interact with others. It is often used to control the actions and attitudes of people.

125. Kenny, a fourth grader, has trouble comprehending analogies, using comparative, spatial and temporal words, and multiple meanings. Language interventions for Kenny would focus on:
    a. Morphology
    b. Syntax
    c. Pragmatics
    d. Semantics

d. is correct.
Rationale: Semantics has to do with word meanings. Semantic tests measure receptive and expressive vocabulary skills.

126. Celia, who is in first grade, asked, "Where is my ball"? She also has trouble with passive sentences. Language interventions for Celia would target:
    a. Morphology
    b. Syntax
    c. Pragmatics
    d. Semantics

b. is correct.
Rationale: Syntax refers to the rules for arranging words to make sentences.

127. Scott is in middle school, but still makes statements like "I gotted new high-tops yesterday," and "I saw three mans in the front office." Language interventions fro Scott would target:
    a. Morphology
    b. Syntax
    c. Pragmatics
    d. Semantics

a. is correct.
Rationale: Morphology is the process of combining phonemes into meaningful words.

128. Which is not indicative of a handwriting problem?
    a. Errors persisting over time
    b. Little improvement on simple handwriting tasks
    c. Fatigue after writing for a short time
    d. Occasional letter reversals, word omissions, and poor spacing

d. is correct.
Rationale: A, B, and C are physical, handwriting problems. D, however, is a problem with language development.

129. All of these are effective in teaching written expression EXCEPT:
    a. Exposure to various styles and direct instruction in those styles
    b. Immediate feedback from the teacher with all mistakes clearly marked.
    c. Goal setting and peer evaluation of written products according to set criteria
    d. Incorporating writing with other academic subjects

b. is correct.
Rationale: Teacher feedback is not always necessary. The student can have feedback from his peers, or emotional response, or apply skills learned to other subjects.

130. Mr. Mendez is assessing his students' written expression. Which of these is not a component of written expression?
    a. Vocabulary
    b. Morphology
    c. Content
    d. Sentence structure

b. is correct.
Rationale: Morphology is correct. Vocabulary consists of words, content is made up of ideas, which are expressed in words, and Sentences are constructed from words. Morphemes, however, are not always words. They may be prefixes or suffixes.

131. Ms. Tolbert is teaching spelling to her students. The approach stresses phoneme-grapheme relationships within parts of words. Spelling rules, generalizations, and patterns are taught. A typical spelling list for her third graders might include light, bright, night, fright, and slight. Which approach is Ms. Tolbert using?
    a. Rule-based Instruction
    b. Fernald Method
    c. Gillingham Method
    d. Test-Study -Test

a. is correct.
Rationale: Rule-based Instruction employs a system of rules and generalizations. It may be taught using the linguistic or phonics approach.

132. At the beginning of the year, Mr. Johnson wants to gain an understanding of his class' social structure in order to help him assess social skills and related problems. The technique that would best help Mr. Johnson accomplish this is:
    a. Personal interviews with each student
    b. Parent rating form
    c. Sociometric techniques
    d. Self-reports

c. is correct.
Rationale: The issue of reliability and validity arises with A, B, and D. C is the best technique.

Sociometric Measures: There are three basic formats. (a) peer nominations based on non-behavioral criteria such as preferred playmates, (b) peer ratings in which students rate all of their peers on nonbehavioral criteria such as work preferences, and (c) peer assessments, in which peers are rated with respect to specific behaviors.

133. In assessing a group's social structure, asking a student to list a classmate whom he or she would choose to be his or her best friends, preferred play partners, and preferred work partners is an example of:
    a. Peer nomination
    b. Peer rating
    c. Peer assessment
    d. Sociogram

a. is correct.
Rationale: Students are asked to nominate their peers.

134. Naming classmates who fit certain behavioral descriptions such as smart, disruptive or quiet, is an example of which type of sociometric assessment?
    a. Peer nomination
    b. Peer rating
    c. Peer assessment
    d. Sociogram

c. is correct.
Rationale: Students are asked to assess their peers' behavior.

135. Mr. Johnson asks his students to score each of their classmates in areas such as who they would prefer to play with and work with. A likert-type scale with non-behavioral criteria is used. This is an example of:
    a. Peer nomination
    b. Peer rating
    c. Peer assessment
    d. Sociogram

a. is correct.
Rationale: Students are asked for their preferences on non-behavioral criteria.

136. Which of these explanations would not likely account for the lack of a clear definition of behavior disorders?
    a. Problems with measurement
    b. Cultural and/or social influences and views of what is acceptable
    c. The numerous types of manifestations of behavior disorders
    d. Differing theories that use their own terminology and definitions

c. is correct.
Rationale: A, B, and D, are factors that account for the lack of a clear definition of some behavioral disorders. C is not a factor.

137. Ryan is 3, and her temper tantrums last for an hour. Bryan is 8, and he does not stay on task for more than 10 minutes without teacher prompts. These behaviors differ from normal children in terms of their:
    a. Rate
    b. Topography
    c. Duration
    d. Magnitude

c. is correct.
Rationale: It is not normal for temper tantrums to last an hour. At age eight, a normal student stays on task much longer than ten minutes without teacher prompts.

138. All children cry, hit, fight, and play alone at different times. Children with behavior disorders will perform these behaviors at a higher than normal:
    a. Rate
    b. Topography
    c. Duration
    d. Magnitude

a. is correct.
Rationale: Children with behavior disorders display them at a much higher rate than normal children.

139. The exhibition of two or more types of problem behaviors across different areas of functioning is known as:
    a. Multiple maladaptive behaviors
    b. Clustering
    c. Social maladjustment
    d. Conduct disorder

b. is correct.
Rationale: Children with behavior disorders do display a single behavior. They display a range of behaviors. These behaviors are usually clustered together, hence, clustering.

140. Children with behavior disorders often do not exhibit stimulus control. This means they have not learned:
    a. The right things to do
    b. Where and when certain behaviors are appropriate
    c. Right from wrong
    d. Listening skills

b. is correct.
Rationale: These children respond to stimuli at almost any place and time. They are not able to stop and think or control their responses to stimuli.

141. Social withdrawal, anxiety, depression, shyness, and guilt are indicative of:
    a. Conduct disorder
    b. Personality disorders
    c. Immaturity
    d. Socialized aggression

b. is correct.
 Rationale: These are all personality disorders.

142. Short attention span, daydreaming, clumsiness, and preference for younger playmates are associated with:
    a. Conduct disorder
    b. Personality disorders
    c. Immaturity
    d. Socialized aggression

c. is correct.
Rationale: These disorders show immaturity. The student is not acting age appropriately.

143. Truancy, gang membership, and a feeling of pride in belonging to a delinquent subculture are indicative of:
    a. Conduct disorder
    b. Personality disorders
    c. Immaturity
    d. Socialized aggression

D. is correct.
Rationale: The student is acting out by using aggression. This gives him a sense of belonging.

144. Temper tantrums, disruption or disobedience, and bossiness are associated with:
    a. Conduct disorder
    b. Personality disorders
    c. Immaturity
    d. Socialized aggression

a. is correct.
Rationale: These behaviors are designed to attract attention. They are Conduct Disorders.

145. Which of these is not true for most children with behavior disorders?
    a. Many score in the "slow learner"
    b. They are frequently behind classes in academic achievement
    c. They are bright but bored with their surroundings
    d. A large amount of time is spent in nonproductive, nonacademic behaviors

C. is correct.
Rationale: Most children with conduct disorders display the traits found in A, B, and D.

146. Echolalia, repetitive stereotyped actions, and a severe disorder of thinking and communication are indicative of:
    a. Psychosis
    b. Schizophrenia
    c. Autism
    d. Paranoia

c. is correct.
Rationale: The behaviors listed are indicative of autism.

147. Teaching children functional skills that will be useful in their home life and neighborhoods is the basis of:
    a. Curriculum-based instruction
    b. Community-based instruction
    c. Transition planning
    d. Functional curriculum

b. is correct.
Rationale: Teaching functional skills in the wider curriculum is considered community based instruction.

148. Disabilities caused by fetal alcohol syndrome are many times higher for which ethnic group?
    a. Native Americans
    b. Asian Americans
    c. Hispanic Americans
    d. African Americans

a. is correct.
Rationale: There is a very high incidence of this syndrome in Native American children on reservations.

149. Which of these would be the least effective measure of behavioral disorders?
   a. Projective test
   b. Ecological assessment
   c. Standardized test
   d. Psychodynamic analysis

c. is correct.
Rationale: These tests make comparisons, rather than measure skills.

150. Which behavioral disorder is difficult to diagnose in children because the symptoms are manifested quite differently than in adults?
   a. Anorexia
   b. Schizophrenia
   c. Paranoia
   d. Depression

d. is correct.
Rationale: In an adult, it may be displayed as age-appropriate behavior, and go undiagnosed. In a child, it may be displayed as not age appropriate, so it is easier to recognize.

REFERENCES

AGER, C.L. & COLE, C.L. (1991). A review of cognitive-behavioral interventions for children and adolescents with behavioral disorders. Behavioral Disorders. 16(4), 260-275.

AIKEN, L.R. (1985). Psychological Testing and Assessment (5th ed.) Boston: Allyn and Bacon.

ALBERTO, P.A. & TROUTHMAN, A.C. (1990). Applied Behavior Analysis for Teachers: Influencing Students Performance. Columbus, Ohio: Charles E. Merrill.

ALGOZZINE, B. (1990) Behavior Problem Management. Educator's Resource Service. Gaithersburg, MD: Aspen Publishers.

ALGOZZINE, B., RUHL, K., 7 RAMSEY, R. (1991). Behaviorally Disordered? Assessment for Identification and Instruction CED Mini-library. Renson, VA: The Council for Exceptional Children.

AMBRON, S.R. (1981. Child Development (3rd ed.). New York: Holt, Rinehart and Winston.

ANERSON, V., & BLACK, L. (Eds.). (1987, Winter). National news: U.S. Department of Education releases special report (Editorial). GLRS Journal [Georgia Learning Resources System].

ANGUILI, r. (1987, Winter). The 1986 Amendment to the Education of the Handicapped Act. Confederation [A quarterly publication of the Georgia Federation Council for Exceptional Children].

ASHLOCK, R.B. (1976). Error Patterns in Computation: A Semi-programmed Approach (2nd ed.). Columbus, Ohio: Charles E. Merrill.

ASSOCIATION OF RETARDED CITIZENS OF GEORGIA (1987). 1986-87 Government Report. College Park, GA: Author.

AUSUBEL, D.P. & SULLIVAN, E.V. (1970) Theory and Problems of Child Development. New York: Grune & Stratton.

BANKS, J.A., & McGee Banks, C.A. (1993). Multicultural Education (2nd ed.). Boston: Allyn and Bacon.

BARRETT, T.C. (Ed.). (1967). The Evaluation of Children's Reading Achievement. In Perspectives in Reading No. 8. Newark, Delaware: International Reading Association.

BARTOLI, J.S. (1989). An ecological response to Cole's interactivity alternative. Journal of Learning Disabilities, 22(5). 292-297.

BASILE-JACKSON, J. The Exceptional Child in the Regular Classroom. Augusta, GA: East Georgia Center, Georgia Learning Resources System.

BAUER, A.M., & SHEA, T.M. (1989). Teaching Exceptional Students in Your Classroom. Boston: Allyn and Bacon.

BENTLEY, E.L. Jr. (1980). Questioning Skills [Videocassette & manual series]. Northbrook, IL. Hubbard Scientific Company. (Project STRETCH [Strategies to Train Regular Educators to Teach Children with Handicaps]. Module 1. ISBN 0-8331-1906-0).

BERDINE, W.H. & BLACKHURST, A.E. (1985). An Introduction to Special Education. (2nd ed.) Boston: Little, Brown and Company.

BLAKE, K. (1976). The Mentally Retarded: An Educational Pschology. Englewood Cliff, NJ: Prentice-Hall.

BOHLINE, D.S. (1985). Intellectual and Affective Characteristics of Attention Deficit Disordered Children. Journal of Learning Disabilities. 18 (10). 604-608.

BOONE, R. (1983). Legislation and litigation. In R.E. Schmid, & L. Negata (Eds.). Contemporary Issues in Special Education. New York: McGraw Hill.

BRANTLINGER, E.A., & GUSKIN, S.L. (1988). Implications of social and cultural differences for special education. In Meten, E.L. Vergason, G.A., & Whelan, R.J. Effective Instructional Strategies for Exceptional Children. Denver, CO: Love Publishing.

BREWTON, B. (1990). Preliminary identification of the socially maladjusted. In Georgia Psycho-educational Network, Monograph #1. An Educational Perspective On: Emotional Disturbance and Social Maladjustment. Atlanta, GA Psychoeducational Network.

BROLIN, D.E. & KOKASKA, C.J. (1979). Career Education for Handicapped Children Approach. Renton, VA: The Council for Exceptional Children.

BROLIN, D.E. (Ed). (1989) Life Centered Career Education: A Competency Based Approach. Reston, VA: The Council for Exceptional Children.

BROWN, J.W., LEWIS, R.B., & HARCLEROAD, F.F. (1983). AV instruction: Technology, Media, and Methods (6TH ED.). New York: McGraw-Hill.

BRYAN, T.H., & BRYAN, J.H. (1986). Understanding Learning Disabilities (3rd ed.). Palo Alto, CA: Mayfield.

BRYEN, D.N. (1982). Inquiries Into Child Language. Boston: Allyn & Bacon.

BUCHER, B.D. (1987). Winning Them Over. New York: Times Books.

BUSH, W.L., & WAUGH, K.W. (1982). Diagnosing Learning Problems (3rd ed.) Columbus, OH: Charles E. Merrill.

CAMPBELL, P. (1986). Special Needs Report [Newsletter]. 1(1). 1-3.

CARBO, M., & DUNN, K. (1986). Teaching Students to Read Through Their Individual Learning Styles. Englewood Cliffs, NJ. Prentice Hall.

CARTWRIGHT, G.P. & CARTWRIGHT, C.A., & WARD, M.E. (1984). Educating Special Learners (2nd ed.). Belmont, CA: Wadsworth.

CEJKA, J.M. (Consultant), & NEEDHAM, F. (Senior Editor). (1976). Approaches to Mainstreaming. [Filmstrip and cassette kit, units 1 & 2]. Boston: Teaching Resources Corporation. (Catalog Nos. 09-210 & 09-220).

CHALFANT, J. C. (1985). Identifying Learning Disabled Students: A Summary of the National Task Force Report. Learning Disabilities Focus. 1, 9-20.

CHARLES, C.M. (1976). Individualizing Instructions. St Louis: The C.V. Mosby Company.

CHRISPEELS, J.H. (1991). District Leadership in Parent Involvement - Policies and Actions in Sand Diego. Phi Delta Kappa, 71, 367-371.

CLARIZIO, H.F. (1987). Differentiating Characteristics. In Georgia Psychoeducational Network, Monograph #1, An educational Perspective on: Emotional Disturbance and Social Maladjustment. Atlanta, GA Psychoeducational Network.

CLARIZIO, H.F. & MCCOY, G.F. (1983) Behavior Disorders in Children (3rd ed.). New York: Harper & Row.]

COLES, G.S. (1989). Excerpts from The Learning Mystique: A Critical Look at Disabilities. Journal of Learning Disabilities. 22 (5). 267-278.

COLLINS, E. (1980). Grouping and Special Students. [Videocassette & manual series]. Northbrook, IL: Hubbard Scientific Company. (Project STRETCH [Strategies to Train Regular Educators to Teach Children with Handicaps], Module 17, ISBN 0- 8331-1922-2).

CRAIG, E., & CRAIG, L. (1990). Reading In the Content Areas [Videocassette & manual series]. Northbrook, IL: Hubbard Scientific Company. (Project STRETCH [Strategies to Train Regular Educators to Teach Children with Handicaps].Module 13, ISBN 0-8331-1918-4).

COMPTON, C., (1984). A Guide to 75 Tests for Special Education. Belmont, CA., Pitman Learning.

COUNCIL FOR EXCEPTIONAL CHILDREN. (1976). Introducing P.L. 94-142. [Filmstrip-cassette kit manual]. Reston, VA: Author.

COUNCIL FOR EXCEPTIONAL CHILDREN. (1987). The Council for Exceptional Children's Fall 1987. Catalog of Products and Services. Renton, VA: Author.

COUNCIL FOR EXCEPTIONAL CHILDREN DELEGATE ASSEMBLY. (1983). Council for Exceptional Children Code of Ethics (Adopted April 1983). Reston, VA: Author.

CZAJKA, J.L. (1984). Digest of Data on Person With Disabilities (Mathematics Policy Research, Inc.). Washington, D.C.: U.S. Government Printing Office.

DELL, H.D. (1972). Individualizing Instruction: Materials and Classroom Procedures. Chicago: Science Research Associates.

DEMONBREUN, C., & MORRIS, J. Classroom Management [Videocassette & Manual series]. Northbrook, IL: Hubbard Scientific Company. Project STRETCH (Strategies to Train Regular Educators to Teach Children with Handicaps]. Module 5, ISBN 0-8331-1910-9).

DEPARTMENT OF EDUCATION. Education for the Handicapped Law Reports. Supplement 45 (1981), p. 102: 52. Washington, D.C.: U.S. Government Printing Office.

DEPARTMENT OF HEALTH, EDUCATION AND WELFARE, OFFICE OF EDUCATION. (1977, August 23). Education of Handicapped Children. Federal Register, 42, (163).

DIANA VS. STATE BOARD OF EDUCATION, Civil No. 70-37 R.F.P. (N.D.Cal. January, 1970).

DIGANGI, S.A., PERRYMAN, P., & RUTHERFORD, R.B., Jr. (1990). Juvenile Offenders in the 90's A Descriptive Analysis. Perceptions, 25(4), 5-8.

DIVISION OF EDUCATIONAL SERVICES, SPECIAL EDUCATION PROGRAMS (1986). Fifteenth Annual Report to Congress on Implementation of the Education of the Handicapped Act. Washington, D.C.: U.S. Government Printing Office.

DOYLE, B.A. (1978). Math Readiness Skills. Paper presented at National Association of School Psychologists, New York. K.J. (1978). Teaching Students Through Their Individual Learning Styles.

DUNN, R.S., & DUNN, K.J. (1978). Teaching Students Through Their Individual Learning Styles: A Practical Approach. Reston, VA: Reston.

EPSTEIN, M.H., PATTON, J.R., POLLOWAY, E.A., & FOLEY, R. (1989). Mild retardation: Student characteristics and services. Education and Training of the Mentally Retarded, 24, 7-16.

EKWALL, E.E., & SHANKER, J.L. 1983). Diagnosis and Remediation of the Disabled Reader (2nd ed.) Boston: Allyn and Bacon.

FIRTH, E.E. & REYNOLDS, I. (1983). Slide tape shows: A creative activity for the gifted students. Teaching Exceptional Children. 15(3), 151-153.

FRYMIER, J., & GANSNEDER, B. (1989). The Phi Delta Kappa Study of Students at Risk. Phi Delta Kappa. 71(2) 142-146.

FUCHS, D., & DENO, S.L. 1992). Effects of curriculum within curriculum-based measurement. Exceptional Children 58 (232-242).

FUCHS, D., & FUCHS, L.S. (1989). Effects of examiner familiarity on Black, Caucasian, and Hispanic Children. A Meta-Analysis. Exceptional Children. 55, 303-308.

FUCHS, L.S., & SHINN, M.R. (1989). Writing CBM IEP objectives. In M.R. Shinn, Curriculum-based Measurement: Assessing Special Students. New York: Guilford Press.

GAGE, N.L. (1990). Dealing With the Dropout Problems? Phi Delta Kappa. 72(4), 280-285.

GALLAGHER, P.A. (1988). Teaching Students with Behavior Disorders: Techniques and Activities for Classroom Instruction (2nd ed.). Denver, CO: Love Publishing.

GEARHEART, B.R. (1980). Special Education for the 80s. St. Louis, MO: The C.V. Cosby Company.

GEARHART, B.R. & WEISHAHN, M.W. (1986). The Handicapped Student in the Regular Classroom (2nd ed.). St Louis, MO: The C.V. Mosby Company.

GEARHART, B.R. (1985). Learning Disabilities: Educational Strategies (4th ed.). St. Louis: Times Mirror/ Mosby College of Publishing.

GEORGIA DEPARTMENT OF EDUCATION, PROGRAM FOR EXCEPTIONAL CHILDREN. (1986). Mild Mentally Handicapped (Vol. II), Atlanta, GA: Office of Instructional Services, Division of Special Programs, and Program for Exceptional Children. Resource Manuals for Program for Exceptional Children.

GEORGIA DEPARTMENT OF HUMAN RESOURCES, DIVISION OF REHABILITATION SERVICES. (1987, February). Request for Proposal [Memorandum]. Atlanta, GA: Author.

GEORGIA PSYCHOEDUCATIONAL NETWORK (1990). An Educational Perspective on: Emotional Disturbance and Social Maladjustment. Monograph #1. Atlanta, GA Psychoeducational Network.

GEREN, K. (1979). Complete Special Education Handbook. West Nyack, NY: Parker.

GILLET, P.K. (1988). Career Development. Robinson, G.A., Patton, J.R., Polloway, E.A., & Sargent, L.R. (eds.). Best Practices in Mild Mental Disabilities. Reston, VA: The Division on Mental Retardation of the Council for Exceptional Children.

GLEASON, J.B. (1993). The Development of Language (3rd ed.). New York: Macmillan Publishing.

GOOD, T.L., & BROPHY, J.E. (1978). Looking into Classrooms (2nd Ed.). New York: Harper & Row.

HALL, M.A. (1979). Language-Centered Reading: Premises and Recommendations. Language Arts, 56 664-670.

HALLLAHAN, D.P. & KAUFFMAN, J.M. (1988). Exceptional Children: Introduction to Special Education. (4th Ed.). Englewood Cliffs, NJ; Prentice-Hall.

HALLAHAN, D.P. & KAUFFMAN, J.M. (1994). Exceptional Children: Introduction to Special Education 6th ed.). Boston: Allyn and Bacon.

HAMMILL, D.D., & BARTEL, N.R. (1982). Teaching Children With Learning and Behavior Problems (3rd ed.). Boston: Allyn and Bacon.

HAMMILL, D.D., & BARTEL, N.R. (1986). Teaching Students with Learning and Behavior Problems (4th ed.). Boston and Bacon.

HAMILL, D.D., & BROWN, L. & BRYANT, B. (1989) <u>A Consumer's Guide to Tests in Print.</u> Austin, TX: Pro-Ed.

HANEY, J.B. & ULLMER, E.J. ((1970). <u>Educational Media and the Teacher.</u> Dubuque, IA: Wm. C. Brown Company.

HARDMAN, M.L., DREW, C.J., EGAN, M.W., & WOLF, B. (1984). <u>Human Exceptionality: Society, School, and Family.</u> Boston: Allyn and Bacon.

HARDMAN, M.L., DREW, C.J., EGAN, M.W., & WORLF, B. (1990). <u>Human Exceptionality</u> (3rd ed.). Boston: Allyn and Bacon.

HARGROVE, L.J., & POTEET, J.A. (1984). <u>Assessment in Special Education.</u> Englewood Cliffs, NJ: Prentice-Hall.

HARING, N.G., & BATEMAN, B. (1977). <u>Teaching the Learning Disabled Child.</u> Englewood Cliffs, NJ: Prentice-Hall.

HARRIS, K.R., & PRESSLEY, M. (1991). The Nature of Cognitive Strategy Instruction: Interactive strategy instruction. <u>Exceptional Children, 57,</u> 392-401.

HART, T., & CADORA, M.J. (1980). <u>The Exceptional Child: Label the Behavior</u> [Videocassette & manual series], Northbrook, IL: Hubbard Scientific Company. (Project STRETCH [Strategies to Train Regular Educators to Teach Children with Handicaps], Module 12, ISBN 0-8331-1917-6). HART, V. (1981) <u>Mainstreaming Children with Special Needs.</u> New York: Longman.

HENLEY, M., RAMSEY,R.S., & ALGOZZINE, B. (1993). <u>Characteristics of and Strategies for Teaching Students with Mild Disabilities.</u> Boston: Allyn and Bacon.

HEWETT, F.M., & FORNESS, S.R. (1984). <u>Education of Exceptional Learners.</u> (3rd ed.). Boston: Allyn and Bacon.

HOWE, C.E. (1981) <u>Administration of Special Education.</u> Denver: Love.

HUMAN SERVICES RESEARCH INSTITUTE (1985). <u>Summary of Data on Handicapped Children and Youth.</u> (Digest). Washington, D.C.: U.S. Government Printing Office.

JOHNSON, D.W. (1972) <u>Reaching Out: Interpersonal Effectiveness and Self-Actualization.</u> Englewood Cliffs, NJ: Prentice-Hall.

JOHNSON, D.W. (1978) <u>Human Relations and Your Career: A Guide to Interpersonal Skills.</u> Englewood Cliffs, NJ: Prentice-Hall.

JOHNSON, D.W., & JOHNSON, R.T. (1990). <u>Social Skills for Successful Group Work. Educational Leadership. 47</u> (4) 29-33.

JOHNSON, S.W., & MORASKY, R.L. <u>Learning Disabilities</u> (2nd ed.) Boston: Allyn and Bacon.

JONES, F.H. (1987). <u>Positive Classroom Discipline.</u> New York: McGraw-Hill Book Company.

JONES, V.F., & JONES, L. S. (1986). <u>Comprehensive Classroom Management: Creating Positive Learning Environments.</u> (2nd ed.). Boston: Allyn and Bacon.

JONES, V.F. & JONES, L.S. (1981). <u>Responsible Classroom Discipline: Creating Positive Learning Environments and Solving Problems.</u> Boston: Allyn and Bacon.

KAUFFMAN, J.M. (1981) <u>Characteristics of Children's Behavior Disorders.</u> (2nd ed.). Columbus, OH: Charles E. Merrill.

KAUFFMAN, J.M. (1989). <u>Characteristics of Behavior Disorders of Children and Youth.</u> (4th ed.). Columbus, OH: Merrill Publishing.

KEM, M., & NELSON, M. (1983). <u>Strategies for Managing Behavior Problems in the Classroom.</u> Columbus, OH: Charles E. Merrill.

KERR, M.M., & NELSON, M. (1983) <u>Strategies for Managing Behavior Problems in the Classroom.</u> Columbus, OH: Charles E. Merrill.

KIRK, S.A., & GALLAGHER, J.J. (1986). <u>Educating Exceptional Children</u> (5th ed.). Boston: Houghton Mifflin.

KOHFELDT, J. (1976). Blueprints for construction. <u>Focus on Exceptional Children. 8</u> (5), 1-14.

KOKASKA, C.J., & BROLIN, D.E. (1985). <u>Career Education for Handicapped Individuals</u> (2nd ed.). Columbus, OH: Charles E. Merrill.

LAMBIE, R.A. (1980). A systematic approach for changing materials, instruction, and assignments to meet individual needs. <u>Focus on Exceptional Children,</u> 13(1), 1-12.

LARSON, S.C., & POPLIN, M.S. (1980). <u>Methods for Educating the Handicapped: An Individualized Education Program Approach.</u> Boston: Allyn and Bacon.

LERNER, J. (1976) <u>Children with Learning Disabilities.</u> (2nd ed.). Boston: Houghton Mifflin.

LERNER, J. (1989). Learning Disabilities,: Theories, Diagnosis and Teaching Strategies (3rd ed.). Boston: Houghton Mifflin.

LEVENKRON, S. (1991). Obsessive-Compulsive Disorders. New York: Warner Books.

LEWIS, R.B., & DOORLAG, D.H. (1991). Teaching Special Students in the Mainstream. (3rd ed.). New York: Merrill.

LINDSLEY, O. R. (1990). Precision Teaching: By Teachers for Children. Teaching Exceptional Children, 22. (3), 10-15.

LINDDBERG, L., & SWEDLOW, R. (1985). Young Children Exploring and Learning. Boston: Allyn and Bacon.

LONG, N.J., MORSE, W.C., & NEWMAN, R.G. (1980). Conflict in the Classroom: The Education of Emotionally Disturbed Children. Belmont, CA: Wadsworth.

LOSEN, S.M., & LOSEN, J.G. (1985). The Special Education Team. Boston: Allyn and Bacon.

LOVITT, T.C. (1989). Introduction to Learning Disabilities. Boston: Allyn and Bacon.

LUND, N.J. * DUCHAN, J.F. (1988)/ Assessing Children's Language in Naturalist Contexts. Englewood Cliffs, NJ: Prentice Hall

MALE, M. (1994) Technology for Inclusion: Meeting the Special Needs of all Children. (2nd ed.). Boston: Allyn and Bacon.

MANDELBAUM, L.H. (1989). Reading. In G.A. Robinson, J.R., Patton, E.A., Polloway, & L.R. Sargent (eds.). Best Practices in Mild Mental Retardation. Reston, VA: The Division of Mental Retardation, Council for Exceptional Children.

MANNIX. D. (1993). Social Skills for Special Children. West Nyack, NY: The Center for Applied Research in Education.

MARSHALL, ET AL, VS. GEORGIA U.S. District court for the Southern District of Georgia. C.V. 482-233. June 28, 1984.

MARSHALL, E.K., KURTZ, P.D., & ASSOCIATES. Interpersonal Helping Skills. San Francisco, CA: Jossey-Bass Publications.

MARSTON, D.B. (1989) A curriculum-based measurement approach to assessing academic performance: What it is and why do it. In M. Shinn (Ed.). Curriculum-Based Measurement: Assessing Special Children. New York: Guilford Press.

MCDOWELL, R.L., ADAMSON, G.W., & WOOD, F.H. (1982). Teaching Emotionally Disturbed Children. Boston: Little, Brown and Company. MCGINNIS, E., GOLDSTEIN, A.P. (1990). Skill Streaming in Early

Childhood: Teaching Prosocial Skills to the Preschool and Kindergarten Child. Champaign, IL: Research Press.

MCLOUGHLIN, J.A., & LEWIS, R.B. (1986). Assessing Special Students (3rd ed.). Columbus, OH: Charles E. Merrill.

MERCER, C.D. (1987). Students with Learning Disabilities. (3rd. ed.). Merrill Publishing.

MERCER, C.D., & MERCER, A.R. (1985). Teaching Children with Learning Problems (2nd ed.). Columbus, OH: Charles E. Merrill.

MEYEN, E.L., VERGASON, G.A., & WHELAN, R.J. (Eds.). (1988). Effective Instructional Strategies for Exceptional Children. Denver, CO: Love Publishing.

MILLER, L.K. (1980). Principles of Everyday Behavior Analysis (2nd ed.). Monterey, CA: Brooks/Cole Publishing Company. MILLS VS. THE BOARD OF EDUCATON OF THE DISTRICT OF COLUMBIA, 348F. Supp. 866 (D.C. 1972).

MOPSICK, S.L. & AGARD, J.A. (Eds.) (1980). Cambridge, MA: Abbott Associates.

MORRIS, C.G. (1985). Psychology: An Introduction (5th ed.). Englewood Cliffs, NJ: Prentice-Hall.

MORRIS, J. (1980). Behavior Modification. [Videocassette and manual series]. Northbrook, IL: Hubbard Scientific Company. (Project STRETCH [Strategies to Train Regular Educators to Teach Children with Handicaps,] Module 16, Metropolitan Cooperative Educational Service Agency.). MORRIS, J. & DEMONBREUN, C. (1980). Learning Styles [Videocassettes & Manual series]. Northbrook, IL: Hubbard Scientific Company. (Project STRETCH [Strategies to Train Regular Educators to Teach Children with Handicaps], Module 15, ISBN 0-8331-1920-6).

MORRIS, R.J. (1985). Behavior Modification with Exceptional Children: Principles and Practices. Glenview, IL: Scott, Foresman and Company.

MORSINK, C.V. (1984). <u>Teaching Special Needs Students in Regular Classrooms.</u> Boston: Little, Brown and Company.

MORSINK, C.V., THOMAS, C.C., & CORREA, V.L. (1991). <u>Interactive Teaming, Consultation and Collaboration in Special Programs.</u> New York: MacMillan Publishing.

MULLSEWHITE, C.R. (1986). <u>Adaptive Play for Special Needs Children: Strategies to Enhance Communication and Learning.</u> San Diego: College Hill Press.

NORTH CENTRAL GEORGIA LEARNING RESOURCES SYSTEM/CHILD SERVE. (1985). <u>Strategies Handbook for Classroom Teachers.</u> Ellijay, GA.

PATTON, J.R., CRONIN, M.E., POLLOWAY, E.A., HUTCHINSON, D., & ROBINSON, G.A. (1988). Curricular considerations: A life skills orientation. In Robinson, G.A., Patton, J.R., Polloway, E.A., & Sargent, L.R. (Eds.). <u>Best Practices in Mental Disabilities.</u> Des Moines, IA: Iowa Department of Education, Bureau of Special Education.

PATTON, J.R., KAUGGMAN, J.M., BLACKBOURN, J.M., & BROWN, B.G. (1991). <u>Exceptional Children in Focus</u> (5th ed.). New York: MacMillan.

PAUL, J.L. (Ed.). (1981). <u>Understanding and Working with parents of Children with Special Needs.</u> New York: Holt, Rinehart and Winston.

PAUL, J.L. & EPANCHIN, B.C. (1991). <u>Educating Emotionally Disturbed Children and Youth: Theories and Practices for Teachers.</u> (2nd ed.). New York: MacMillan. PENNSYLVANIA ASSOCIATION FOR RETARDED CHILDREN VS. COMMONWEALTH OF PENNSYLVANIA, 334 F. Supp. 1257 (E.D., PA., 1971), 343 F. Supp. 279 (L.D. PA., 19972).

PHILLIPS, V., & MCCULLOUGH, L. (1990). Consultation based programming: Instituting the Collaborative Work Ethic. <u>Exceptional Children.</u> 56 (4), 291-304.

PODEMSKI, R.S., PRICE, B.K., SMITH, T.E.C., & MARSH, G.E., IL (1984). <u>Comprehensive Administration of Special Education.</u> Rockville, MD: Aspen Systems Corporation.

POLLOWAY, E.A., & PATTON, J.R. (1989). <u>Strategies for Teaching Learners with Special Needs.</u> (5th ed.). New York: Merrill.

POLLOWAY, E.A., PATTON, J.R., PAYNE, J.S., & PAYNE, R.A. 1989). <u>Strategies for Teaching Learners with Special Needs,</u> 4th ed.). Columbus, OH: Merrill Publishing.

PUGACH, M.C., & JOHNSON, L.J. (1989a). The challenge of implementing collaboration between general and special education. Exceptional Children, 56 (3), 232-235.

PUGACH, M.C., & JOHNSON, L.J. (1989b). Pre-referral interventions: Progress, Problems, and Challenges. Exceptional Children, 56 (3), 217-226.

RADABAUGH, M.T., & YUKISH, J.F. (1982). Curriculum and Methods for the Mildly Handicapped. Boston: Allyn and Bacon.

RAMSEY, R.S. (1981). Perceptions of disturbed and disturbing behavioral characteristics by school personnel. (Doctoral Dissertation, University of Florida) Dissertation Abstracts International, 42(49), DA8203709.

RAMSEY, R.S. (1986). Taking the practicum beyond the public school door. Journal of Adolescence. 21(83), 547-552.

RAMSEY, R.S., (1988). Preparatory Guide for Special Education Teacher competency Tests. Boston: Allyn and Bacon, Inc.

RAMSEY, R.S., DIXON, M.J., & SMITH, G.G.B. (1986) Eyes on the Special Education: Professional Knowledge Teacher Competency Test. Albany, GA: Southwest Georgia Learning Resources System Center.

RAMSEY R.W., & RAMSEY, R.S. (1978). Educating the emotionally handicapped child in the public school setting. Journal of Adolescence. 13(52), 537-541.

REINHEART, H.R. (1980). Children I Conflict: Educational Strategies for the Emotionally Disturbed and Behaviorally Disordered. (2nd ed.). St Louis, MO: The C.V. Mosby Company.

ROBINSON, G.A., PATTON, J.R., POLLOWAY, E.A., & SARGENT, L.R. (Eds.). (1989a). Best Practices in Mental Disabilities. Des Moines, IA Iowa Department of Education, Bureau of Special Education.

ROBINSON, G.A., PATTON, J.R., POLLOWAY, E.A., & SARGENT, L.R. (Eds.). (1989b). Best Practices in Mental Disabilities. Renton, VA: The Division on Mental Retardation of the Council for Exceptional Children.

ROTHSTEIN, L.F. (1995). Special education Law (2nd ed.). New York: Longman Publishers.

SABATINO, D.A., SABATION, A.C., & MANN, L. (1983). Management: A Handbook of Tactics, Strategies, and Programs. Aspen Systems Corporation.

SALVIA, J., & YSSELDYKE, J.E. (1985). Assessment in Special Education (3rd. ed.). Boston: Houghton Mifflin.

SALVIA J., & YSSELDYKE, J.E. (1991). Assessment (5th ed.). Boston: Houghton Mifflin.

SALVIA, J. & YSSELDYKE, J.E. (1995) Assessment (6th ed.). Boston: Houghton Mifflin.

SATTLER, J.M. (1982). Assessment of Children's Intelligence and Special Abilities (2nd ed.). Boston: Allyn and Bacon.

SCHLOSS, P.J., HARRIMAN, N., & PFIEFER, K. (in press). Application of a sequential prompt reduction technique to the independent composition performance of behaviorally disordered youth. Behavioral Disorders.

SCHLOSS, P.J.., & SEDLAK, R.A.(1986). Instructional Methods for Students with Learning and Behavior Problems. Boston: Allyn and Bacon.

SCHMUCK, R.A., & SCHMUCK, P.A. (1971). Group Processes in the Classroom. Dubuque, IA: William C. Brown Company.

SCHUBERT, D.G. (1978). Your teaching - the tape recorder. Reading Improvement, 15(1), 78-80.

SCHULZ, J.B., CARPENTER, C.D., & TURNBULL, A.P. (1991). Mainstreaming Exceptional Students: A Guide for Classroom Teachers. Boston: Allyn and Bacon.

SEMMEL, M.I., ABERNATHY, T.V., BUTERA G., & LESAR, S. (1991). Teacher perception of the regular education initiative. Exceptional Children, 58 (1), 3-23.

SHEA, T.M., & BAUER, A.M. (1985). Parents and Teachers of Exceptional Students: A Handbook for Involvement. Boston: Allyn and Bacon.

SIMEONSSON, R.J. (1986). Psychological and Development Assessment of Special Children. Boston: Allyn and Bacon.

SMITH, C.R. (1991). Learning Disabilities: The Interaction of Learner, Task, and Setting. Boston: Little, Brown, and Company.

SMITH, D.D., & LUCKASSON, R. (1992). Introduction to Special Education: Teaching in an Age of Challenge. Boston: Allyn and Bacon.

SMITH, J.E., & PATTON, J.M. (1989). A Resource Module on Adverse Causes of Mild Mental Retardation. (Prepared for the President's Committee on Mental Retardation).

SMITH, T.E.C., FINN, D.M., & DOWDY, C.A. (1993). Teaching Students With Mild Disabilities. Fort Worth, TX: Harcourt Brace Jovanovich College Publishers.

SMITH-DAVIS, J. (1989a April). A National Perspective on Special Education. Keynote presentation at the GLRS/College/University Forum, Macon, GA.

STEPHENS, T.M. (1976). Directive Teaching of Children with Learning and Behavioral Disorders. Columbus, OH Charles E. Merrill.

STERNBURG, R.J. (1990). Thinking Styles: Key to Understanding Performance. Phi Delta Kappa, 71(5), 366-371.

SULZER, B., & MAYER, G.R. (1972). Behavior Modification Procedures for School Personnel. Hinsdale, IL: Dryden.

TATEYAMA-SNIEZEK, K.M. (1990.) Cooperative Learning: Does it improve the academic achievement of students with handicaps? Exceptional Children, 57(2), 426-427.

THIAGARAJAN, S. (1976). Designing instructional games for handicapped learners. Focus on Exceptional Children. 7(9), 1-11.

THOMAS, O. (1980). Individualized Instruction [Videocassette & manual series]. Northbrook, IL: Hubbard Scientific Company. (Project STRETCH [Strategies to Train Regular Educators to Teach Children with Handicaps]. Module 14, ISBN 0- 8331-1919-2).

THOMAS, O.(1980). Spelling [Videocassette & manual series]. (Project STRETCH [Strategies to Train Regular Educators to Teach Children with Handicaps]. Module 10, ISBN 0-83311915-X).

THORNTON, C.A., TUCKER, B.F., DOSSEY, J.A., & BAZIK, E.F. (1983). Teaching Mathematics to Children with Special Needs. Menlo Park, CA: Addison-Wesley.

TURKEL, S.R., & PODEL, D.M. (1984). Computer-assisted learning for mildly handicapped students. Teaching Exceptional Children. 16(4), 258-262.

TURNBULL, A.P., STRICKLAND, B.B., & BRANTLEY, J.C. (1978). Developing Individualized Education Programs. Columbus, OH: Charles E. Merrill.

U.S. DEPARTMENT OF EDUCATION. (1993). To Assure the Free Appropriate Public Education of all Children with Disabilities. (Fifteenth annual report to Congress on the Implementation of The Individuals with Disabilities Education Act.). Washington, D.C.

WALKER, J.E., & SHEA, T.M. (1991). Behavior Management: A Practical Approach for Educators. New York: MacMillan.

WALLACE, G., & KAUFFMAN, J.M. (1978). Teaching Children with Learning Problems. Columbus, OH: Charles E. Merrill.

WEHMAN, P., & MCLAUGHLIN, P.J. (1981). Program Development in Special Education. New York: McGraw-Hill.

WEINTRAUB, F.J. (1987, March). [Interview].

WESSON, C.L. (1991). Curriculum-based measurement and two models of follow-up consultation. Exceptional Children. 57(3), 246-256.

WEST, R.P., YOUNG, K.R., & SPOONER, F. (1990). Precision Teaching: An Introduction. Teaching Exceptional Children. 22(3), 4-9.

WHEELER, J. (1987). Transitioning Persons with Moderate and Severe Disabilities from School to Adulthood: What Makes it Work? Materials Development Center, School of Education, and Human Services. University of Wisconsin-Stout.

WHITING, J., & AULTMAN, L. (1990). Workshop for Parents. (Workshop materials). Albany, GA: Southwest Georgia Learning Resources System Center.

WIEDERHOLT, J.L., HAMMILL, D.D., & BROWN, V.L. (1983). The Resource Room Teacher: A Guide to Effective Practices (2nd ed.). Boston: Allyn and Bacon.

WIIG, E.H., & SEMEL, E.M. (1984). Language Assessment and Intervention for the Learning Disabled. (2nd ed.). Columbus, OH: Charles E. Merrill.

WOLFGANG, C.H., & GLICKMAN, C.D.(1986). Solving Discipline Problems: Strategies for Classroom Teachers (2nd ed.). Boston: Allyn and Bacon.

YSSELKYKE, J.E., ALGOZZINE, B., (1990). Introduction to Special Education (2nd ed.). Boston: Houghton Mifflin.

YSSELDYKE, J.E., ALGOZZINE, B., & THURLOW, M.L. (1992). Critical Issues in Special Education (2nd ed.). Boston: Houghton Mifflin Company.

YSSEDLYKE, J.E., THURLOW, M.L., WOTRUBA, J.W., NANIA, PA.A (1990). Instructional arrangements: Perceptions From General Education. Teaching Exceptional Children, 22(4), 4-8.

ZARGONA, N., VAUGHN, S., 7 MCINTOSH, R. (1991). Social Skills Interventions and children with behavior problems: A review. <u>Behavior Disorders, 16</u>(4), 260-275.

ZIGMOND, N., & BAKER, J. (1990). Mainstream experiences for learning disabled students (Project Meld): Preliminary report. <u>Exceptional Children, 57</u>(2), 176-185.

ZIRPOLI, T.J., & MELLOY, K.J. (1993). <u>Behavior Management.</u> New York: Merrill.

XAMonline, INC. 21 Orient Ave. Melrose, MA 02176

Toll Free number 800-509-4128

TO ORDER Fax 781-662-9268 OR www.XAMonline.com

ILLINOIS TEACHER CERTIFICATION SYSTEM - ICTS - 2006

PO#   Store/School:

Address 1:

Address 2 (Ship to other):

City, State Zip

Credit card number_____-_____-_____-_____   expiration_____

EMAIL _____

PHONE   **FAX**

13# ISBN 2007	TITLE	Qty	Retail	Total
978-1-58197-977-0	ICTS Assessment of Professional Teaching Tests 101-104			
978-1-58197-976-3	ICTS Basic Skills 096			
978-1-58197-996-1	ICTS Elementary-Middle Grades 110			
978-1-58197-997-8	ICTS Elementary-Middle Grades 110 Sample Questions			
978-1-58197-981-7	ICTS English Language Arts 111			
978-1-58197-991-6	ICTS Family and Consumer Sciences 172			
978-1-58197-987-9	ICTS Foreign Language- French Sample Test 127			
978-1-58197-988-6	ICTS Foreign Language- Spanish 135			
978-1-58197-992-3	ICTS Library Information Specialist 175			
978-1-58197-983-1	ICTS Mathematics 115			
978-1-58197-989-3	ICTS Physical Education 144			
978-1-58197-995-4	ICTS Principal 186			
978-1-58197-993-0	ICTS Reading Teacher 177			
978-1-58197-994-7	ICTS School Counselor 181			
978-1-58197-978-7	ICTS Science- Biology 105			
978-1-58197-979-4	ICTS Science- Chemistry 106			
978-1-58197-673-1	ICTS Science- Earth and Space Science 108			
978-1-58197-999-2	ICTS Science: Physics 116			
978-1-58197-982-4	ICTS Social Science- History 114			
978-1-58197-985-5	ICTS Social Science- Political Science 117			
978-1-58197-986-2	ICTS Social Science- Psychology 118			
978-1-58197-975-6	ICTS Special Education Learning Behavior Specialist I 155			
978-1-58197-998-5	ICTS Special Education General Curriculum 163			
978-1-58197-990-9	ICTS Visual Arts Sample Test 145			

	SUBTOTAL	
FOR PRODUCT PRICES GO TO WWW.XAMONLINE.COM	Ship	$8.25
	TOTAL	

CPSIA information can be obtained at www.ICGtesting.com
Printed in the USA
BVOW052155131111

276027BV00001B/4/A